The Intellectual Origins of Modernity

The Intellectual Origins of Modernity explores the long and winding road of modernity from Rousseau to Foucault and its roots, which are not to be found in a desire for enlightenment or in the idea of progress but in the Promethean passion of Western humankind. Modernity is the Promethean passion, the passion of humans to be their own master, to use their insight to make a world different from the one that they found, and to liberate themselves from their immemorial chains. This passion created the political ideologies of the nineteenth century and made its imprint on the totalitarian regimes that arose in their wake in the twentieth.

Underlying the Promethean passion was modernity—humankind's project of self-creation—and enlightenment, the existence of a constant tension between the actual and the desirable, between reality and the ideal. Beneath the weariness, the exhaustion, and the skepticism of post-modernist criticism is a refusal to take Promethean horizons into account. This book attests the importance of reason, which remains a powerful critical weapon of humankind against the idols that have come out of modernity: totalitarianism, fundamentalism, the golem of technology, genetic engineering, and a boundless will to power. Without it, the new Prometheus is liable to return the fire to the gods.

David Ohana is Professor of Modern European History at the Ben-Gurion University of the Negev, Israel. He has been affiliated with the Hebrew University, Jerusalem, Israel, the Paris-Sorbonne, Harvard University, and the University of California at Berkeley. He specializes in comparative national mythologies.

Routledge Studies in Social and Political Thought

Experiencing Multiple Realities
Alfred Schutz's Sociology of the Finite Provinces of Meaning
Marius I. Benţa

Human Flourishing, Liberal Theory and the Arts
Menachem Mautner

Rethinking Liberalism for the 21st Century
The Skeptical Radicalism of Judith Shklar
Giunia Gatta

Norbert Elias and the Analysis of History and Sport
Systematizing Figurational Sociology
Joannes Van Gestel

Progressive Violence
Theorizing the War on Terror
Michael Blain and Angeline Kearns-Blain

Democracy, Dialogue, Memory
Expression and Affect Beyond Consensus
Edited by Idit Alphandary and Leszek Koczanowicz

Common Sense as a Paradigm of Thought
An Analysis of Social Interaction
Tim Delaney

The Intellectual Origins of Modernity
David Ohana

For a full list of titles in this series, please visit www.routledge.com/series/RSSPT

The Intellectual Origins of Modernity

David Ohana

NEW YORK AND LONDON

First published 2019
by Routledge
52 Vanderbilt Avenue, New York, NY 10017

and by Routledge
2 Park Square, Milton Park, Abingdon, Oxon, OX14 4RN

Routledge is an imprint of the Taylor & Francis Group, an informa business

© 2019 Taylor & Francis

The right of David Ohana to be identified as author of this work has been asserted by him in accordance with sections 77 and 78 of the Copyright, Designs and Patents Act 1988.

All rights reserved. No part of this book may be reprinted or reproduced or utilized in any form or by any electronic, mechanical, or other means, now known or hereafter invented, including photocopying and recording, or in any information storage or retrieval system, without permission in writing from the publishers.

Trademark notice: Product or corporate names may be trademarks or registered trademarks, and are used only for identification and explanation without intent to infringe.

Library of Congress Cataloging-in-Publication Data
Names: Ohana, David, author.
Title: The intellectual origins of modernity / David Ohana.
Description: New York, NY : Routledge, 2019. | Series: Routledge studies in social and political thought ; 138 | Includes bibliographical references and index.
Identifiers: LCCN 2018052284 (print) | LCCN 2019001577 (ebook) | ISBN 9781351110518 (Master) | ISBN 9781351110501 (Adobe) | ISBN 9781351110495 (ePub) | ISBN 9781351110488 (Mobi) | ISBN 9780815363125 (hbk) | ISBN 9781351110518 (ebk)
Subjects: LCSH: Civilization, Modern—Philosophy. | Political science—Philosophy.
Classification: LCC CB358 (ebook) | LCC CB358 .O43 2019 (print) | DDC 909.8—dc23
LC record available at https://lccn.loc.gov/2018052284

ISBN: 978-0-8153-6312-5 (hbk)
ISBN: 978-1-351-11051-8 (ebk)

Typeset in Times New Roman
by Apex CoVantage, LLC

Contents

	Prologue	1
1	From Rousseau to Tocqueville: Janus Face of Modernity	29
2	1848: "We Are Sitting on a Volcano"	80
3	From Marx to Lenin: A Red Future	111
4	Anarchism, Nihilism, Racism	168
5	Foucault and Beyond	204
	Epilogue	218
	Bibliography	222
	Index	234

Prologue

The Promethean Passion of Modernity

The Intellectual Origins of Modernity suggests that modernity and Enlightenment, far from being synonymous, are separate, different, and sometimes even contradictory concepts. Modernity is humankind's consciousness in the last two to three centuries, of being able to form themselves with their own hands. Some have sought do this in a context of freedom, and some in a context of repression. The Enlightenment, on the other hand, which typified major thinkers of the seventeenth and eighteenth centuries, promoted the idea of the universality of mankind, the principle of the liberty and equality of all, and the theory of progress whereby morality and the spirit of rational criticism were spread through education and the dissemination of knowledge. Modernity is a period marked by the Promethean desire to master the world, whereas the Enlightenment was a normative outlook on the world. Modernity could be enlightened, but it could also rebel against the values of the Enlightenment.

Modernity and Enlightenment have had a continuous history of friction between them. The paths of modernity were tortuous, and its roots are not to be found in a desire for enlightenment or progress but in the Promethean longing of Western humankind to be their own masters, to impose their own rationality, and consequently to mold the world in a form different from that in which they received it. In order to carry out the project of modernity, its representatives made use of the Enlightenment—rationality, universality, progress, and science—but solely for the purposes of the Promethean passion. This passion motivated the political ideologies of the nineteenth century and engendered the forms of the regimes that followed in the twentieth. These ideologies and regimes were modern in that they sought to create a political and social reality in the image of humanity. The Promethean passion of modern humankind, which developed from a desire for independence to a desire for unbridled power, is the hallmark of our time.

It is some small consolation that the twentieth century—the century of mass extermination—was a short one. The century, which began late, in 1914, ended early, in 1989. It began with a total mechanized war, the first of its kind, which obliterated the difference between soldiers and citizens, a war without content—a "Nietzschean republic", as one of its participants called it—and it ended with the collapse of the last surviving totalitarian ideology of those that sprang up between the two world wars. What were the intellectual roots of the totalitarian nihilism, which reached its climax in the twentieth century?

The Intellectual Origins of Modernity investigates the question: what happened to modern human, the Prometheus who created his own world, when he became his own ruler? What happened to Prometheus unbound? Is not modern humankind, freed from all restraint, liable to create a new Golem? Does not the inner logic of unlimited rationality and unbridled freedom finally engender enslavement to oneself, a human-monster like Frankenstein? The myth of Prometheus is like a thread running through Western culture, a central axis along which one may perceive the changes that take place in mankind.

The human experience in the twentieth century was bound up with the metamorphoses of modernity from a desire for liberty to a will to power, from Promethean humanism to Prometheus released from his chains. We are faced with the Promethean paradox: from the classical world to modern times, Prometheus was a symbol of humanism. How did he become a Caesar in the twentieth century? An explanation of the matter requires a distinction between modernity and enlightenment, two concepts that have been confused to the point of becoming identical. How was it that modernity rose against Enlightenment in the twentieth century? In the light of this, it would seem that Prometheus's fate was a degeneration. He abandoned his humanity for hubris and herein resembled other myths in Western thought: the Golem, Faust, the sorcerer's apprentice, and Frankenstein. Examples of Prometheus unbound are science that changed in the modern age from a contemplation of nature to a will to power, technology that became an instrumental rationality without rational content, and the attempt to create a new human through totalitarian ideologies or genetic engineering.

This dual aspect of modernity lies at the heart of the Promethean passion. Our power has increased in the modern age, but the results of our actions come toward us like a hostile and alien force, an independent force not subject to our influence. Jean-Jacques Rousseau and Alexis de Tocqueville, two French political thinkers, were the first to criticize the supposed identity of modernity and enlightenment.[1] Hence Rousseau's proposal to condition modern education in his book *Émile*; hence the possibility envisaged by De Tocqueville in his works on modern democracy in France and America that democratic despotism could be a consequence of radical liberty. Rousseau and De Tocqueville perceived the ambivalence of progress, the contradictory tendencies of modernity, and the paradox of freedom in modern times. The failed revolutions of 1848 were the starting point of an attempt to translate social aspirations into political terms. The fears of the liberal conservative De Tocqueville of a Promethean socialism that would give birth to a new man were at the same time the hopes of revolutionaries like Karl Marx and Auguste Blanqui. The year 1848 was a parting of the ways in which the prophecies concerning revolutionary socialism saw it as a new servitude or the hope of society. From the mid-1800s to the turn of the century, the optimistic revolutionary mentality changed to a sense of decadence, a feeling that the modern world was heading toward destruction.

In *The Intellectual Origins of Modernity*, the universal and particular aspects of one modern ideology, Marxism, are studied in the revolutionary approach of Marx and in Vladimir Lenin's view of nationalism. Marx examined the history of political revolution from the 1789 revolution onward during a hundred years of French history. According to Marx, this political revolution, a revolution of the bourgeoisie, was supposed to pave the way for a class revolution, the revolution of the proletariat. The Revolution of 1789, the Revolution of 1848, the Louis Napoleon regime, and the Paris Commune of 1871 were examined by him in the light of future revolutions that could only take place in modern socioeconomic conditions. Marx said that the modern economy "rivets the laborer to capital more firmly that the wedges of Vulcan did Prometheus to the rock".[2] But the modern worker created a history of liberty over and above the envisaged outcome. The seventy years of Bolshevik history—a distorted mutation of Marxist ideology—showed that, in the Soviet Union, Prometheus rebelled against Caesar. Lenin, Marx's Russian disciple, wished to carry out a universal class revolution in a single country at the height of the First World War. Rapid modernization, which required the subordination of means to ends and adapting the social situation to the ideology, enslaved a whole nation to a party for seventy years. But parallel with the organized collective revolutionary path of the party and nation, there sprang up on the revolutionary left an individual revolutionism that sought to hasten redemption through explosives. From the anarchistic propaganda-through-action at the beginning of the nineteenth century to the nihilistic conclusion that the world cannot be repaired but only destroyed, the way was not a long one. Was the logic that led from Bakunin to Nechayev the same mode of thought that led from Sartre to Fanon and also to Beider–Meinhoff? And apart from those who despaired of achieving utopia in the modern world, there were thinkers such as Ernst Bloch, Herbert Marcuse, and Hannah Arendt, who condemned the metamorphoses of the Promethean utopia in the twentieth century as distortion, repression, and banality.

Metamorphoses of the Myth of Prometheus

According to David Hume, the task of the historian of ideas is to trace the history of the human consciousness. Voltaire added that it is more important to know how people thought in times gone by than to know how they acted. The myth of Prometheus is an inseparable part of modern thought. The critical modern reader takes a distance from the naive beliefs that gave birth to myth so that only its symbolic meaning remains. In modern times, mythical texts are not regarded as sacred or objective but are viewed as contributing to humanity's self-knowledge. The hermeneutist Paul Ricœur said that there is no need to disprove myths, to reject myth as such because of its primitive character—in fact, de-mythicize it—but one must decipher the symbolism it contains. Hermeneutics, which is a midrashic and innovative deciphering of texts, permits modern humankind to recapture the message of a myth through its interpretation.³ In this, Ricœur is close to Claude Lévi-Strauss, who claimed that myths—logical and linguistic structures—think themselves through us.

Instead of the religious message of a myth—in theological terms, its *kerygma*—the deconstruction of a myth into its component parts reveals a kind of human consciousness. The structural analysis of a myth, like that of Prometheus and its representation in various cultures, illuminates the unity of the human race and the intellectual closeness of different peoples in the face of similar problems of existence.⁴ When a text is detached from its author and his cultural context, it becomes a challenge for an up-to-date reading and a novel interpretation. The great task of hermeneutic interpretation in the historical context is to bridge the gap between the cultural reality of the past, in which the mythical text is anchored, and the modern reader living in the present. From being a symbol of Greek man who constructed his future in the kingdom of secularism, cut off from transcendental horizons, Prometheus became the image of a Caesar who sought to replace God. Renaissance humanism, Romanticism, and the Enlightenment gave revolutionary meanings to Prometheus, who became the symbol of man who puts himself in God's place and even boasts of creating a man in his image.

There is a series of myths in Western culture—Prometheus, the Golem, Faust and Frankenstein—that express the ambivalence of human knowledge, of boundless desire, with its attractive and threatening possibilities, whose culmination is the creation of a new human. For many thinkers of the eighteenth and nineteenth centuries, Prometheus was the supreme symbol of the liberation of humankind, the equality of all, the crossing of human boundaries and the discovery of new horizons. As the representative of the human race who stole fire from the gods and spread the light of knowledge and reason among humankind, he was the standard-bearer of universal human values. This was the man who rose against the gods, took their place, and himself attempted to embody divinity. His revolt against the father of the gods was a protest against a situation in which there were absolute values beyond man. The myth of Prometheus was first introduced by the poet Hesiod at the turn of the eighth and seventh centuries BCE in the "Thenogia" and in "Acts and Days" and by the dramatist Aeschylus in "Prometheus Bound", the only surviving tragedy from the fourth century BCE.⁵ The tale of Prometheus is the story of the birth of humankind and its attempt to sever its umbilical cord from its metaphysical parent: a story of rebellion, sin, and punishment, and also a story concerning the limitations of humans and their attempts to transcend them.⁶

In the Greek mythological universe, Uranus is considered the first ruler. A war of succession took place between King Cronos and the titans on the one hand and his son Zeus (Jupiter), together with various monsters, on the other. At first, Prometheus fought against Zeus and advised the titans, who represented anarchic tendencies, to be careful and sparing in the use of force. The titans refused to listen, and Prometheus decided to transfer his allegiance to Zeus. Finally, with the help of the Olympian gods, Zeus, the father of the gods, overcame the titans. In return for his help to Zeus, the gods gave Prometheus the task of creating man. Prometheus's intellectual qualities (his name meant "forethought") made him wiser than the gods. His brother Epimetheus (meaning "afterthought") changed his mind all the time and behaved the same way with people. At the end of the apportioning of gifts to the different creatures, Epimetheus did not leave anything for humans, and he was full of remorse and called for his brother. Prometheus responded to the challenge by creating a human who was greater than an animal. In those days, the cultural level of humans was close to that of animals. Hoping to create a higher culture, Zeus wished to eradicate inferior beings and produce a higher human strain. In his compassion for the human race, Prometheus created an erect man in the image of the gods. He subsequently rose to the heavens, lit a torch, and brought it down to earth. Prometheus instructed humanity in arts and crafts and taught men not to fear death by blurring their consciousness, but Zeus repaid him for his sin in stealing the light by binding him to a rock.[7]

Plato, in his "Protagoras" dialogue, supports the tradition that ascribes the creation of man to Prometheus:

> There was once a time when there were gods, but no mortal creatures. And when to these also came their destined time to be created, the gods moulded their forms within the earth, of a mixture made of earth and fire and all substances that are compounded with fire and earth. When they were about to bring these creatures to light, they charged Prometheus and Epimetheus to deal to each the equipment of his proper faculty.[8]

Another mythological source of the origin of humankind is the legend of the five ages in which the gods themselves created the human race. The creation of humanity was performed in laboratory conditions through types of metals, from precious to inferior ones. In the first age, humans were made from gold. They were ordinary mortals but devoid of pain like the gods. In the silver age, men were wolves to one another and lacking in wisdom. The third race, formed from brass, loved war; the fourth race was made up of heroes resembling the gods. The fifth race, made of iron, was wicked from youth onward. Hesiod thought that human culture went from bad to worse, but Aeschylus believed that humanity progressed from a barbarous to a civilized state.

Whatever the case, in the golden age there were no women in the world. Women were created later on the orders of Zeus as a punishment for Prometheus, who benefited mankind and deceived the gods when offering sacrifices intended for gods and men. Instead of the good sacrificial meat intended for the gods, Prometheus deceitfully gave them bad meat. When choosing between two piles, a pile of meat covered with intestines and a pile of bones covered with fat, Zeus chose the pile covered with fat that Prometheus had provided. In revenge, Zeus created Pandora, who was outwardly beautiful but was really a curse for the human race. After punishing mankind, Zeus revenged himself against Prometheus, the chief of sinners. His servants, force and violence, dragged Prometheus to the Caucasus, bound him with chains to a rock, and an eagle was sent to eat his liver. This was the treatment meted out to the man who loved the human race and honored mankind.[9]

Despite the tortures, Prometheus's spirit was strengthened, and he refused to yield to the savage creatures. From Greece to modern times, Prometheus has personified the human rebellion against tyranny; he is the symbol of the creative human spirit, the representative of critical thought.[10] It is not known how or when Prometheus was liberated, whether it was because Hercules killed the eagle or because the centaur Chiron, who was immortal, chose to die in his place. The tragedy "Prometheus Unbound", which is lost, was written after "Prometheus Bound" and "Prometheus the Fire-Bearer". In this play, Prometheus, for a long period, was spared imprisonment in Tartarus, but he was bound to the rock in the Caucasus. Zeus delayed Prometheus's liberation until the latter granted his request and revealed to him the name of the mother who would give birth to the son of the father of the gods who wished to depose his father and take his place. The end of the lost tragedy was paradoxical: the liberated Prometheus saw Zeus as the protector of humanity.

From Fichte and Schelling to Marx and Camus, Prometheus's seizure of the light represented man rebelling against arbitrary forces beyond himself. He was the symbol of the German philosophy of idealism.[11] Fichte, for example, wrote:

> You need nothing outside of yourself; not even a God; you yourself are your own God; you are your Messiah and savior [. . .] A worthy image of this way of thinking is the presentation which an ancient poet makes of Prometheus.[12]

The revival of classical culture in the early nineteenth century was a meeting point of Enlightenment and Romanticism. Schelling contributed to seeing Greek mythology in a modern and universal way:

> Prometheus [is] will unconquerable [. . .], which for that reason can resist God [. . .] Prometheus is the thought in which the human race, after it has brought forth the world of gods out of its inner being, returning to itself, becomes conscious of itself and its fate.[13]

August Wilhelm Schelling enunciated a Promethean imperative: "Even if everything appears to conspire against you, [your] inner power shall nevertheless prove itself triumphant".[14] Karl Marx, of course, read Fichte and Schelling, and also Schlegel, who was his teacher in two courses in the University of Bonn. His doctrinal thesis was dedicated to Karl Friedrich Koppen, who in turn dedicated to Marx his work on Frederick the Great and the Enlightenment. This is how Koppen quoted Frederick the Great: "[The Enlightenment] was Prometheus who brought the heavenly light to earth in order to enlighten the blind, the people".[15]

In his personality and literary output, the exemplary figure of Goethe embodied the Promethean Enlightenment. In his great poem "Prometheus", the gods are rejected for considering themselves superior to Prometheus. The self-esteem of modern humankind, released from the chains of the gods, gives Goethe the strength to challenge them. Prometheus finds within himself the spiritual means to overcome the pains of life without the aid of metaphysics. This independence does not constitute absolute liberty or a clear victory over suffering but is a sign of self-awareness.[16] The cosmos surrounding humanity is created in their image: it is the universe that humans have made. Prometheus does not consecrate the world to the gods but creates it for himself alone. The classics scholar Càroli Kerényi thought that "Goethe's Prometheus is [. . .] the impartial prototype of man as the original rebel and affirmer of his fate. The original inhabitant of the earth, seen as an anti-god, as Lord of the Earth".[17] He was endowed with three qualities: creativity, independence, and courage.

Did Goethe's Faust personify the rebellious Prometheus who now made a pact with the devil? With Goethe, Faust gained a new, modern meaning: he represented the development of the human race. The quest for new horizons ended in tragedy, in expulsion from the Garden of Eden. The first work on Faust, the *Historia von Doktor Johann Fausten* (Story of Doctor Johann Faust), published by Johann Spies in 1587, already condemned a desire for knowledge outside the confines of the Church. An antireligious tendency began to be in evidence about twelve years later, in G. R. Widmann's reediting of Spies's work on Faust. The renown of the magician and sorcerer who gained supernatural powers through a pact with the devil traveled westward from Germany. Lessing, who in the eighteenth century first raised the possibility of saving Faust's soul, saw his thirst for knowledge as a leading principle of the Enlightenment. Nickolaus Lenau, in his poem "Faust" (1836), and Paul Valéry, in *Mon Faust* (My Faust) (1946), pointed out the dangers of a correlation between a thirst for absolute knowledge and a desire for the power to attain it.[18] Thomas Mann, in his novel *Doktor Faustus*, which described the corruption of the chief character and of German society through a pact that they made with the National-Socialist devil, drew a historical conclusion.

An innovation of Goethe's was the idea that the outstanding feature of Faustian man is action and that persistence has a value in itself, regardless of its aims. This idea is closely connected with that of the continuous and ever-changing interrelationship of modernity and enlightenment and of humankind as a self-created entity that indefatigably seeks the truth. Goethe was doubtful of the basic assumption of the premodern religious philosophers that the nature of a human being is a static "being", that a person's transient existence is like a husk in a world of arbitrary changes, and the true "essence" will only be revealed in eternity. In contrast to this view, Goethe saw action as the true nature of humanity, revealed in movement, development, and growth. Humanity is not homeless in the world but a product of time and the universe. The Promethean desire to possess the tree of knowledge of good and evil is expressed in Goethe's words: humans know themselves only to the degree that they know the world.[19] Is there not in Goethe's Prometheus a suggestion of the structural connection between Faust and Mephistopheles, between modern humans and the Satan that lies in wait for them?

Many commentators have noticed the points of similarity between Prometheus and Satan, and the poet Shelley went further and revealed the strong resemblance between them. Zvi Werblowsky, in his book *Lucifer and Prometheus*, analyzed the deep archetypical and mythical points of identity between these two literary figures.[20] After reading Milton's *Paradise Lost*, he concluded that in every human action there is a certain hubris, Promethean or satanic: Lucifer, the lord of hubris, is deeply entrenched in Prometheus's desire to be liberated from his chains. The Promethean myth is ambivalent: fire illuminates but it also burns, destroys and entices like Lucifer himself. In this respect, the Promethean myth could refer either to Jesus or to the Devil: every human action contains an element of sin, and in Christianity there is no escape except through the intervention of divine grace. This suggests a closeness between the suffering and desire of Prometheus and those of Jesus and Lucifer. In all desire for knowledge, there is inevitably an element of pride, sin, and human suffering. Goethe was fond of the romantic poet, Byron, who wrote as follows:

> And be the new Prometheus of new men, Bestowing fire from Heaven, and then, too late, Finding the pleasure given repaid with pain.[21]

Romanticism praised the "new man" who was born in an aesthetic context. Friedrich Schiller, who continued this line of thought, gave a good account of the special quality of Prometheus: "A pure consciousness can only give and not receive". This is the universal power of giving, like the power of God. This power is the essence of God within us, God within mankind. In satisfying hunger, in giving to the weak, Schiller's Promethean self finds God in humanity and arrives at a reflective consciousness of man as a creator of values, as a giver, as the embodiment of the power: "Love places [its center] out of itself in the axis of the universal whole".[22]

Mankind's Promethean consciousness, which extends over time, is at the heart of the Hegelian philosophy of history. Man advances from the world of the ancient East to the modern world. Reason is the measure of history: the rational is progressively realized in history. In the introduction to his *Philosophy of Law* (1821), Hegel enunciated his dual principle: "Whatever is rational is real, and whatever is real is rational". In this double sentence, Hegel describes the relationship between the actual and the desirable. Hegel's 1819 manuscript (discovered over ten years ago) supports the view that it is no accident that rational radicalism comes first in the double sentence while the conservative justification of the existing order only appears at the end. And this is how it is expressed: "*Was vernünftdig ist, wird wirklich, und das wirkliche wird vernünftig*" (Whatever is rational becomes real, and the real becomes rational).[23] Rationality is not identified with reality, and the intention is a process whereby the rational becomes real.

Historical reality is a process in which the Promethean passion, from being a principle, becomes a realization. It is people who make history and not forces outside them. Historical insight became a metaphysical system: after Kant, Hegel sought to create an all-embracing system in which truth was only possible within the framework of a complete and comprehensive view of things. But the Golem (politics) rose against its maker (historiography): in the nineteenth and twentieth centuries, Hegel's disciples split into the political left and right. The idea of having a total comprehension of historical reality, and hence a desire to construct the future on a totalitarian political model, is facilitated by a neglect of details and a sanctification of ends. From the point of view of the lord of history who, like the owl of Minerva, looks at changing events only at the onset of darkness—at the end of the historical process—the details, the means or the values are of little importance.

For the young Marx, philosophy was above all Hegelian philosophy, a way of seeing, a desire to know the completion that would achieve human totality. In a famous letter to his father on the 10th of November 1837, he acknowledged his Hegelianism:

> Philosophy makes no secret of it. The confession of Prometheus: "I hate the packs of god" [phrase originally in Greek] is its own confession, its own aphorism against all heavenly and earthly gods who do not acknowledge human self-consciousness as the highest divinity. It will have none other beside.[24]

The myth of the fall, the suffering, and the self-redemption of Prometheus created a dramatic model for Marxism as a modern ideology of redemption.[25] When reality is represented as a story of redemption, history undergoes a dramatization. The classicist Kerényi already showed that the Greeks did not appreciate the redeeming figure of Jesus as much as they appreciated the need for redemption: hence the pretension of modern humans to embody divinity themselves. Modern humankind takes its place in the arena of sanctity: a new surveillance by a supreme eminence that cannot tolerate any authority other than its own.

The Nietzschean Prometheus is a parting of the ways. Nietzsche did not have a progressive philosophy of history and consequently rejected the ideology of redemption. His criticism of rational progress on the one hand and of the regressive religious view on the other left Nietzsche with a cyclical immanent view of history.[26] Nietzsche rejected both the metaphysics of the religious church and of the secular church of the Enlightenment. In Nietzsche's Promethean myth, humans deal with the fire voluntarily and do not receive it from heaven. They raise themselves progressively and acquire their culture themselves. The rise of the individual is bound up with the decline of the gods and represents a rebellious faith in a capacity to create people and to destroy the Olympian deities. The tragic foundation of the Promethean myth is the fact that humans acquire the good for themselves by means of sin. Punishment is meted out to the human race because of its aspiration to rise too high: the Greek original sin is the first philosophical problem and reveals an insoluble contradiction between humanity and its aspiration to divinity. This contradiction, according to Nietzsche, is at the root of all culture. The Promethean dilemma of the sinning and suffering individual is his heroic aspiration to totality and his desire to be the one eternal being. Nietzsche warned of the liberated Prometheus who was liable to turn rebellion into despotism and culture into a new barbarism:

> I point to something new: certainly for such a democratic type there exists the danger of the barbarian, but one has looked for it only in the depths. There exists also another type of barbarian, who comes from the heights: a species of conquering and ruling natures in search of material to mold. Prometheus was this kind of barbarian.[27]

Through a genealogy of ideas, Nietzsche concluded that modern humankind is the creator of light. The God of light, fire, and humanity does not really exist but is a metaphor. Nietzsche's radical interpretation was that through world-creating aesthetics, humans controlled their god from the beginning, and therefore they can easily kill him:

> Did Prometheus have to fancy first that he had stolen the light and then pay for that—he finally discovered that he had created the light by coveting the light and that not only man but also the god was the work of his own hands and had been mere clay in his hands?[28]

God has been killed, but the *Übermensch* has not yet been born. Modern humanity is faced with the consciousness of nihilism. They are homeless, and the question is where can they turn now? Nihilistic criticism paved the way to the will to power, the desire for independence. This is the modern situation: a world created in one's own image without reference to God. The Nietzschean revolution is the reflective self-awareness of the modern human who constructs the world out of personal creativity. The axis of the revolution is not reason but aesthetics; not Judeo-Christian morality but the principle of the will to power; not knowledge but creation; not essence but existence. The death of God is the announcement of the possibility of the birth of modern humankind.

What Is There Between Modernity and Enlightenment?

Modernity is humanity's desire in modern times to mold itself and its fate with its own hands. The idea of modernity could be described as the triumph of critical reason over the hallowed principles of the old world, whose foundations were religious salvation, metaphysical redemption, and the Lord of history.[29] The new principle of modern society was that everything may be judged and criticized: the social order, the political system, economic activities. Modernity is made up of all the products of rational activity: scientific, technological or administrative. If the hallowed old order was based on a total concept, the modern order was divided into separate critical categories that consequently were essentially secular. The social differentiation of politics, economics, and family affairs led at the same time to different critical categories. Religion was no longer the sole principle according to which life was organized and the motive force behind everything. In its place, one had divisive and subversive reason.

Modernity is identified above all with the process of secularization. Criticism of secularism, which is the very heart of modernity, is based on three main arguments. One denies the possibility of a modernity founded on secular norms and values and claims that these inevitably lead to revolution, violence and nihilism. According to this view, the separation of modern culture from its religious source must necessarily lead to self-destruction. The second argument denies the concept of historical development and doubts the possibility of exchanging theology for historicism or replacing religious redemption with secular progress. The third argument is that there can be a messianic or transcendental significance to history only on a religious basis, and one consequently cannot hope to create a secular future as envisaged by the great secular mass ideologies.[30] This represents a protest against the very idea of secular modernity, secular historicism, and the secular ideologies filling the gap left by the decline of religion.

Max Weber described modernity as a process of intellectualization, meaning that modernity is a break with the finality of the religious spirit.[31] The religious vision hopes for a final accomplishment of God's plan and thus expects an end of history. Historicism, on the other hand, finds meaning in historical events but not beyond them. Modernity is the contrary of the idea of an end to history and can be described as an end of prehistory. Prehistory is the totality of the events and personalities of traditional society, the feudal system, the royal dynasty, aristocratic privileges, of traditions, beliefs and prejudices. In the seventeenth and eighteenth centuries, the modern consciousness, utilizing reason, differentiation, and criticism, believed it was promoting universal objectives.

The Enlightenment was characterized by three elements: reason, nature, and progress. The main contribution of the Enlightenment to human thought was the universalization of reason. Reason related to all human beings in the same way. Allan Bloom wrote that what distinguished the Enlightenment from all previous philosophies was its intention of extending to everyone what had previously been the property of a few: a life based on reason. This was not idealism or optimism but a new science, a new type of political science.[32]

The intellectual origins of political science are already to be found in the classical world, in the Platonic enterprise of creating the conceptual model of a perfect state, and in the world of the Renaissance, in Macchiavelli's project of separating politics from religious or moral criteria. The revolutionary innovation of modernity was the creation of a rational model of politics for all of humankind. A scientific theory of this kind lay behind the attempts of Hobbes (1651) and Rousseau (1762) to propose a rational conditioning of all citizens through an unquestioning acceptance of Leviathan (the state), or the general will.[33] For the Englishman Hobbes in the seventeenth century and the Frenchman Rousseau in the eighteenth, any bourgeois or sacred social or political order had to be based on a free choice expressing the general will identified with reason. Like all Enlightenment thinkers, Rousseau refused to see divine Providence as supreme and replaced it with reason. The West lived out the concept of modernity as a revolution, rational modernity as the image of Prometheus unbound. Modernity's challenge to build a rational or scientific society led revolutionaries, from France in the eighteenth century to Russia in the twentieth, to create a new society and a new human in the name of reason. Rational principles called for the absolute monarchies to be replaced.

In September 1784, Moses Mendelssohn was the first person to answer the question asked by the German journal, *Berliner Monatsscrift*: "What is enlightenment?"[34] He thought that the task of enlightenment was to create a positive correlation between the function of man as an individual and his function as a citizen. Man as an individual had no need of culture (*Kultur*), but he needed enlightenment (*Aufklärung*). If the Scottish Enlightenment focused on morality and the French Enlightenment focused on politics, the German Enlightenment focused on education (*Bildung*) and culture. Four months later, Immanuel Kant, in the same journal, defined enlightenment as follows: "*Sapere aude*— have the courage to use your brain! That is the slogan of the Enlightenment".[35] This definition made Kant one of the first thinkers to distinguish between the Enlightenment—humans leaving their immaturity through the use of their brains without any external assistance—and modernity: the struggle for self-determination. Since then, the definition of enlightenment has been dependent on its relationship to history. To paraphrase Michel Foucault: modern philosophy has become obsessed with this question, which it could neither solve nor ignore.[36] The question of enlightenment has been part of political philosophy from the triumph of rationalism in the modern era to its subversion in postmodernist thought.

The rational discourse that appeared in the seventeenth century was the turning point of the Enlightenment. The autonomy of the individual in Descartes, based on thought and not on tradition, and Newton's laws of nature disconnected from theological justification, were the factors that paved the way for the Enlightenment, but the secular challenge of defining enlightenment plunged Kant into a Copernican revolution. According to Yehoshua Arieli, this revolution was about humanity's claim to be the sole source of authority and legitimacy and the sole judge of values, norms, and ideas, just as they are the source of history itself. Seen in this way, humanity was the initiator, creator, and changer of reality, and its dynamic force had only just begun to be revealed. Humanity was Prometheus unbound.[37]

In the view of the Enlightenment thinkers of the eighteenth century, social conditions, the cultural background, and the legal system hindered the spread of rational ideas among the majority of people. The Church, economic backwardness, poverty, and deformity combined to prevent the expansion of reason.

Voltaire, a representative critic of the age, saw the Christian Church as the main culprit for leading humanity astray. This was caused by its transcendental and supernatural source of justification that placed faith and salvation above reason and criticism. The term *philosophe* (philosopher) was defined by the French *encyclopédistes* as follows: "Reason is for the philosopher what grace is for the Christian". Just as grace was available to every believing Christian, so everyone could have access to reason in certain environmental conditions. John Locke (1690) laid the philosophical and psychological foundation on which the *philosophes* based their faith in reason. The human is born a *tabula rasa* (an empty slate). If one directs and controls one's experience of life, one can form one's own consciousness and character. "Cultural engineering" could improve all human beings through a change of environment and especially through education.[38] Helvétius (1758) thought that all people have an equal capacity of understanding. Condorcet (1795) went further and claimed that Westerners were in the final stage of a full rational understanding of the world.[39]

The second element in the Enlightenment, nature, was dependent on reason. It was reason that enabled humans to reveal nature. Nature was the antithesis of two concepts. One, the supernatural, included miracles, salvation, and the revealed truths of religion, which were products of the human imagination and kept humans ignorant and brutish; and the other, the unnatural, which unlike the supernatural really existed, included the artificial forms, the harmful customs and irrational traditions that had developed in the course of history with evil consequences. The question of how the natural became the unnatural was hard for the human of the Enlightenment to resolve just as the question of why the omnipotent and omniscient God permitted Adam to bite the apple remained unanswered. Whatever the case, nature was identified with the good, a body of ethical and aesthetic criteria that were not essentially different from those of the Judeo-Christian tradition. Perhaps the reason for this was the strong Hellenic presence in the eighteenth century, as well as that of the Puritan presence and of other schools of thought that sought to create perfect models of society. The main task in gaining acceptance for the concept of nature and the concept of reason was bringing humanity into unity with the universe:

> "Nature" therefore does not so much signify a given group of objects as a certain "horizon" of knowledge, of the comprehension of reality. To nature belongs everything in the sphere of "natural light" everything whose understanding and confirmation require no other aid than the natural forces of knowledge. [. . .] There need be no opposition between belief and knowledge, between revelation and reason. [. . .] The realm of grace does not negate the realm of nature. Though the former, so to speak, overshadows the latter, it does not impinge on the existence of the latter as such: "Grace doesn't abolish Nature, but completes it".[40]

Religious ethics were replaced by the theory of the laws of nature. There was an aspiration to a natural order of things represented by the ethical and aesthetic dimensions. Nature was "the great dream of the century: humanity living at peace with itself and with the world, and in spontaneous harmony with the universal order". The moderns sought a "natural" model for a rational understanding of society, whether it was mechanical, organic, or cybernetic, or was based on a conceptual system, a general theory, or a scientific comparison. Humans were to be subject to the laws of nature alone. Rousseau sought *transparence* (clarity),[41] and the philosophy of the Enlightenment was chiefly a search for clarity, the light that distinguishes between good and evil, truth and falsehood, science and religion. And, indeed, the verb "to enlighten" (*aufklären*) was the linguistic source that revealed the philosophical intention of the movement. Universal values were definitive because they were seen as scientific. Rousseau's theory of the social contract and Marx's *Kapital* replaced the old absolute authority; the *Jacobins* wished to embrace Rousseau just as the Bolsheviks clasped Marx to their bosom. They wished to apply the "scientific" theory to politics.

"Primitivistic" thinkers and writers in the second half of the eighteenth century believed that the state of nature existed in history and that, in that state, humans lived free and innocent lives. The state of nature was located in classical times, in the Hellenic golden age, or in places remote from the European continent, but many others did not believe in the historical reality of the ideal state of nature. Even Rousseau thought that the state of nature was, in our terms, a myth, a kind of propaganda for a new order. The social contract and life according to reason promoted "natural" ethics and natural rights, and these represented the comprehensiveness of humanity, the universality of mankind.

The third element in Enlightenment thought was the theory of progress. The Judeo-Christian tradition fostered a mentality that transcended the here and now, like the belief in heaven. The Christian outlook, represented by Augustine in his *Civitate Dei* (City of God) required a belief in a better society, but this would not be achieved through a continual improvement of humanity in this world but would only come about with the second advent of Christ. The Hellenic tradition developed various theories of cyclical time, and the humanists of the Renaissance and the Protestants of the Reformation adopted models from the past that in their opinion were suitable to the present.

The question asked at the beginning of the modern age, at the time of the "*querelle des anciens et des modernes*" (dispute of the ancients and moderns) in France and the "battle of the books" in England, was a literary one: did the writers of the end of the seventeenth century create works that were of equal value or perhaps superior to those of the great writers of Greece and Rome?[42] In a lecture at the Sorbonne in 1750, the French economist and statesman Turgot put forward a theory of infinite progress that would represent eternity in this world. In the view of his friend and disciple Condorcet, this was an optimistic utopia, a kind of "natural salvation". In the hope of achieving it, the thinkers of the Enlightenment, from Locke and Rousseau to Pestalozzi, wrote major works of educational theory. The *praxis* of education was in fact based on the theory of progress. In Rousseau's work, *Émile*, reason, nature, and progress were combined. Good, progressive education enabled human reason to gradually reveal nature.

Did modernity—the self-creation of humanity and their world—and enlightenment—moving this creation toward universality—go hand in hand in modern times, or did they part company in the twentieth century? Was there a historical and epistemological split between modernity and enlightenment, between politics, technology, communications, and industrialization and the human contents that all these were supposed to serve? Did instrumental reason overcome universal values?

Modernity gave the role of divine providence to science instead of God. The challenge posed by modernity was that of rationalization, which meant the destruction of all the old social relationships that owed their justification to a nonrational source: status, preferential treatment, lineage, inheritance, and the like. Rationalization was the agent of modernization: not a class or a special category but universal reason that made historical development possible.[43] Modernization was not the achievement of an enlightened despot, a popular revolution or a ruling class, but of reason embodied in science, technology, and education. The origins of this mode of thought were in Greek philosophy.

Socrates, the first of the intellectuals, sought a correlation between knowledge and virtue and between lack of knowledge and error, deficiency, sin, and perversion. Knowledge as a tool was seen as an infrastructure for ethics: a person who through reason knows that the good will avoid doing evil. The basic assumption of the rationalist intellectual tradition from Socrates and Plato to Kant and Hegel was that intellectuals were the guardians of rational concepts and moral values. This was also the assumption underlying the condemnation—from Julien Benda's *Le Trahison des clercs* (The Betrayal of the Intellectuals) to Raymond Aron's *L'Opium des intellectuels* (The Opium of the Intellectuals)—of thinkers who abandoned the legacy of the Enlightenment.

Major philosophical currents in the twentieth century such as existentialism, the Frankfurt school, and post-modernism declared that the modern reality is not necessarily identical with reason.[44] From Nietzsche to Foucault, there has been a question mark over the universality of reason and over the autonomy of values. If the universalist status of reason disappears, so does the universalist status of morality, and the universalization of the Enlightenment also collapses. The communicative rationality of Jürgen Habermas seeks to answer this postmodernist claim. Habermas does not see the identification of modernity with enlightenment as self-evident but updates the Enlightenment to the end of the twentieth century by promoting a civil society and a public sphere in which there is room for rational discourse (communication), democratic norms, and collective identity.[45]

The ever increasing correlation between the human productive capacity and mass destruction, the rise of the totalitarianism of the left and right at the beginning of the twentieth century, the dominance of consumerism, one-dimensional advertising and the communication media, the gap between the prosperous north and the poor south, the menacing power of modern technology, the flowering of religious fundamentalism and particularistic nationalism: all this bears witness to a growing gulf between the desirable and the real, between the theoretical and the actual. Modern humankind does not act as expected according to the universal rules of the Enlightenment. Reason has risen against itself.

Max Horkheimer stressed the contribution of Max Weber to the triumph of instrumental reason over fundamental reason. Horkheimer declared that the meaning of reason had long been the exercise of understanding and the internalization of eternal values that were said to be the proper objectives of mankind. Today, he thought, we witness an opposite process.[46] The means have replaced the ends, and people have become dependent on the political, economic, technological, and communicative powers that they themselves unleashed and that they were supposed to control. What can modern humans do to find themselves again? Are they capable of acting without any guiding, accompanying, directing, and restraining forces? Are they able to control their own powers that have exceeded their limits?

The Promethean Golem

The French Revolution was the turning point in society's relation to itself. It gave birth to modern politics, which desired to be liberated from the chains of Church, privilege, and prejudice, and believed humanity's fate to be determined by its own strength. But, just around the corner, a dangerous parallel option lay in waiting: humanity, who knew its great powers, sought to build the City of God in the vale of tears. Next to the ideas of universal liberty of 1789, one had the terrorism of the here and now of 1793.[47] Between the French Revolution and the century of blood and iron, there were the nineteenth-century political ideologies. All of them—nationalism, liberalism, socialism, Marxism, racialism, among others—tried to mold the modern reality in accordance with their outlook. The events of the twentieth century were a rupture of civilization that raised threatening human possibilities, created radical political concepts and was the negative climax of modernity: man's presumption to rule the cosmos. The deep crisis of Western culture in the first third of the twentieth century revealed a bureaucratic murderousness, the cynical outcome of Western rationalism that Hannah Arendt called "nihilistic banality". [48] The twentieth century witnessed the first attempt—National Socialism—to found a political Church on nihilism. On the other side, in the Soviet Union, the Marxist ideology was voided of its content in the Soviet concentration camps. The system changed from one of government by people to an administration that saw people as objects (reification). The totalitarianism of the left and right sought "empires of objects".

Rational dialogue between men was replaced by a monologue, a sort of perfect totalitarian language: the rulers spoke and gave orders, and the subjects were silent and obeyed. The monologues of the despots who ruled over their subjects were godlike, a discourse of one, as in George Orwell. The aim of the new discourse was to reduce the scope of thought: the revolution would be completed when the language was completed.[49] Arthur Koestler repeated this idea in his critique of communism: "Not only our thinking but also our vocabulary was reconditioned".[50] Herbert Marcuse revealed a similar way of thinking in the 1960s, when he remarked on the one-dimensionality of consumerist and technical language, corresponding to the one-dimensionality of the consumer society.[51] The triumph of instrumental reason as expressed in modern technology is likely to empty life of all transcendental meaning and to leave a world in which the only value is power for power's sake. It would seem that De Tocqueville's prophecy of a new despotism took on flesh and blood in the first half of the twentieth century: hence the great power of bureaucracy, hence the isolation and loneliness. Until the twentieth century, no political force was organized with the aim of destroying the bodies and souls of masses of human beings. Such nihilism was an extreme example of the modern practice of simplifying existential problems and solving them by technological means. Martin Heidegger saw this as a case of modernization and nothing more.[52]

In his book, *The Philosophical Discourse of Modernity* (1985), Jürgen Habermas examined in depth the influence of Nietzsche on post-modernist thought. He saw how Nietzsche's aesthetic view of the world became a criticism of the Enlightenment in Heidegger and Derrida and a subversion of reason in Foucault and Georges Bataille. The perspectivist approach and the Nietzschean genealogical method that undermined the validity of the concepts of "good" and "evil" gave rise to the post-modernist discourse that, according to Habermas, is based on a demonstrative critique of reason that positions itself outside rationalism.[53] Nietzsche's aphoristic method was different from the usual forms of philosophical self-criticism that had accompanied modernity from the beginning. The Nietzschean rhetoric attempted to uproot all attempts to gain acceptance for the "dialectic of enlightenment" and impose it. Nietzsche particularly disliked Kant's "practical reason" and Hegel's idea of the reassembling of fragments of the modern reality by means of a dialectical superstructure. An aesthetic escape from reality, said Habermas in reference to Nietzsche, can lead to dangerous simplistic conclusions.[54]

Modernity tends to distinguish between different dimensions of existence. Kant's critical trinity—science, ethics, and aesthetics—are three means of instruction that permit a reexamination and a critical assessment of reality. Max Weber, following Kant, saw modernity as a change from the total way of thinking of religion and metaphysics to a mode of thought that creates rational divisions: understanding of the universe (science), normative behavior (ethics), and aesthetic judgment (art).[55] The aestheticization of the whole of life is a dominance of one principle over the others, and it therefore cannot be critical and operates against modernity. Walter Benjamin and Marshall MacLuhan warned of the consequences of abandoning critical reason for an aestheticization of modern life. In totalitarianism as an aestheticization of politics[56] and in the communication media as an aestheticization of technology, form replaced content, myth replaced criticism, and one had experience in place of ideology.

The basis of the nihilist order was the experience of the absolute and nothingness, and it was likewise the foundation of the totalitarian regimes and ideologies. In the chapter, "Prometheus Becomes Napoleon, Napoleon Prometheus" in his *Work on Myth*, the philosopher Hans Blumenberg described the complex relationship of Goethe to Prometheus and Faust by means of a dialectic of the absolute and nothingness. Napoleon was an example of the danger of raising humans to the level of the absolute and sacrificing everything in order to realize an idea.[57] The concept of the absolute and nothingness took on flesh and blood in the twentieth century. This is how Trotsky described the project of the "new man" of permanent revolution:

> It is difficult to predict the extent of self-government which the man of the future may reach or the heights to which he may carry his technique. Social construction and psycho-physical self-education will become two aspects of one and the same process. All the arts—literature, drama, painting, music and architecture will lend this process beautiful form. More correctly, the shell in which the cultural construction and self-education of Communist man will be enclosed, will develop all the vital elements of contemporary art to the highest point. Man will become immeasurably stronger, wiser and subtler; his body will become more harmonized, his movements more rhythmic, his voice more musical. The forms of life will become dynamically dramatic. The average human type will rise to the heights of an Aristotle, a Goethe, or a Marx. And above this ridge new peaks will rise.[58]

Trotsky's Promethean vision, according to Michael Allen Gillespie in his *Nihilism Before Nietzsche*, was a development of Fichte's idea of absolute liberty.[59] The attempt to turn this idea into a reality produced a nightmare, from which we awakened only thirty years ago with the collapse of the last of the totalitarian ideologies. The principle complementary to the creation of the new revolutionary man in Trotsky's militaristic program was the organization of Soviet society as an army camp and transforming the Russian population into a disciplined and bureaucratic army of workers. Did the totalitarian ideologies exemplify the ancient Faustian sin in translating modern presumption into political terms?

The totalitarian ideologies provided comprehensive explanations of history and accordingly conceived vast programs of social transformation.[60] These ideologies were like secular religions, but unlike religions they set no limits to the powers of humankind. The despotic ideological regimes boasted of doing something that previously had only been ascribed to God: to create reality, to produce life, to create a new human. The a-historical and nonhumanistic character of instrumental rationality was in keeping with the nonhumanistic character of the totalitarian urge itself, and at the same time one should remember that one is speaking of a historical reality produced by human beings. This is how Albert Camus described the Promethean rebel who became a Caesar:

> Here ends Prometheus' surprising itinerary. Proclaiming his hatred of the gods and his love of mankind, he turns away from Zeus with scorn and

approaches mortal men in order to lead them in an assault against the heavens. But men are weak and cowardly; they must be organized. They love pleasure and immediate happiness; they must be taught to refuse, in order to grow up, immediate rewards. Thus Prometheus, in his turn, becomes a master who first teaches and then commands. Men doubt that they can safely attack the city of light and are even uncertain whether the city exists. They must be saved from themselves. The hero then tells them that he, and he alone, knows the city. Those who doubt his word will be thrown into the desert, chained to a rock, offered to the vultures. The others will march henceforth in darkness, behind the pensive and solitary master. Prometheus alone has become god and reigns over the solitude of men. But from Zeus he has gained only solitude and cruelty; he is no longer Prometheus, he is Caesar.[61]

Totalitarianism was a product of modernity. The roots of totalitarianism are to be found in the structure and logic of modern society, just as the phenomenon and roots of nihilism are to be found in Western society. Modern subjectivity has been revealed to be a Promethean will to power that soon became a purposeless endeavor. Parallel with this, many intellectuals in the twentieth century saw modernity as a humanistic self-realization, taking responsibility for a humanization of the social reality, fixing the world through new forms of productivity, social solidarity, and gradual improvement. Progress and rebellion were at the heart of the Western enterprise: it was a confirmation of the value of man. Humanism is an awareness of the potential of each person, the exercise of human liberty, a daily enactment of Prometheus. But as soon as modern man began to mold reality according to his understanding, he discovered that he was enslaved.

Post-modernists like Foucault and Jean-François Lyotard sought to expose the will to power of Western culture, the illusion of progress, the depressing backstage of modernity, the dark side of enlightenment.[62] Modern politics were founded on the basis of what Lyotard called the metanarrative of progress, of enlightenment. This, of course, is not the whole picture of humanism. It is one conceivable aspect, but one should not close one's eyes to the contradiction that exists in humanism or ignore one aspect of it. The will to power, which passed from the individual to society, gave birth to the Golem that rose against its maker.

Frankenstein was the eldest son of Prometheus unbound. Two years before the appearance of the anonymously published novel, *Frankenstein, or the Modern Prometheus* (1818), the poet Shelley, his wife Mary, and Lord Byron traveled together to the Swiss Alps. One evening, the two men discussed the scientific possibility of creating an artificial man. The effect of the conversation on Mary Shelley was so deep that on that same night she had a nightmare about the creation of a murderous man-monster. Two years later, a novel in the form of letters was published, in which a ship's captain named Walton told his sister the story of a Swiss scientist, Victor Frankenstein. After Walton had saved him from drowning, Frankenstein told him how he had created an artificial man from parts of a body stolen from a cemetery. The scientist who, contrary to nature, had created a new man with his own hands, experienced an emotional storm:

> Life and death appeared to me ideal bounds, which I should first breakthrough, and pour a torrent of light into our dark world. A new species would bless me as its creator and source; many happy and excellent natures would owe their being to me. No father could claim the gratitude of his child so completely as I should deserve theirs.[63]

The affair had a bad beginning. Frankenstein's assistant, Igor, mistakenly stole the brains of a criminal for the creation of the artificial man, and when he came into being, he was a man-monster who murdered all the inhabitants of the town and persecuted his maker obsessively. At the heart of the book was an insatiable thirst for knowledge: it could only be satisfied by taking Frankenstein's life. Although Frankenstein was motivated by his brain and the monster was actuated by his feelings, they were two sides of the same coin—humanity. The author was alarmed by modernity, which subverted enlightenment and warned the scientist that the monstrous product of his hands would rise against him.

The Golem who rises against his maker and becomes uncontrollable is the theme of both the legend of the Golem of Rabbi Elijah of Chelm and of Goethe's ballad of the legend of the sorcerer's apprentice. The ballad was written after a visit by the poet to the Altneuschul in Prague, the site of the Jewish legend ascribed, no doubt wrongly, to the Maharal of Prague.[64] According to the legend, the Maharal crated a Golem that served him on every day of the week except for the Sabbath. On every Sabbath eve, the Maharal removed the Ineffable Name from the Golem, and in that way he became lifeless. On one Sabbath, he forgot to do this. When the congregation chanted the Psalm for the Sabbath Day, the Golem began to act wildly and to destroy everything in its path. The Maharal was immediately summoned, and before the Sabbath began, he was able to remove the Ineffable Name. In the Maharal version of the story, the Golem collapsed and turned into dust, a lifeless clod of earth. In the Elijah of Chelm version, the Golem was stopped, but a piece of the matter he became fell on the rabbi and killed him. Thus, the Golem is a symbol of man's destructive power that grows immeasurably and can destroy the world. When the Golem is not restrained by the Holy Name and the rules of propriety, he is liable to strike out blindly and destructively.

The concept of the Golem passed through many metamorphoses in the history of ideas. In Jewish literature, the concept first appears in the *Book of Psalms* (139:16): "Thy eyes beheld my unformed substance; in thy book were written, every one of them, the days that were formed for me, when as yet there was none of them". The Midrash and the Talmud associated the concept with Adam, the "natural man", half-formed, created out of "the dust of the earth".

In the Hassidic tradition of the twelfth and thirteenth centuries, the Golem was an artificial man. There was a significant development in Kabbalistic circles in Provence and Spain when the Golem changed from being an artificial man to a symbolic representation of the world in a human form. Later, in Lurian Kabbala, the original man was created, but he was also a creator. He was the purpose of the creation, but at the same time infinite. Here, the concept of the "Golem" (the material of the body at the time of its formation) was connected with the concept of the "image" (the "form" of the human body).

As long as the divine spark was not supreme in humankind, the human was no more than a Golem. God was able to create the human from dust and implant the spark through the power of his Being and his Holy Wisdom, on the lines of "in his image made he him". The starting point of the argument was the celebrated saying in the Ethics of the Fathers (3:18):

> He (Rabbi Akiva) used to say: "Beloved of God is man, in that he was created in the divine image, but still greater was the love shown him, in that it was made known to him that he was created in the image of God, as it is said, For in the image of God made he man".

Man is the image (*icon*, or in the biblical equivalent, *tselem*) of God.[65] The view that humans are created in God's image makes God present in them, or, that is to say, makes them an extension of God. The Talmudic tradition took a truly revolutionary step. It asserted that rather than God was human, humanity was divine. It is precisely in their creative activity that humans demonstrate their divinity, for the concept of the imitation of God (*imitatio dei*) implies a totality. Humankind wishes to continue the immemorial work of God. One has here a kind of dual image: the human was made in the image of God, and the Golem was made in the image of the human.

Science embodies the modern Golem created through reason. Gershom Scholem spoke of biological and spiritual descendants of the Maharal: famous scientists like Theodor von Karman, the engineer-scholar who applied mathematics to space travel; John von Neumann, the physicist of quantum mechanics and game theory in economics; and Norbert Wiener, the mathematician who founded cybernetics.[66] Henri Atlan continued Scholem's line of thought and pointed out, among other things, that magic prepared the way for modern science, which seeks to comprehend the laws of nature, change it, and even control it.[67] Pico della Mirandola, for example, used magic and Kabbala in order to control the fate of the world by means of science. The "modernity" of the Renaissance—the intellectualization of magic—was personified by Giordano Bruno, the disseminator of the ideas of Copernicus sentenced to death by the Church like Prometheus bound to the rock by the gods.

Science, which had been theoretical speculation, became a will to power and a concrete influence on the world. In the story of the Golem, the myth portrayed the relationship between the knowledge of nature and the control of nature as ambivalent and contradictory. Eating from "the tree of knowledge of good and evil" meant that knowledge of the world gave men control of it. The tree of knowledge, which brings man close to God, fulfills the *raison d'être* of humans in the image of God. The ambiguous truth that the tree of knowledge is also the source of death and destruction has accompanied the experience of knowledge from its gnostic and monotheistic origins to early science, the Renaissance, and modernity. Scientific achievement is the apex of the idea of the imitation of God: in order to truly understand humanity, we must be able to create it.[68] The natural sciences provided inspiration for the social sciences: political science, beginning with modernity and the Enlightenment, sought to create a new man as the crown and necessary realization of a knowledge of human nature.

The "mad father" in Bruno Schulz's story *Tailor's Dummies*, wished to reach "Faustian heights", or, as Moshe Idel claimed: The second creation of men is achieved in the same way a tailor uses his dummy.[69] But unlike this modern human, separated from the divine sphere, the wise men of the Middle Ages were audacious and did not fear the theological consequences of humankind's creative powers. They wished to produce something that would reflect the creation of humanity through a magical experience that would attain spiritual plenitude. The Jewish philosopher André Neher remarked, in his book *Faust and the Maharal of Prague* (1987), on "the basic identity of the structure of the Golem and the Faustian soul of modern and post-modern man".[70]

Faust represents a pact with the devil, and the Golem reflects the ambivalence of human nature, the ambiguity of the sciences, which is the hallmark of modernity. In the words of Gershom Scholem, "The Golem [. . .] became a technical servant of man's needs".[71] Was this the intention of the Frankfurt School when they revealed the instrumental rationality of modernity? Prometheus's contemporary counterpart is to be found in the scientist, the engineer, and the technician who create their Golems in laboratories and duplicate them.[72] Science is criticized by its creator, but it is liable to liberate the dangerous tendencies it contains, overrule its critic, and develop destructive qualities. Jewish tradition in ancient times held that the earth has a spirit of its own. The gnostic sources of this tradition warned of the danger of making the Golem an uncontrolled independent body, a creation that is its own authority. The question of the creation of man has long ago left the esoteric sphere of magic for that of science, which determines boundaries.[73] This is perhaps the secret of the connection between the philosopher Hans Jonas's study of the gnostics in his youth and his later search for "an ethics for a technological civilization". His conclusion was that "Prometheus was undoubtedly released from his chains when science revealed previously unknown powers".[74]

The conclusions of a presidential commission published in the United States in 1982 described the dialectic of genetic engineering.[75] The members of the committee relied on the myth of the Sorcerer's Apprentice, the myth of the Golem and the Frankenstein story while formulating their conclusions. The twentieth century had the Promethean urge to control nature, to mold the cosmos, and to create a new human. The problem was the great gulf that exists between the ever increasing powers and possibilities of the modern human and our impotence, the price we pay for our liberty and the disasters we create with our own hands. The achievements of modern humankind seem amazing by any historical standard, and they have been attained due to our previously unparalleled powers. However, these powers do not succeed in giving people true happiness or the feeling that they are in control of their fate or their lives. The power always seems to be uncontrolled or in the possession of someone else.[76]

Our powers have risen against us and determine the conditions of our existence with an independent dynamic that perfects itself in its own way. We are blind to it, and it finally causes us lethal damage. It seems that with every new medicine, we create a previously unknown illness, that every technological development demands an ecological price, that the potential for quality of life provided by nuclear reactors is immediately revealed to be the danger of nuclear annihilation. We destroy species, pollute sources, unload populations on the face of the earth, pierce the ozone layer, spread cancer and AIDS, cause poverty and unemployment, and increase racial and ethnic hatreds. One can no longer blame the Greek *moira*, a predetermined fate, bow down before God or place hope in transcendental powers. These are not unavoidable disasters, punishments from heaven: these are the long-term consequences of human actions, of our wishes and desires. We ourselves lower our world into the pit, we drive the engine lunging into the abyss.

The Advisory Committee for Bio-Ethics of the United States advised Congress to allow the cloning of human embryos for research purposes. Following success in duplicating a sheep by gene cloning, there was a debate about making improvements through genetic engineering. Genetic technology and social planning permit a change in the ratio of men to women, the choice of the sex of a child, the production of desirable qualities, and even the cloning of a man. The Nazis' experiments in eugenics were the first fruits of a perverted reality in which a dehumanization took place when modernity rose against enlightenment. Ever since the success in duplicating the sheep by genetic cloning, governments and presidents have appointed committees of thinkers and scientists to examine the ethical, legislative, and practical consequences of human genetic cloning. Professor Michel Revel of the Weizmann Institute recommended cloning only in particular cases and warned of it becoming a social technology. One cannot prevent individual precedents from speeding up research in an endless race that could end in disaster. It should be remembered that the success of evolution until now has not been the result of planning but was accidental and arbitrary.

Is the oldest desire of all, the desire to create a new human through our own powers, connected with the death of God? One of the oldest sources of the Golem legend relates that the prophet Jeremiah studied *Sefer Yetzira* (The Book of Creation). Through a Kabbalistic combination of letters, a man was created on whose forehead were written the letters יהוה אלוהים אמת ("*Yahweh elohim emet*", the Lord is the true God, Jeremiah 10:10). But the man erased with a knife the א [aleph] of אמת (true), and there remained מת (*met* = dead).

The meaning was a desecration of the Holy Name whereby God was shown to be dead. This is how Gershom Scholem, who told the story, summed it up: "It is indeed significant that Nietzsche's famous cry, 'God is dead', should have gone up first in a Kabbalistic text warning against the making of a Golem and linking the death of God to the realization of the idea of the Golem".[77]

The metamorphoses of the story of the Golem and the modern myth of Frankenstein and its progeny hint at the possibilities threatening the man who has created himself from the dust of God, modern humans who have freed themselves from their restraints. In Fritz Lang's film *Metropolis* (1928), inspired by Gustav Meyrink's novel *The Golem*, the hero of the film and the ruler of the city of Metropolis, together with the scientist who worked for him, created a robot in the form of a woman. Technology, personified by the woman-robot who transforms the human and spiritual into the industrial and mechanical, becomes "an autonomous god-like force demanding prostration, surrender and ritual sacrifice".[78] In the film *Blade Runner*, made in the 1980s, the director Ridley Scott produced robots with a short life span who rose against their creators and destroyed them, as in the Kabbalistic legend. Isaac Asimov, a popular writer of science fiction, for his part created a new genre of robots that were positive and effective, in contrast to the Frankenstein tradition.

Modernity—man's attempt at self-creation—also acquired a monstrous Frankenstinian quality. The communist faith engendered Stalinism, and modern technology created the atom bomb and Zyklon B. If the objective sanctifies values, the latter lose their absolute character and become relative. This was the conclusion reached by thinkers such as Leo Strauss and Eric Voegelin in politics: a nihilistic relativism of values lies at the heart of the modern consciousness.[79] A relativism of values permits a distortion of values and finally a loss of values. Prometheus's betrayal was a sort of distortion of the ideas of the Enlightenment: nationalism as the assertion of the universal right to self-determination became a murderous form of nationalism; the revolution of "liberty, equality, fraternity" was succeeded by the totalitarian revolutions of the twentieth century; a liberating and progressive science turned into a technology of destruction and the ruination of nature; the technical possibility of universal abundance and wealth produced an all-engulfing Metropolis, a totalitarian Leviathan; positive, progressive, and enlightened ways of thinking were replaced by the tragic idolatry of modern hubris. In his book, *Main Currents in Sociological Thought* (1965), Raymond Aron analyses this phenomenon:

> To understand historical man as Promethean is to understand him in terms of what seems important to us, man's meditation on his own destiny. [. . .] [F]or to be able to call historical man Promethean, one must assume that he questions himself, his values, his vocation.[80]

The American Air Force is preparing for the wars of the future in which we will seek to control natural forces. The technologies of the future will create a certain weather, foment natural disasters, produce rainstorms, divert rivers, create clouds for camouflage, create mists and fogs. Neotechnology (the reorganization of atoms and molecules) will create mists to confuse the movements of the enemy, floods out of nothing in a given area for a given time, and storms that will turn into hurricanes that will devastate whole regions. There are studies on how to cause an instability in the atmosphere that creates artificial chambers of storm and on planning changes in the ionosphere that will confuse the enemy and improve the connections with friendly forces.

This pronounced modern arrogance is revealed as a form of nihilism that suppresses criticism, effaces the individual, rejects the other, destroys dialogue, and voids the present in favor of a hypothetical future, a mythical model, or a virtual reality. In such an intellectual environment, which fosters extremism, one must develop a critical view of the situation. The longing for nothingness leads to a will to absoluteness expressed in totalitarian structures.

Socrates, that indefatigable intellectual subverter, represents what we need: an essential commitment to the good and the true in a situation that is liable to lose its philosophical compass and its moral conscience. Despite the critique of modernity that has made its way to places beyond its limits, one must try to understand modernity in a spirit of critical involvement and not seek out anti-rational and anti-modern escape routes. A critical Promethean enlightenment is required, based on a philosophical reading and a distinction between truth and falsehood; a universal ethic and a distinction between good and evil, a historical understanding, an environmental and aesthetic sensitivity, and a social solidarity among the humans that make up the family of mankind.

Notes

1 Matthew W. Maguire, *The Conversion of Imagination: From Pascal Through Rousseau to Tocqueville*, Cambridge 2006.
2 Karl Marx, "Capital: Critique of Political Economy", in *Karl Marx–Friedrich Engels: Collected Works*, vol. 1, Institute of Marxism-Leninism, Moscow and New York 1975, 645.
3 Paul Ricœur, "Qu'est-ce qu'un texte? Expliquer et Comprendre", *Hermeneutik und Dialektik*, II, Tubingen 1970, 181–200.
4 Moshe Idel, *Golem: Jewish Magical and Mystical Traditions on the Artificial Anthropoid* (Suny Series in Judaica), New York 1990; Olga Raggio, "The Myth of Prometheus—Its Survival and Commonplace", *Journal of Warburg and Courtauld Institutes*, 21 (1958): 44–62.
5 Hesiod, *Hesiod: Theogony, Works and Days, Testimonia*, trans., Glenn W. Most, Loeb Classical Library, no. 57, Cambridge, MA 2006; Aeschylus, *Aeschylus: Persians. Seven Against Thebes. Suppliants. Prometheus Bound*, trans., Alan H. Sommerstein, Loeb Classical Library, no. 145, Cambridge, MA 2009.
6 There is a scholarly debate over the authenticity of Aeschylus's *Prometheus Bound*. For further reading on the subject, see C. J. Harrington, *The Author of Prometheus Bound*, Austin, TX 1970; Reginald Pepys Winnington-Ingram, *Studies in Aeschylus*, Cambridge 1983.
7 Hesiod, *Theogony*.
8 Plato, *Laches. Protagoras. Meno. Euthydemus*, Loeb Classical Library 165, Cambridge, MA 1977, 129.

9. Leon Golden, *In Praise of Prometheus: Humanism and Rationalism in Aeschylean Thought*, Chapel Hill, NC 1966.
10. Jacqueline Duchemin, *Promethe: Historie du mythe, de ses origines orientales a ses incarnations modernes*, Paris 1974; Raymond Trousson, *Le theme de Promethee dans la literature europeenne*, 2 vols., Geneva 1964.
11. Hans Urs von Balthasar, *Prometheus: Studien zur Geschichte des deutschen Idealismus*, Heidelberg 1947.
12. Johann Gottlieb Fichte, "Die Anweisung zum seligen Leben oder auch die Religionslehre", in *Sammtliche Werke*, vol. V, 1806, 504.
13. Friedrich Wilhelm Joseph Schelling, *Einleitung in die Philosophie der Mythologie oder Darstellung der rein-rationalen Philosophie in Schellings Werke*, ed., Schroder M., 6 vols., Munich 1927–1928, vol. V, 663–664.
14. August Wilhelm Schlegel, *Prometheus*, 1979; appeared first in Friedrich Schiller, *Musen-Almanach*, Tubingen 1798, 54.
15. Karl Friedrich Koppen, *Friedrich der Gross und seine Widersacher*, Leipzig 1840, 30.
16. W. Meschke, ed., "Prometheus", in *Gedichte Goethes, veran-schaulicht nach Form und Strukturwandel*, Berlin 1957, 83.
17. Károly Kerényi, *Prometheus: Archetypal Image of Human Experience*, trans., R. Manheim, New York 1963.
18. Philip M. Palmer and Robert P. More, eds., *The Sources of the Faust Tradition, from Simon Magus to Lessing*, London 1936; Geneviève Bianquis, *Faust a travers quatre siecles*, Paris 1955.
19. T. J. Ridd, Goethe (Past Masters), Oxford 1984; E. C. Mason, *Goethe's Faust: Its Genesis and Purpose*, Berkley 1967; Lesley Sharpe, ed., *The Cambridge Companion to Goethe*, Cambridge 2006; Barker Fairley, *Faust: Six Essays*, Oxford 1953.
20. Raphael Judah Zwi Werblowsky, *Lucifer and Prometheus—A Study of Milton's Satan*, London 1952.
21. George Gordon Byron, *The Works of Lord Byron*, London 1905, 269.
22. Friedrich Schiller, "The Theosophy of Julius," *The Works of Friedrich Schiller*, IV, Poems and Essays, New York 1906, 294.
23. Georg Wilhelm Friedrich Hegel, *Philosophie des Rechts—Die Vorlesung von 1919–20 in einer Nachschrift*, D. Henrich, ed., Frankfurt 1983.
24. Marx and Engels, *Collected Works, vol. 1, Marx: 1835–1843*, New York 1973, 30.
25. Roger Wells, *Insurrection: The British Experience 1795–1803*, Gloucester, MA 1986.
26. David Ohana, *The Nihilist Order: The Intellectual Roots of Totalitarianism*, Eastbourne 2016, 15–55.
27. Friedrich Nietzsche, *Digitale Kritische Gesamtausgabe Werke und Briefe*, NF-1885, 34[112]—Nachgelassene Fragmente April–Juni 1885.
28. Ibid, *Die fröhliche Wissenschaft*: § 300. Erste Veröff. 10/09/1882.
29. Zeev Sternhell, *Anti-Enlightenment Tradition*, trans., David Maisel, New Haven, CT 2009.
30. Yehoshua Arieli, *Individualism and Nationalism in American Ideology*, Cambridge, MA 1964.
31. Max Weber, *The Protestant Ethic and the Spirit of Capitalism*, trans., Stephen Kalberg, Oxford 2010.
32. Alan Bloom, *Closing of the American Mind: How Higher Education Has Failed Democracy and Impoverished the Souls of Today's Students*, New York 2012.
33. Thomas Hobbes, *Hobbes: Leviathan (Revised student edition)*, ed., Richard Tuck, Cambridge 1996; Jean-Jacques Rousseau, *On the Social Contract (Hackett Classics)*, trans., Donald A. Cress, Indianapolis, IN 1988.
34. Moses Mendelssohn, *Ueber die Frage: was heißt aufklären?* Berlin 1784.
35. Immanuel Kant, *Beantwortung der Frage: Was ist Aufklärung?* Berlin 1784.
36. Michel Foucault, *History of Madness*, trans., J. Khalfa, ed., J. Murphy, New York 2006.

37 Yehoshua Arieli, *Individualism and Nationalism in American Ideology*, Cambridge, MA 1964, 199–200.
38 John Locke, *Second Treatise of Government* (Hackett Classics), Indianapolis, IN 1980.
39 Marquis des Condorcet, *Esquisse d'un tableau historique des progres de l'esprit humain*, Paris 1795.
40 Ernst Cassirer, *The Philosophy of the Enlightenment*, Princeton, NJ 1951, 39–40.
41 Jean Starobinski, *Jean-Jacques Rousseau, La Transparence et l'obstacle*, Paris 1982; Gianni Vattimo, *The Transparent Society*, Cambridge 1992.
42 Robert J. Nelson, "The Quarrel of Ancients and the Moderns", in Denis Hollier, ed., *A New History of French Literature*, Cambridge, MA 1989.
43 Talcott Parsons, *The System of Modern Societies*, Englewood Cliffs, NJ 1971.
44 Martin Jay, *The Dialectical Imagination: A History of the Frankfurt School and the Institute for Social Research 1921–1950*, London 1973.
45 Richard J. Bernstein, ed., *Habermas on Modernity*, Cambridge, MA 1985.
46 Max Horkheimer and Theodor Adorno, *The Dialectic of Enlightenment*, New York 1974, VII.
47 François Furet, *La Revolution 1770–1880. Historie de la France*, vol. IV, Paris 1988.
48 Hannah Arendt, *The Origins of Totalitarianism*, New York 1968, 454.
49 Jeffrey C. Issac, *Arendt, Camus, and Modern Rebellion*, New Haven, CT 1992.
50 Arthur Koestler, "The Initiates", in Richard H. Crossman, ed., *The God That Failed*, New York 1950, 39–40.
51 Herbert Marcuse, "The End of Utopia", in *Five Lectures: Psychoanalysis, Politics and Utopia*, trans., J. J. Shapiro and S. M. Weber, Boston 1970.
52 M. E. Zimmerman, *Heidegger's Confrontation with Modernity: Technology, Politics, Art*, Bloomington, IN 1990.
53 Jurgen Habermas, *The Philosophical Discourse of Modernity*, trans., Frederick G. Lawrence, Cambridge, MA 1987, 96.
54 Idem, "The Entry into Post-Modernity—Nietzsche as a Turning Point", ibid., 105.
55 Max Weber, *Gesammelte Aufsatze zur Reigionssoziologie*, Tubingen 1922–1923, 15–25.
56 Walter Benjamin, "The Work of Art in the Age of Its Technological Reproductibility", in Edmund Jephcott, Howard Eiland, and others, trans., Michael W. Jennings and Howard Eiland, eds., *Collected Writings*, Cambridge, MA 2002, 96–101; Marshall McLuhan, "Myth and Mass Media", *Daedalus*, 2 (Spring 1959), 339–348.
57 Hans Blumenberg, *Work on Myth*, trans., R. M. Wallace, Cambridge, MA 1985, 497.
58 Leon Trotsky, *Literature and Revolution*, ed., William Keach, Ann Arbor, MI 1960, 256.
59 Michael Allen Gillespie, *Nihilism Before Nietzsche*, Chicago 1995, 172.
60 Alain Touraine, *Critique of Modernity*, Oxford 1995, 318–320.
61 Albert Camus, *The Rebel: An Essay on Man in Revolt*, trans., Anthony Bower, New York 1992, 244–245.
62 Michel Foucault, *Surveiller et punir*, Paris 1975; Jean-Francois Lyotard, *La condition post-moderne: rapport sur le savoir*, Paris 1979; Scott Lash, *Sociology of Post-Modernism*, London 1990.
63 Mary Shelley, *Frankenstein: Or the Modern Prometheus*, San Diego 2015, 42.
64 Gershom Scholem, *Origins of the Kabbalah*, trans., Allan Arkush, Princeton, NJ 1987, 102–103; idem, "The Golem of Prague & the Golem of Rehovoth", *Commentary*, January 1, 1966; Moshe Idel, *Golem: Jewish Magical and Mystical Traditions on the Artificial Anthropoid (Suny Series in Judaica)*, New York 1990.
65 Yair Lorberbaum, *In God's Image: Myth, Theology, and Law in Classical Judaism*, Cambridge 2015.
66 Scholem, "The Golem of Prague & the Golem of Rehovoth".
67 Henri Atlan, Preface, in Moshe Idel, *Le Golem*, trans., Cyrille Aslanoff, Paris 1992, 11–28.

68 Ibid., Altan, 25.
69 Ibid., Idel, 29.
70 André Neher, *Faust et le Maharal de Prague: Le mythe et le réel* (Questions) (French Edition), Paris 2015, 198.
71 Gershom Scholem, *The Messianic Idea in Judaism and Other Essays*, New York 1995, 338.
72 Jean-Jacques Salmon, *Le destin technologique*, Paris 1922, 19.
73 Dominique Lecourt, *Promethee, Faust, Frankenstein—Fondements imaginaries de l'ethique*, Le Plessis-Robinson 1996.
74 Hans Jonas, *Le principe responsabilite: une ethuque pour la civilization technologique*, Paris 1990.
75 Byron L. Sherwin, *The Golem Legend*, New York 1952, 29.
76 Hanna Fenichel Pitkin, *The Attack of the Blob—Hannah Arendt's Concept of the Social*, Chicago 1981, 7–8.
77 Scholem, "The Golem of Prague & the Golem of Rehovoth".
78 Andreas Huyssen, "The Vamp and the Machine—Technology and Sexuality in Fritz Lang's Metropolis", *New German Critique*, 24–25 (1981–1982): 221–237.
79 Leo Strauss, *Natural Right and History*, Chicago 1965; Eric Voeglin, *The New Science of Politics*, Chicago 1987.
80 Raymond Aron, *Main Currents in Sociological Thought*, vol. I, London 1965, 208.

1 From Rousseau to Tocqueville

Janus Face of Modernity

A. Jean-Jacques Rousseau and the Promethean Chains

Already in his first essay, *Discours sur les sciences et les arts* (Discourse on the Sciences and Arts) (1750), Jean-Jacques Rousseau exposed the paradoxical process whereby modernity subverted the Enlightenment:

> The sciences, letters, and arts [. . .] spread garlands of flowers over the iron chains with which they are laden, throttle in them the sentiment of that original freedom for which they seemed born, make them love their slavery, and fashion them into what is called civilized peoples.[1]

Modern man—the fettered Prometheus casting off his chains—was his own prisoner. The image of chains runs like a thread through the writings of Rousseau and reflects the snare of modern freedom.

The version of the Prometheus fable that Rousseau cites in the First Discourse is drawn from Plutarch's "How to Profit from One's Enemies", an essay that accompanied Rousseau throughout his life. Unlike the versions of Aeschylus, Hesiod, and Plato, which stressed the pains of Prometheus's knowledge that accompanied the gift of light he received, Plutarch emphasized the advantages of fire for those who know how to use it. Rousseau internalized both the lessons of Hesiod, Aeschylus, and Plato and that of Plutarch and saw the dual face of Prometheus:

> Prometheus's torch is the torch of the Sciences made to quicken great geniuses; that the Satyr who, seeing fire for the first time, runs towards it, and wants to embrace it, represents the vulgar who, seduced by the brilliance of Letters [. . .] that the Prometheus who cries out and warns them of the danger is the citizen of Geneva.[2]

This article presents a phenomenological inquiry into the eidetic structures of modernity. The method of the inquiry will be a hermeneutical and comparative study of Jean-Jacques Rousseau's texts as both partly foundational and representative of the character of modernity as Promethean passion. The usage of mythological metaphors is designed to provide a nonrationalistic explanation of the phenomena—an explanation that attempts to grasp the phenomena using a form of understanding that would put modernity in a broader context than itself and would enable an essential understanding of modernity without first committing to its rationalistic variation. I examine Rousseau's writings as characteristics of the general tendency of modernity to create human beings anew—especially using the myth of Prometheus. To conduct the following investigations, I assume the innate openness of Rousseau's writings to contradictions that are characteristic of modernity itself and thus provide an avenue toward the essence of modernity. It is not the purpose of this article to provide a new, coherent, and satisfactory interpretation of Rousseau's thought—on which there is plenty of excellent research elsewhere. The aim here is to provide a reading of Rousseau whose center lies outside his thought as an individual; more precisely, to illuminate the nature of modernity using mythical insights.

In his book on education, *Émile, ou de l'éducation* (Émile, or On Education) (1762), Rousseau developed the theme of chains in connection with the alumnus or the citizen: "To reduce him all of a sudden to a soft and sedentary life would be to imprison him, to enchain him, to keep him in a violent and constrained state".[3] And he also wrote: "All the chains of opinion are broken for me; I know only those of necessity. I learned to bear these chains from my birth, and I shall bear them until my death, for I am a man".[4] The conclusion Émile finally reached after going on his travels with his teacher was to:

> remain what you have made me and voluntarily to add no other chain to the one nature and the laws burden me. The more I examine the work of men in their institutions, the more I see that they make themselves slaves by dint of wanting to be independent and that they use up their freedom in vain efforts to ensure it.[5]

Alluding to Plato's analogy of the cave, Rousseau asked in his "Discourse on the Sciences and Arts", "Are we, then, destined to die tied to the edge of the well into which truth has withdrawn?"[6]

Twelve years later, in *Le contrat social* (The Social Contract) (1762), Rousseau wrote one of the most striking openings in the history of political thought: "Man is born free, and everywhere he is in chains".[7] The distance from Rousseau's diagnosis that the source of the evil was inequality to the revolutionary Marxist conclusion or to educational radicalism was not a long one: the workers or pupils have nothing to lose but their chains.

Rousseau can be viewed as a contemporary thinker.[8] The tensions in his political and educational outlook are the contradictions of modernity. He was an intellectual who was contemptuous of intellectuals, who glorified sentiment in the name of reason, a thinker of the Enlightenment who despised the idea of progress. The ego and the collective clash within him; freedom and equality disturb his peace; he criticizes the arts and sciences but writes a learned article for the Academy of Arts and Sciences. He overrides the personal will of people of flesh and blood in the name of the abstract principle of the general will; the purpose of his essays was the good of the individual, yet his ideal was a small political community reflecting a social contract established through a perpetual referendum. Did Rousseau forestall a particular kind of modern intellectual: one who seeks to decipher hidden codes and tensions in the spiritual climate of his period?

It is usual to see Rousseau as the father of progressive education. In his book, *Émile, or On Education*, "natural education" is the heart of his educational-anthropological system. Here are some principles of Rousseau's modern progressive education: the autonomy of childhood, an emphasis on the individual, a stage-by-stage preparation of the child and the youth for the life of society, education through nature, the use of "negative education" for educational purposes. The innovative methods he advocated established his reputation as a radical critic of bourgeois, normative, conventional education, a thinker who championed the "natural" man. But in contrast to the liberal interpretation of *Émile*, this educational tract can be seen as a two-way text that offers each generation a democratic education but also a totalitarian one, freedom but also servitude, individuality, but, no less, conformity.

The Rousseauist freedom is paradoxical: it is a freedom that subjugates itself to the aims and purposes of objective reason. Rousseau praises a free education, but another reading of his pedagogical essay shows that what we have before us is a model of educational conditioning. Émile's instructor Jean-Jacques says that the person instructed can do what he or she wants but can only want what the instructor wishes him to do. Rousseau's view of education reflects the interrelationship of the Enlightenment and modernity and the paradoxical concept of freedom in his teachings. Modern humans who seek to form their own world can form it in accordance with the principles of the Enlightenment or in opposition to them. There is an immanent gap between the ideal and the reality. In this respect, *Émile* is a mirror of the paradoxes of modern thought in both the political and the educational spheres.

Rousseau is a many-sided thinker who forestalled with his insights the main intellectual signposts on the intersections of modernity. Before Kant, he sought a positive correlation between reason and morality;[9] he forestalled Hegel in the distinction between "civil society" and the state;[10] he heralded Marx in seeing property as the foundation of the political order and in his desire for a universalization of freedom.[11] He preceded Darwin in the theory of evolution, preceded Nietzsche in perceiving the origins of good and evil in historical and philological genealogy.[12] Before Freud, he was skeptical of culture, progress and art; before existentialism, he saw the alienation in man's desire to resemble his neighbor. He was a pioneer of the structural revolution, and it is not surprising if Claude Lévi-Strauss saw him as the anthropologist among the philosophers.[13] Before de Tocqueville, he identified the danger in the power of public opinion, and before the Frankfurt School he perceived the "cultural industry" of industrial civilization. Before Jacques Ellul, he exposed the lethal potential of science and technology, and he preceded both the existentialists, the Frankfurt School, and the post-modernists in his criticism of the one-dimensionality of the Enlightenment and of its schematic assumptions of the inevitability of progress and the exclusivity of reason.[14]

It is not surprising if opposing thinkers and currents of thought have in modern times taken hold of Rousseau and refused to let him go. Kant, who regarded Rousseau as "the Newton of morality", claimed that he cured him of the idea that the glory of the human race was its intellectual development. Rousseau liberated him from his prideful attitude toward the common citizen who had no part in this intellectual progress. Kant wrote that Rousseau taught him to respect humanity, and the only picture in his bare room was a portrait of Rousseau. Kant and Rousseau were both outstanding figures of the Enlightenment, but Rousseau sought to get away from it. He wished to transform reason à la Kant into the general will, into spontaneous knowledge, into a social contract and an educational experience. Kant learned from Rousseau that virtue is a precondition for man to be man and that the law of nature is the "world of morality". Virtue is the human's capacity to aspire to the ideal, to direct consciousness toward a universal objective that is simultaneously rational and moral. In the instructor's call to his protégé Émile to "widen the law of knowledge", there is the idea of extending the laws of nature to human morality. In this way, Kant's categorical imperative owes a debt of antecedence to Rousseau. Rousseau, however, made the opposite impression on Nietzsche in his *Twilight of the Idols*:

> But Rousseau—to what did he really want to return? Rousseau, this first modern man, idealist and rabble in one person—one who needed moral "dignity" to be able to stand his own sight, sick with unbridled vanity and unbridled self-contempt. This miscarriage, couched on the threshold of modern times, also wanted a "return to nature"; to ask this once more, to what did Rousseau want to return?[15]

To Nietzsche's question about the character of Rousseau's "return to nature"—his famous cry—there are several different answers. Nietzsche claimed that in every act of value in art or life, there is a creative overcoming of raw nature. In rationalism, there is also an attempt to transcend the raw material, a transcendence from nature to what is beyond it, to what is no longer nature.

In 1762, the year of the publication of the *Social Contract* and *Émile*, Rousseau gave two opposite answers to the question, "What is human nature?"[16] This anthropological-political curiosity about the nature of man is linked in Rousseau, as in many thinkers of his generation, with the distinction made by the Enlightenment between the "state of nature" and the "political state". Were these actual historical states or hypothetical alternatives? Rousseau's "natural man" in a "state of nature" does not relate to a historical human being but to a model, a criterion, a point of comparison. The figure of the "natural man" served as an inspiration to modern anthropologists, who found it a useful model for a comparative study of societies.

In Rousseauian terms, man in his wild state is not the natural man. Rousseau can admire the noble savage as a type that is uncorrupted, but he is not an ideal. Modern man cannot return to the condition of the noble savage. Rousseau's intention was more complex than that: to transcend the ideal of man in his wild state and to educate toward the ideal of the natural man. Modern man cannot return to a primitive state, but he can look at the infancy of mankind as a model, as a kind of nonlost paradise. The question is how modern man can improve himself, and Rousseau believed this is only possible in a dialectical fashion. He can progress if he has before him the vision of the natural man: freedom and not alienation, partnership and not enslavement, direct experience and not life according to the book.

Voltaire, a contemporary of Rousseau's and an outstanding representative of the age of modernity and enlightenment, understood Rousseau's "return to nature" as a return to the primitive stage of humanity.[17] Nietzsche was closer to the mark than Voltaire, inasmuch as he realized that Rousseau's modernity lay in his moral ambivalence, in the fact that he was both "idealistic and degraded". In Nietzsche's opinion, this ambivalence also characterized the French Revolution, which gave birth to modernity:

> I still hate Rousseau in the French Revolution: it is the world-historical expression of this duality of idealist and rabble. The bloody farce which became an aspect of the Revolution, its "immortality", are of little concern to me: what I hate is its Rousseauan morality.[18]

In his *Antichrist*, Nietzsche listed Rousseau among the spiritual zealots: Savonarola, Luther, Robespierre, Saint Simon, the pathological foundation of whose teachings made them "the opposition-type of the strong spirit who has become free".[19] Nietzsche, like Robespierre himself, saw Rousseau as the spiritual father of Robespierre, who in the French Revolution wanted to impose a mechanical equality on all humans, to subjugate them within their state of freedom.

Marx also perceived Rousseau's influence on Robespierre and the French revolutionaries, but his attack on Rousseau was made from the other side of the fence. In Marx's opinion, Rousseau's and Robespierre's failure to relate to the dominant economic class finally left them as idealists who adhered to the principle of will. All that Rousseau and the revolutionaries were able to accomplish, according to Marx, was a political revolution without economic significance, and it therefore had no chance of bringing about real social change. Marx was stubborn in not recognizing Rousseau's influence on him, but it undoubtedly existed, if only to a limited degree. Although Marx's innovation was his emphasis on an understanding of the economic-social mechanism in the historical context, one can easily see a great similarity between the "Communist Manifesto" and Rousseau's *Second Discourse*.[20] Rousseau saw at an early stage the Promethean fetters of modern man.

The writer of *The Social Contract* has also been subjected to criticism from the radical wing of the "nihilist-totalitarian" current. To anti-Enlightenment intellectuals of the late nineteenth and early twentieth centuries, Rousseau was the greatest intellectual adversary of all. Georges Sorel, the theoretician of violence and myth, said that the Enlightenment, represented by Rousseau, adopted the philosophy of nature, which was essentially religious and pantheistic. According to Sorel, the "utopian" philosophies of the eighteenth century turned to the concept "nature", which to them represented wholeness and absolute harmony. The Enlightenment replaced the religious concept "God" with the modern concepts "nature" and "reason" and in this way made harmonious, deterministic basic assumptions that Sorel totally rejected. Sorel found signs of religiosity and Christianity in the ideas of the Enlightenment. He said that "some of Rousseau's ideas about nature are essentially biblical and Calvinistic".[21] He saw the rational ideal of the Enlightenment as in no way different from the religious ideal: both of them seek to exchange this world, with its contradictions, for an alternative structure devoid of oppositions. In Sorel's opinion, Rousseau exemplified Jacobin abstraction, the offspring of rationalist despotism and begetter of political utopias like the French Revolution.[22]

Rousseau was aware of the paradoxes that his writings could engender. In *Émile* he warned, "Common readers, pardon me my paradoxes. When one reflects, they are necessary and, whatever you may say, I prefer to be a paradoxical man than a prejudiced one".[23] With self-mockery, he said in the same vein in his most important work: "I would wager that on this point a thousand people will again find a contradiction in *The Social Contract*. This shows that there are more readers who have to learn to read than there are writers who have to learn to be consistent". This awareness of Rousseau of the paradoxical character of human nature is modernity's contribution to political and educational thought.

Rousseau's first essay, "Discourse on the Sciences and Arts", is a prophecy of twentieth-century humanity and a warning that modernity is in danger when science subverts the human race. This piece, which won the Dijon Académie des sciences et belles lettres prize, discusses the question put by the academy: did the creation of the sciences and arts contribute to an improvement of morals? Rousseau's answer, in total contradiction to what one might expect from a man of his time, completely rejected what is considered the heart of the Enlightenment—the belief in education and progress—as expressed, for example, in the *Encyclopédie* (Encyclopedia) of his friend Diderot. In his opinion, science, art, and popular education were harmful to morality. Moreover, the souls of human beings were corrupted by the progress of science. The correlation between education and corruption, he said, was a phenomenon that "has been observed in all times and places". Examples of this historical "law" could be found in ancient Egypt, Greece, Rome, Byzantium, and modern China. Unlike these civilizations, uneducated peoples such as the Persians, the Germans, the early Romans, and the Swiss were virtuous. Individuals, unlike peoples, can be both wise and virtuous, and Socrates, who attacked the sciences and arts, was an outstanding example of this.

Rousseau makes a sharp distinction between virtue and sterilizing enlightenment. Human knowledge and conventional education contain our errors from the beginning, and it is therefore dangerous to rely on them. He enumerates certain problems that deserve to be mentioned: learning through conjecture, refutation, and confrontation do not necessarily contribute to achieving the required goal, which is knowledge. There is no connection between the great scientific discoveries and the education of citizens to be virtuous, and there is even a negative correlation between the "mass of philosophers" and the value of philosophy.

Inequality develops among men on an artificial basis that is not conducive to virtue. Those unable to attain scientific achievements have to be artists, and the others, who are able to be true intellectuals, have no need of teachers. The sciences and arts can be enriched only when political power and scientific knowledge are interwoven and interdependent, and thus philosophers such as Newton, Descartes, and Bacon should be the counselors of kings. Plato made a distinction between the ideas of the majority of men and true knowledge, which is given to only a very few. The norms of society are uncritically upheld by the body of citizens: "As for ourselves, vulgar men, to whom Heaven has not vouchsafed such great talents and whom it does not destine for so much glory, let us remain in our obscurity".[24] Very few people devote their lives solely to the pursuit of wisdom, critical of norms and skeptical of common beliefs.

In this initial essay, Rousseau made a distinction between knowledge and ideas, a dichotomy that corresponds to that between philosophy and politics. According to the republican-Platonic way of thinking, an ideal political order would be achieved under a philosopher-king, but the paradox is that, by nature, the philosopher has no inclination toward ruling but rather toward direct investigation of the truth.[25] Philosophy means casting doubt and ceaselessly striving for wisdom, qualities antithetical to a will-to-power.

The task of the philosopher is to be counselor to a ruler and not a popular educator. Philosophers failed in their mission because they did not have an understanding of the contradiction between philosophy and politics, which can be bridged only by classical political thought.[26]

Philosophy is not understood by the masses, who are not practiced in casting doubt on common ideas. On the other hand, education, politics, and patriotism enable most people to make a clear distinction between good and evil, a distinction that applies in specific cases in particular historical societies.[27] Thus, stable normative values are possible in a small community of citizens who place the public good above their own interests. Political or pedagogical virtue exists when a small minority of philosophers or educators are able to exist in a society without subverting the beliefs of the majority, but this can only happen in a city-state like those of the ancient world, an example of which was Rousseau's birthplace, Geneva. In a large society, the citizens cannot know one another and work for the common good. Sparta and the Roman republic are examples of good political communities with the appropriate qualities: patriotism and virtue.

Rousseau, like Nietzsche, angrily condemned those who pride themselves on their education: "Suspicions, offences, fears, coolness, reserve, hatred, betrayal, will constantly hide beneath this even and deceitful veil of politeness, beneath this so much vaunted urbanity which we owe to the enlightenment of our century". Because popular education corrupts, the education of the masses should be directed toward the acquisition of suitable qualities: love of one's country and concern for others.

The "Discourse on the Sciences and Arts" is a critique of the modern view of politics. Only the classical thinkers who distinguished between knowledge and ideas, between philosophy and politics, were aware of the possibility of creating a virtuous political community. The good and modest qualities of the citizen are preferable to the education of the philosopher. What was important in political life, thought the young Rousseau, was active participation and not subjective consciousness or intellectual development. The concept of freedom in the ancient world gained its validity from the capacity of the citizen, unlike in the past, to participate in the political experience. As against this, the concept of freedom in modern times gains its validity from singling out the individual within the collective or from the possibility of not participating in the political experience.

The Greeks and Romans would undoubtedly have felt at home in Rousseau's republic. The ideal of that republic is the soldier rather than the merchant, the disciplined trainee rather than the intellectual, universal altruism rather than private interests. If Rousseau had to choose, he would have chosen the French Revolution, which placed the sovereignty of the people at the top of its agenda, and not the American Revolution, which sought to secure the freedom of the individual and his right to happiness. The correct approach to politics, according to Rousseau, is one that derives the legitimacy of rule from the idea that it is subordinate to virtue, to the law of nature, to universal morality, to impersonal laws that are directed to the common good. But in the final analysis, it is human beings who interpret laws, and these are liable to distortion because of the strength of selfish desires. Underlying Rousseau's thinking is a paradox that illuminates the tension between philosophy and politics, a tension that Plato understood very well and that the philosophers of the Enlightenment disregarded.[28]

Although Rousseau developed some of the political concepts of the classical authors, and although he anticipated or hinted at some of the philosophical concepts of the post-modernists, he remains, as Nietzsche said, the first modern man. One cannot identify modernity, which has been in existence for two hundred years now and which is still at its height, with the rational consciousness, the universal view of mankind, moral improvement, or the theory of progress. In other words, modernity cannot be identified with the Enlightenment. The critique of the concept of progress accompanied the age of modernity and enlightenment from its inception, and Rousseau is an outstanding example of this. The "counter-Enlightenment" is also an integral part of modernity despite the fact that it cast doubt on some of the basic assumptions of the Enlightenment.[29]

Rousseau's seemingly rational principles do not necessarily make him modern, just as Nietzsche's seemingly irrational principles do not necessarily make him post-modern. It is not the primacy of reason that makes both of them modern thinkers par excellence but their perception that man is a creature who is perpetually creating himself. Modernity is the consciousness, the challenge and the capacity of humanity in modern times to create its destiny with its own hands. The ideologies, the social utopias, and the political myths are "modern" inasmuch as they have sought to mold reality in the form and image of man.

Does the capacity of humans to create their society, their education, their economics—our definition of modernity—necessarily correspond to the principle of freedom? Or could it be that the movements, ideologies, and totalitarian regimes of the twentieth century that declared war on freedom are no less modern? Whatever the case, modern despotism is the result of the radicalism of freedom: totalitarianism was born with the first modern human. For the first time in history, in the twentieth century there was the technological possibility of realizing an enslaving ideology in the name of freedom. Many intellectuals have desired an integration of society and have presumed to speak in society's name in accordance with Rousseau's saying, "They will compel him to be free".

Rousseau based himself on premodern traditions because he felt that his modern age stood above a chasm, but a hundred and eighty years after his time, his prophecies came to pass. German thinkers such as Schopenhauer, Freud, Sombart, Schmitt, and Jünger combined technological modernity with counter-Enlightenment political radicalism. They wished to resolve the apparent paradox of modernity and political mythology by means of a reactionary modernism.[30] But the very expression "reactionary modernism" suggests a defective modernism. There is in it the hidden assumption that normative modernism requires progress, but that is not the case: Rousseau has already taught us that a denial of progress did not make him less modern or less enlightened.

Together with Rousseau's critique of progress, we have his concept of virtue. Virtue is one of the elements in the attempt of the Enlightenment to create a scale of values for man's development, a way of assessing what is desirable or what is not desirable.[31]

From Socrates and Plato to the thinkers of the Enlightenment, thinkers tried to correlate reality (modernity) with the desirable (enlightenment). Reality must be made to correspond to the ideal. Rousseau's modernity is focused on the institutionalization of classical virtue in the reality of modern times. Rousseau is characterized by the ambiguity of modernity: the rational and the sensory, the moral and the amoral, virtue and "the other side", progressivism and romanticism dwell side by side in his writings.

It is not surprising if Rousseau is open to all interpretations: everyone—Jacobins, socialists, liberals, nationalists, communists, post-modernists—reads him as one of themselves. Rousseau is one more proof of the idea that a great thinker should not be judged by any particular system of thought but by his capacity to reflect reality with all its contradictions. Thus, Rousseau can be seen as a crossroads of modernity with its different ideological possibilities.

In the Presence of the Statue of Glaucus

Glaucus, the Greek sea god, dwelt in Delos, and Apollo gave him the gift of prophecy. Once a year he left his place of residence, sailed to the islands of the Aegean, appeared before kings with his lean body covered in shells and seaweed, and foretold disasters. That was perhaps the cause of his melancholy and ill-fated loves. There are many legends about him. One relates that he was originally a humble fisherman who, one day, on returning from fishing, left his catch among the plants near the shore and saw that the fishes were jumping about and throwing themselves back into the sea. When he too tasted the plants, he turned into a triton, leaped into the sea, and became one of the sea gods.

Glaucus was an inspiration to philosophers from Plato to Rousseau. The image of the sea god as it took on form helped Plato in his Republic to represent the contrast between the pure state of the soul and its actual state:

> We have seen her [the soul] only in a condition which may be compared to that of the sea god Glaucus, whose original image can hardly be discerned because his natural members are broken off and crushed [. . .] so that he is more like some monster than he is to his own natural form [. . .] We must look [. . .] at her love of wisdom. Let us see whom she affects, and what society and converse she seeks in virtue of her near kindred with the immortal and eternal and divine; also how different she would become if [it] disengaged from the stones and shells and things of earth and rock which in wild variety spring up around her [. . .] Then you would see her as she is, and know whether she has one shape only or many, or what her nature is.[32]

Some 2,300 years after Plato, Rousseau used the figure of Glaucus to illustrate the original, natural state of man:

> Like the statue of Glaucus which time, sea, and storms had so disfigured that it less resembled a God than a ferocious Beast, the human soul, altered in the lap of society by a thousand forever recurring causes, by the acquisition of a mass of knowledge and errors, by the changes that have taken place in the constitution of Bodies, and by the continual impact of the passions, changed in appearance to the point of being almost unrecognizable.[33]

In 1753, four years after the "Discourse on the Sciences and Arts", Rousseau submitted the *Discours sur l'origine et les fondements de l'inégalité parmi les hommes* (Discourse on the Origins and Foundation of Inequality Among Men) for a competition of the Dijon Academy, but this time he did not receive the prize. In order to demonstrate how the inequality of rich and poor does not prevent people from feeling equal in their servitude, Rousseau drew upon his own life and reached conclusions from his personal biography about universal human experience. He did not draw the materials for his work from an ivory tower but offered brilliant insights reflecting a sensitive awareness of conflicting episodes of his life and memories of childhood, diagnoses made with a comparative anthropological glance at different societies. Rousseau is revealed as the herald of historical sociology: a correct understanding of society is possible only if one investigates its traces.[34] The search for the sources of unhappiness in man was made through a genealogy of good and evil in society. The starting point of Rousseau's discussion develops the image of Glaucus:

> For how can the source of inequality among men be known unless one begins by knowing men themselves? And how will man ever succeed in seeing himself as nature formed him [. . .] and to disentangle what he owes to his own stock from what circumstances and his progress have added to or changed in his primitive state?[35]

This recognition of the dynamic nature of humankind reveals Rousseau's modernity, but, as in his first essay, Rousseau does not identify modernity with enlightenment. In contrast with the view held by the Enlightenment, Rousseau did not think that humankind was inevitably moving toward equality or moral improvement but the opposite: there was equality in the beginning, and there was later a deterioration. Machiavelli had already said, "Take the clothes off the aristocrat and you will see that nature created men equal. Nature is democratic". Rousseau declared that now, at the height of the age of modernity and enlightenment, inequality prevailed, and people were alienated from one another. The distinction between the natural and the corrupted, between the original and the later state, between the primeval and the modern, is a distinction of values in Rousseau and lies at the heart of his essay. No wonder that the essay is preceded by the following quotation from Aristotle: "What is natural has to be investigated not in beings that are depraved, but in those that are good according to nature".[36]

Rousseau thought that the philosophers and educators had failed thus far to reveal the true nature of man, which was to be found only in his natural state before the creation of human society. The experience of the original man was basic to his investigation. Man in his wild state functioned in a direct fashion: he ate his fill under the oak tree, quenched his thirst from the stream, lay down to sleep under the tree that provided him with his food. Rousseau's conclusion up to this point: nature behaved as the Spartan law behaved toward the children of the citizens. It strengthened those with a good constitution and abandoned the rest. Due to a lack of necessity and challenge, civilized man is incapable of many things:

> If he had an axe, could his wrist have cracked such solid branches? If he had a sling, could he have thrown a stone as hard by hand? If he had had a ladder, could he have climbed a tree so nimbly? If he had had a horse, could he have run as fast?[37]

Man, who functioned without society solely according to his natural instincts, indifferent to educational values, lived his life in a direct way and was a happy animal. More recent commentators suggest that Rousseau's notion of self-loving is itself an appropriation of stoic and Augustinian notions, namely the same desire that allows for the "noble savage" to be happy on the one hand, while on the other hand corrupting the cultured man. The same desire allows for different appropriations and hence functions as an explanation for the human situation and is foundational for any moral constitution.[38]

Rousseau criticized the limitations of the wild state and acknowledged that modern man has broader horizons. Man in his wild state knew only his immediate sensations, and "his thinking was heavy and dull". What distinguished men from animals was not brains but free will, or, in other words, freedom. The source of the instinctive actions of the animal is nature alone, but man forms his own behavior as a free creature. Nevertheless, despite the opinion of moralists, human reason owes a great deal to the desires in the absence of which man does not use his brain.

Man in his wild state is unable to master his desires or use his life experience for educational purposes or the collective memory. Rousseau hints at the way humans' collective consciousness is formed. Modern anthropology has come to the conclusion that the collective consciousness and its transmission from generation to generation is very rare in primitive societies. They relate to the past, but this is not the historical past but a mythical one. In many societies, there is no continuity between the mythical past and the present. While the historical past represents a consciousness that seeks to perpetuate a certain moment in time, myth is ever present. The mythical event is an experience that does not have the dimension of consciousness, a kind of once-only happening that cannot be reinterpreted but is a precedent that recurs again and again. Even if the natural man were a "philosopher" who discovered the truth about his life, what use, asked Rousseau, could the human race make of this metaphysics, which could not be transmitted further and was lost with the individual who conceived it?

Parallel with the ahistorical consciousness of the natural state, one had the amoral consciousness. Rousseau thought that primitive man did not have degenerate characteristics or good qualities: he was neither good nor bad. In this, he contradicted Hobbes's belief that because there was no concept of good, man was by nature bad. Man in his natural state was a human animal who did not harm others unless he himself was endangered. Rousseau thought that the fact that he did sometimes harm others was the reason Hobbes claimed there was an immanent state of war among men. Hobbes, he said, ascribed to the natural man qualities like pride and fear of violent death, qualities due to society, not to nature. The Hobbesian war of all-against-all was the result of historical development, not the true natural state. Like Hobbes, the classical thinkers of the West—Rousseau named Aristotle, Cicero, and Thomas Aquinas—erred in their claim to reveal the true nature of man and achieve a true understanding of the law of nature.

Rousseau was a tireless subverter. His subversion is evident in his treatment of the "grand tradition" of Western thought, a tradition derived from medieval culture, of which Thomas Aquinas was the outstanding representative. The king, the nobility, and the Church—the Holy Trinity, the foundations of premodern society—depended on the sacred character of the monarchy, the elitist character of those with special rights, and the unquestioned authority of Christian dogma. All of them single-mindedly prescribed the historical, social, and moral duties of humankind. Already in the seventeenth century, this "grand tradition" had begun to be undermined: the secular and naturalist philosophies of Hobbes, Spinoza, and Locke questioned the rational basis of concepts such as political justice and ecclesiastical education. In their unorthodox way, they claimed that social and political justice should be based on more solid foundations than a rationale full of errors and prejudice. The alternatives they proposed were the concepts "nature" and "natural philosophy", which in the seventeenth and eighteenth centuries were the foundations on which the basic assumptions of the Enlightenment were built. The basic problem of political philosophy was the nature of humankind and the character of the law of nature. What was the starting point of inequality?

In the natural state, claimed Rousseau, there was equality. The natural man had no ambitions but only capacities. He was a lazy and happy animal that enjoyed his life, protected himself, and was devoid of cruelty, free to act and without social or political allegiances. "Social" or "political" or "civilized" man created civil society, which was non-natural, not free, and not egalitarian.[39] Thus, the significant change in man's nature took place in history, in the change from the natural state to the political. As the philosopher Allan Bloom suggested, here, for the first time, history became an integral part of a political theory.[40] More recent research has suggested, following Frederick Neuhouser, that Rousseau is not committed to any historical state of affairs but merely uses history as an instrument to demonstrate the different elements that composite the psychology of human beings in an allegorical manner.[41] However the case may be, it is contended that the situation in which man is enslaved to his neighbor is a result of some sort of "enflaming" of the *amor proper*[42] and is not "dependent" on any situation as such and not a natural-immanent one. The historical man who lives for himself now lives for others. Social conflict was born when the gap was created between those who have and those who do not (Bloom) or when a certain psychological trigger activated the direction of the *amor proper* (Dent).

Immanent nature was no longer everything: society or the direction of the desire is what matters now. The alienated man who wishes to imitate the desires and experiences of others replaced the free man who is actuated only by his own immanent will. Desire was replaced by the will-to-status; autonomy was replaced by the will-to-power; and freedom was replaced by education. Rousseau puts the cart before the horse. Hobbes was right in saying that "man is a wolf to man" but was wrong in thinking that this was due to the state of nature. The truth is rather that it is the competitive political state that turns the natural man into an alienated wolf. Locke was right in saying that the purpose of civil society is the protection of property but was wrong in thinking that property was natural to man. Man is free by nature, but civil society takes his freedom away from him. The citizen is dependent on the law, and the law is made for the benefit of the rich.[43]

Inequality comes into being with the establishment of civil society. Long-drawn-out changes in the various races led to the building of huts, the founding of families, and the development of language, art, trade, and agriculture. A distribution of land and labor were inevitable consequences. The stronger obtained more employment, the more proficient got better results, the more intelligent found ways of cutting down the time of work, the farmer needed more iron, the blacksmith needed more wheat. One received more than another for the same amount of work, and the latter found it difficult to make ends meet. In the natural state—the state previous to the political state—everyone was his or her own judge; there was no distribution of rights, no separation of authorities or any factor that regulated social activity. The transition from the natural state to the political, social, and civic state can be located at a certain point:

> The first man who, having enclosed a piece of ground, to whom it occurred to say, this is mine, and found people sufficiently simple to believe him, was the true founder of civil society. How many crimes, wars, murders, how many miseries and horrors Mankind would have been spared by him who, pulling up the stakes or filling in the ditch, had cried out to his kind: Beware of listening to this impostor; you are lost if you forget that the fruits are everyone's and the Earth no one's.[44]

The Marxist interpretation of the formation of the unequal society is perfectly in accordance with this passage. One of its representatives, Jean Starobinski,[45] described the establishment of the political society as a reprehensible pact to protect property owners who preferred order to violence and the appearance of justice and order to uncertainty. Socialization is only possible when there is a real threat. Thus, the pact was based on feelings of fear and superiority, the presumption of inequality, and the institutionalization of the privileges of the wealthy. The laws to protect property or economic exploitation, which did not exist in the natural state, were invented in order to protect the rich, who translated their economic power into political power. The social contract was a crass manipulation that gave legitimacy to flagrant inequality.

Apart from the case of the particular society he knew in the eighteenth century, there was the basic question: is society as such, as an institution based on wealth, good for the human race? Rousseau's conclusion was that society corrupted man precisely because it developed his talents. Society is a collection of selfish individuals who see other individuals as reflections of themselves. Their alienation from their essence is its salient sociological characteristic. Rousseau distinguished between *amour de soi*—self-love—and *amour propre*, selfish love of self. Individuals become a society when self-love becomes a selfish love of self, when altruism changes into egoism. Later, Hegel was to distinguish between the family, which is particular altruism, civil society, which is universal egoism, and the state, which is universal altruism. The agreement between Rousseau and Hegel comes down to the idea that civil society is a collection of people actuated by personal motives.

Unlike Hegel, who saw the state as the apotheosis of modernity because it was only in its framework that freedom could spread from the dominant group to all citizens, Rousseau felt that the present political state still lacked the positive content of freedom: the leviathan was essentially negative, universal principles were replaced by particularistic ones, the rich were protected and the poor oppressed, the many labored for the few, money replaced virtue, and self-preservation destroyed a desirable life, which was the purpose of self-preservation. The hopes of the Enlightenment, which corresponded in this case to the hopes of modernity, were disappointed: scientific progress and the acquisitive society did not increase men's happiness, poverty was not mitigated by wealth, nature was not conquered by science, progress did not bring about artistic progress. Rousseau exposed the illusions of the Enlightenment and at the same time undermined them. The starting point of the Enlightenment was Rousseau's turning point: bourgeois civil society was based on inequality and enslavement, and therefore prejudice did not disappear with education. Rousseau now made a surprising, unexpected move.

Educational Conditioning

Rousseau did not, as it is usual to say, advocate a return to nature, a reconstruction of the past, or an escape into romanticism. Rousseau's move was more clever, more dialectical than that. He said one has to get away from both the natural state in which man is a happy individual and from civil society in which man is an alienated social creature, and move toward a connecting experience of a new kind in which rational and moral virtue is the general rule: "Form an enclosure around your child's soul at an early date. Someone else can draw its circumference, but you alone must build the fence".[46]

In 1760, Rousseau began to write *Émile* and *The Social Contract*, but *Émile* was not his first essay on education. The *Projet pour l'éducation de M. de Sainte-Marie* (Project for the Education of Monsieur de Sainte-Marie) (1740) was a youthful essay that contained the principles that were fully developed twenty years later in his major educational work. Émile, the pupil in *Émile, or On Education*, was an orphan who grew up in a village remote from civilization and was put in the exclusive care of his instructor Jean-Jacques, which of course was Rousseau's Christian name. Émile was not a wild creature who lived in a desert or jungle but a wild creature who was destined to live in a town. He was not born in the natural state but in society. Rousseau was not interested in a special, exceptional, isolated type, anachronistic to the political condition, but focused on an average pupil as a suitable anthropological model. Accordingly, he wrote in a letter to Philibert Cramer on the 10th of October 1764, two years after the publication of *Émile*, that the main subject of the educational novel that he wrote was not the pedagogical question but the elucidation of the anthropological question.[47] It was not Émile, the particular, empirical pupil who was at the center of things but the model of the "new man".

The stage of infancy in the education of Émile lasted to the age of five. The suckling of the infant would eventually help in harmonizing the natural feelings of the citizen for his neighbor, for, in the future, parents would have to provide "people for humanity, citizens for the state". A nurse or instructor can replace the parents, but this is not recommended "Man must be trained like a school horse; man must be fashioned in keeping with his fancy like a tree in his garden",[48] that is, developing plants by working on them, or developing people through education. Babies are born. Apart from giving the child room to play, the instructor favors a Spartan education: the child must not become a burden. It is better that a baby should die than that it should remain sick or dependent: it must be washed in cold water in winter and summer, prevented from forming habits or taking artificial medicines, and must be taught to disregard pain or sickness. One should not pander to its whims and should encourage self-control and bodily discipline.[49]

The correct form of education is the "natural" education. The meaning of "natural" for Rousseau is the preservation of the "core" of a man before he is corrupted by normative culture and the alienated society—that is to say, all that is spontaneous, direct, and experiential. Hence the natural education is a negative education: there is no education in values as such or in norms. The natural education is also a total education. Total education means not only the supremacy of reason as understood by the Enlightenment but an all-inclusive experience of life: "To live is not to breathe; it is to act; it is to make use of our organs, our senses, our faculties, of all the parts of ourselves which give us the sentiment of our existence".[50]

The "natural education", which is "negative" in the first stage and "total" in all stages, is a radical expression of humanism:

> In the natural order, since men are all equal, their common calling is man's estate [. . .]. On leaving my hands, he [the student] will, I admit, be neither magistrate nor soldier nor priest. He will, in the first place, be a man. All that a man should be.[51]

This human-centeredness of Rousseau's is universal, unconditioned by the laws of religion, economics, or history, *a priori* self-evident. Until the Enlightenment, there had never been such a clear assumption of the universal nature of man without any need for extra justification. The basis for this universal concept of man was a social contract among free individuals. The essential precondition for the social contract was an education based on the "recognition of necessity". Education is thus a means of conditioning a person to accept the general will, to internalize it, and to live in accordance with its demands.

The total education that molds all the different elements of a person has necessity as its starting point, and this leads automatically to freedom. The pedagogical aim is not to train a person to be different but to accustom him/her to be her-/himself, "to goad him or restrain him with ropes of necessity" and bring him into the law of necessity. Education should not be a matter of chance, good intentions, arbitrariness, or the spontaneous gesture but should be the result of planning, orders, and commands guided by necessity. Only when the instructor has conditioned the pupil to accept the yoke of natural, objective necessity do objective necessity and personal freedom become separate concepts.

From the stage of infancy, Rousseau proceeds to the stage of childhood, which lasts from the age of five to the age of twelve. Guidance, direction, and conditioning are the basis of the negative education of people of this age group, and their purpose is to protect the child from harmful influences. The "recognition of necessity" places the burden of education on the instructor and not on the child. The instructor represents reason, nature, society, and the aim is to gradually introduce the child to the principles of the conceptual and educational system. The child at the beginning of the path is an empty vessel, a tabula rasa, which is formed like raw material by the instructor. Émile obeys, gives up his independent judgment, his critical sense, overcomes his inclinations, tames his desires, and abandons himself completely to the omnipotent authority that does with him as it pleases. Thus, the instructor and his charge become a holistic, undivided entity. The dichotomy between the individual will and the general will, between the individual and society, between the individual and the state is blotted out. The free, natural and negative education is revealed to be an enslaving, normative and totalitarian education. The whole system of education is seen as a deceit, a way of internalizing the values of others, a form of outright enslavement.

Rousseau's approach to education derives from his conception of politics. In both cases, the law takes precedence over man: "If there is any means of remedying this ill in society, it is to substitute law for man and to arm the general will with a real strength superior to the action of every particular will".[52] The "general will", identified with natural law, automatically eliminates evil. Objectivity overcomes subjectivity, and the most effective means of training is conditioning, not prohibition: "Without forbidding him to do harm, it suffices to prevent him from doing it".[53] Rousseau liberates the child from the duty of adopting values: "To know good and bad, to sense the reason for man's duties, is not a child's affair".[54] The significance of the "negative education" is that it prevents the child from knowing good and evil: "The first stage of education must be one of negative purification. The whole principle of this is not the learning of morality and truth but protecting the heart from bad influences". In other words, the essence of education is not discernment, study, choice, but conditioning "in order to prevent the birth of evil".[55] The conditioning is not achieved by preaching, threatening, or promising but by temptation, manipulation, and directing the child toward results that the instructor has envisaged from the start.

The instructor is the sole authority that determines the needs of the child. The instructor sets the limits of freedom, and freedom depends on responding to necessities. The relationship between the instructor and the child is one-sided: there is no dialogue and no discussion. Authority stems from control. The instructor identifies himself with reality, and the necessity of reality is the necessity of the instructor, for "nobody rebels against a necessity that he recognizes".

One ought not to get involved with raising a child if one does not know how to guide her or him where one wants by the laws of the possible and the impossible alone. The sphere of both being equally unknown to him, they can be expanded and contracted around him as one wants. One enchains, pushes, and restrains the child with the bond of necessity alone without letting out a peep.[56] "We will do and then we will hear" is the pedagogical principle of the stage of childhood. "Treat your pupil according to his age. At the outset put him in his place, and hold him there so well that he no longer tries to leave it".[57] But one should not use orders and commands:

> Command him nothing [. . .] Do not even allow him to imagine that you might pretend to have any authority over him. Let him know that he is weak and you are the strong, that by his condition and yours he is necessarily at your mercy.[58]

In this way, the child becomes patient, agreeable, mild, calm, and all this is achieved, according to Rousseau, through a conditioned will, the force of reality, and the recognition of necessity. The instructor expects Émile to learn through a direct recognition of reality, but the person who reveals nature to the child is the instructor. The child reads, but this is not really the book of nature but the book of the instructor. Rousseau's ideal was a total experience and not alienating intellectualism, learning by rote. It follows that his preferred method of instruction was through the senses. Spartan education was an example of total education and was the one that Rousseau favored most.

Two examples that Rousseau gives of the philosophy of Jean-Jacques show that the pedagogical episodes described by the instructor are intended to condition the child through social isolation, learning through punishment and the inculcation of conformity and obedience. In the first example, Jean-Jacques helps Émile to create a garden, and he convinces him that the garden is his. But the gardener Robert, to whom the area sown with beans belongs, uproots the newly sown shoots on the grounds that he has sown the area with watermelons first. The scene with the gardener was, of course, staged and arranged together with the instructor. In this way, Émile internalizes the concept of property as a result of work and the meaning of punishment for breaking the social contract.

The second episode concerns a real event in which Rousseau was involved as an educator. He taught a lesson to a spoiled child from a wealthy home, the son of a French nobleman, who insisted on taking walks at hours inconvenient for the instructor. The instructor encouraged the child in a manipulative manner to take his walks alone, which caused the child to experience ridicule and hostility from an unfriendly crowd. Rousseau's use of "natural punishment" caused the spoiled child to change his ways and taught him a lesson through the failure of his rebellion against the lawgiver-instructor and through the breaking of an unwritten social contract.

The main concern in the stage of childhood is to make the freedom of the child identical with obedience to the instructor. Education is the art of temptation through various means: by encouraging a child to be curious but in a way that is directed by the instructor, by molding the child's future, guiding his wishes, deciding on his fate. This becomes the instructor's "life's-work". This educational project is only possible if the supervision of the child is intensive, based on thorough acquaintance, total surveillance, and boundless trust. What is important is that the subjugation and supervision should be disguised as freedom, as the illusion of freedom:

> Let him always believe that he is the master, and let it always be you who are. There is no subjection so perfect as that which keeps the appearance of freedom. Thus the will itself is made captive. The poor child who knows nothing, who can do nothing, who has no learning, is he not at your mercy? Do you not dispose, with respect to him, of everything which surrounds him? Are you not the master affecting him as you please? Are not his labors, his games, his pleasures, his pains, all in your hands without his knowing it? Doubtless he ought to do only what he wants; but he ought to want only what you want him to do. He ought not to make a step without your having foreseen it; he ought not to open his mouth without your knowing what he is going to say.[59]

The third stage in Émile's education is that of adolescence, which lasts from the age of twelve to the age of fifteen. This is "the time of work and study". The boy does not choose his profession of carpentry; the instructor does in accordance with the tendencies he has fostered in the adolescent. In adolescence, Émile learns to combine the physical and the intellectual, to understand the meaning of happiness, and to aim at long-term objectives. He does not learn for the sake of learning but for the sake of the experience of learning. He draws maps and employs tools not for the sake of acquiring knowledge but in order to learn how to study the world through deduction, comparison, concentration. As in the earlier stages, here, too, the main thing is conditioning. The instructor decides on selective, useful knowledge, and guides the boy's studies toward his own view of things. He does this through the boy's absorption of materials, the means by which they are conveyed and the categorization of thought:

> Remember always that the spirit of my education consists not in teaching the child many things, but in never letting anything but accurate and clear ideas enter his brain. Were he to know nothing, it would be of little

importance to me provided he made no mistakes. I put truths into his head only to guarantee him against the errors he would learn in their place.⁶⁰

The effectiveness of the conditioning depends on its being disguised as freedom and on its inculcation in successive stages in a pleasant manner: "But this attention ought always to be produced by pleasure or desire, never by constraint".⁶¹ The adolescent must in each stage absorb only what is suitable to that stage. The compartmentalization of knowledge, selectivity, and progressiveness are the characteristics of education at the stage of adolescence.

Rousseau's conditioning of Émile reveals the character of the educational project of modernity: he intends to raise him to the level of a man.⁶² The laws of history, ancestral traditions, or economic mechanisms cannot create a "new man". Only an education such as Émile's, bound up with a new conception of politics (the social contract), can deal with a human challenge of this kind. The aim of Émile's education is not to equip him for the social status quo, to prepare him for life, or to provide him with a profession. Rousseau's aim in education is very far-reaching: the conditioning is the expression of the radical political philosophy that underlies this total and natural education. Behind Rousseau's radical thought, in education as in politics, is the idea of the construction of a human, a new anthropological model, the formation of a human being in the light of abstract pedagogical principles different from all previous empirical models.

In this educational scheme, the ideal book for the adolescent to read is *Robinson Crusoe*, which is lavish in its praise of the autarchy (self-sufficiency) of the isolated man, who gets to know his surroundings through the principle of use, creates himself with his own hands, relates to life as a whole rather than to its parts, and keeps his distance from the restless crowd.⁶³ One may ask whether Robinson really represents "authentic autarchy", as Rousseau thinks, or whether he carries the whole of civilization with him to his desert island. Whatever the case, it is Jean-Jacques who forms the existential authenticity of the isolated adolescent, first of all by his choice of books—or rather the only book allowed the adolescent Émile—and then by its prolongation in a conditioned isolation.

Émile is thus not a "noble savage", as the anti-modernist romantics would say, but a universal human model, the product of modernity. He is a criterion for himself, not for others. He is gifted with the capacity to learn, to understand the significance of his actions, and to find satisfaction in his beliefs, but he does not arrive at this capacity, this understanding, or this satisfaction alone. Apart from the effect of the conditions in which the boy grew up, the instructor chooses the path he is to take.

In *Émile*, Rousseau constantly distinguishes between "ornamental" knowledge and the principles of enlightenment. Knowledge does not bring happiness, science does not mean progress, study does not lead to truth. On the contrary, these are the causes of alienation, mendacity, and self-deception:

> Since all our errors come from our judgements, it is clear that if we never needed to judge, we would not need to learn. We would never be in a

position to be deceived. We would be happier in our ignorance than we can be with our knowledge. Who denies that the learned know countless true things which the ignorant will never know? Are the learned thereby closer to the truth? On the contrary, they get farther from it in advancing; because the vanity of judging makes even more progress than enlightenment does, each truth that they learn comes only with a hundred false judgements. It is entirely evident that the learned companies of Europe are only public schools of lies.[64]

Education is the means of avoiding the snare of knowledge that creates alienated people. The normal alienated education is part of a comprehensive culture, bookish and ornamental, which itself is the result of a politics based on a distorted approach to one's neighbor and to society. The accepted system of education produced someone who was a slave to learning, weak, hypocritical, miserable, and lacking self-knowledge. He was a prisoner of himself. The image of the prisoner in chains clearly reflects freedom as the thread that runs through Rousseau's writings. The fourth stage in the educational project of Émile is that of youth, which lasts from the age of fifteen to the age of twenty. Youth is like a second birth:

We are, so to speak, born twice: once to exist and once to live [. . .] This is the second birth of which I have spoken. It is now that man is truly born to life and now that nothing human is foreign to him.[65]

Paradoxically, the instructor develops the self-knowledge of the person educated. The source of the rebirth is the self-love that the pupil manifests at that age, and that self-love is broadened until it embraces the whole of humanity. The youth discovers his need for his neighbor and his social proclivities, and, together with that, "he begins to sense his moral existence". The instructor prefers to expose him to human misery and to develop his sense of social solidarity rather than to encourage him to be successful and so stir up jealousy and rivalry. His intellectual, aesthetic, historical, emotional, sexual, and social education permits Émile to disregard utilitarian considerations and submit to "the knowledge of necessity", to reason and the "general will".

The age of reason is the age of activity and study, participation and experience. For example, the study of history can be a learning experience, a kindling of the imagination and a lesson in morality. Before Nietzsche, Rousseau encouraged one to learn from great historical figures and from historians like Thucydides, whom he called a "model historical writer". In revealing historiography's aim of objectivity and in emphasizing its educational value, Rousseau also preceded Nietzsche: the instructor was the overseer of history in the sense that he told the youth which examples to take from it.

The educational ideal is not the product of dialogue, free experiment, or choice but reflects the world outlook of the instructor who "moulds the form" of the youth and "forms him out of nothing". The instructor gives him instruction in the "civil religion", in the principles of aesthetics, in sexual education. The instructor encourages initiative, the giving of charity and help to the needy. Personal experience and social participation teach good and evil in a direct manner. The instructor's ideal is a pupil who is uninfluenced by public opinion, is interested in his social environment, is content with what he has, is free from prejudice, and is not dependent on others.

The education of the girl Sophie who was to marry Émile is intended to make her an ideal companion, a dutiful housewife, and a mother to her children. Her existence is an adjunct to that of the man Émile. The mutuality is false, her relationship with Émile is one-sided and is characteristic of the life of girls. For this purpose, Sophie learned housework, learned music and dancing in order to entertain her husband, took care of her appearance and manners in order to please him, and cultivated the qualities of fidelity, devotion, and modesty in order to restrain his desires. Sophie became a tool in the hands of the instructor, who used her in order to dominate Émile through her at the end of his formal education. Her marriage was postponed for two years in order for the formal education of her future husband to be completed.

The political education of Émile was mainly studying the state legal system, and traveling in Europe. In this way, he learned the laws and internalized them, and his conclusion was that the principles of politics and the principles of education were identical: both conditioned the pupil or the citizen to accept the necessity of freedom. "My teacher", the youth confesses to his instructor, "you have made me free". Stage by stage, Rousseau brings his pupil to abandon his personal will for the sake of the general will identified with reason, the reason of the lawgiver-instructor. Freedom is necessity, and this must be very forcefully impressed on the pupil-citizen, and in Rousseau's famous words in *The Social Contract*, "Whoever refuses to obey the general will shall be constrained to do so by the entire body: which means nothing other than that he shall be forced to be free".[66] Here we have the paradox of Rousseau's conception of freedom. As Jacob L. Talmon so aptly said:

> On the one hand, the individual is said to obey nothing but his own will; on the other, he is urged to conform to some objective criterion. The contradiction is resolved by the claim that this external criterion is his better, higher, or real self, man's inner voice, as Rousseau calls it [. . .] for in fact he is merely being made to obey his own true self. He is thus still free [. . .]. Every exercise of the general will constitutes a reaffirmation of man's freedom.[67]

The educational project has now come to an end. Jean-Jacques and Émile, in a festive ceremony, make "a sacred pact which cannot be violated", and in it the instructor for the first time reveals to his pupil the principle of conditioning that was central to his pedagogical thinking. Jean-Jacques declares that he is about to end his task, but Émile promises always to obey his rules in absolute freedom, for that is "his immutable will". Rebellion against his instructor is perceived as rebellion against the necessity of reason, and Émile asks him to compel him to be free. The instructor replies, and his answer deserves to be regarded as Rousseau's pedagogical credo:

> My young friend, you lack experience, but I have fixed things so that you would not lack reason. You are in a position to see the motives of my conduct in all things. To do so, you have only to wait until you are calm. Always begin by obeying, and then ask me for an account of my orders. I shall be ready to give you a reason for them as soon as you are in a position to understand me, and I shall never be afraid of taking you as the judge between you and me. You promise to be docile, and I promise to make use of this docility only to make you the happiest of men. I give you as a guarantee of my promise the fate that you have enjoyed up to now.[68]

Émile declares that he will need his instructor forever. The permanent education he received transcends the particular case of Jean-Jacques and applies to the whole of education in society. Émile is a particular case of "every man's will" who submits with those like him to Jean-Jacques' "general will". The subjective conforms to the objective, identified with reason. In this, Rousseau resembles Plato and is opposed to Nietzsche. The Platonic philosopher in the cave represents the transcendental ideals; Rousseau's instructor represents the "general will" embodied in the rational, but Nietzsche's Zarathustra who leaves his country and isolates himself in a cave represents only himself. Plato, who lived in the classical period but had the ideas of the Enlightenment, and Rousseau, who pointed out the tension between enlightenment and modernity, both had the idea of a correct, objective education. The climax of this educational idea was the "new man".

The "New Man"

The French Revolution as the climax of a historical process was a proclamation of the birth of modernity: humanity's challenge to form itself in its own image, to give birth to humanity once again. Dissatisfaction with the existing culture has long given rise to dreams of creating a new humanity, from the "second coming" of Jesus to the millenarian visions and humanistic ideas, and, finally, to the utopias of the early modern age and the political ideologies of the twentieth century. But only since the French Revolution have the conditions existed in which modern politics and education were able to form a new model of humanity. In this way, the revolution served as a crossroads for different possibilities of human models.

A single thinker has never been as closely identified with a revolution as the writer of *The Social Contract* was with the revolution of 1789. In particular, Rousseau is considered the intellectual progenitor of the Jacobins. In 1790, his statue and a copy of *The Social Contract* were placed in the hall of the National Assembly. In December of that year, the proposal was made for the first time by members of the Assembly to give him some mark of public honor, but only in August 1791, in a petition in which he was called "the father of French legislation", was the demand formulated to confer on him "a mark of honour from the nation-at-large". Although Robespierre made speeches for the "cult of the Supreme Being" in which he praised Rousseau's ideas, and although he and Saint-Just made speeches in his honor, Rousseau's ashes were only later deposited in the Panthéon by those who overthrew Robespierre.[69] Until 1795, the leaders of the revolution identified with Rousseau's ideas, which were widely disseminated. Before 1789, there were thirteen editions of *The Social Contract*, twenty-three editions of *Émile*, and fifty editions of *The New Heloïse*.

Two basic principles of the revolution—the supremacy of politics and general education—drew their inspiration from Rousseau, among other things. The "Declaration of the Rights of Man and of the Citizen" was universal in its character and language, and it is not surprising that the words "France" or "French" were not mentioned there. Although the American Revolution had already issued a "Declaration of Rights", the French Revolution had a pedagogical intent that was bound up with political radicalism. Its disconnection from the legitimacy of all previous legislation and from historical continuity necessitated a reliance on some other form of legitimacy and that was found in reason, and reason was general and not specifically French. The "Declaration", like *The Social Contract* or *Émile*, was not confined to France but was intended to create a "new man", and that required a legislative and educational revolution that drew its justification from natural rights, not hereditary privileges.

The "Declaration", which was drawn up by property owners, did not contain any social rights and did not have the radical-social spirit of Rousseau in his *Discourse on the Origins of Inequality* or the radical-pedagogical spirit of *Émile*. The "Declaration" spoke only of the rights of the citizen and did not mention his duties. The legislative and institutional establishment of rights—the right to life, to protection from the arbitrariness of rulers, to freedom of speech, to freedom of conscience and religion, to general education, welfare, unemployment pay—was liable to efface the boundaries and limitations of society, the law, and the state. The state is not coercive but exists to serve the rights of the citizen. The true test, however, was not the right to freedom or universal suffrage but the right to property. Was political freedom and education for all possible without property? In the "Declaration", the right to property is assured, but not a word is said about the poor citizens who need to be given property so that their freedom, their education, and their security will be genuine.

If Montesquieu said that government is the province of the aristocracy, and if Voltaire claimed that it belongs to the upper bourgeoisie, as against Montesquieu or Voltaire, Rousseau handed the sovereignty to the people. The principle of equality distinguishes Rousseau from Voltaire, from the *encyclopédistes*, and from the majority of thinkers of the Enlightenment. Diderot, Holbach, and D'Alembert were concerned with concrete reforms, with improvements that would constitute progress. All of them thought that, with such a formidable enemy as the establishment, one cannot wage an all-out war. Unlike them, Rousseau was eager for battle. He demanded that the state should "eradicate the sins of property", as the historian Albert Soboul put it, and create a social equilibrium through laws of inheritance and progressive taxation. From this point of view, the legislation of 1783 had a pedagogical character and was directly in the line of Rousseau. For example, the article dealing with the right to work declared that the state had to provide employment, and if it was unable to do so, it had to provide financial aid. De Tocqueville stated a truth when he said that the French Revolution had two passions: a hatred of inequality and a desire for freedom. It aimed "to create a society whose members, as far as human nature allows, will resemble one another, and conditions of equality". The "new man" was a revolutionary attempt to reconcile the two polarities of equality and freedom.

The passion to give birth to history itself led to the creation of a revolutionary calendar. The new calendar was born with the secular challenge of creating a "new man", but unlike the sanctified territorial space of the revolution, the Panthéon, which has survived until now, the new revolutionary division of time did not endure.[70] The revolutionary calendar was adopted by the Convention on the fifth of October 1793 and abandoned on the first of January 1806. Already at the beginning of the revolution, on the 15th of July 1789, the day after the fall of the Bastille, the revolutionaries began to issue documents and certificates dated "the second day of freedom". Apart from the attempt to simplify time, there was a pedagogical message here: that of remembering and commemorating the revolution as the beginning of a new history, a noncontinuity of time. If everything has been changed, how can one continue with the old calendar as if nothing has happened? Modern times have begun, in which the "new man" establishes his freedom in an egalitarian society and has an equal status among free men. The calendar expressed the modern idea in which nature and history became one, in which the dream of giving birth to oneself came true in the here and now.

Hannah Arendt is of the opinion that the abandonment of the revolutionary calendar divested the revolution of its special character and brought it back into the course of history.[71] But even this abandonment is some kind of evidence of the profound logic of the chronological reform. The hope of a new life based on a new calendar was not entirely dead. In addition to the anticlerical declaration, there was something positive: the dream of the "new man", so central to the revolution, brought about the liberation of the old man from his chains and made him into a citizen. From now on, the citizen was to be conditioned by new images, unifying rituals, constructive traditions. In order to make this positive pedagogy possible, time had to be rebuilt. The republican calendar was a tool to cement the new loyalties of the citizen and create a nation of new people.

In Rousseau and in the French Revolution as well, the "people" were a "nation", and the private individual was a citizen. The legislation of 1793 declared that sovereignty lies with the people: it is one and indivisible. The sovereign people consists of the citizens of France as a whole. The individual was assimilated to the nation, society was swallowed up in the state. The individual transferred his or her sovereignty to the citizens as a whole and then received validity from the nation and became an indivisible part of the community. This being the case, the "sovereign nation of citizens" was not the sum of the individuals that composed it but a new comprehensive entity the source of whose legitimacy was in itself.

Ten years after *The Social Contract* and *Émile*, Rousseau wrote his last essay, *Considérations sur le gouvernement de la Pologne* (Considerations on the Government of Poland) (1772). In a special chapter on national education, he concluded:

> It is education that must give souls the national form, and so direct their tastes and opinions that they will be patriotic by inclination, passion, necessity. Upon opening its eyes, a child should see the fatherland [. . .], that is to say love of the laws and of freedom, with his mother's milk. [. . .] This love makes up his whole existence; he sees only his fatherland, he lives only for it; when he is alone, he is nothing: when he no longer has a fatherland, he no longer is, and if he is not dead, he is worse than dead.[72]

One sees the similarity of the education that makes the patriot of the Polish nation, the citizen of the social contract, and Émile among the pupils, assimilate themselves to something else—be it the nation, society, or reason—renounce their individual will before the duty of the citizen and identify the individual with the law. In his essay on Poland, Rousseau said he wished to learn from the great legislator-educators of history—Moses, Lycurgus, and Numa Pompeius—who discovered the means to make the citizens adhere together as a nation. The inculcation of patriotism through a national education places one's country at the center of things. The Polish national existence was achieved through unified governmental education and public control. The institutionalization of a collective way of life was brought about by military service, the abandonment of voluntary traditions, the holding of ceremonies, and the emergence of national leaders. In other words, it was brought about by a return to history and by molding it in a revolutionary manner.

Historical time was an educational factor in the making of the "new man", which was done in a pedagogical framework. Hence the importance of Rousseau as an educator: Émile is the model of an empirical laboratory for the modern man who was constructed in stages, step by step, conditioned to a new world, guided from station to station until he reached maturity. The construction was achieved in the dimension of time, and in the words of the writer Edgar Quinet, "Time must be elevated". The "new man" is formed within history, but in a new history whose conditions are created by revolutionaries and educators. The education is to the point, moral conditioning, total control. The Promethean passion to create a new humanity is what gave the French Revolution its character as a model for future revolutions and for many regimes of the next two hundred years. Anyone who supports the creation of a "new man" also supports the canceling out of the division between the individual and the collective, declares war on his adversaries, and is completely absorbed in a pedagogical strategy. It is therefore not surprising if the "new man" of modernity went the whole way from the "enlightened man" to the "barbarian".

Notes

1. Jean-Jacques Rousseau, "Discourse on the Sciences and Arts or First Discourse", in Victor Gourevitch, ed., and trans., *The Discourses and Other Early Political Writings*, Cambridge 1997, 6.
2. Ibid., "First Discourse, Replies", 90. See also 16, at the beginning of part II, where Rousseau relates to "an ancient tradition passed on from Egypt to Greece, a God inimical to men's repose was the inventor of the sciences". Rousseau also showed at the beginning of his First Discourse an illustration of Prometheus warning the satyr not to touch the fire lest he is burned.
3. Rousseau, "Introduction", *Émile, or On Education*, Book V, trans. and ed., Allan Bloom, New York 1979, 432.
4. Ibid., 472.
5. Ibid., 471.
6. Rousseau, "Discourse on the Sciences and Arts", 16.
7. Rousseau, "The Social Contract", in Victor Gourevitch, ed., and trans., *The Social Contract and Other Later Political Writings*, Cambridge 1997, 41; See especially, Christopher Bertman, *Rousseau and the "Social Contract"*, London 2004.
8. Maurice Cranston, *The Noble Savage: Jean-Jacques Rousseau, 1754–1762*, Chicago 1991; Nicholas J. H. Dent, *Rousseau*, London 2005.
9. Georges Vladchos, "L'influence de Rousseau sur la conception du contrat social chez Kant et Fichte", *Études sur le "Contrat Social" de J.-J. Rousseau*, Paris 1964, 459–480.
10. Stanley Rosen, *G.W.F. Hegel: An Introduction to the Science of Wisdom*, South Bend, IN 2000, 175–176, 180–182, 198–199, 209–212.
11. Galvano della Volpe, "Critique marxiste de Rousseau", *Études sur le "Contrat Social" de J.-J. Rousseau*, Paris 1974, 503–513.
12. Friedrich Nietzsche, "Beyond Good and Evil", in *The Portable Nietzsche*, ed., and trans., Walter Kaufmann, New York 1968.
13. Samuel Baud-Bovy, ed., *Jean-Jacques Rousseau*, Neuchâtel 1962.
14. Bryan Garsten, ed., *Rousseau, the Age of Enlightenment and Their Legacies*, Princeton, NJ 2014.
15. Friedrich Nietzsche, "Twilight of the Idols", in *The Portable Nietzsche*, ed., and trans., Walter Kaufmann, New York 1968, paragraph 48.
16. See Rousseau's letter from January 1962, *Letters*, in *Présentation, choix et notes de Marcel Raymond*, Lausanne 1959, 168–185, and in the subchapter "Educational Conditioning".
17. G. R. Havens, *Voltaire's Marginalia on the Pages of Rousseau*, Columbus 1933.
18. Friedrich Nietzsche, *Twilight of the Gods*, paragraph 48.
19. Friedrich Nietzsche, "The Antichrist", in *The Portable Nietzsche*, paragraph 54.
20. Jean Starobinski, *Jean-Jacques Rousseau—Transparency and Obstruction*, Chicago 1971, 24.
21. Georges Sorel, "Jean-Jacques Rousseau", *le mouvement Socialiste*, XXI (Juin 1907): 507–532; see also David Ohana, *The Nihilist Order: The Intellectual Roots of Totalitarianism*, Eastbourne 2016, 259–260.

22 David Ohana, *Homo Mythicus*, Eastbourne 2009, 37–38.
23 Rousseau, *Émile or On Education*, Book II, 93.
24 Rousseau, "Discourse on the Sciences and Arts", Part II, 27. See also Joshua Cohen, *Rousseau: A Free Community of Equals*, Oxford 2010.
25 Jacob Neidelman, *Rousseau's Ethics of Truth*, London 2017.
26 Allan Bloom, "Jean-Jacques Rousseau", in Leo Strauss and J. Cropsey, eds., *History of Political Philosophy*, Chicago 1987, 559–580.
27 Jacques Juillard, *La faute à Rousseau*, chapter 6, Paris 1985.
28 Jean-Louis Lecercle, *Jean-Jacques Rousseau: Modernité d'un Classique*, Paris 1973.
29 Isaiah Berlin, *Against the Current: Essay in the History of Ideas*, ed., Henry Hardy, London 1979.
30 Jeffrey Herf, *Reactionary Modernism: Technology, Culture and Politics in Weimar and the Third Reich*, Cambridge 1984.
31 David Gauthier, *Rousseau: The Sentiment of Existence*, Cambridge 2006.
32 Plato, *The Dialogues of Plato*, Republic, Book X, 611, trans., B. Jowett, Oxford 2005.
33 Rousseau, "Discourse on the Origin and Foundations of Inequality", *preface*, 124.
34 Emil Durkheim, "Montesquieu and Rousseau", in *Forerunners of Sociology*, Ann Arbor, MI 1960.
35 Rousseau, "Discourse on the Origins and Foundations of Inequality", preface, 124.
36 Aristotle, *Politics*, Book 2, quoted in Rousseau, *Second Discourse*, 113.
37 Rousseau, "Discourse on the Origin and Foundations of Inequality", part I, 135.
38 Christopher Brooke, "Rousseau's Second Discourse, Between Epicureanism and Stoicism", in Stanley Hoffmann and Christie MacDonald, eds., *Rousseau and Freedom*, Cambridge 2010, 44–57.
39 David Lay Williams, *Rousseau's Social Contract*, Cambridge 2014.
40 Allan Bloom, "Jean-Jacques Rousseau", 577–579.
41 Frederick Neuhouser, *Rousseau's Critique of Inequality*, Cambridge 2014.
42 Nicholas Dent, "Rousseau on amour-propre", *Aristotelian Society Supplementary*, 72:1 (1998): 57–74.
43 Jean Starobinski, *Jean-Jacques Rousseau*, 23–32.
44 Rousseau, "Discourse on the Origin and Foundations of Inequality", 161.
45 Starobinski, *Jean-Jacques Rousseau—Transparency and Obstruction*, 24.
46 P. H. Meyer, "The Individual and Society in Rousseau's *Émile*", *Modern Language Quarterly*, 19 (1958): 99–114.
47 Eliyahu Rosenaw, "Rousseau's *Émile*, An Anti-Utopia", *British Journal of Educational Studies*, XXVIII:3 (1980): 212–224.
48 Rousseau, *Émile*, 37.
49 Ibid., 38.
50 Ibid., 42.
51 Ibid., 41–42.
52 Ibid., 85.
53 Ibid., 8.
54 Ibid., 90.
55 Ibid., 94.
56 Ibid., 92.
57 Ibid., 91.
58 Ibid.
59 Ibid., 120.
60 Ibid.
61 Ibid., 172.
62 Ibid., 196.

63 Denise Schaeffer, "The Utility of Ink: Rousseau and Robinson Crusoe", *The Review of Politics* (2001): 121–148.
64 Rousseau, *Émile*, 204.
65 Ibid., 211–212.
66 Rousseau, *The Social Contract and Other Later Political Writings*, Book I, chapter 7, 53.
67 Jacob L. Talmon, *The Origins of Totalitarian Democracy*, London 1952, 40.
68 Rousseau, *Émile*, 326.
69 Gregory Dart, *Rousseau, Robespierre and English Romanticism*, Cambridge 1999.
70 François Furet and Jacques Ozouf, *Reading and Writing: Literacy in France from Calvin to Jules Ferry*, Cambridge 1982.
71 Hannah Arendt, *The Origins of Totalitarianism*, New York 1973, 199.
72 Rousseau, "Considerations on the Government of Poland", *The Social Contract and Other Later Political Writings*, 189.

B. Alexis De Tocqueville: The Prophecy of the Modern World

A Prophet in His Own Town

The work of Alexis de Tocqueville (1805–1859) resulted from his study of the crisis of modernity. The stages of his personal biography are test cases of the presence of Western civilization in the modern age, or in other words, of the interrelationship between modernity and enlightenment. His *De la Démocratie en Amérique* (Democracy in America) (1835), was written after the 1830 revolution in France, which led him to his celebrated voyage of discovery in the United States; his *Recollections* (Memoirs) (1850) were set down in the shadow of the events of 1848, and his *L'Ancien Régime et la Révolution* (The Ancien Régime and the Revolution) (1856) was conceived against the background of the rise of Louis Napoleon. De Tocqueville, who sought to learn the lessons of the recent past, wrote a pragmatic history of modernity.

As a late and critical descendant of the Enlightenment, De Tocqueville foresaw the subversive and conflicting tendencies inherent in modernity.[1] Did the responsibility of modern humankind for molding its own destiny—our definition of modernity—necessarily result in liberty, or did it not also result in contrary tendencies opposed to liberty that were also part of modernity? Here he examined the modern nexus as the paradoxical but logical conclusion of the quest for liberty: Prometheus freed from his chains was liable to turn against himself. De Tocqueville's insights concerning the defects and drawbacks of American democracy today look like prophecies of the future of the modern world.

De Tocqueville can be considered a prophet of the crisis of the modern state. His prophecies of the emergence of a new form of despotism in the modern era, his forecast of the future great powers (the United States and Russia), his warning of the existence of a racial problem, his fears of the arbitrary nature of public opinion and a tyranny of the majority, his perception of the development of a mass society and a bureaucratic state, his views on modern armies and their role in a total war, his call for a separation between the industrial barons and the ruling powers, his descriptions of the fundamentalist tendencies of a state-as-a-religion or a religion-as-a-state, his recognition of "individualism" as an objective of the modern age, his indication of the contradictions that had developed in American society and of the discrepancies between liberty and equality—all this and more give De Tocqueville a place of honor in the pantheon of political philosophy.[2]

Among the many definitions of a prophet, that of Martin Buber is particularly appropriate in the case of De Tocqueville: he is a thinker who places two alternatives before us and calls upon us to choose one of them, like the prophets of the Bible: "I have put before you heaven and earth, life and death, a blessing and a curse. Choose life!" De Tocqueville pointed to two political alternatives of the democratic era. One was a revolutionary, radical democracy, which begins with abstract ideas and the utopia of the creation of a new man and ends in a regime of violence and terror, and which subjects reality to an *a priori* model. De Tocqueville already found the seeds of this new democratic tyranny in the managerial state created by the Ancien Régime in France. The French Revolution merely improved on it. The other alternative was a liberal, democracy supported by free institutions. De Tocqueville asked his readers to choose the model of American democracy over the threatening indigenous model of the French Revolution, but as he was far from national preferences or political simplification, he showed that in the American alternative as well there were currents and tendencies that could result in the political paradox of a democratic tyranny.

De Tocqueville began his celebrated journey to North America in 1831, at the age of twenty-six. In 1835, he published the first part of *Democracy in America* and published the second part five years later.[3] When the first part of that monumental work appeared, he declared in a letter to his friend Keyorlay that the movement toward equality was inevitable and that the chief problem of the period was to find out if that direction was consistent with liberty:

> For nearly ten years I have thought a great deal about what I have just told you. I traveled to America only to clarify this point. The penal system was simply a pretext. I saw it as a passport by means of which I could enter any place in the United States.[4]

One should notice the words, "For nearly ten years". De Tocqueville, who was born in 1805, wrote this in 1835: that is to say that, according to him, he was only twenty years old when he began to think about complex intellectual matters.

De Tocqueville did not do anything or write anything for pleasure. All his energy was devoted to investigations and reaching conclusions. He was not an aesthete but a pragmatic historian, and his journey to America, like the works he wrote on the history of France and on Britain,[5] was a kind of experiment conducted in an inductive and deductive spirit.[6] If the question that preoccupied him all his life concerned him at such a young age, it was because it was not theoretical but existential. The young De Tocqueville was oppressed by the traumatic collective memory of the French Revolution and regarded it as a warning.[7] His grandfather, who defended King Louis XVI before the revolutionary tribunal, was one of the victims of the guillotine.[8] In the same way as his contemporaries, De Tocqueville felt that his world was disappearing like his aristocratic family doomed to extinction by the march of history.

He gave this feeling a literary form and drew the relevant conclusions. The romantic concept of "fate" was developed by him into a system. He saw the victory of democracy as a stroke of fate, an unquestionable basic assumption and the starting point of his thinking. But while accepting the triumph of the democratic spirit, he was worried by the implications of equality, the slogan of the French Revolution. The problem of the legacy of the French Revolution disturbed all French liberals in the period of the Restoration. The victory of democracy in France and in the world at large involved the dual character of the revolution as both a liberal and an antiliberal legacy: that of 1789 but also that of 1793, that of lofty rhetoric but also that of *la terreur*.[9]

Democracy in America is not read today as it was read in the "springtime of the peoples" in 1848 or in the Cold War about a hundred years later. Each generation reads it in the light of its own situation and problems. As soon as it was published, the book was praised by many people, including Lamartine, Guizot, Royet-Collard, and also by foreigners such as Cavour, John Stuart Mill, and John Quincy Adams. Royet-Collard called De Tocqueville "the Montesquieu of the nineteenth century who has written a new *Esprit des Lois*". John Stuart Mill regarded the book as the first theory of representative democracy; the founders of the Third Republic in France sought in it the golden mean between liberty and equality. It is still read today as a relevant work of political philosophy. Guizot focused on the problems of his time, but De Tocqueville went beyond them. His historical sociological analyses gave rise to significant debates on the subjects of liberty and despotism, producing insights that have nourished political thought for generations.

If, as De Tocqueville maintained, democracy was on the rise and was irreversible, how does one explain the reaction of Napoleon III? Why did the first democratic election in history end with the establishment of the Second Empire in the mid-nineteenth century? And how does one explain the totalitarianism in Europe between the two world wars and in one of the great powers after the end of the Second World War? De Tocqueville gave an interesting explanation, Modern societies are democratic by nature, but the democratic state can develop in two possible directions, one being liberal and empirical and the other, totalitarian. Totalitarianism, as the outstanding political phenomenon of the twentieth century, was not inconsistent with the modern era but was the ultimate conclusion of the modern mass society that had lost traditional restraints, was incapable of coping with unbridled liberty and so abandoned freedom. The radicalism of the French Revolution was the beginning of this phenomenon.

When, at the end of his life, De Tocqueville examined the history of French radicalism in his book *L'Ancien Régime et la Révolution* (The Ancien Régime and the Revolution), he made a new and provocative assertion:

> Radical as it was, the Revolution introduced fewer innovations than has been generally supposed, as I shall have occasion to show hereafter. [. . .]

yet it was the mere natural result of very long labors, the sudden and violent termination of a task which had successively engaged ten generations of men".[10]

This evolutionary idea that the monarchy laid a basis of concentration and that administration and the revolution merely added layers to it was a surprising one. Until then, it had been accepted that the revolution was decentralized, essentially anarchic and antireligious in spirit and in its early days had inscribed the freedom of the individual on its banner. According to De Tocqueville's analysis, France under the Ancien Régime was divided horizontally so that it was possible to supervise the periphery from the center, and perpendicularly, so that the country could be administered through a gradation. Next to the king, the king's council served as a ministerial body, and the government in the center stood above the periphery. Beneath it was the general supervisor of the national administration; beneath the supervisor were the *intendants* responsible for the provinces; and beneath them were those responsible for the secondary districts. The officials of the centralized public administration collected taxes, recruited for the army, sustained the needy, and were responsible for public works and public order. The centralized administration of the monarchy inherited the feudal order in which the aristocracy was the custodian of the subjects. The government began to replace the aristocracy when the latter abandoned its task of serving the public and became a closed sect intent on preserving its privileges. Supervision, concentration, and unity were the characteristics of the royal administration and prepared the way for a centralized revolution.

There was a great deal of involvement of the central administration.[11] In the cities, it imposed customs duties, raised taxes, and set up businesses. In the villages, it arranged village meetings and reduced its representatives to two. In the Church, it made the priests into government officials and made the Church a participant in the acquisition of land. And in legislation, the legal and administrative systems were mixed together, and the central government drew on their authority and supervised their activities. The centralization replaced an institutional public pluralism and social voluntarism, and thus there was an absolute dependence of all small institutions, voluntary bodies, and local authorities on the central administration. The modern administrative state already existed in the time of the Ancien Régime, and this concentration under the monarchy was replaced by a revolutionary concentration.[12] Both were based on a centralized administration that was more an instrument of government than a mediator between the government and the requirements of the people, the traditional role of the aristocracy, which had vanished from the scene. Paris, which represented the entire country, enabled a single revolt to become a general revolution because the whole system of the national government was concentrated there.

With the breakup of the class structure, there began a process of unification of the people reflected in a unification of the law. Identical regulations were issued on the orders of the King's Council; there was an equalization of districts and classes in accordance with the interest of the central government in abrogating special rights and suppressing local forces that threatened its authority. There was a spread of education that tended to reduce the differences between the aristocrats and the bourgeoisie. All this represented a tendency to unification, which undermined the uniqueness of each citizen and finally gave rise to social alienation. The processes of centralization and bureaucratization, which had begun under the Ancien Régime and came to a head with the Revolution, voided the "civil society"[13]—a concept coined by Adam Ferguson and developed by Hegel—of its soul and created an alienating social atomization. Parallel with this unification and as a result of it, the individuals, who had formerly belonged to social groups, began to stand on their own feet. The isolation of the classes from each other prepared the way for the isolation of the individual in modern society. The alienating individualism on the one hand and the unification on the other made it easier for the central government to rule the citizens, who closely resembled one another but at the same time were distant from one another.

The French Revolution continued the tendencies of the monarchical regime. It established a democratic despotism that disregarded social interconnections, stifled voluntarism and public spirit, increased its power by appropriating the authority of local bodies, and created a bureaucracy in place of the traditional functionaries. These developments were largely possible due to the ideas of the Enlightenment. The new philosophy not only created a discrepancy between society as it was and the society it envisaged, but it fostered the illusion that it would one day bring about the utopia it had promised. The atmosphere of atomization favored abstraction over tradition and replaced the authority of the king and religion with the rule of reason and the individual.

Democratic Tyranny in the New World

While in France, as the representative of the Old World, the opposition between the Church and democracy, religion and liberty was most in evidence, American society succeeded in combining the power of religion with the power of freedom.[14] The settlers in America, who had fled from religious authority, brought to the New World a form of Christianity that De Tocqueville described as "a democratic and republican religion". By abandoning equality in the Catholic faith for equality of opportunity in society, this type of Christianity enabled public opinion to establish a republican democracy. The American Catholics were the most submissive believers and the most independent citizens. As a minority, the adherents of the Catholic faith wished their rights to be respected by the state, and Protestantism generally encouraged its followers to be independent rather than equal.

Where direct influence was concerned, De Tocqueville said that the United States did not have a single religious doctrine hostile to democratic and republican institutions and that, with regard to indirect influence, religion taught the

Americans the art of being free: "The Americans are one of the most free and enlightened peoples in the world, and enthusiastically fulfill all the practical precepts of religion". The clerics supported the rights of the citizens although their role made them take a distance from political matters and party controversies. The clerics in the United States, who foresaw that political power involved a reduction of religious influence, were the first to favor a separation of church and state.

Critical enlightenment and religious faith were not contradictory in America. Religion did not interfere in the governance of America, but it acquired a taste for liberty: "Despotism can forgo religion, but freedom cannot". De Tocqueville believed that religion was necessary in order to strengthen moral relationships in a democracy when political relationships were weakened. At the same time, he disliked the one-dimensional atheistic kind of enlightenment, which claimed that religious extremism would disappear as freedom and education increased.

De Tocqueville's variety of liberalism toward religion and the state was crystallized when he observed the events of 1848 in France: For him, the February revolution must be Christian and democratic, and it cannot be social. These words summarize for Tocqueville the whole of his thought. Christian morality served as a protection against the liberalism of *laissez-faire*: religion restrained capitalism. But, religion, according to De Tocqueville, was not the sole litmus test to distinguish between the dogmatism at home and the desired model beyond the Atlantic. French democracy was imposed from above by means of an omniscient philosophy, an omnipotent bureaucracy, and a radical form of politics that subordinated means to ends, while American democracy sprang up from below without direction, in an unofficial manner and in an authentic way. On an infrastructure of small societies and associations—the townships—independent governing institutions and principles of political equality were interwoven. The genealogy offered by De Tocqueville for the democratic mechanism in France and in America provides us with a sociological key to explain the different character of the regimes.

In *The Ancien Régime and the Revolution*, De Tocqueville made a critical analysis of the intellectual abstraction and political radicalism that were one facet of the dual face of the French Revolution. In *Democracy in America*, which preceded the appearance of *The Ancien Régime and the Revolution* by a generation, he asked why the Americans were less enthusiastic than the French about general ideas in political matters, and he explained it by a kind of sociology of opinion. The difference between the empirical approach of the Americans and the French approach was due to the fact that the latter had a tendency to ideology because for hundreds of years they were unable to take part in public affairs: the royal and revolutionary bureaucracy stifled public spirit. The less one participated in public affairs, the more the tendency to develop theories increased: abstraction and theory were incompatible with negotiations, and thus one had French radicalism instead of American pragmatism. America succeeded where France failed due to the Anglo-Saxon tradition and political culture that was able to institutionalize voluntarism as an axiom. This was done through economic associations, independent communities, and local churches, autonomous administrations, principles of volunteering and a nongradated political structure. The visit to America was a confrontation with the democratic mechanism itself, a study of the concept of equality in practice.[15] Jacksonian America revealed the nature of democracy.

In his study of American society, De Tocqueville discovered that the source of the idea of the sovereignty of the people—the main characteristic of American democracy—was to be found in the historical background of the English settlement in America. The immigrants to the New World brought with them from England their political culture, which was the infrastructure for the Anglo-American social regime and laid the basis for an equality of social conditions. This regime was outstandingly democratic from the beginning. When the American nation was just beginning, a unique democratic political culture, which was also an excellent model for other democracies, already came into being due to the special historical background. Two possibilities were open to people in a democratic regime: a compromise between the sovereignty of all individuals or placing the governance in the hands of one person.[16]

The republican idea was dominant in the United States, just as the monarchical idea was dominant in the France of Louis XIV. In France, all power had been concentrated in the hands of a single person, but in the United States the power was spread through all sections of the population, which meant that the people were sovereign. The belief underlying the American social regime was that divine providence had given to each individual a minimum of wisdom by means of which he could live his life. This principle bound the head of the family to his children, the master to his servants, the state to the province, the province to the local authority, the local authority to those it administered, and the Union to the various states. When it embraced the entire nation, it became the principle of the sovereignty of the people.[17] In this way, the principle on which the republic was established was the principle that directed most human activities.

The principle of the sovereignty of the people was also expressed in the legal system in general and in the institution of trial by jury in particular. The function of the jury revealed a very republican side of the administration. De Tocqueville saw two aspects to the jury: it was both a legal institution and a political institution. The jury, in his opinion, was first of all a political institution, in that it sought to encourage the belief that the true leadership of the state was in the hands of the ruled and not of the ruler. The jury raised the people itself to the seat of judgment, and thus it has to be seen as one of the expressions of the sovereignty of the people. Every citizen of the United States could serve on a jury.[18]

Unlike in France and despite a tendency to social conformity, political freedom was preserved in America. The reason for this was the voluntarism and the social and institutional pluralism that were basic features of American politics. Organization was not imposed from above as in the days of the Ancien Régime in France but depended on the various sections of American society. The Americans organized themselves in community affairs as in religious matters.[19]

Freedom of association exists on three levels: the freedom to write, the freedom to gather together, and political organization. The many elections to the House, to the Senate, to the presidency, to the governorship of the states necessarily created a fermentation in political life and a continual involvement of the citizens in matters of administration and society. The emergence of public servants from among the masses of the people was a guarantee that the administration was in the hands of the people and not outside it. The people who managed the administration of public affairs in the United States were often less talented and moral than those whom an aristocracy might have chosen, but their personal interest was in keeping with that of the majority of citizens.[20] Everything was centered on the task and not on the official. In the view of the democrats in America, government was never good but was a necessary evil. De Tocqueville accepted the Jeffersonian proposition: "What government is good? The one that governs least". The bureaucratic administration represented the views of most of the people and the common general interest, and thus public officials did not need to advance the interest of any particular candidate. Their work was comprehensive, consistent, and benefited the whole population.

The chief matter that troubled De Tocqueville was the institutionalization of the freedom of the individual in a democracy. In a society connected by bonds of command to the state, to the aristocracy, to the Church, people develop a hunger to demand the legitimate expression of their natural rights. On the other hand, a democracy, in order to survive, must give the desire to live well not merely to a group of people but to all and in so doing must convince people to devote some of their energy to the good of the community. Democracy can allow itself to neglect lofty objectives. Self-interest is regarded as the good of all, and the good of all is the justification of democracy.[21] This utilitarian approach also found expression in the attitude to rights. Individuals in America attached great importance to the rights of the state because they themselves benefited from them. They refrained from harming the rights of others so that others would not harm their own. In other words, De Tocqueville associated the principle of rights as practiced in the United States with the interest of the individual and the utilitarian approach of the English political thinker Jeremy Bentham.[22]

What were the advantages that De Tocqueville found in democracy? It is a society that heads the order of preferences in a democracy, and thus the laws, customs, and institutions of a democracy have a general human purpose. Democracy does not have an aristocratic tradition of legislation, and one cannot please everyone, but the task of democracy is to satisfy people's desires as far as possible. Unlike in an aristocracy, in which the interests of the officials and the inhabitants are not the same, the lack of competition between classes in a democracy and the identity of interests of the officials and the people create an enlightened state devoid of bad intentions.

De Tocqueville thought that a democratic society could be an enlightened one if one cultivates its good points. The foundations of democracy are a recognition of political rights, an encouragement of public life, a general equality, a restriction of bureaucracy, and respect for the law. The respect for the law derives from the universal approach of the individual: each individual relates to the law as if he or she had created it. Democracy is not something learned by rote, an abstract creation dependent on the benevolence of a king, a religious command, or historical determinism, but is an institutionalization of the training of character and an educational-political process.

At the same time, De Tocqueville found ten weak points in American democracy: the excessive influence of the legislature on the executive, the unsatisfactory method of electing the president, the supreme court's infringement on the independence of the state, the difference in the composition of the Senate and the House of Representatives, the lack of a natural democratic tradition, the instability of the law and the frequency of elections, a separatist and alienating individualism, the conformism of the majority, the danger of an extreme form of central government, and the lack of a religious spirit.

The United States was freed from the burden of history, alien to abstract conceptions, adverse to all that was doctrinaire and opposed to the domination of a single truth. According to De Tocqueville, democracy, with all its virtues, could also become something repulsive. It was liable to revolt against the values of the Enlightenment in the name of the majority, develop a conformist character, and be a kind of enslavement. These factors caused De Tocqueville to suggest improvements in the structure of American democracy.

The improvements that De Tocqueville proposed were suitable for all democratic regimes and would directly affect any people who wished to construct a political regime on new social foundations. They were intended to protect the state from internal and external dangers that could destroy the republic and undermine the social structure. The names of regimes, like empires, kingdoms, constitutional monarchies, republics, and the like, made no impression on De Tocqueville. He accepted all regimes provided they ensured the existence of parliamentary institutions.

The excessive influence of the legislature on the executive (and on the president as its head) constituted a misuse of the laws of the republic and a dangerous blurring of the differences among the three powers. Like previous political thinkers, De Tocqueville knew that the precondition for an enlightened regime was a distribution of authority, a separation of powers, and the total independence of each one. In order to counter the danger of excessive intervention by the Senate in the work of the president—an intervention that could lead to the neutralization of the executive—De Tocqueville recommended the establishment of two executive bodies. One would represent the people directly, and the other, the Senate, would be elected by the people independently and represent its delegates.

De Tocqueville feared the effects of the practice of reelecting the president. The American attached great importance to the office of the president as a counterweight to the laws of the legislature, which could be influenced by the caprices of the masses. But, in practice, the president, instead of focusing on affairs of state, was concerned with reelection and acceptability to the legislators and the masses. De Tocqueville therefore suggested that the president could be elected by secondary electoral bodies.

The Supreme Court was an institution with enormous legislative power, with greater juridical authority than that of the states, and it therefore endangered the independence of the states and the existence of the federation. This situation threatened the delicate balance between the federal jurisdiction and the local jurisdiction, between the constitution and the laws of the states.

De Tocqueville saw another weak point in the different composition of the two legislative bodies, the House of Representatives and the Senate. The difference was that the House of Representatives was elected directly by the people and thus in certain respects represented superficial aims, while the people who sat in the Senate were selected by special electoral bodies. The senators, who were chosen by representatives, had particularly suitable qualities. De Tocqueville thought that the election of both houses should be organized in such a way that there would be only outstanding representatives in the legislature.

Tyranny is the power to dominate completely, whether in a dictatorship or a democracy. De Tocqueville believed that the tyranny of the majority was the great danger threatening the United States because the officials, judges, soldiers, and police all represented the opinion of the majority. A government is only democratic when the legislature and executive are chosen by the majority but not subordinated to its will, for that is like a spiritual inquisition. In place of the power of the majority, De Tocqueville proposed a body composed of people who were respected and eminent in their professions, a body that could be coordinated with the institutions of a democracy. Only such an "oligarchic" class could serve as a brake on the democratic deluge. Another institution of this kind was the jury that contributed the citizen's faculty of judgment and thus molded public opinion.

The instability of American law and the frequent elections were undoubtedly connected to the lack of a political tradition in the United States. It was the only country in which the law had no antiquity, and this fact was connected with the rapid replacement of the members of the legislature. The laws were created in accordance with the changing will of the citizens, and in modern democratic regimes in general and in America in particular, this tendency increased in times of crisis.

In face of the danger of the fragmentation of the population into isolated individuals, there stood the free institutions. Only through societies, communities, and free associations could the isolated individual connect with others and promote his personal interests. The religious spirit also neutralized the alienation of individuals. Centralized rule is a danger to freedom. De Tocqueville did not oppose centralized rule in all cases: it is necessary at a time when government projects or the mobilization of the nation require it, but he feared a centralized state when taken to an extreme. After the French Revolution, the local authorities in most countries were abolished in favor of the new ruler. In such a regime, there was a conformist unity in all areas of life, and the central government increasingly intervened in the affairs of the individual. Enlightened regimes try to preserve the sovereignty of the people and avoid absolute control despite the desire of the people to be guided and dominated.

Enlightenment in De Tocqueville went hand in hand with his modernity. Association based on a social rationale for purposes of welfare had replaced historical and tribal relationships: "The spirit of man is developed through small common efforts [. . .] the great connection between the whole human race is strengthened". In the final analysis, democracy is more productive than despotism. It does everything less effectively, but it utilizes intellectual and moral activities for material ends and the promotion of welfare. It favors rationalism rather than genius, peaceful practices rather than heroism.

Another outstanding quality in American democracy was the spread of welfare activities throughout the social and political fabric—the forms of civil, political, and juridical intervention. The citizens' awareness of all that takes place around them was reflected in social life. The intervention of the American citizen recalled the intervention of the citizen in the Greek *polis*. Out of the 43,000 citizens of Athens, 6,000 served each year in the popular law courts, 500 served with the members of the Council of State, and more than a 1,000 served in various political offices. The positions were for one year, and most of the inhabitants of Athens occupied them at least once in their lives. In the villages and urban neighborhoods, there was an active public life, and once a week there were popular assemblies. The member of the *polis* participated in the life of his city-state not only in theory but in practice. It was a continuous participation.[23] But it should be remembered that the great majority of people in the *polis* were slaves.

De Tocqueville saw his ideas as an extension and an amendment of Montesquieu's theory concerning ancient republics.[24] In a section that does not appear in the two parts of *Democracy in America* but in the notes preparatory to the second part, he compared his interpretation of American democracy with Montesquieu's view of the ancient republics: "We do not have to understand Montesquieu's idea only in a narrow literal sense". Montesquieu thought that a republic could remain in existence only through the society's influence on itself, and the meaning he gave to the concept *virtu* (virtue) was the moral force that each individual brings to bear on himself, a force that prevents him from infringing on the rights of others. De Tocqueville thought that Montesquieu was right when he spoke about ancient *virtu* and also in the things he said about the Greeks and Romans that applied to the Americans as well. There are, of course, significant differences between Montesquieu's idea of a republic and that of De Tocqueville.[25] For De Tocqueville, the typical ancient democracy was egalitarian but aspired to *virtu*—that is, of moral excellence and a high standard in civil life, while a modern democracy was industrial and commercial, and self-interest was consequently dominant in modern societies. If Montesquieu's ideas were applied to modern democracy in the context envisaged by De Tocqueville, the criterion would be interests, not moral excellence.[26]

De Tocqueville thought that American democracy was in danger of becoming an anonymous society of alienated individuals or, as it was later called, a mass society, a consumer society or a one-dimensional society. Hence his fear of the danger of a tyranny of the majority. When he spoke of the omnipotence of the majority in the United States or of the dangerous consequences of its omnipotence in the future, he was speaking of a situation in which "the very nature of democratic government is the absolute rule of the majority, for in a democracy there is nothing that can confirm its rule except a majority".[27]

In order to illustrate this observation, De Tocqueville examined most of the American laws and institutions and came to the conclusion that they aimed at artificially increasing this natural power of the majority. There were two starting points to this exposition. First, the will of the majority found very effective expression in the legislature because the Americans wanted its members to be directly elected by the people and appointed for only a very short time and thus would be continually under their influence. Second, the legislature was the strongest power, and its influence overshadowed that of the other two powers. The law thus increased the strength of the strong power and made the weak powers even weaker. Apart from laws, the proof of the absolute power of the majority was also to be found in customs. Custom that had struck root in the United States overruled the principle of representative government. Electors who dictated a certain conduct to their candidates could be compared to a mass of people buying and selling in a market: "Due to special circumstances, the majority protrudes and dominates to such a degree in America that it cannot be opposed".[28]

The idea on which the concept of the moral superiority of the majority was based, according to De Tocqueville, is that many special people have more wisdom and education than a single individual and that many jurists have more than a chosen few. The first immigrants brought to the United States the view that the majority, through the power of its intelligence, has the right to rule the country. This view gained strength in American society and was instituted in local frameworks and habits of life. De Tocqueville rejected the two principles that in his opinion guided the Americans in founding the rule of the majority: (1) the majority can never be mistaken, and (2) the interests of many are to be preferred to those of a few. According to De Tocqueville, the people who settled in America were all equal, and there was therefore no conflict of interest.

According to him, the dynamic underlying the American regime in the sphere of legislation was a liability to democratic government because it contributed to its instability. The representatives of the people were reelected every year, and this resulted in perpetual changes of direction in the most important decisions. In examining the American legislation of his time, De Tocqueville noticed that the laws in America had a shorter time frame than those of any other country, and this had a negative influence on the implementation of the laws and administration. Moreover, because it was important to please the majority, which was the only source of power, as soon as the attention of the majority turned from one matter to another, it lost its interest in the matter and forgot its importance. This was not the case in Europe: because in Europe the executive did not depend on the legislature, the legislator's will was carried out even when he was occupied with other matters. The liberal aristocrat De Tocqueville was not a revolutionary. He saw enthusiasm as something momentary and transient, which could not be allowed to dictate the pace of legislation or the nature of political life. His approach, which resembled that of Edmund Burke, was close to the English school, which called for a step-by-step improvement and renewal within a tradition.

He felt that omnipotence as such was dangerous and bad and that it was beyond the capacity of man to use it.[29] No government in the world is so revered, or whose rights are so sacred, that it could be allowed unlimited power, action without criticism, or restriction. De Tocqueville compared the majority to an individual with his aspirations and affairs, and the minority to another individual with aspirations and affairs of his own. Anyone with unlimited power can make an immoral use of it against his adversaries, and this also applies to a majority. The idea that in government the majority of the people has the right to do anything is basically indefensible, but, nevertheless, De Tocqueville made the government of the state dependent on the will of the majority. When individuals organize themselves as a majority, they do not change their character and do not become more tolerant.

He also disbelieved in the effectiveness of a Polybius-type "mixed constitution". He claimed that there could not be a mixed form of government because in every society there was a dominant activating principle to which other principles are subordinate. Among the different social forces one must identify the one that is dominant, but it must be fenced round with restrictions to moderate it. Like Montesquieu, De Tocqueville supported the principle of a separation of powers that balance and restrain one another. Social forces embodied in associations and institutions could oversee the dominant majority and restrain it by democratic means. John Stuart Mill was also aware of the danger to society of mob rule, of placing the power of political decision in the hands of broad sections of society that had not been trained in the use of the right to vote and that were liable to use it irrationally.[30]

De Tocqueville's ideal was a moderate constitutional regime, whether a limited monarchy or a limited republic. In a place where the balance of powers was lacking and voluntary societies were not active, as in the Ancien Régime in France, there was a danger that a democratic regime would degenerate into a mass society. In the United States, the voluntary associations prevented power from being concentrated in a single source.

All areas of life in the United States were characterized by the principle of the majority. The individual who suffered a misfortune could not appeal to an authoritative body because all of them—whether public opinion, the legislature, the executive, the army, or the jury—represented the views of the majority. Even the judges in some states were elected by the majority. The omnipotence of the majority was institutionalized in the legislature and the executive, which were instruments of the will of the majority within the framework of the government. The concept "majority" is meaningless until it is embodied in an official framework that is able to exert influence, unlike the concept "the masses", which, owing to its undefined nature, is far more dangerous. Because the majority was institutionalized in official bodies, it prevented any criticism of it on the grounds that "we are the rulers". The majority, which had an unlimited right to make laws, to supervise their execution, and to control the governors and the governed, saw the officials as instruments to serve it and relied on them to do its bidding. De Tocqueville perceived two main dangers in the omnipotence of the majority: a legitimized despotism of the legislature and an accepted arbitrariness of government officials.[31] This despotism was not widespread in the United States of the 1830s, but in order to prevent its dominance it was necessary to restrict the power of each body as far as possible, erect barriers between the different bodies, and restrain the despotism in the civil and political tradition through criteria and norms rather than by enacting new laws.

Comparing the absolute regimes of certain European states in which there was a consciousness of a critical opposition with a democratic regime like that of the United States, in which an overwhelming majority was liable to stifle the criticism of the minority and take it under its wing, De Tocqueville saw greater danger in the latter. In the first kind of regime, "The monarch has only a physical power that acts on deeds and cannot reach wills", but in a democratic regime, "the majority is vested with a strength simultaneously physical and moral, which acts on the will as well as on actions and which at the same time prevents the deed and the desire to do it".[32] De Tocqueville's assertion is somewhat sweeping and contains a certain exaggeration deriving from the lack of previous critical debate on the matter, but the very fact of pointing out this kind of danger in a democratic society specifically is a refreshing innovation in political thought. De Tocqueville did not disregard controlling and supervisory mechanisms like the legal system and local government. The influence of the majority in the United States was most in evidence in the sphere of consciousness. De Tocqueville did not know of any country in which there was "less independence in the majority and less true freedom of discussion than in America". This radical formulation was intended to reveal a problem: in America, thought was threatened by the majority. A conformist writer was accepted and at liberty, but he was persecuted and harmed if he went outside the system. It was therefore not surprising, said De Tocqueville, that no great writer had come out of America. Conformist thinking did not have as much importance in political life in the United States as it had in molding the American national character. Thus, there were few outstanding people in the American political scene at the beginning of the nineteenth century, unlike the great number of them at the time of the revolution. De Tocqueville predicted that if American liberty would ever be lost, it would not be because of weakness but because of a depressing conformism that would bring minorities to such despair that it would cause them to fight. Then anarchy would be let loose, and it would be the result of despotism.

In the United States, the principle of the majority was dominant, but it lacked the tools to impose a tyranny. In De Tocqueville's opinion, the power in American democracy was not concentrated in a single political source. There was a central government but not a concentration of administration. De Tocqueville gave three examples of the division of power. The federal government only dealt with major problems of policy, and it permitted the body of citizens to deal with secondary matters. The majority did not increase the authority of the central administration and did not give it the tools to act in all areas. The government was centralized, and the majority was represented in it, but there were also restraining factors such as the townships, the states, and the various associations.

The greatest obstacle to distortions of democracy was the authority given to jurists and their influence on the government and the public.[33] The jurists' opposition to the revolutionary spirit of democracy derived from their liking for habit, order, legality and from their systematic way of thinking. De Tocqueville considered the jurists an aristocratic element in the social-democratic fabric of the United States, and they helped to rectify the natural deficiencies of democracy. The law courts were their most effective instruments. They filled most public positions, the legislature, and the administration; they influenced legislation; and, above all, they brought the judicial spirit to the public. The judicial spirit, which was expressed in the institution of the jury, tempered the omnipotence of the majority. It communicated to the public the prestige of a judge, taught all classes to respect the decisions of the court, trained people to act honestly and not to evade responsibility, taught every citizen to value his own judgment, made everyone aware of his duties to society, made everyone a partner in government, and encouraged practical intelligence and an active political sense.

While Karl Marx saw alienation as the great problem of modern industrial society, De Tocqueville considered individualism the main defect of modern democratic society.[34] Individualism, a product of democracy, which came into existence with the growth of conditions of equality, destroyed the gradations and connections between the social strata that characterized feudal-aristocratic society.[35] When individuals isolate themselves from society as a whole, individualism causes them to hand over the whole power of government to some central factor. As social conditions become increasingly identical, people are less unique, and the state becomes a Leviathan. Every citizen resembles the others and is swallowed up in the mass, and only the generality is visible. The democratic revolution, which in the United States resulted in an equalization of conditions, brought it about that individuals sought themselves within themselves. In other words, they no longer depended on factors outside themselves and were no longer burdened with the life experience of their ancestors, the commands of aristocrats or the charisma of their leaders.[36] The American formula for overcoming individualism was to get the citizens to participate in public affairs. As a consequence of this, there were bodies that mediated between the individual—who tended toward individualism and anarchy—and the public at large. To make use of a Hegelian concept, De Tocqueville's was particularly interested in the strengthening of the "civil relationship" between the state and the individual and his or her family.[37]

In his analysis of the influence of public opinion in the United States, De Tocqueville came to the conclusion that the more equal and similar the citizens became, the less able they were to believe in a particular person or class. On the other hand, when conditions were not equal, individuals tended to take the intelligence, charisma, and initiative of a particular person or class as a guide. In a time of equality, people have no belief in one another because of their similarity, but it is precisely this similarity that gives them an almost unlimited faith in public opinion, a belief that the truth is to be found in the opinion of many. According to De Tocqueville, public opinion in a democratic society is a tremendous force of a special kind, which aristocratic societies never conceived of. One may therefore suppose that in the United States the majority took it upon itself to supply individuals with many ready-made ideas and so relieved them of the necessity of thinking for themselves. Thus, the majority dominates society with its way of thinking, and in the future the domination of the majority would become a manipulation of the majority by public opinion.[38]

The contradiction that De Tocqueville pointed out in American society was a tendency to individualism and separatism side by side with the tyrannical influence of public opinion and the omnipotence of the majority. This dialectical combination could be the foundation of a new democratic absolutism. The American model of democracy, however, succeeded in successfully combining these two contrary principles by dividing the power into many subsidiary parts. These different components served as a brake on administrative centralization on the one hand and an institutionalization of the tyranny of the majority on the other, but there was no guarantee that in the future there would not be a far more sophisticated form of tyranny than there has ever been before. The tyranny of the Roman Empire was cruel but was limited by being premodern, but the tyranny foreseen by De Tocqueville was the opposite of the Roman model:

> This is how it makes the use of free will less useful and rarer everyday; how it encloses the action of the will within a smaller space and little by little steals from each citizen even the use of himself. Equality has prepared men for all these things; it has disposed men to bear them and often even to regard them as a benefit.[39]

In modern government, whose salient features are education and equality, rulers can easily combine the components of power and constantly intervene in the affairs of the individual in a more effective way than rulers in ancient times.

After molding the individual to his or her liking, the ruler does something similar to all sections of society. The molding of society and the stifling of the individual are not performed through the violence and compulsion that typified absolutist regimes in the past: "Chains and executioners, those are the crude instruments formerly used by tyranny; but today civilization has perfected even despotism itself, which seemed however to have nothing more to learn".[40] The new democratic despotism was an orderly and comfortable enslavement of people, "an enslavement of internal peace". This was the great calamity to be feared, and it was De Tocqueville's discovery: when tyranny appears, its violent nature rouses people to criticism and action, but—as Marx and Marcuse were to say after him—when the consciousness is blurred, apart from the fact that it is liable to send people to sleep, it represents a danger for the future: the creation of an omnipotent state as an all-powerful guardian, educator, and redeemer.

Democracy in America sets De Tocqueville among the pioneers of the analysis of the problem of democracy. He was the first thinker in modern times to investigate in a comprehensive manner the way in which the principle of democracy—equality—emerges as the first cause and shaper of every aspect of modern society. This was different from the method of the political thinkers of the seventeenth and eighteenth centuries who began their investigations by studying human beings and then examined their status as citizens within a given regime. In De Tocqueville's opinion, the study of politics begins with an examination of the condition of society. As we would say, he combined sociology with political science within a historical context.[41]

Democracy in America sought to demonstrate how a certain social situation, a situation of equality, affected the political institutions of the nation and the traditions, customs, and intellectual habits of the citizens. This social situation is brought about by the nature of democratic regimes. That was "the basic fact from which everything else derives". One can thus understand De Tocqueville's call for a "new science of politics", which has to be adopted in order to comprehend the new conditions created by the victory of democracy. Equality, which was on the rise, did not necessarily mean the victory of democracy or progress, as many people think. Equality could also lead to a "one-dimensional society", as Herbert Marcuse says, or to a "totalitarian democracy", as described by Jacob Talmon.[42]

In his book *One-dimensional Man*, Marcuse depicted American society of the 1960s as a conformist consumer society that used hidden means of supervision and control in the name of the majority and on behalf of the majority. The aim was to bring the individual into conformity with the one-dimensional society that suppressed any ideological alternative or critical rejection. In this society, a modified pluralism existed through an integration of culture and sex, and a functionality of the written and spoken language. Orders were not given from a royal court, and executioners were not welcome in a society of this kind. The press appeared to be free, the individual was allowed to do as he pleased, but the society was conditioned by the despotism of a majority of individuals who were alike and equal in their one-dimensionality. It was a self-sufficient totalitarianism that had no need of an external despot. It was sophisticated, refined, and in no way resembled the absolutism of the past that had become outmoded, but for that very reason it was all the more dangerous. Despite the differences between the ideological outlooks of De Tocqueville and Marcuse (one being a nineteenth-century liberal conservative and the other a twentieth-century Marxist), the points of convergence in their analyses of American society are remarkable. There are, of course, many differences between them both in the starting points of their analyses and in the conclusions they come to, but the main difference is that Marcuse examined in practice something that De Tocqueville feared could happen but against which he thought that the Americans had developed suitable safeguards.

Jacob Talmon also thought that dictatorship in modern times is essentially different from previous dictatorships because it is based on the democratization of the masses and depends on the increasing power of equal citizens, not on chosen elites as in the past. It is true that he examined European society and not American, but in his idea of "totalitarian democracy" he based himself first and foremost on the hypothesis-prediction of De Tocqueville:

> So I think that the type of oppression by which democratic peoples are threatened will resemble nothing of what preceded it in the world; our contemporaries cannot find the image of it in their memories. I seek in vain myself of an expression that exactly reproduces the idea that I am forming of it; the thing that I want to speak about is new, and men have not yet created the expression which must portray it. The old words of despotism and of tyranny do not work. The thing is new, so I must try to define it, since I cannot name it.[43]

De Tocqueville teaches us how human beings can be free and equal at the same time through government by the people, representative institutions, the separation of powers, and he also shows us that the real force driving democracy—the passion for equality—can also lead to despotism. An omnipotent state dominating all areas of life in a paternalistic way can exist simultaneously with the official institutions of democracy. Unlike many contemporary thinkers who say that increased equality goes together with the final eradication of the possibility of despotism in our time, De Tocqueville understood that the democratic principle is vulnerable to manifestations of power like public opinion, factors that did not exist previously.[44]

In the sociological style of Montesquieu, De Tocqueville sought to catch the essence of a certain society, the spirit of the American nation, by means of a comprehensive examination of a historical tradition, a geographical area, and the influence of the laws and the leaders. That was the De Tocqueville of the first part of *Democracy in America*, but in the second part he examined America as an ideal example of democracy in modern societies. Raymond Aron discerned two sociological approaches in De Tocqueville: one, the portrayal of a particular collective, and the other, the delineation of an abstract tendency and the description of a general problem.[45] In other words, De Tocqueville's sociopolitical analysis was bound up with theoretical conclusions. De Tocqueville concluded: freedom depends on people's leaders and beliefs, not on exemplary laws. Free institutions are essential, but people also need a sense of independence, a certain feeling of opposition to power, and a considerable degree of liberty.

De Tocqueville thought that democracy would not give birth to a new kind of human. He feared two things. On the one hand, he was rightly afraid that democracy would foster mediocrity, would favor interests rather than *virtu* (virtue), and would encourage the common denominator, and on the other hand he was very fearful that politics would become a religion and *virtu* would become coercion. He was a political sociologist, not a moralist.[46] He wished to prevent modern democracy from developing a desire to change humankind: one must recognize that there could be a good life without distinction or greatness, and it would always be endangered. Raymond Aron pointed out ironically that we always think that only left-wing people are humanists, but De Tocqueville believed that the radicals in France, the extreme republicans, were not humanitarians but revolutionaries inebriated by ideology and ready to sacrifice millions of people for their ideas. He therefore preferred the American model of democracy, although he also pointed out its dangers. He was an aristocrat and a humanist, a sociologist who did not shrink from passing judgment in the best tradition of classical political thought.

He was a modern prophet in political thought. For better or worse, he chose the democratic experience in America as a test case and as a model of the future of the modern world. The collapse of the totalitarian ideology of communism ten years before the end of the twentieth century places De Tocqueville's unique status as a thinker in a historical perspective. His prophecy was more on target than that of Marx. De Tocqueville warned against a centralized economy, a monolithic state, a one-party government, an atheism that arose on the ruins of faith, or, in other words, a socialism that in the name of class equality put its trust in a dangerous concentration of power instead of a liberal democracy on a voluntary basis. One can observe the vicissitudes of the forecasts of De Tocqueville and Marx if one makes a historical analysis of the events in France in the year 1848. De Tocqueville thought that socialist ideas were reactionary because they strengthened a pathological tendency of both the Ancien Régime and of revolutionary France: the tendency to bureaucracy and a concentration of power. He looked with suspicion at the new elites of bureaucrats and party activists and was repelled by a democracy that restricted human liberty in the name of an economic determinism. In his view, America was the opposite of all this.

De Tocqueville protested against the breakup of social solidarity and communal relationships and the neglect of the value of citizenship. He understood that an effective democracy attempts to disperse power and that the new elements of power had to be social bodies that bore the burden of self-administration. He knew that the only antidote to the defects of a democratic society—its commercialism, its shallowness, its promotion of the average—lay in the moral act of self-administration, the maximum dispersion of the political system.

In this way, political responsibility in the United States could be seen as a moral commitment. No thinker has gone further than De Tocqueville in warning about the connection between the disposal of power and moral dangers. He did not begin his social and historical researches with assumptions about human nature, as the classical philosophers did, and although he did not base his work on the methodology of the social sciences like the theoreticians of the nineteenth century—Marx, Durkheim, and Weber—De Tocqueville can be regarded as a thinker, observer-participant, and prophet. His thought, his testimony, and his prophecy seized upon America as the crossroads of modernity and enlightenment at the point where democratic modernity tends either toward enlightenment or against it, "towards slavery or freedom, towards education or barbarism, towards abundance or deprivation".

Notes

1 Cheryl B. Welch, ed., *The Cambridge Companion to Tocqueville*, Cambridge 2006.
2 Dana Richard Villa, *Teachers of the People: Political Education in Rousseau, Hegel, Tocqueville, and Mill*, Chicago 2017.
3 Richard Reeves (ed.), *American Journey: Traveling with Tocqueville in Search of Democracy in America*, New York 1983; George Wilson Pierson, *Tocqueville and Beaumont in America*, New York 1938; Jon Elster, *Alexis de Tocqueville: The First Social Scientist*, Cambridge 2009.
4 François Furet, "La Decouverte de L'Amerique", *Magazine litteraire*, 236 (Decembre 1986), 35; See correspondence between Tocqueville and Kergorlay: Alexis De Tocqueville, *Correspondence Tocqueville-Kergorlay*, Tome XIII, vols. 1, 2, Paris 1977.
5 Seymour Drescher, *Tocqueville and England*, Cambridge, MA 1964; Adah Tsemah, *Alexis de Tocqueville on England*, Notre Dame 1951.
6 Yehoshua Arieli, *Individualism and Nationalism in American Ideology*, Cambridge, MA 1964.
7 Hugh Brogan, *Alexis de Tocqueville: A Life*, New Haven, CT 2007.
8 See especially de la Fournier X, *Alexis de Tocqueville, un monarchist independent*, Paris 1981; André Jardin, *Alexis de Tocqueville*, New York 1986.
9 François Furet and Mona Ozouf, eds., *Dictionnaire Critique de la revolution francaise*, Paris 1981, 1021–1032.
10 Alexis de Tocqueville, *The Old Regime and The Revolution*, trans., John Bonner, New York 1856, 36.
11 Robert T. Gannett, *Tocqueville Unveiled: The Historian and His Sources for the Old Regime and the Revolution*, Chicago 2003.
12 Richard Herr, *Tocqueville and the Old Regime*, Princeton, NJ 1962.
13 Bob Edwards, Michael W. Foley, and Mario Diani, eds., *Beyond Tocqueville: Civil Society and the Social Capital Debate in Comparative Perspective*, Hanover 2001.
14 Joshua Mitchell, *The Fragility of Freedom: Tocqueville on Religion, Democracy and the American Future*, Chicago 1995.
15 James T. Schleifer, *The Making of Tocqueville's Democracy*, Chapel Hill, NC 1980.
16 De Tocqueville, *Democracy in America*, trans., James T. Schleifer, Indianapolis, IN 2010, 90.
17 Ibid., 633–634.
18 Ibid., 179, 445–446.
19 Ibid., 302.
20 Ibid., 380.

21 Jean-Claude Lamberti, *La notion d'individualisme chez Tocqueville*, Paris 1970.
22 Jeremy Bentham, *An Introduction to the Principles of Morals and Legislation*, eds., J. H. Burns & H. L. A. Hart, London 1982.
23 Donald Kagan, *Pericles of Athens and the Birth of Democracy*, New York 1991.
24 Raymond Aron, *Main Currents in Sociological Thought*, vol. I, London 1965.
25 Pierre Birnbaum, *Sociologie de Tocqueville*, Paris 1955.
26 Paul O. Carrese, *Democracy in Moderation: Montesquieu, Tocqueville, and Sustainable Liberalism*, Cambridge 2016.
27 De Tocqueville, *Democracy in America*, 402.
28 Ibid.
29 De Tocqueville, *Democracy in America*, 402–407.
30 John Stuart Mill, *Considerations on Representative Government*, London 1861.
31 De Tocqueville differentiates between arbitrariness and tyranny: tyranny guided by the law—which is governance without arbitrariness, and arbitrariness—which could be favorable for the citizens and is without inherent tyranny.
32 De Tocqueville, *Democracy in America*, 417.
33 Ibid., 431–442.
34 Nestor Capdevila, *Tocqueville ou Marx: Democratie, Capitalisme, Revolution*, Paris 2012.
35 Arieli, *Individualism and Nationalism in American Ideology*, 184–190, 193–204.
36 De Tocqueville, *Democracy in America*, 885–889.
37 Ibid., 885–894.
38 Ibid., 717.
39 Ibid., 1251.
40 Ibid., 418.
41 Jack Lively, *The Social and Political Thought of Alexis de Tocqueville*, Oxford 1965.
42 De Tocqueville, *The Democracy in America*, 415; Herbert Marcuse, *One-Dimensional Man: Studies in the Ideology of Advanced Industrial Society*, Boston 1991; Jacob L. Talmon, *The Origins of Totalitarian Democracy*, New York 1970.
43 De Tocqueville, *Democracy in America*, 1248–1249.
44 Jean Claude Lamberti, *La notion d'individualisme chez Tocqueville*, Paris 1970.
45 Aron, *Main Currents in Sociological Thought*, vol. I, 183–232.
46 Jean-Louis Benoit, *Tocqueville moraliste*, Paris 2004.

2   1848
"We Are Sitting on a Volcano"

A. De Tocqueville: Socialism as a New Servitude

Alexis De Tocqueville clearly discerned the Promethean passion of the Paris workers in 1848, was frightened by it, and warned of it in advance. As a liberal conservative. he did not believe the slogans about a "new man", about worldwide revolution and a change in the order of things. Promethean socialism was likely, in his opinion, to develop into a new form of servitude.

According to the personal testimony of Henry Reeve, in 1837 De Tocqueville called himself "an instinctive aristocrat", and this provided the key to his thinking and political activities:

> They absolutely want to make me a party man and I am not that in the least; they assign to me passions and I have only opinions, or rather I have only one passion, the love of liberty and human dignity. All forms of government are in my eyes only more or less perfect ways of satisfying this holy and legitimate passion of man. They alternately give me democratic or aristocratic prejudices. [. . .] I came into the world at the end of a long Revolution, which, after having destroyed the old state, had created nothing durable. Aristocracy was already dead when I started life and democracy did not yet exist, [. . .] I was living in a country that for forty years had tried a little of everything without settling definitely on anything; therefore I was not susceptible to political illusions.[1]

The year 1848 was not a political illusion. The thinker enamored of liberty and fearful of radicalism was conscious that France on the eve of 1848 was a land on the edge of a volcano. After his visit to the United States, he was aware of the danger of mass-despotism in a situation of equal political rights. His liberal outlook did not prevent him from having social feelings in his own country. As a prophet in his own town, before the rebellion broke out, he identified its Promethean modernity: in practice, the social question was all-important. Only a few days before the revolutionary events began, in a famous speech on the 27th of January 1848 in the National Assembly, he warned of a potentially disastrous combination of social radicalism and political radicalism. This combination, he said, would not only cause a political upheaval but a real revolution that could change the foundations of Western society.[2]

In these days, he thought that the working classes are not troubled by political ambitions but by social passions. He warned that the ideas that were in the air will shake the foundations of society: the idea that anyone above them is not fit to govern, that the distribution of resources is unjust. These ideas, when they go to the root of things, sooner or later will lead to the worst kind of revolution. Tocqueville claimed: "We are sitting on a volcano. Can't you see that the earth is trembling again? A revolutionary wind is blowing, a storm is gathering on the horizon".[3] This tempestuous spirit made Marx and Engels, a few months earlier, write the "Communist Manifesto". In 1848, for the first time in history, the working classes unsuccessfully demanded a redistribution of resources.

De Tocqueville first wrote about the French Revolution in 1836 in John Stuart Mill's newspaper. His article, "The Social and Political Situation in France Before and After 1789", was the result of his travels in Britain, travels that molded his social and political consciousness.[4] In 1835, at the height of the social and industrial changes in Britain, he foresaw the problems that would be caused by the growth of industry and the democratic movement. The journey across the English Channel was important for his intellectual development like Engel's visit to Manchester in 1844.

His reflections on the Industrial Revolution led him to the conclusion that "the human spirit is corrupted here and a cultured man becomes wild".[5] De Tocqueville was shocked at the importance given to money: "Money not only represents wealth here, but power and glory". On the relationship of workers and bosses, he wrote: "On this side you have the workers and on that side, the boss. On this side you have the wealthy and on that side, the masses". As a member of the French postrevolutionary generation, he was surprised at the nonviolent character of the unfolding of English history and ascribed this to the English nobility. By way of contrast, the great mistake of the French aristocracy was that it exploited its political privileges and neglected the workers, who in a parallel fashion built up their own political strength. This happened at a time when capital became necessary for economic success, but the aristocracy continued to rely, as in the past, on petty trading and industry.

The downfall of the aristocracy did not happen because it neglected the laws. Its downfall was due to a decline in the psychological motivation of the whole class. At that period, the commercial classes did have this motivation. De Tocqueville thought that this decline in aspiration was more important than any legal factor. The middle class within the Third Estate began to develop the traits of the aristocracy, in particular its ambitiousness.

The rise of the middle class was depicted by De Tocqueville as a kind of new creation, the entry of a fresh foundation into the history of the nations. This "new nation" was not only destined to gain an important place in society, but it threatened to eradicate the excessive rights of the aristocracy. Moreover, it intended to eradicate the very concept of an aristocracy. De Tocqueville did not think that it is possible to dispense with the elite of a functioning society.[6] The opposite was true: one of the main principles operating in history was the principle of guidance and communication belonging to the aristocracy in all societies. Birth, wealth, and knowledge are the attributes of an aristocracy: one cannot have a society in which all are aristocratic, educated, and wealthy. Of these qualities, the French aristocracy of the eighteenth century had only birth. Its downfall was due to its neglect of its political and social functions.

The main feature of the eighteenth century, which was already described in this early article, was the decline of the aristocracy and the rise of the middle class. De Tocqueville concluded from this that a democratic state in which there were great differences in wealth could not be expected to endure. Such conditions would compel the possessors of capital to use force and would perpetuate the subjugation of the proletariat. Apart from the failure of the aristocracy to provide for the nation, De Tocqueville pointed to two major developments: the movement toward equality became the main tendency, and the power of the state continually increased in the centuries preceding the revolution. The lack of a responsible aristocracy made the French people defer to the government as the central authority, and the middle class, which found itself without an effective leadership, supported the crown in order to destroy the aristocracy. The citizens, unable to govern themselves, gave all power to the state.

Thus, the arbitrary state had absolute power, and, parallel with this, there was an increase of selfishness and individualism. De Tocqueville assumed that the idea of personal liberty had to be combined with free institutions. His study of French history led him to the conclusion that, despite the good intentions of the people, it was liable to bring on despotism. The article "France Before and After 1789" was written between the publication of the first volume of *Democracy in America* (1835) and the publication of the second volume (1840).

In his speech to the Académie française in 1842, De Tocqueville expanded on the idea of free institutions. He looked at French history from the perspective of Count of Cessac, a previous member of the Academy. Cessac had held a public position in the Ancien Régime, during the revolution and during the rule of Napoleon. As a senior official, he laid the foundation of the bureaucratic and centralized state which reached its zenith in the time of Napoleon. In his speech, De Tocqueville pointed to two tendencies that emerged from this source of the nineteenth century: one led to free institutions and the other to absolute power.[7]

De Tocqueville was one of the first historians in the nineteenth century to undermine the myth of Napoleon. This subversive historiographical tendency was not in keeping with the spirit of the time, for two years earlier, in 1840, Napoleon's bones had been brought from Saint Helena for burial in Les Invalides. De Tocqueville thought that the Napoleonic myth was a burden on the French people: "Napoleon owes his greatness more to accident than to his personality". Thus, in De Tocqueville's speech, Cessac's public career became a testimony to the great revolution that began with the hope of liberty and ended in tyranny.

In 1843, De Tocqueville was asked to prepare a report on the moral tendencies of contemporary society, basing himself on the voluminous literature calling for a social transformation. The institution that ordered the report was the

Académie des Sciences Morales et Politiques (Academy of Moral and Political Sciences), of which De Tocqueville was a member. He sought the assistance of Count Artur de Gobineau before he published his famous book about race. In the report, De Tocqueville looked at the historical influences on the revolutionary character of his period. His aim was to examine the nature of modernity as reflected in the new socialist theories that put forward new doctrines concerning man and society completely unconnected with the Christian religion.[8]

The final test of every revolution, said De Tocqueville, is the totality of its intention: that is to say, a new understanding of the world. The weakness of Christianity was its neglect of political and social matters. De Tocqueville recognized the legitimacy of a demand for social reform, the need to abolish poverty and to improve the material conditions of mankind. These demands, he said, must be motivated by the spirit of Christianity. As against this, the radical Gobineau wanted to build a new world based on absolute principles.[9] The paths of the two friends De Tocqueville and Gobineau parted, and the report was shelved.

In 1847, De Tocqueville wrote the manifesto, "On the Middle Class and the People", for the National Assembly. He wished to write the history of France from the "July revolution" in 1830 to November 1847, and by that means to point to the lack of vitality in political life in France. In his opinion, the success of the 1830 revolution prevented the development of parties whose task was to endow the skeleton of politics with flesh and blood. "The revolutions of 1789 and 1830 were only episodes in the long, violent struggle between the old feudal nobility and the middle class".[10] This struggle gave the revolution its large parties and its controversial record. The victory of the middle class in 1830 arrested the impetus of the revolution and dampened its spirit. The two classes were now separated by a chasm in their traditions, interests, and ideas. The year 1830 was thus one point in the continuity of the French revolutionary tradition. The homogeneity of interests in the middle class gave rise to a general drowsiness, but in the future, predicted De Tocqueville, there would be a revolutionary change in which there would be a demand for the abolition of the privileges of wealth—privileges that the French Revolution did not touch.

The right to property was the last barricade of the old world of politics. It was defended only by the board members of the National Assembly. De Tocqueville was convinced that the next revolution in France would be in the social sphere: "There is reason to believe that the struggle between the political parties will shortly be between those who have and those who have not. The battlefield will be property".[11] At the time he wrote these words, Marx was dealing with the final proofs of the "Communist Manifesto".

De Tocqueville was the only thinker to treat the ideas of Owen, Saint-Simon, Fauré, and Louis Blanc seriously. He did not reject them as utopian dreams but carefully considered their significance. This resulted in the two main proposals in the manifesto: one was to extend political rights to the lower classes as well. In his opinion, the monopoly of political power by the middle class would disappear, whether voluntarily or through a revolution. The second proposal concerned the duty of the state to care for the social welfare of its citizens through its capacity to improve the conditions of the lower classes while preserving the right to property. The manifesto, which was not published, reflected De Tocqueville's political education at the time of the July monarchy. His social sentiments and his observations on the future of France primarily reflect the historian he was rather than the public representative.

Important events in history, thought De Tocqueville, come about through long inner developments, which are accelerated at a certain moment by particular events. There were several general reasons for the uprising of 1848. The first was the development of the Industrial Revolution in France in the thirty years before the revolutionary events. De Tocqueville did not make an exact assessment of the effects of industrialization on the French economy, but in Paris he was aware of a new population of members of the working class and unemployed proletarians. They were easily influenced by socialist theories based on positivist laws. Although they were not organized on a class basis and lacked a common strategy, they served as the raw material for a social uprising.

In addition to these general causes, there were aggravating factors. The reforms demanded by the opposition aroused forgotten desires that only a rebellion could satisfy. Conservative historians have explained France's bad situation at the time by its inability to set up a functioning monarchy in the years 1815–1848. One had an impotent government unable to carry out its plans, and the "senile stupidity" of Louis-Philippe, as De Tocqueville put it, bore witness to its weakness. His failure was the last example of that of a long line of kings—Charles I, Louis XVI, and Charles X—who failed to adapt to the politics of modernity.[12]

The lack of distance in time did not prevent De Tocqueville, unlike his contemporaries, from analyzing the significance of the events of 1848 against the background of the long history of the French Revolution. He was a witness to the violent and tortuous journey that began in 1789. On the 24th of February 1848, he thought that the revolution had reached its conclusion. He listened in a depressed state to his contemporaries' prophecies about the end of civilization. He felt that a new radical foundation was about to change the organization of society and that this change in the course of modern history was to be ascribed to economic and social factors rather than the political factors that were the causes of revolutions in the past. At quite an early stage, he realized that the key to 1848 was an understanding of its social character.[13] Although he was not an economist, he accepted in a general way the theory of Adam Smith but was wary of blindly supporting *laissez-faire*.

The uprising of 1848, in his opinion, represented the fusion of a certain idea with power: the idea of social reform with the power of the masses and their demand for economic equality. In June 1849, he supported the dictatorship declared by the minister of defense Cavaignac. In that same year, he reached the peak of his political career: his appointment as minister for foreign affairs. After the resignation of Louis-Napoleon's government in October 1849 and until the coup d'état of the 2nd of December 1850, he attempted unsuccessfully to prevent the breakup of the Second Republic. His political experience during the Revolution of 1848 and the change in his life from theory to practice enabled him to understand the permutations of French society, but in the course of time his liberal ideas grew weaker. The events had a dialectical influence on him: his vision impelled him to political activity, but the activity dulled his vision.

Like Marx, De Tocqueville saw the bourgeoisie and the proletariat as allies in the first stage of the uprising. Hence the popular character of that revolution and its lack of hatred. Little by little, however, when the proletariat united and developed a consciousness that it was not the agent of a higher class, it began to act independently and contrary to the wishes of the bourgeoisie. There began to be a polarization between the two classes that made up French society. One of the sides in the struggle, said De Tocqueville, was not content with victory but sought "to impose a whole social science, I would almost say a philosophy, an easily-acquired and tested religion on all mankind".[14]

He saw class warfare as a constant factor in history, but what he meant by it was the struggle between rich and poor. The February revolution provided an additional proof: "Socialism is the dominant feature of the February revolution and its most alarming characteristic. The republic is only a means and not the final goal".[15] France was at the height of the egalitarian impetus of the modern age, and he foretold that it would not end with the republic. There would be an earthquake that would not only change the laws but would overturn the principles behind the laws.

Socialism, claimed De Tocqueville, was the intellectual crane that shifted the center of gravity from the political plane to the social plane. The bourgeoisie, which De Tocqueville described as having one end in the upper class and the other end in the lower, lacked a backbone. It therefore exploited the anger of the masses who had turned against the monarchy. The bourgeoisie joined the masses against the government, the same government that served the interests of the bourgeoisie. Both Marx and De Tocqueville noticed that on this occasion the bourgeoisie was saved by the skin of its teeth from socialist ideas, but the disappointment of the communist was the hope of the liberal.

In order to study the mood of the Parisian middle class at close quarters, De Tocqueville watched King Louis-Philippe with great attention and came to the conclusion that all his feelings were only a matter of ambition. In his memoirs, he summed up the period of his rule as follows: "In principle, what was missing in the political world was political life itself".[16] Behind the consensus of the Guizot government there were 200,000 people who decided the fates of 35 million French citizens. When asked about it, Guizot answered: "Work and enrich yourselves, and you will become voters". Naturally enough, De Tocqueville felt a stranger in such a political environment: the February revolution rescued him from boredom. The success of the Paris workers was mainly due to the non-intervention of the petty-bourgeois National Guard. The provisional government extended the right to vote to 9,5 million French citizens, but in setting up "national workshops" and recognizing "the right to work", it moved too far to the left. When it imposed a land tax of forty-five centimes, it raised against it the farmers, the small landowners, and the property-owning bourgeoisie. The republican bourgeoisie therefore gained a majority of five hundred members, the monarchical opposition had three hundred, and the socialists had only a hundred. The workers revolted on the 23rd of June, but from the beginning the uprising had no chance. Minister of Defense Cavaignac appeared as the rescuer of society and private property after three days of shedding the blood of the Paris workers.

De Tocqueville did not participate in the battles of June 1848, but he foresaw them in his capacity as a mediator between the National Assembly and the National Guard. He was shaken by what he called *la terreur de la mort* (the terror of death), sensed the depth of the hatred between the rival camps, and was amazed at the intolerable lack of seriousness with which they treated murder and destruction. He revealed his preconceptions when he described a socialist as "a drunkard who spends all his time in a tavern, and, when not there, beats his wife". Caustically, he described the significance of the events in June: "June was not exactly a political struggle, but a class conflict. A kind of civil war".[17]

He regarded the June revolution as a social one. De Tocqueville did not blame certain groups or personalities with radical ideas, as he did in the case of the July monarchy. France, he felt, had lost control. The knowledge that Thermidor would reoccur at the end of the 1848 Revolution was less disturbing to him than the thought that France was sick and longing for order and security. Having abandoned his previous belief that the "July workers" were wicked and thieves, he came to the conclusion that the workers' "religion" could not be defeated by bayonets alone.

Although he participated in drafting the law enacted on the 4th of November 1848, he avoided taking part in the great controversy regarding the insertion of the article about the "right to work". He feared the scale of the obligations that the state took upon itself and opposed setting up an omnipotent state, or a welfare state as we would call it, and preferred to give more power to communities: "The state must be allowed to oversee—within a minimal and necessary centralized government—just those things that concern the state, and no more".[18]

On drafting the November legislation, De Tocqueville wished to follow the American model and create two legislative bodies in France. In his opinion, the history of the republic showed that a centralized government and a single legislative body did not work together for the benefit of the citizens. Fear of the despotism of one legislative body would make the other a curb on a harmful distribution of powers. The two legislative bodies would not prevent revolutions, but they would be a guarantee against bad government that would cause revolutions.

In his search for mechanisms to restrict power, De Tocqueville succeeded in canceling the automatic right of the president to be reelected: the president would now be elected by a relative majority of at least 2 million votes. He opposed any system that did not give the people the initial right of electing the president. Only a decisive majority could cause the president to be elected, and, in the absence of such a majority, the National Assembly would decide. The president would choose his ministers who would have ministerial responsibility: "The president must have decisive and active power and he must therefore have freedom and strength". De Tocqueville likewise opposed the creation of a house of representatives which he felt was not suitable for France. The requirement that a three-quarters majority was needed to change the law proved to be an obstacle and served as a pretext for Louis Napoleon in his coup d'état in 1851.

De Tocqueville's contribution to the work of the legislative committee was a result of his attitude to the masses. He refused to deprive the masses of their political power but was conscious of their unpreparedness. This feeling caused him to believe that they could easily fall victim to a state that treated its citizens as subordinates. His devotion to liberty did not prevent him from fearing its exploitation by the masses who were not ready for it. His fears of an omnipotent state were due to the threatening shadow of a "Leviathan". One must distinguish in his case between his understanding of revolution, by which government would reach its fulfillment in the establishment of a welfare state, and his refusal to recognize its justification.

According to De Tocqueville, socialist thought has three characteristics: an excessive catering to people's material desires, an attack on property—or, as Proudhon put it, "Property is theft"—and a totalitarian view of the individual and society: "The characteristics of Socialism in all its colors is their lack of faith in liberty and human reason. This is the idea that the state should not only govern the society, but should master all the individuals as well. In short, Socialism, to my understanding is a complete new form of servitude".[19]

Surprisingly, De Tocqueville found the affinity of socialism to be not with the French Revolution but with the Ancien Régime. Both of them had an oppressive political mechanism. The legitimacy of socialism could not be found in the 1789 revolution because the revolutionaries consecrated the right to property. Tens of millions of landowners defended the revolutionary tradition against the claims of socialism. Socialism cannot go together with democracy: a political system that treats people as numbers cannot be reconciled with the democratic principle. He concluded: "There is no certainty that the February revolution is a socialist one. It takes courage to say that". He explained that his acceptance of the February revolution as a historical fact was meant to confirm that it was the last one. The restoration and the July monarchy institutionalized the privilege of election by a small group of voters, and the February revolution corrected the anomaly and completed the work of the Great Revolution.

In emphasizing the Christian aspect of the February revolution, De Tocqueville wished to appeal to his Catholic audience and at the same time to give a certain magnanimity to politics, as against the "religious" character of the socialist gospel. Socialism, in his opinion, was missionary, nonliberal, coercive, nondemocratic, centralized and not dispersed. In short, socialism in its essence aspires to totalitarianism.

De Tocqueville examined the events of his time in a historical perspective. When he first encountered socialist literature, he examined its historical significance by searching for its roots in the rise of Christianity. When he examined the crisis of the Second Republic, he looked at the crisis of the Western world in the fifth century. When he revealed the problems of democracy, he looked at the French Revolution, which created both the new plebeian democratic order and the new plebeian despotic order. Modernity includes both the Enlightenment and its enemies.

Notes

1. Roger Boesche, ed., *Alexis de Tocqueville—Selected Letters on Politics and Society*, trans., J. Toupin and R. Boesche, Berkley 1985, 115–116.
2. Alexis De Tocqueville, "Discours Prononce a l'Assemblee Constituante dans la Discussion du Projet de Constitution (12 Septembre 1848)", *Oeuvres Completes*, 520–532, Paris 1864–1875.
3. For more projections and predictions, see especially Olivier Zunz and Alan S. Kahan, eds., *The Tocqueville Reader: A Life in Letters and Politics*, Oxford 2002.
4. De Tocqueville, "The Social and Political State of France Before and After 1989", *London and Westminster Review* (1836).
5. De Tocqueville, "Voyages en Angleterre, Voyage de 1835", *Oeuvres Completes*, VIII, 369.
6. Francis G. Wilson, "Tocqueville's Conception of the Elite", *The Review of Politics*, IV (1949): 271–286.
7. Alexis De Tocqueville, "Discours de Reception a l'Academie Francaise", *Oeuvres Completes*, IX, 16.
8. De Tocqueville, *The European Revolution and Correspondence with Gobineau*, ed., and trans., J. Lukacs, Gloucester, MA 1968, 190–195.
9. Arthur De Gobineau, *The Inequality of Human Races*, trans., A. Collins, New York 1967.
10. Ibid., 515.
11. Ibid., 517.
12. Edward T. Garden, *Alexis de Tocqueville: The Critical Years 1848–1851*, Washington, DC 1955, 55–69.
13. De Tocqueville, *Souvenirs*, ed., Luc Monnier, Paris 1942, 83.
14. Ibid., 80.
15. Ibid., 83.
16. Ibid., 27–31.
17. Ibid, 135.
18. De. Tocqueville, "Discours Prononce a l'Assemblee Constituante dans la Discussion du Projet de Constitution (12 Septembre 1848)"; Jacques Cohen, *La Preparation de la Constitution de 1848*, Paris 1925.
19. Ibid., 540–541.

B. Marx: From a Fusion of Opposites to Class Warfare

The Promethean passion that De Tocqueville saw arising out of the barricades of the revolutionaries of 1848 was reason for hope for Marx. The fears of the liberal were the desires of the revolutionary. At the same time, with historical clear-sightedness, Marx knew that the 1848 Revolution was not a proletarian revolution because it happened too early and conditions were not yet ripe. According to Marx, a political revolution like that of 1848 was only a partial one. On the other hand, a proletarian revolution, when it happened, would be a Promethean revolution that destroyed the old world and built a new, proletarian, egalitarian one in its place.

As a historical strategist, Marx led his troops from a position of hindsight. In reviewing the events of the 1848 revolution, he did not intend to make a scholarly historical analysis but a commentary that was itself a political instrument by means of which one learned how to read the map. According to Marx, the map of France in February 1848 showed that the political revolution, which placed the bourgeoisie and the proletariat in the same camp, did not have the capacity to replace the rule of the bourgeoisie with that of the proletariat. The events of May 1848 showed that the lesson of separation from the bourgeoisie had been learned from the failure in February.

An analysis of the history of France in the years 1848–1850 led Marx to the conclusion that a combination of the structural crisis in public relations, class consciousness, and the intensification of social differences in France, together with localized crises such as the potato famine in 1845 and the commercial and industrial crisis in England, brought about the revolution of February 1848. In the Revolutions of 1848–1849, Marx sought negative proof of his idea of a correlation between economic crises and revolution.

> In their analyses of the causes of the February revolution, one finds evidence of a difference of outlook between Marx and Engels. In his introduction to *The Class Struggle in France, 1840–1850*, Engels ascribed to Marx the view that the political crisis of 1848 was a by-product of the economic crisis of 1847: What he [Marx] had hitherto deduced, [. . .] that the world trade crisis of 1847 had been the true mother of the February and March revolutions, [. . .] prosperity which had been returning gradually

since the middle of 1848 and attained full bloom in 1849 and 1850 was the revitalising force of a restrengthened European reaction.[1]

Engels decided that:

> The work republished here was Marx's first attempt to explain a piece of contemporary history by means of his materialist conception, on the basis of the prevailing economic situation. [. . .] to demonstrate the inner causal connection in the course of a development [. . .] to trace political events back to effects of what were, in the final analysis, economic causes.[2]

This mechanistic-economic approach ascribed to Marx by Engels was completely different from Marx's real approach to the Revolutions of 1848–1849 in France. Marx really thought the opposite: he sought to prove that it was precisely the lack of an economic-structural crisis in 1848 that partially explained the February collapse, a political revolution doomed to failure from the start. Marx only drew attention to the economic crisis of 1847 as an accelerating factor in the series of events leading up to the February revolution. He came to the conclusion that:

> The various quarrels in which the representatives of the individual factions of the Continental party of Order now indulge and mutually compromise themselves, far from providing the occasion for new revolutions are, on the contrary, possible only because the basis of the relationships is momentarily so secure [. . .] *A new revolution is possible only in consequence of a new crisis. It is, however, just as certain as this crisis*.[3]

In his analysis of the mechanism of the July monarchy—the monarchy that led to the February revolution—Marx showed that the aristocracy of wealth was the group with the political power behind King Louis-Philippe. The proliferation of debts by the state, the profiteering of the upper bourgeoisie, and a weak foreign policy postponed urgent reforms and caused the bankruptcy of the petty bourgeoisie. There was an inevitable buildup: clashes between the people and the army, demonstrations for reform of the electoral law, the hesitation of the king, and the passivity of the National Guard—these led to the paralysis of the army, the fall of the monarchy, and the establishment of a provisional government as a compromise between the various classes. There was a radicalization of the revolution; instead of there being a limited bourgeois revolution, all classes entered the fray: "all classes of French society were suddenly hurled into the orbit of political power, forced to leave the boxes, the stalls and the gallery and to act in person upon the revolutionary stage!"[4] With the fall of the monarchy, the dividing line between the political power and civil society also disappeared. The proletariat subjugated the republic and aroused the bourgeoisie against it, and in that situation, in Marx's opinion, two directions were open to the February republic: it could solidify and institutionalize the role of the bourgeoisie, or the exposure of the revolutionaries could speed up the political development of the proletariat and peasantry.

Following the subjugation of the republic by the proletariat, Marx said that there had been some progress in its class consciousness and political activities: In July, the workers had gained the bourgeois monarchy as an ornament to republican institutions, and in February they had gained a republic embellished with social institutions. But Marx was doubtful about the present capacity of the proletariat to rebel. He said that the French working class is not yet ready to carry out its own revolution. There were four reasons for this: the fusion of opposites between the proletariat and the bourgeoisie created a false fraternity and prevented a revolution; France was not prepared for a long European war, a war that would speed up the revolutionary process; the farmers and the petty bourgeoisie, the classes between the bourgeoisie and the proletariat, lacked consciousness and direction; French industry, which was still in its infancy, had not yet created a strong bourgeoisie and an active proletariat.

The complex interrelationships between the bourgeoisie, the proletariat, and the farmers were examined through the prism of the national workshops. The government had expected that the establishment of the workshops, which were imposed on it, would create a second proletarian army against the proletariat, but this hope was disappointed. The workshops were like millstones round the government's neck and constituted a potential army of rebellion. The promises and concessions made by the government to the proletariat were chains that had to be broken. The government decided on the method of "divide and rule", raised up an internal army among the proletariat in the form of the Mobile Guard, and incited the farmers against the proletariat. Against the background of these relationships, the events for Marx were first tentative encounters in the great class war that the bourgeoisie hides under its wings. Paradoxically, the defeat of the socialist and democratic camp in the elections to the National Assembly that met on the 4th of May was a revolutionary achievement. The general suffrage gave the middle classes the opportunity to shed their illusions and stripped the mask from the face of the bourgeoisie. In accordance with his historiographical interpretation and political position, Marx wrote:

> What succumbed in these defeats was not the revolution. It was the pre-revolutionary traditional appendages, [...] persons, illusions, conceptions, projects from which the revolutionary party before the February Revolution was not free, from which it could be freed not by the victory of February, but only by a series of defeats. [...] In a word: the revolution made progress, forged ahead, not by its immediate tragi-comic achievements, but on the contrary by the creation of a powerful, united counter-revolution.[5]

The February revolution, which was carried out by the workers with the passive assistance of the bourgeoisie, set up a bourgeois republic, but the provisional government was under pressure from the proletariat to declare itself a republic with social institutions. Now, said Marx, the government must be totally victorious. "The Assembly broke immediately with the social illusions of the February Revolution; it roundly proclaimed the bourgeois republic, nothing but the bourgeois republic".[6] The rigidity of the National Assembly and its draconian laws—particularly the restrictions placed on the national workshops—caused an uprising of the workers that was suppressed on the 22nd of June: "Modern society is divided by a great battle between the classes, a struggle over the survival or the end of the bourgeois regime". The fraternity of the classes had become a civil war. While the February revolution, the pleasant one, mixed together the opposing classes and presented them to the monarchy, the June revolution, the unpleasant one, stressed the opposition of interests and polarized the classes. Marx thought that the June uprising revealed the true face of the bourgeoisie.

The events in June taught Marx about the relationship between a proletarian revolution and a national one and led him to the conclusion that the French bourgeoisie needed to preserve peace with other nations in all situations in order to wage a civil war at home. The proletarian revolution therefore had to break down the barriers between the national states: "The new French revolution is forced to leave its national soil forthwith and conquer the European terrain".[7] Marx's views in the "Communist Manifesto" on the universality of the proletarian revolution and his opposition to separate nationhood are well-known. The proletariat is a national class because it is a universal class:

> The Communists do not form a separate party opposed to other working-class parties. [. . .] In the national struggles of the proletarians of the different countries, they point out and bring to the front the common interests of the entire proletariat, independently of all nationality. [. . .] The working men have no country.[8]

The First World War disproved this idea.

After the defeat in June, Marx said that what had happened was that there had been a modern class war between rivals who had gained self-awareness. Until then, there had been political revolutions that reflected subjective factors and disregarded socioeconomic forces. The social failure of the 1789 revolution was repeated in 1848: once again it appeared that a political revolution did not have the capacity to change the socioeconomic reality. The failure of the Blanquist revolt in Paris and the failure of Friedrich Hecker's revolt in Baden could be judged by the same criterion: the Jacobin illusion that a political revolution could bring the proletariat to power was finally shattered. The importance of the June defeat lay in the conclusion that the proletariat is a socioeconomic force that by its very existence is opposed to the bourgeoisie. The failure deepened class consciousness, set the classes against one another, and finally benefited the revolutionary process.

In theory, the bourgeois reaction aimed to cancel out the achievements of the revolution, and for that purpose it used a double mechanism: military dictatorship (Cavaignac) and conservative republican legislation on the one hand

and giving the proletariat the right to vote on the other. Marx pointed out the tactical error of his opponents in instituting universal suffrage. There was an internal contradiction: the bourgeoisie, which was supposed to institutionalize the demands of the workers, endangered itself by giving the proletariat political power to the point of cutting off the branch on which it was sitting. Another consideration with regard to the right to vote was that the obligation to use it mentioned in the "Communist Manifesto" (in order to make the proletariat the ruling class and overtake democracy) and viewing it as a legitimate weapon of class warfare did not justify parliamentarianism. The right to vote was not the main thing, and dispelling the illusion was liable to lead to sterile anarchy. It was a manipulative tool of the political authorities represented by Napoleon III. The right to vote would exist as long as the people kept to the rules of the game and voted for Louis Napoleon, but as soon as it no longer justified its purpose—as on the 10th of March and the 28th of April 1850—it would be annulled. The defeat gave rise to a sober evaluation:

> Universal suffrage had fulfilled its mission. The majority of the people had passed through the school of development, which is all that universal suffrage can serve for in a revolutionary period. It had to be set aside by a revolution or by the reaction.[9]

Despite its failure, the June uprising was the first purely socialist rebellion in Europe, and it was consciously aimed against legitimists and liberals. Isaiah Berlin summed it up well: "for the first time revolutionary socialism revealed itself in that savage and menacing aspect in which it has appeared ever since to its opponents in every land".[10] June, the culmination of the revolutionary development, proclaimed the beginning of the summer. On the 10th of December 1848, the peasantry destroyed the achievements of the revolution.

In the years 1848–1849, the peasantry was a perpetual victim of the mounting deficit that necessitated the imposition of new taxes. The strong grew stronger and the weak grew weaker. The peasantry bore the consequences of the February revolution and thus were the first to mount a counter-revolution. The peasants' revolt against the republic was expressed in their support of Louis Napoleon on the 10th of December 1848: "The republic had announced itself to this class with the tax-collector; it announced itself to the republic with the Emperor".[11] Capital exploited both the peasantry and the proletariat, and thus Marx thought that the peasants would be liberated only with the collapse of capital, but the right to vote was the thing most important to the peasants and proletariat: "Beneath the voting slips lie the stones of the street". The institution of monarchy returned by the front door in the person of Louis Napoleon, and the vote of the peasantry on the 10th of December turned out to be a reactionary revolution.

The National Assembly was the last source of power for the republican bourgeoisie. Marx discerned three aspects to the struggle between Louis Napoleon and the National Assembly: the legal aspect (the salt tax showed the deceived peasantry the monarchical side of Louis Napoleon); the political aspect (Louis Napoleon gave the government of Odion Barrat plenty of provocations such as the disbanding of the mobile guard, the prohibition of clubs, and the proposal to dismiss the National Assembly in the case of an insurrection); and the aspect of foreign affairs (the military intervention of Cavaignac in Italy was due to his wish to receive religious legitimacy from the Pope in order to gain the favor of conservative French society).

Louis Blanc saw the struggle between the members of the National Assembly and Louis Napoleon as a classic struggle between the legislature and the executive. But here Marx touched the root of the matter. The members of the assembly, who saw that the Napoleonic republic was turning into a monarchy, had to shelve their republican-bourgeois dream. The real struggle took place between the illusion and its destruction. Against the background of the elections to the legislative assembly, each faction feared to lose the tactical support of the republic to its rival.

In the French Revolution, there was a process of radicalization in which each event in the series of events was more violent and revolutionary than the previous one. Marx, in his "Class Warfare in France", spoke of an opposite process: the course of events in 1848–1850 from a liberal revolution to the setting up of an imperial despotism was a process of continual retreat. At its beginning, the petty bourgeoisie abandoned the proletariat, the petty bourgeoisie was later abandoned by the bourgeoisie, and finally the aristocracy of wealth and landowners abandoned the bourgeoisie and ingratiated themselves with the army and Louis Napoleon. June 1849 was a caricature of June 1848: 1848 marked the uprising of the proletariat, and June 1849 was a revolt of the petty bourgeoisie against the bourgeois republic.

We mentioned Marx's opinion that universal suffrage was likely to be annulled in a revolution or a reaction. In the struggle of the "party of order" against the proletariat, the National Assembly had to increase the power of the executive—that is to say, of Louis Napoleon—and in so doing it accelerated its self-destruction. With the annulment of universal suffrage, the circle was closed that was opened with the February revolution, and in this respect there was a close resemblance to the Revolution of 1789, which evolved into the first Napoleonic empire. If Edmund Burke foresaw there would be a despotism at the end of the French Revolution, Marx retrospectively saw a similar process in 1849.

In summing up the record of the 1848–1849 revolutions, Benedetto Croce concluded that every historical event is also a defeat, inasmuch as it never corresponds to the ideal. The past is never anything but an experiment for those acting in the present. But it is not a real defeat unless the principle is abandoned by the principles of those who adhere to it.[12] The Revolution of 1848 failed according to Marx because from the beginning it was a caricature of its older sister. Historically, it was nothing special, and it did not carry a new message. As a romantic revolution, essentially lukewarm and imitative in its actions, it attempted without much success to reduplicate the experience of the great revolution. Marx reached the conclusion that the social revolution took place before its time because mid-nineteenth-century France was not yet ready for a revolution of classes. The radicalization of events and the politicization of the classes gave rise to a reactionary direction. Although the peasantry voted for the first time in history, it voted of its own free will for a new despotism. Marx's analysis was essentially a study of the lessons of defeat. The defeat disproved the illusion of fraternity among the classes, increased social disagreements, polarized the classes, concentrated the other classes around the proletariat, abrogated universal suffrage, and caused the politicization of whole classes that had not yet been in the political melting pot. A political revolution is not enough to change a given economic situation: that was the lesson to be learned from the Revolutions of 1789 and 1848.

Notes

1. Frederick Engels, *Karl Marx and Frederick Engels—Collected Works*, "Introduction [To Karl Marx's *The Class Struggles in France 1848 to 1850*] [1895]", vol. 27, Moscow 1990, 507.
2. Ibid., 506.
3. Karl Marx, *Karl Marx and Frederick Engels—Collected Works*, "The Abolition of Universal Suffrage in 1850", vol. 10, Moscow 1978, 135.
4. Ibid., 54.
5. Ibid., 47.
6. Ibid., 66.
7. Ibid., 70.
8. Marx, *Karl Marx and Frederick Engels—Collected Works*, "Manifesto of the Communist Party", vol. 6, London 2010, 497–502.
9. Ibid., "The Abolition of Universal Suffrage in 1850", vol. 10, 137.
10. Isaiah Berlin, *Karl Marx: His Life and Environment*, Oxford University Press 1996, 161.
11. Marx, *Karl Marx and Frederick Engels—Collected Works*, "The Abolition of Universal Suffrage in 1850", vol. 10, 80.
12. Benedetto Croce, *History of Europe in the Nineteenth Century*, trans., Henry Frust, New York 1933.

C. Blanqui and Blanquism: The Revolutionary Experience

The 1848 "revolution of the intellectuals", as it was called by the historian Lewis Namier, was doomed to failure from the start.[1] Intellectuals like Alphonse de Lamartine, Auguste Ledru-Rollin, Louís Blanc, Étienne Cabet, François-Vincent Raspail. Victor Considérant, and Louis Blanqui did not know how to use force at the right moment and were hesitant in view of the fatefulness of the hour. Their lack of flexibility, their perplexities, the slogans they put out, their embrace of the revolutionary past—all this was a disadvantage to them. Their intellectual propensity to replace the old regime with a radical new one by means of words rather than bayonets was more a fad than a practical possibility. As intellectuals, they suffered from an excessive consciousness of history: they were paralyzed by the revolutionary myth of 1789. They were a striking example of how a consciousness of history can hinder action. Their Promethean passion was impotent: the intellectuals continued to interpret the world, but they had no capacity to change it.

A few intellectuals like Louís Auguste Blanqui (1805–1881) paid for their ideas with their liberty. About forty of his seventy-six years were spent behind bars because he opposed all the regimes: the monarchy, the Empire, and the two republics. He went from intellectual criticism to political activities and urged perpetual revolution against all feudal, religious, and capitalist institutions. He was the personification of nineteenth-century revolution, the embodiment of the revolutionary avant-garde and the living image of the romantic rebel. His life was a legend, and he helped to form his own legend. An "ism" was added to his name: Blanqui became Blanquism—that is to say, a Jacobin political culture of dedicated revolutionaries who had self-awareness and a tradition of subversion at any price, revolutionaries well versed in the use of myth, and ritual in French radical politics.[2]

Everyone has his own Blanqui. He is a proletarian, a revolutionary, an early communist, a Jacobin, a democrat, a secularist, and a patriot. The socialist tradition in France, from the radical left to the communists, saw him, after the Paris *Commune*, as a reflection of its outlook. Communism took him to its bosom after Marx in 1852 called him "one of the true leaders of the proletarian party and the true communists".[3] There are some who have diagnosed him as an early case of Marxist-Leninism, although two minimum Marxist conditions were missing: an interest in the daily economic struggle of the workers and a scientific concept of revolution.

The main principles of Blanquism—an avant-garde organization of professional revolutionaries and dictatorship after the revolution—have been seen as Leninist perversions of true Marxism. Stalin regarded him as a man of practicality, deficient from the theoretical point of view. The victory of the Bolshevist current of socialism at the beginning of the twentieth century aroused a new interest in Blanqui.[4]

Some have called him an "ultra-Jacobin" whose socialism was an expression of revolutionary republicanism without a proletarian affinity or a concept of class warfare. Georges Clemenceau, a Blanquist in his youth, described him as a "democratic angel", a man of action and consistent thinking who even after his imprisonment under the Third Republic supported a broadening of democratic institutions. In a letter to Clemenceau in 1879, he asked the latter to commit himself to freedom of speech and of the press, enlightened secularism, and abstention from militarism and made no mention whatsoever of socialism.[5] Blanqui supported the parliamentary system and was almost elected that year parliamentary deputy for Bordeaux. He could be described as a political revolutionary whose ideas on socialism could be summarized as sympathy for the proletariat and viewing formal democracy as a revolutionary objective. Despite this, he supported in his writings basic social and economic changes that would be achieved in his opinion through a violent struggle of the proletariat within the framework of class warfare.[6]

Many modern French socialists and republicans have seen him as a social reformer who was active in the historical context of the social upsurge in nineteenth-century France. Blanqui himself regarded himself as a socialist, by which he meant "a true republican [. . .] who is not a monarchist, and a democrat who is not an aristocrat".[7] Socialism, for him, meant social justice.

He has also been seen as an enlightened thinker: radical but enlightened. A society, he said, is enlightened if it gives priority to education, but communism cannot wait until the victory of universal education. One cannot establish a communist economy until the people are prepared for it, and even then it would be adopted voluntarily.[8] In the events of 1848, in which he was known as one of the radicals among the revolutionaries, Blanqui preferred pure democracy to socialism. This was shown by the manifesto of the "Club Blanqui" addressed to the government in the first week of March 1848. It contained demands in the best bourgeois-democratic tradition. To demands for freedom of speech and freedom of the press, there was added a demand for social legislation and the drafting of unemployed workers in the National Guard. One of the revolutionary meetings at which he was present ended with a demand for "victory through words".[9] When he was tried in 1849, he declared that "from now on, only one task remains to me: to be a man of controversy".[10]

Blanqui the patriot was revealed when the Prussians were at the gates of Paris in 1870. His wavering between his commitment to the individual and his commitment to society was now set aside in the face of a matter of life and death. At that moment, he did not think, like the Marxists, that a patriotic war had to be made into a civil war.

Louis Auguste Blanqui was the son of a Girondist who was a senior official in Napoleon's government. He was sent with his brother Adolphe to study in Paris, where he befriended subversive elements. His entry into politics in the period of the Restoration is often explained by his subversive outlook: he regarded the underground cell of a secret society such as the Carbonari as the ideal form of political activity. The background to his initial activities was the period of Louis-Philippe, which was full of restlessness. In the revolution of July 1830, he was the parliamentary correspondent of the economic journal *Le Globe*. He later joined the opposition to the July monarchy, and with a minority of young republicans demanded an immediate social revolution: he saw political struggle as a means to social struggle.[11]

The history of the republican underground in France from the July monarchy to 1848 is that of a struggle between the Montagnards—the popular republicans—and the Girondins, who favored an American type of democracy. The former were social democrats who wanted a centralized dictatorial government, and the latter were political democrats, republicans who wanted a centralized democratic government. Blanqui supported the former, radical school.

In 1832, when he joined the Société des Amis du Peuple (Friends of the People Society), Blanqui described his occupation as follows: "I am a proletarian [...] one of the thirty million Frenchmen who live from their work".[12] Here, it seems, is the proof of his lack of a consciousness of class warfare and his preference for the distinction between "rich" and "poor". But if one follows Blanqui's statements, one discovers a point of view different from that of the "many" against the "few". In a letter to a liberal friend in 1831, he expressed anger that the bourgeoisie had been victorious in the July revolution and set up a "government of the bourgeois class", a concept that shows that he did have a class consciousness after all.[13] Despite the hope of a reconciliation between the classes, Blanqui remained pessimistic. The future revolution frightened him, as had the previous unavoidable one in 1789.

It is reasonable to suppose that in his famous reply, "I am a proletarian", Blanqui was referring to the needy and oppressed, but his comparison of the confrontation between the bourgeoisie and the feudal aristocracy with the new struggle between the proletariat—the "new form of slavery"—and the contemporary middle class is clear proof that he had a modern class consciousness. And indeed, this is what he said in a speech to the Friends of the People Society in 1832: "There is no point in concealing the fact that there is a life-and-death struggle between the classes that divides the nation".[14] This was despite the fact that Blanqui, who gave an account of French history from 1815 onward, refrained from analyzing the struggle between the bourgeoisie and the proletariat in economic terms.[15]

One could regard the concept of exploitation in Blanqui as a litmus test for the definition of class: there are those who live from it and those who suffer from it. The proletariat ceased to be identified with the people, an idea that prevailed in the eighteenth century. The proletariat was now the class of workers, not the Third Estate. The correlation between the economic classes and political forces was examined in relation to reforms: Blanqui identified those who supported the right to property as promoting the freedom to exploit, free enterprise, and the freedom of the workers to starve. Thus, economic improvements, like legislative reforms, were of no use. "The state is a regime of the rich against the poor",[16] he said, and it was served by the press and the Church, the slaves of capitalism. As a result, there could not be enlightened education as long as the political forces represented capital, the army, and the Church. The conclusion was that the revolution had to have the capacity not to create a social future but to make it possible. A portrait of the egalitarian society could not be painted before the revolution had ended the old society. In this way, Blanqui took himself out of the tradition of utopian socialism. Although he was influenced by utopians, especially the historical and economic ideas of Saint-Simon, Blanqui belonged to a different tradition, the tradition of Jacobin communism. His socialist theory and his revolutionary practice derived from the spirit of 1793.[17]

In 1834, Blanqui, with Armand Barbès, founded the Société des Familles (Society of Families).[18] a secret society that had 1,200 members and was divided into "families" of ten members for each cell. Its program was one of social radicalism and violent rebellion. Its members regarded propaganda and revolution as the purpose of the society, and they even set up small enterprises in Paris for the production of gunpowder. Blanqui identified radical republicanism with socialism: "I am a republican as long as the republic supports social change [. . .] If the republic destroys this hope, we will no longer see ourselves as republicans". A year later, he declared that political rights gained in elections were only means to a radical change in society. A year after that, he wrote in the Society of Families' manifesto:

> What is a people? A people is a mass of working citizens. What is the fate of the proletariat in a regime of the rich? A life of exploitation and suffering. Does the individual have to engage in a political or social revolution? He has to engage in a social revolution.[19]

In 1837, Blanqui founded the Société des Saisons (Society of Seasons). This secret society was constructed in a gradated way and was based on leaders of small groups that were given the names of seas, months, and seasons. Blanqui's revolutionary outlook went through a change from radical republicanism to proletarian republicanism. He assumed that a postrevolutionary society would still need a revolutionary government. Blanqui's extremism operated on all levels: the social foundation of his politics shifted from the educated bourgeoisie to the workers, his form of subversion went from propaganda to secret cells, and his objective changed from opposition to the monarchy, and the bourgeois aristocracy turned to the creation of a revolutionary government, the dictatorship of a minority on behalf of the proletarian majority. Thus, Blanqui embodied the stages of his transition to communism.[20]

In 1839, Blanqui and Barbès led an abortive revolt. (They later quarreled about its failure. Blanqui was head of the Central Republican Society, and Barbès led the Club of Revolutionaries. The two men, who for years occupied the same prison cell before and after 1848, were bitter enemies.) On the 12th of May 1839, the two of them brought five hundred men to the Paris municipality with the aim of fomenting a popular uprising and toppling the regime in one day of revolution. The attempted revolt was rapid and unsuccessful, and the hope that the workers would join it was disappointed.[21] The idea of a revolution was embraced by only a small minority of intellectuals and members of secret societies, not by the masses.

The death sentence imposed on Blanqui was commuted to a life sentence on Mont Saint-Michel. In the "February days" in 1848, he was released from prison, and as soon as he reached Paris, he began to lead the radical group, the Central Republican Society, in organizing processions and making rousing speeches. In that same period, a libel was brought against him that he was a spy planted by the police. The source of the libel, the "Taschereau document",[22] was shown to be a forgery, and Blanqui continued his activities, advocating the construction of a revolutionary force. What angered him more than anything else was the renunciation of the red flag by the leftist camp: "Today the symbol, tomorrow the principle, and soon the reality!" For an intellectual of his kind, the symbols were no less important than the contents.

On the 17th of March, Blanqui brought a 100,000 demonstrators to the Hôtel de Ville (City Hall) to prevent countrywide elections to the legislature for fear that they would result in a conservative majority. He preferred a pressure group for a provisional government threatened by the Paris workers, provided it was not dominated by the bourgeoisie, which would make it "a regime of the rich against the poor". His fears were confirmed in April: this intellectual who spoke in the name of the people did not trust the people's democratic decision. He thought that, after such a long period of conditioning, the masses were not capable of making free decisions. Hence the decisive importance he gave to education, and he therefore believed there was a need for a temporary dictatorship. Like many intellectuals after him, for the sake of liberty, he consecrated the means to reduce it. On the 15th of May, Blanqui led a demonstration that made its way to the Hôtel de Ville in order to proclaim a new provisional government.[23] The uprising was suppressed, and he was sent to prison for ten more years.

Blanqui belongs to the tradition of Jacobin communism whose roots lay in French history from 1792 onward and that combined absolute equality with political activism. It was a blend of popular enthusiasm and revolutionary violence that existed from the time of the *enragés*, the *Hébertistes*, and Gracchus Babeuf in the great revolution, up to the Carbonari organizations, the republican movement, revolutionary syndicalism, and the Communist Party. The Blanquists were a source of inspiration because it was felt that they completed the unfinished business of the French Revolution. Jacobinism was the connecting thread of the French radical tradition.

The Jacobin revolutionary club in Paris gave rise to the idea of "Jacobinism", denoting a revolutionary elite of political radicals, the characterization of a revolutionary organization, a description of the centralized leadership of Robespierre. It was a symbol of revolutionary fidelity and was identified with the policies of the Committee of Public Safety. Its rivals saw Jacobinism as a perpetual threat to the existing order, a kind of political fundamentalism associated with the left.

The Jacobins were national, democratic, social, and republican.[24] They had a commitment to the national interest that was above that of the party and called for a solidarity of the oppressed of the nation and of the world. Like the Italian Mazzini, the Hungarian Kossuth, the Polish Mickiewicz, and the Russian Herzen, Blanqui as a Frenchman believed in the universal mission of his people. In his activities, however, he was not cosmopolitan but French. Apart from his references to figures from the classical world, people of his own language predominate in his writings, and his ideas were mainly aimed at the French reader. His deep patriotism derived from his birth in the period of Napoleon and the memory of foreign troops invading his country. His universal side—France had given the European peoples the "principle of equality"—was due to the fact that the eyes of the whole world were on revolutionary Paris. The worse the situation of the proletariat became, the more necessary it was to rebel and not to believe in an inevitable gradual improvement. These expectations weighed upon the Paris revolutionaries who, having no choice, took the world revolution upon themselves.

The Jacobins called for a direct democracy, and the meaning of politics for them was participation and intervention.[25] According to them, democratic obligation required a sense of social responsibility and limits to the poverty and wealth of the citizens. Examples of political leaders who gave them constant inspiration were Robespierre, Danton, Hébert, Napoleon, Ledru-Rollin, Giambetta, and Blanqui. Blanqui believed that the guarantee of the success of an uprising was the revolutionary spirit of the masses and its preservation through liberty, strikes, and propaganda.

The Jacobins were republicans, in perpetual opposition to the institutions of the Ancien Régime. The republican divide between liberals and democrats characterized the revolutionary legacy in the nineteenth century. The liberals supported a moderate republican model based on the dominance of property owners and the parliamentary system that existed in the constitutional monarchy in 1791, the constitutional republic in 1795, and the July monarchy of 1830. The democrats, on the other hand, in the revolutionary days of July 1830, February 1848, and September 1870, based their radical republican model on an extension of equality, social and economic reform, and universal suffrage.

A division arose among the Jacobins from a disagreement about the correct form of revolutionary action: political guidance such as was advocated by the Montagnards or the kind of inspiration favored by the Hébertists. Blanqui and the Blanquists saw themselves as a continuation of the Hébertists and the opponents of Robespierre, whom they called an "early Napoleon". Blanqui condemned Robespierre chiefly because of his religiosity, which he viewed as a betrayal of the atheism of the revolutionaries. The cult around him and his ruthlessness repelled him: "The Jacobin club was no more than a Church, and Robespierre was its high priest".[26] Blanqui hated "the impartiality of the guillotine", the way revolutionaries were executed by other revolutionaries. He believed that the characteristic quality of the Hébertists was their total devotion to revolution shown by their close relationship to the Parisian masses and their uncompromising atheism. In 1864, Blanqui wrote the introduction to Gustave Tridon's book *Les Hébertistes*.[27] Another reason to admire the Hébertists was the political festivals associated with their name.

The Blanquists created the aesthetics of the revolutionary experience. They developed a politics of days of remembrance and institutionalized the drama of revolution. They went on pilgrimage to the cemeteries where the heroes of the revolution lay, erected monuments to its martyrs, marched to the sites in Paris sacred to the revolutionary movement, wrote memoirs and newspaper articles, made a calendar based on memories of the revolution, drew attention to the images of famous revolutionaries in the cemeteries, especially Père-Lachaise, and engaged in a cult of the dead. This culture of memory of a small sect succeeded in the 1880s in attracting many people in social solidarity.

The Blanquists played an active part in two events. The first was the Parisian commune in 1871.[28] The myth of the Commune was in keeping, on the one hand, with the historical model of the popular uprising in 1793 and, on the other hand, with the future model of the dictatorship of the proletariat envisioned by Marx or the soviets of Lenin. The Blanquist myth of the Commune provided the left with an image of a future democratic republic and strengthened the image of the Blanquists as the authentic heirs of the revolutionary tradition.

The second event was the founding of the Boulangist movement in 1886–1889.[29] The mixture of Blanquists, populists, and radicals under the dubious leadership of General Boulanger made its mark as part of a new technique in politics: there were modern forms of publicity, the organization of election campaigns and mass processions. All this did not prevent the disintegration of the movement or a blow to its revolutionary image. The Commune and Boulangism exposed the Blanquists' belief in the myth of the revolution, a myth that they themselves had created.

Revolutionary fervor was no less prized by Blanqui and the Blanquists than social or political content. In the absence of revolutionary situations, they sought to preserve the flame of revolution in their hearts by means of a constant preoccupation with myth and ritual. The more the despair of the intellectuals increased, the more they promoted the cult of the memory of the revolutionary experience.

Notes

1 Lewis B. Namier, *1848: The Revolution of the Intellectuals*, New York 1946.
2 Maximilien Le Roy, Loïc Locatelli Kournwsky, *Ni Dieu ni maître. Auguste Blanqui, l'enfermé*, Tournai 2014.

3 Karl Marx, "The Eighteenth Brumaire of Louis Bonaparte", in V. Adoratsky, ed., *Selected Works*, vol. 2, New York 1939, 323; A. Marty, *Quelques aspects de l'activite de Blanqui*, Paris 1951, 19–28.
4 Joseph Stalin, "Lenin as the Organizer and Leader of the Russian Communist Party", in Lenin, ed., *Selected Works*, vol. 1, Moscow 1950, 34.
5 Sylvain Molinier, *Blanqui*, Paris 1948, 69; G. Clemenceau, *Le Journal*, November 27, 1896.
6 Louis-Auguste Blanqui, *Défense du citoyen Blanqui devant la cour d'assises*, Paris 2018.
7 Bibliotheque Nationale, Blanqui MSS, Nouvelles acquisitions francaises, Files 9578–9598.
8 Blanqui, *Critique Sociale*, 2 vols, Paris 1885, 184–187.
9 Ibid., Bibliotheque Nationale, Blanqui MSS, File 9581, 143–145.
10 A. B. Spitzer, *The Revolutionary Theories of L. A. Blanqui*, New York 1957, 86.
11 Samuel Bernstein, *Auguste Blanqui and the Art of Insurrection*, London 1971.
12 Roger Garaudy, "Le Neo-blanquisme de contrebande et les positions anti-leninistes d'Andre Marty", *Cahiers du Communisme* (January 1953), 39.
13 Letter from Blanqui to Mongolafaie, August 1906.
14 Ibid., Bibliotheque Nationale, Blanqui MSS, File 9592, 17–26.
15 Blanqui, *Oeuvres de Louis Auguste Blanqui*, Editions la Bibliothèque Digitale 2012; idem., *The Blanqui Reader*, eds., Peter Hallward, Philippe Le Goff, trans., Mitchell Abidor, Memphis 2018.
16 Ibid., Blanqui, *Critique Sociale*, 78.
17 Henri Berna, *Du socialisme utopique au socialisme ringard*, Paris 2015.
18 Jean-Noël Tardy, *L'Age des Ombres. Complots, conspirations et sociétés secrètes au XIXe siècle*, Paris 2015.
19 Bernstein, *Auguste Blanqui and the Art of Insurrection*, 70–76.
20 Ibid., 77–80.
21 Camille Leymaire, "Barbes et Blanqui a Belle-Ile", *La Nouvelle revue*, CXII (1898), 358.
22 *Reveu Retrospective* (Paris 1848), 3–10.
23 Ibid., Bibliotheque Nationale, Blanqui MSS, File 9581, 66.
24 Patrick H. Hutton, *The Cult of the Revolutionary Tradition: The Blanquists in French Politics, 1864–1896*, Berkeley 1981, 3–6.
25 André-Jean Tudesq, *La Democratie en France depuis 1815*, Paris 1971.
26 Albert Mathiez, "Notes inedites de Blanqui sur Robespierre", *Annales historiques de la Revolution Francaise* (1928), 305–321.
27 Gustave Tridon, *Les Hebertistes*, Paris 1864.
28 Jacques Rougerie, *Proces de Communards*, Paris 1964.
29 Zeev Sternhell, *La Droite revolutionnaire, 1885–1914*, Paris 1978, 33–60.

D. Modernity as Decadence

The first line of Paul Verlaine's poem *Langueur*, written in 1883—"*Je suis l'Empire à la fin de la decadence*" ("I am the Empire at the end of the decadence")—expresses the mood in France after the failure of the revolution of 1848 and the internal and external reverses the country had experienced. Artists, writers, and cultural critics felt that there was a moral degeneracy in French society, a sense of alienation, weariness, and despair. Many people looked for a new and radical style in art and literature, turning their backs on political activism. They were drawn as if spellbound to literary decadence, which at the turn of the century was considered the modern avant-garde. The true opposite of decadence was not provided by the adherents of progress but by proponents of rebirth. Barbarians, including modern ones, were regarded as agents of rebirth: they counteracted decadence. Nietzsche warned against both decadence and its vanquisher, the "Prometheus who is a sort of barbarian".

The idea of decadence is very old.[1] Matei Călinescu, in his classic work, *Modernism, Decadence, Kitsch, Post-modernism* (1987), described the metamorphoses of the concept of decadence. Its fatal quality of descent over time is a constant motif in all mystico-religious traditions. Although the Latin term *decadentia* (falling down) was not used before the Middle Ages, the Platonic cave was already a metaphorical symbol of decadence: an inferior and degenerate world as against the perfect, unchanging world of ideas. The misfortunes of time mark it out. The concept of time among the Greeks was a continual decline, a fall from an ideal initial situation.[2]

In contrast to the passive view of time among the Greeks, the Christian perception of time was active. The closeness of the Day of Judgment created a sense of crisis. The Jewish and Christian philosophy of history gave rise to messianic and eschatological conceptions. The meaning of the Greek word *eschata* is "the doctrine of last things". The "last day" is connected with decline and is overshadowed by the satanic power of the Antichrist.[3] The expectation of universal disaster around the year 1000 CE reflected the concept of the end of history in millenarianism.[4]

This Christian perception was overtaken by the Renaissance view of time, which was divested of its sanctity. A modern secular millenarianism began to make an appearance in the utopias of the Renaissance and later periods.

Dissatisfaction with Christian culture and later with modern industrial culture gave birth to revolutionary utopias. It is no accident that the Marxist utopia is umbilically linked to the fall of capitalism.[5]

Decadence is associated in our minds with the fall of all phenomena, such as races, nations, religions, and arts, in which there is a sequential development: hence terms like "decline", "descent", "twilight", "attrition", "degeneration", "autumn".[6] This presents a contrast to terms like "sunrise", "spring", "youth", generally used in connection with decadence in biological analogies. As in the case of every organism, there are the stages of infancy, maturity, withering, and death. The organic affinities of the idea of decadence show that the concept of progress is not a true opposite. Progress is a concept derived from mechanics, not from biology. There is an interrelationship between decadence and progress, not an opposition. For instance, the decadent feelings of loss and alienation are sometimes the results of progress reflected in a high degree of technological development. And in any case, both of them are relative concepts. Decadence exemplifies growth and withering, maturity and decomposition, aging and rebirth, beauty and ugliness, while progress represents a linear development of time.

The basis of progress is the idea that the course of time is unlimited: continual improvement is possible because time is endless.[7] The idea of progress is based on the assumption of improvement: we begin with the bad and move toward the good. Kant distinguished between the human world and the metaphysical world. In his transcendental world, God began with the good, but in our world we begin with the bad. Progress is a matter of repair. The true opposite of decadence is not progress but regeneration. If the early Christian historians conceived of history in theological terms so that decadence was a punishment from heaven, the philosophers of progress—Jean Bodin, Charles-Louis Montesquieu, Anne Robert Jacques Turgot, Immanuel Kant, Marquis de Condorcet, Auguste Comte—maintained that periods of decadence are mere accidents in an inevitable progress. Rousseau was of a different opinion: civilization, he believed, is by its very nature decadent. A long series of thinkers, from Ibn Khaldun and Giambattista Vico to Jacob Burkhardt and finally to Oswald Spengler, saw decadence as an aspect of a cyclical concept of civilization and decline. Spengler forecast at an early stage the decline of Western civilization, and it is now worth reading him again in the light of the postmodernist criticism of the arrogance of Western culture.[8]

The optimistic philosophy of progress of the eighteenth century was replaced by the pessimistic view of nineteenth-century historiography. The writers who spoke of the decadence of Bourbon France or Victorian England made analogies with the Roman decadence. From the mid-eighteenth century, historical studies began to be published in England of the fall of the greatest power in the ancient world, the most famous of them being Edward Gibbons's *Decline and Fall of the Roman Empire*. In 1734, when he was describing the reasons for the fall of Rome, Montesquieu claimed that modern wealth and literary achievements were a sign that decadence was at hand.[9] In 1756, Voltaire also spoke of decadence in connection with the decline of the ancient empire. Madame de Stael, who had the Enlightenment's naive belief in the end of barbarism, saw decadence as a thing of the past.

The French conservative critic Désiré Nisard was less optimistic than Madame de Stael. In his book on the poetry of the late Roman Empire, published in 1834, he already distinguished between decadence itself and the theoretical concept of a "decadent style".[10] Such a style only made an appearance at the end of the nineteenth century and was associated with modernity.

Charles Baudelaire, the supreme poet of decadence, dedicated his collection of poems, *Les Fleurs du Mal* (The Flowers of Evil), to Théophile Gautier. Joanna Richardson's contemporary biography of Baudelaire sheds new light on the Baudelaire–Gautier relationship.[11] In the first edition of *Les Fleurs du Mal* (1857), Baudelaire identified himself with a style that was decadent, spiritual, and modern. Two years later, making a direct connection between decadence and modernity in his article "Philosophical Art" (1859), Baudelaire wrote that the chief characteristic of decadence was a systematic attempt to dissolve the boundaries between the various arts. Max Nordau, in his book *Degeneration* (1892), saw this multidimensional synthesis of impressions received through different senses as a symptom of the sickness of a decadent culture. Bernard Shaw, on the either hand, in his essay, "The Sanity of Art", denied any connection between good art and moral health. Nordau and Shaw, each of whom rejected the view of the other, both denied the paradoxical quality ascribed to decadence.

In his introduction to Baudelaire's works (1868), Gautier regarded his poetry as the apex of modern art. He said that the poet of *Les Fleurs du Mal* exemplified what was unjustifiably called "the style of decadence", which was only art that had reached a stage of extreme maturity, a stage to which the setting suns of aging cultures are obliquely drawn. It was a style, full of subtleties and hints, that takes its color from the whole spectrum, attempts to communicate thoughts that cannot be expressed in words and whose expression is misty and elusive.[12]

Decadence is one of those vague and misleading terms. Have the many commentators succeeded in dealing with the elusiveness of the phenomenon, explaining the nebulous charm that decadence still has for us? The French writer and critic Paul Bourget, in his article "A Theory of Decadence" (1881), took an aesthetic and philosophical approach to decadence as a style, not as a condition.[13] Bourget, influenced by social Darwinism, claimed that energetic "organic societies" are subject to the demands of a total mechanism, while in "decadent societies", there are hierarchical relationships between the different elements of society that are largely individual. The supposition that individualism can be central to a society—contrary to De Tocqueville's idea—leads him to the conclusion that decadent periods are not nationalistic or military and encourages an aestheticization of life. Comparing decadence with barbarism, Bourget preferred the former.

But these two possibilities are not necessarily opposed. Very often, they coincide or are two aspects of the same phenomenon. Bourget himself was a good example. With him, there was a blurring of boundaries between an intellectual recognition of the existence of decadence and an aesthetic commitment to political absoluteness. Thus, there was a relativity in him that was beyond modernity. The style of decadence, in his opinion, rejected authoritative categorizations such as unity, hierarchy, objectivity. Was Bourget an early postmodernist? Whatever the case, Bourget was a member of Action française, the French proto-fascist national-monarchist movement. His play *La Barricade*, which was staged, was a re-working of Georges Sorel's *Réflexions sur la violence* (Reflections on Violence).[14] The style of decadence ended with a call for new barbarians.

So we may conclude that aestheticism and violence were not contradictory. The novel *À Rebours* (Against the Grain) (1884) by Joris-Karl Huysmans was the most comprehensive and conscious attempt to effect an aestheticization of decadence. Aestheticism is not disconnected from the social and political sphere. Thus, the decadent style was open to revolutionary ideas: Stéphane Mallarmé in France and Oscar Wilde in England tended toward anarchism.

One of the reasons for the lack of dialectical discussion in the phenomenon of decadence was the choice of Arthur Schopenhauer as a starting point. For example, there was a reliance on Schopenhauer's principles for understanding the forces that govern the mood of a situation because of the inability of man to know how things really stand. But the key figure did not have to be Schopenhauer: it could have been Nietzsche. The one-dimensional, excessively pessimistic Schopenhauer emphasized only the will. The choice of this philosopher lacked the elasticity necessary for a concept that embodied pessimism but passed beyond it.

The dialectical quality of Nietzsche's discussion of decadence was due to his experience of life. As a sick man, he was able to appreciate the literal truth of the metaphor that good health is a treasure. It is in this context that his assertion must be understood that decadence is required by life itself so that it can be overcome. Decadence, he claimed, is a necessity of nature, and thus decadence is not something to be fought against: it is absolutely necessary because it is to be found in every period and every people.[15]

But decadence can be seen as a social degeneracy and a sickness that lowers the stature of mankind and is harmful to the health of a culture. Nietzsche's conclusion was that nihilism has the function of uprooting the decadent values of a culture. Consequently, "nihilism is not the cause of decadence but only its logic".[16] The importance of nihilism lies in its exposure of the true face of decadence. The cure turned out to be a sickness: religion, morality, and reason, as weapons against nihilism, only increase the alienation: "What have been regarded until now as the causes of degeneracy are only its results. But, likewise, what are regarded as medicines against degeneracy are only palliatives against those same results: The 'healers' are only a different kind of degenerate".[17] Nietzsche is telling us that the aim of ridding the world of sicknesses finally encourages them. This is a dialectical analysis of decadence and an insight into the kind of policy that seeks to eradicate it.

Decadence as an aesthetic category cannot exist without the temptation to overcome it. According to Nietzsche, a true tragic consciousness exists only in the context of decadence because it is life on the edge of the abyss. In the depths, the nothingness that underlies the fear, there is some sort of solution, and that is the dark magic secret of decadence.

If Baudelaire is the starting point for a discussion of decadence, Wagner is its culmination. Nietzsche wrote: "Wagner encapsulates modernity [. . .] There is nothing else to be done—one has to be a Wagnerian first".[18] In his opinion, Wagner represented the romantic spirit of the decadence. He was the greatest of liars: "His music is never real". "Real" in the Nietzschean sense meant that music as an autonomous art is aesthetically justified by its independence. Wagner was mentioned by Nietzsche in the context of music used for non-musical purposes. In this way, Nietzsche internalized the theory of decadence as it had been developed since Nisard. Nisard accused Victor Hugo of painting with words, which was an attempt to create an illusion, but Nietzsche's perception—"Wagner is the Victor Hugo of music as language"[19]—is deeper than that of the theoreticians of decadence such as Nisard, Bourget, and Gautier. Apart from their "elitist" approach to decadence, Nietzsche pointed out their criticism of the masses and warned against politicization.

Wagner, in Nietzsche's opinion, represented "cultures in decline [. . .] Modernity leads to theatricality".[20] Do we have here an early intimation of a strategy of experience without content, art for art's sake, an appeal to the masses, modern politics as theater? The director Francis Ford Coppola was right on target when he chose Wagner's music to accompany the fire-spitting helicopters in the film *Apocalypse Now*.

Notes

1. For further reading, see the excellent books by Matei Calinescu, *Five Faces of Modernity—Modernism, Avant-Garde, Decadence, Kitsch, Post-Modernism*, Durham 1987; Norberto Bobbio, *The Philosophy of Decadentism*, trans., David Moore, Oxford 1948; Pierre Chaunu, *Historie et Decadence*, Paris 1981; Julien Freund, *La Decadence: Historie sociologique et philosophique d'une categorie de l'expression humaine*, Paris 1984.
2. Arthur Oncken Lovejoy and George Boas, *Primitivism and Related Ideas in Antiquity*, New York 1965, 155–168.
3. Gerhard von Rad, "The Origin of the Concept of the 'Day of Y'", *Journal of Semitic Studies*, 4 (1959): 97–108.
4. Norman Cohn, *The Pursuit of the Millennium*, New York 1961.
5. Leszek Kolakowski, *Main Currents of Marxism*, trans., P. S. Falla, Oxford 1978.
6. Johan Huizinga, *The Autumn of the Middle Ages*, Chicago 1997.
7. George Sorel, *The Illusions of Progress*, trans., J. Stanley and C. Stanley, Berkeley 1969, V–VIII.
8. Oswald Spengler, *The Decline of the West*, 2 vols., trans., C. F. Atkinson, New York 1947.
9. Charles de Montesquieu, *Considerations sur les causes de la grandeur des Romains et de leur decadence*, Paris 1734.
10. Desire Nisard, *Etudes de moeurs et de critique sur les poetes latins de la decadence*, 2 vols., Paris 1888.

11. Joanna Richardson, *Baudelaire*, London 1994.
12. Theophile Gautier, *Portraits et souvenirs litteraires*, Paris 1881.
13. Paul Bourget, "Theory of Decadence", in *Décadence*, Essais de psychologie contemporaine, Paris 1883.
14. Idem, *La Barricade*, Paris 1910.
15. Friedrich Nietzsche, *The Will to Power*, trans., and ed., Walter Kaufmann, New York 2011, paragraph 41.
16. Ibid., paragraph 43.
17. Ibid., 42.
18. Nietzsche, eKGWB/NF-1888, 16[29]—*Nachgelassene Fragmente Frühjahr—Sommer 1888*.
19. Nietzsche, *The Gay Science*, trans., Josefine Nauckhoff, Cambridge 2001, paragraph 347.
20. Calinescu, *Five Faces of Modernity*, 192.

3 From Marx to Lenin
A Red Future

A. Marx and the Promethean Revolution

The Marxist Promethean Urge

In his doctoral thesis, "The Difference Between the Philosophy of Nature of Democritus and Epicurus" (1840), Karl Marx wrote: "Prometheus is the noblest saint and martyr in the philosopher's calendar".[1] Prometheus was the saint of philosophy, and Marx regarded philosophy as a sacred sphere that represented a striving for absolute freedom and a passion for absolute equality. Marx's Promethean philosophy rejected the gods, and, as a result, his revolutionary atheism sought to transfer the sanctity from the world of the gods to modern man.

The modern Promethean revolution was a proletarian revolution. In *Das Kapital* (Capital) Marx analyzed the modern economy that oppressed the proletariat "Finally, the Jaw which always holds the relative surplus population or industrial reserve army in equilibrium with the extent and energy of accumulation", said Marx, "rivets the worker to capital more firmly than the wedges of Hephaestus held Prometheus to the rock".[2] Marx's economic philosophy was impregnated with the legend of Prometheus as a model for the liberation of the proletariat and the whole of mankind from the fetters of capital.[3]

In Marx, the Promethean idealism of Hegel became Promethean materialism. Because life forms consciousness, the all-important question is, "Who owns the means of production?" The workers would rise against their employers and create a universalization of power. An analysis of modern capitalist society and the solution in the form of a social revolution are Marx's contribution to the image of the proletarian Prometheus.

The proletarian is Prometheus bound and also the redeeming Prometheus. The proletariat, which personifies the universal idea, was regarded as the only force that could bring about an egalitarian revolution, or, in other words, redemption. The proletarian had the mission of universal redemption and had to sacrifice her- or himself for the sake of the whole of humanity.[4] There is a great similarity between Christian martyrdom and the philosophy of equality of the Enlightenment. Both are motivated by a passion for justice and are marked by suffering and a search for self-fulfillment. Dialectical materialism took on the character of the drama of redemption: myth and logos, science and gnosis, drama and economics, spirit and matter, proletariat and bourgeoisie—all of them coalesced in Marx's vision of redemption.[5]

What would the modern Promethean worker do after casting off the chains? From the point of view of Marxist prophecy, there can only be authentic values at the end of history. Until then, values are subordinated to the revolution. Until the bourgeois class has disappeared, political manifestations like violence and dictatorship can be used in the service of the revolution, or, in other words, they are relative. In all his writings, Marx was inspired by a Promethean vision of the liberation of humanity: from the chains of historical interpretation that justified the present oppressive system, from the means of production that always remained in the hands of someone else, from others who alienate you for their own benefit, from the trades that repress humankind's spirit and change its character.

At the entrance to the edifice of Marxist Promethean aspiration stood Lenin and Stalin. They created an armed empire, made the philosophy into a doctrine, founded a party that became a church, imposed a nation—Russia—on its neighbors, used state terror as a habitual mechanism, reduced the universal model to "socialism in one country", and deepened the estrangement between fellow humans and between humankind and the state, a police state. The vision of classlessness was distorted into a situation of perpetual siege. The Promethean revolution rose against its children: by his own hands, Prometheus was once again bound to the rock.

The Varieties of Socialism

The different varieties of socialism can be classified according to their attitude to revolution—from social democracy, which seeks to improve the social conditions of life within the existing capitalist order, through reforms, legislation, and education, to communist socialism, which seeks to destroy capitalism by revolutionary means.[6] When Marx and Engels formulated their party's manifesto in 1848, they intentionally chose the word "communism"—which expresses the idea of the revolutionary struggle—in order to distinguish their views from "socialism". There is a schematic distinction between modern socialism, which is "scientific", and the earlier socialism, which was "utopian": the distinction should be between revolutionary and evolutionary socialism. Communist or Marxist socialism is the revolutionary branch of nineteenth- and twentieth-century socialism. Before that, socialism was liberal, reformist, utopian, constitutional, experimental, or parliamentary.

Socialism is a social ideology that seeks human justice, social solidarity, and a decrease in the inequality between people. The word "socialism" reflects the emphasis on social relations, as opposed to "liberalism", which emphasizes the individual. Socialism is a constant striving for a more just society—that is, a society in which people's social tendency has more weight than their individualist tendency. Socialism's point of departure is thus revolutionary with respect to human nature.

The heralds of socialism were many and varied, and scholars tend to list them in an order that reflects their interpretive perspective. Some scholars note that the first modern use of the word "socialism" occurred in 1826, in Robert Owen's *Cooperative Magazine*, while others claim that the word was first used in 1832 by a Saint-Simonist in the French journal *Le Globe*. But movements with a socialist flavor existed at least since the Peasants' Rebellion in 1525 under the leadership of Thomas Munzer, the Anabaptist rebellions, such as that in Munster in 1534, and the civil wars in England in 1642–1652, which produced the Diggers under the leadership of Gerrard Winstanley. Radical movements of the Cromwell revolution, such as the Levelers, were more rebellious than revolutionary.[7]

The socialist utopias of the Renaissance were essentially revolutionary texts, calling for the radical construction of an ideal society with new human beings. Such a revolutionary change in human nature is a condition for a perfect socialist society in which all the details of people's lives are shaped in a total manner. Thomas More's *Utopia* (1516) is a social critique of property differences and the eviction of the farmers from their land; More advocates democratic socialism. Tommaso Campanella's *Civitas Solis* (1623) describes a communist sort of life. In Francis Bacon's *The New Atlantis* (1627), on the other hand, it is science that solves social problems. The utopia as a literary genre considered itself a microcosm of human society as a whole.[8]

The idea of revolution had not yet arisen in the millennarist movements and the utopian literature. Their notions were sentimental, and they maintained the model of early Christianity, which advocated a poor man's socialism. Not until the eighteenth century were there a development of capitalism, an accumulation of wealth, and an organization of the working class with a revolutionary consciousness. It was only the combination of the political consciousness of the French revolution and the social change initiated by the Industrial Revolution that created modern socialism with its revolutionary branches, namely Marxism and Anarchism.

At the time of the French revolution, the "social problem" arose as an ideological issue, not a moral one. Previously, eighteenth-century Enlightenment thinkers had discussed the philosophical and ethical aspects of the problem: Mably and Morelly wrote about utopian socialism, while Jean-Jacques Rousseau, in his *Discourse on the Origin and Foundations of Inequality Among Men* (1755), claimed that the growth of property rights was responsible for the decline of civilization. In Rousseau's view, the egalitarian natural situation of man was replaced by a political situation in which the excess privileges of the rich were established by law. The laws protecting property and allowing economic exploitation made the rich a strong political force. This revolutionary social analysis by Rousseau was not adopted by the initiators of the French Revolution, who chose to make their revolution bourgeois rather than socialist.

The Marxist interpretation is that the French Revolution was a political one, which established subjective will rather than a socioeconomic revolution, because France's preindustrial character prevented the development of a working class. In the absence of the appropriate economic conditions, political tenor was the only means available to the revolution. Marx believed that the French Revolution was a bourgeois political revolution of the civil society, which had separated itself from the political state. The French Revolution's contribution to socialism was thus the fact that it constituted a structural and mental stage that paved the way for the next stage—the socialist revolution.

The French constitution of 1793, which was the most socialist of the revolution's constitutions, was never actualized. Gracchus Babeuf aspired to bring it about, and for this purpose he sought to establish a dictatorship of the Parisian workers. The Conspiration des Equal of 1793 was accomplished through organized revolutionary means. It was the first to reveal the radical socialism at the margins of the revolution, although this was not its central trend. Babeuf was the originator of the concept of the proletariat as a revolutionary force. The French Revolution did not actualize socialism as a systematic social movement, but it developed the opposition between the rich and the poor into a political struggle for the first time. This was the first time that maximum prices were established, food hoarding limited, and exorbitant prices forbidden. But the revolutionaries who *were* busy abolishing the feudal order considered their goal to be the expansion of property rights. Babeuf's movement did not become a popular revolution because the urban proletariat was weak and small in numbers. Nevertheless, the revolution paved the way for the prolonged social struggles in nineteenth-century Europe, out of which modem socialism developed.[9]

In the manifesto *On the Middle Class and the Nation*, which Alexis de Tocqueville wrote in 1847 for the French Parliament, he predicted a revolutionary change that would lead to a demand for abolishing excess property rights. The right to property was the last barricade of the old political world: "There is reason to believe that the struggle among political parties will soon become a struggle *between* the haves and the have nots. The arena will be property". At the same time that de Tocqueville *was* writing about socialism as a modem "slave rebellion", Marx was reading the final proofs of the "Communist Manifesto".

The intensive social changes brought about by the industrial revolution—such as urbanization, modernization, and the growth of the proletariat—led to a hatred of technology, which was reflected in such *acts* as the destruction of machines by the Luddites in the 1810s; the growth of a utopian socialist literature; and an increase in the revolutionary consciousness of the working class, which was accompanied by the development of revolutionary socialism, otherwise known as Marxism.

The new social problems associated with urbanization and industrialization were attributed to the acquisitive character of private ownership. This encouraged nineteenth-century socialist thinkers to move from the political to the economic realm. The French Revolution's failure to reshape human relations by political means led to a renewed interest in society, shifting the emphasis from event to process and from making political revolutions to understanding economic systems, which are nonrevolutionary by nature. Postrevolutionary disappointment led people to turn their backs on the political side of reforms and to concentrate on the problems of inequality, poverty, ignorance, education, and social conditions such as health, pensions, working hours, and unemployment. These were the problems that made it necessary to maintain a stubborn socialist struggle, far from the spotlights of revolution.

Utopian socialism claimed that changing from private to collective ownership and organizing the community into voluntary unions could solve a considerable number of social problems. In contrast with eighteenth-century socialism, which was based on the understanding of natural laws, utopian socialism relied on intellectual understanding, moral values, interclass fraternity, and practical economic experiments in the form of socialist communities. The utopias were not programs for a general reorganization of society, nor did they associate themselves with any popular or proletarian movement for the realization of their visions. The social principles shared by Saint-Simon, Fourier, and Owen were opposition to competition, suspicion of politics, and belief in communitarianism and creativity. All three supported socialization in education, economic planning, and cooperation in behavior, while attacking inequality and demanding restrictions on property rights. They did not, however, believe in a proletarian revolution against the bourgeois state.[10] The economist Jérôme Blanqui, in his *Description of the Beginnings of Political Economics* (1839), was the first to call them "utopian socialists", a name that was quickly adopted by Marx and Engels.

Shades of the French Revolution could be detected in the Revolutions of 1848 in Europe—the "revolution of the intellectuals", as it was called by the historian L. B. Namier. The utopias of the mid-nineteenth century, which sought to construct the Heavenly City, added a collectivist element to the individualism that characterized eighteenth-century thought, and they transmitted this new element to the nationalist and socialist movements of their time. An important revolutionary in the 1848 events was Auguste Blanqui, who gave his name to the radical revolutionary trend of Blanquism. This trend, which involved great humanistic fervor, extended from the radical revolutionary groups—the *Enráges*, the *Hébertistes*, and Babeufand, the secret societies of the Carbonari—through the neo-Jacobean movements—such as Young Europe, the Amis de la Verite, and the Amis de Peuple—to the early republican movement, the ideology of revolutionary Syndicalism, and the SocialDemocratic and Communist Parties.[11]

Socialism developed differently in nineteenth-century England[12]—more practically than ideologically.[13] An empirical social trend developed gradually, from Locke's theory of natural rights, Ricardo's "Homo Oeconomicus", Charles Hall's nationalization of agrarian socialism, theories of surplus value, and class struggle, Thomas Hodgkin's labor theory of values, John Gray's circulation theory, and William Thompson's iron law of wages, to the utopian socialist ideas of Robert Owen, the greatest figure of English socialism. From 1830 to 1848, for the first time in the history of English socialism, the Chartist movement combined political action, class consciousness, legislative change, and social work. At the same time, the first socialist international organization was founded—the Society of Fraternal Democrats. In 1884, Sidney Webb and George Bernard Shaw in London founded the Fabian Society, which rejected the revolutionary paradigm of the "class war".[14] They fought poverty and want, as well as the exploitation and selfishness that stem from acquisitiveness. They believed that the historical necessity of the transition to socialism was not solely the responsibility of the working class and that it was important to persuade all the political parties to join the struggle for gradual socialist reform. Consequently, they emphasized activity on the municipal level and in the trade unions, and they played an important role in forming the Labor Party and developing the idea of the welfare state.

In Germany, socialism was more abstract and theoretical than in France and England, due to the conservative structure of German society and the lack of an organized working class. Lassile, a socialist and nationalist, demanded cooperation between the proletariat and the state. In 1863, he succeeded in founding the first independent labor party, the Allgemeiner Deutscher Arbeiterverein. German socialism became a powerful revolutionary force in the Second International, which was established in 1889. Nevertheless, the German socialist movement was severely persecuted, and Bismarck's *socialistengesets* of 1878–1890 prevented it from growing.[15] Later, German democratization and economic growth made the Social-Democratic Party one of the strongest forces in the country. The most serious threat to Marx's revolutionary system was the democratic evolutionism proclaimed by Eduard Bernstein in 1889. This reformist socialism combined Fabian and Marxist ideas, claiming that the situation of the working class could be improved gradually without a social or economic revolution. Although the party remained loyal to Karl Kautsky's conservative revolutionary line, its practical policies became more and more revisionistic.[16]

In France and Italy, the development of socialism in the late nineteenth century led to the formation of the Syndicalist movement, while in England it led to trade-unionism. Whereas the English trade unions were primarily interested in improving the laborers' wages and working conditions, the Syndicalists had revolutionary educational aspirations. Syndicalism was a special sort of revolutionary socialism that was not based on historical determinism or economic mechanism, as Marxism was, but rather on the direct action of the workers, as well as political general strikes. Militant streams in French and Italian revolutionary Syndicalism also led to the beginnings of Fascism.

The socialist movement in nineteenth-century Russia formed the basis for a wave of revolutionary anticzarist activity. It began with the liberal socialism of thinkers such as Herzen and Lavrov, which later divided into various streams. The Social-Democratic Party, which was founded by Plekhanov in 1898, was Marxist, while the Social Revolutionary Party, despite its name, opposed revolution of the Marxist variety. A hybrid of socialism and Jacobinism was first tried in the twentieth century, during the Bolshevik Revolution. According to

Lenin's definition, a Social-Democrat is a Jacobean who has adopted socialism. Lenin claimed that in the twentieth century it was impossible to attain a just regime, as the Jacobeans had sought in their time, without public ownership of the means of production and the direction of the economy. Seventy years of Communism in Russia proved that there is still a wide gap between the enlightened, universal ideas of nineteenth- and twentieth-century socialism and the distortion of these ideas in a totalitarian, bureaucratic, nationalistic historical experiment.[17]

Marxism and Revolution

Friedrich Engels eulogized Karl Marx by saying, "Just as Darwin discovered the law of evolution in organic nature, so Marx discovered the law of evolution in human history".[18] Marx's evolutionary approach to history led to revolutionary ideologies. Until Marx, philosophers had seen their role as merely interpreting history; the Marxists took on the role of revolutionizing it. What the Marxists took from their intellectual predecessors was not only a philosophy of history but also the practical conclusion of avoiding collaboration between the classes. This separated Marxism from socialism.

In their book, *The German Ideology* (1845–1846), Marx and Engels claimed that revolutions are cataclysmic leaps from one means of production to another. A historical period is distinguished from the preceding one by the development of a new mode of production, which leads to a struggle between the class that represents the old order of the forces of production and the one that represents the new order.[19] Engels wrote that "the final causes of all social changes and political revolutions are to be sought [. . .] in changes in the modes of production and exchange". The outcome of the "socialist revolution" will be equality between the old exploitative class and the new dominant class—that is, a classless society. Until then there will only be "bourgeois revolutions"—such as the British, American, and French ones—that are motivated by the need for expansion of the new capitalist forces of production.

Revolutionary France in the eighteenth and nineteenth centuries was a laboratory of historical materialism. However, in contrast to Engels's interpretation, Marx did not consider France an arena for a socialist revolution. Rather, France's history served for him as a proof by *reductio ad absurdum* of the lack of class consciousness. The French Revolution of 1789 and the Revolution of 1648, as well as the Paris Commune, were a historical lesson and warning that economic conditions were not ripe for a socialist revolution.

Around 1848, Marx as editor of the *Neue Rheinische Zeitung*, wrote more about democratic radicalism than about proletarian revolutions. His conclusion—that the workers' movement must undergo a bourgeois revolution—was adopted by Russian Marxists in the early twentieth century. Nevertheless, Marx's and Engels's political activities were clearly revolutionary: they joined the First International as "Bund der Kommunisten" and even wrote the "Communist Manifesto" for it, describing the proletariat as "the only revolutionary class".[20]

Around 1900, a crisis occurred among the European Marxists, with far-reaching implications for the first quarter of the twentieth century. The growing awareness that Marxist predictions were not being fulfilled in practice led to the conclusion that there was some serious flaw in Marxist analysis in the guise of scientific socialism. The revolution had not yet arrived, in spite of the economic, political, and sociological processes that were supposed to bring it about. The agents of modernization, such as progressive education, the universal right to vote, and compulsory army service, which had been expected to lead to class consciousness and motivate revolutionary action among the proletariat, served instead as a means for national and cultural integration and as catalysts for the growth of patriotism and a retreat from antimilitarism. The nonarrival of the expected proletarian revolution, combined with the growing nationalist trends, were a severe shock to the Marxists. This led to two revisions in Marxism, whose common denominator was the goal of forming an egalitarian, classless society: Eduard Bernstein pointed out the possibility of realizing socialism by playing the rules of the parliamentary game, without a social revolution, while Vladimir Lenin strove to bring about the revolution through a revolutionary elite organized into party cadres. The view associated with Bernstein, known as revisionism, cast doubt on the inevitability of the socialist revolution.

Karl Kautsky and Georgi Plekhanov further developed the Marxist view of the proletariat as a universal revolutionary class.[21] They claimed that objective historical necessity requires stages of developed capitalism and polarization of the classes. At a certain point in human evolution, due to the relations between the classes, the forces of production are faced with the decreasing absorptive capability of their products. This socioeconomic contradiction creates social forces that are united in their revolutionary ideology, which brings down the old order and substitutes a new system of production. The revolutionary social order creates the social forces that will later bring it down: every revolution expands the base of the regime it sets up. The antifeudal bourgeois revolution created the proletariat, which is the last revolutionary class.[22]

If the economy is not yet ready for a revolution, no takeover of political power, such as that of Blanquism, will lead to the destruction of capitalism. There is no connection between objective economic laws and spontaneous violence, as illustrated by the Jacobin dictatorship and the Paris commune. Revolutions, in Kautsky's view, are not one-shot aggressive acts, violent rebellions, or civil wars, but the conscious takeover of political power by an organized proletariat when capitalism has reached a certain level of development. Here one can find the seeds of Kautsky's disagreement with Lenin. In contrast to Kautsky, who claimed that a communist society would spring up as soon as the capitalist structure collapsed, the Bolsheviks believed that Russian communism was a revolutionary transition stage and that the Russia of 1919 was in one stage of this transformation.

Kautsky opposed the Russian October Revolution of 1917, rejecting Lenin's idea of the dictatorship of the proletariat. He based his view on Marx's opposition to the Bakunists' attempt to foment a communist rebellion in 1873 in Spain, as well as Marx's attitude to the Paris Commune. Kautsky claimed that the Bolsheviks, like the Jacobins, were trying to solve economic problems by mass terror, which they wrongly called the dictatorship of the proletariat. In 1875, Marx announced in the Gotha Program that between the capitalist and communist society lies a period of revolutionary transformation from one to the other. Corresponding to this is a political transition period during which the state can be nothing other than the revolutionary dictatorship of the proletariat. In 1919, Kautsky wrote that if the dictatorship of the revolution was to continue in Russia, it would end up in militarization, bureaucratization, and totalitarian rule.[23] Lenin, on the other hand, accused Kautsky and the leaders of the Second International of being revolutionaries in language but reformists in practice.

The activists, whose spokespersons were Labriola, Goldmann, and Gramsci, held a "philosophy of action", rejecting the Plekhanovist view of historical inevitability.[24] They believed that the combination of the historical situation and social consciousness could lead to changes in the world. Following Marx, they claimed that the motivating force of the socialist revolution is the alliance of the suffering proletariat and the intellectuals. Thus Gramsci called the Communist Party "the intellectual collective". Revolutionary ideologies turn sociological explanations into political forces: Marxism tried to make a revolutionary class out of the suffering of individuals.

Lenin developed a new view of revolutionary Marxism that did not wait for economic conditions to be ripe.[25] He claimed that the party must take advantage of revolutionary situations and direct revolutions. The failure of the Russian Revolution of 1905 repeated the failure of the Revolutions of 1848 in Western Europe, leading to the conclusion that a strategy of permanent revolution must be adopted: there must be a continual thrust from bourgeois revolutions to socialist ones.

Leon Trotsky, who after 1917 became the People's Commissar for War, believed that the democratic revolution in Russia would lead to a social-democratic regime that would necessarily continue the revolutionary trend toward socialism. Since the bourgeoisie was weak, the revolution would have to be led by the proletariat, and therefore it would not stop at the bourgeois stage. Russia's economic situation would cause the bourgeois revolution to turn into a socialist one immediately, and the revolutionary trend would spread from Russia to all of Europe, and from there to the entire world. If this did not happen and socialism would remain confined to one country, the revolution would not be maintainable.[26] In 1924, Stalin formulated the expression, "Socialism in one country", which was directed against Trotsky and the idea of the "permanent revolution".[27] However, when Russian communism failed to expand the revolution, it did indeed become a static power.

Bolshevism represented an attempt to change an evolutionary theory into a revolutionary practice. It combined the revolutionary elements in Marxism with the unique conditions in Russia: forced industrialization, Russification of the population. a pony dictatorship and class terror as a transition stage between capitalism and socialism, state socialism, the collectivization of the peasants, the exile and destruction of the Kulaks, and the adaptation of Taylor's methods of "scientific" management. The communist end was supposed to justify all the revolutionary means.

While Marxist ideology was mainly theoretical, the revolutionary Bolshevik doctrine became a political practice carried out by a military and police organization. The revolutionary effort was concentrated on destroying the remnants of the bourgeois class and constructing the foundations of a Communist society. However, the revolutionary transition stage turned into a totalitarian reality for seventy years of Bolshevism. Kautsky accused Lenin and the Bolsheviks of maintaining their own rule through terror. The dictatorship of the proletariat, which Marx had considered a postrevolutionary transition stage, had become a dictatorship of the party. The great danger of using revolutionary means was the establishment of the revolutionary force to the point of centralizing bureaucratic power, violence, terror, and the army.

Trotsky and Rosa Luxemburg both believed that a hierarchical, centralist party of professional revolutionaries contradicted the fundamental Marxist principle that the working class can liberate itself without outside help. Luxemburg's uncompromising revolutionary activity and her criticism of the socialists' defection in 1914 turned her into the principal opponent of both the revisionists and the bureaucratic establishment of Russian Marxism. In the "reformism vs. revolution" debate, she took the position that there is no contradiction between reform, which is a means, and the struggle for political power, which is an end in itself. The essence of reform is different from that of revolution; reform is not a stage of revolution. Luxemburg's blind faith that workers are naturally revolutionaries led her to place revolutionary spontaneity above organized party activity.[28]

The Soviet Union, which considered itself the spearhead of the international revolution, was actually a disguise for Russian nationalism.[29] Marxism, as well as the Marxism-Leninism that followed it, examined nationalism from the viewpoint of historical relativism: an independent national state is a structural part of the bourgeois revolution and a precondition for the victory of democracy. The fundamental economic assumption of the two doctrines is that the bourgeoisie, in order to achieve full control of production, dominates the local market by uniting territories into a state. The two consider the formation of "bourgeois nations" to be a historically progressive step. However, modern developments have shown that imperialism cannot exist with colonialist exploitation.

The Austrian Marxists, especially Otto Bauer and Karl Ranner, devoted a great deal of thought to the problem of nationalism from the viewpoint of the communist revolution.[30] The Bolsheviks claimed that internationalism is the continuation of nationalism. The demand for national and racial equality played a more crucial role than the struggle for communism in the worldwide communist propaganda.

Lenin advocated expanding the revolutionary movement to the colonial world.[31] The Soviet Union inflamed nationalist struggles, moving them from Europe to the Third World. The fact that rightist military regimes supported by the West were in control of most of the countries of Asia and Africa left the revolutionary arena for the Russian communists, who described themselves as the only effective alternative. After the Second World War, there was wide acceptance of the Soviet theory that socialism could spread throughout the world even during peacetime.[32] This thesis was adopted at the same time as the competition with Maoism for the leadership of the world socialist revolution.

The Revolution after Leninism: The Revolutionary Phase of Soviet Marxism

Many Marxists began to investigate postrevolutionary cultural, psychological, and sociological issues, beginning in the 1930s. For example, the Frankfurt school, which combined the methods of Marx and Freud, used the Marxist view of the revolution as a starting point for diagnosing cultural and social conditions in which people lost their humanity in capitalism's "industrial culture". They aspired to formulate a critical theory that would expose the false consciousness of the proletariat. According to Herbert Marcuse, the proletariat has become part of the "one-dimensional society", which has lost its revolutionary imagination: the workers have become an inseparable part of the capitalist consciousness, which has neutralized the revolutionary option.

Maoism—the peasant's Marxism—is an ideological revolutionary branch that was adapted to the historical circumstances prevailing in China.[33] The Maoists disagreed with the "orthodox" Chinese Marxists, who advocated the Comintern's conservative line and remained loyal to the Soviet strategy, in which the revolution relies mainly on workers' strikes and rebellions in large industrial areas. In his 1940 article, "On New Democracy", Mao wrote that the Chinese revolution was essentially a peasant revolution relying on the peasants' demands, but the culture of the new democracy would develop under the leadership of the proletariat.[34] At that time, Mao's plan was similar to the first stage of Leninism: a peasantry led by the Communist Party and a dictatorship of the proletariat. But soon, on the basis of the same internal logic that had prevailed in the Soviet revolution, the Chinese revolution as well turned into the totalitarian structure of a centralist, bureaucratic political power. In the Cultural Revolution of 1965, the radicals, led by Mao, tried to suppress the conservatives, who represented bourgeois ideology, especially in the universities. The proletarian revolution is not only political but also cultural. When Antonio Gramsci, the leader of the Communist Party of Italy, analyzed the revolutions of the nineteenth century, he distinguished between "active rebellions", such as that of Mazzini and "passive revolutions", such as that of Cavour, but claimed that both of them were necessary for post-1848 Europe. Gramsci did not consider a revolution to be a technical matter of taking over power.

The revolution is not proletarian and communistic because it destroys the institutions of the old regime or because it calls its activists "communists" but because it liberates the existing productive forces and leads to the development of a society in which class distinction disappears. Forces must be found to transform the productive class from an instrument of suppression to an instrument of liberation. The role of the Communist Party is to help liberate the proletariat, thus bringing the revolution closer.

György Lukács concentrated on explaining the revolutionary principle in theory and practice.[35] For this purpose, he used the word *totalitat* to describe the facts of the world as a "concrete whole". In this view, the truth of the parts is to be found in the whole: the whole is the motor of the revolutionary principle. According to Lukács, Lenin's greatness was that he understood this at the time of the Bolshevik Revolution. Lenin identified the revolutionary moment in all the events of his time, uniting all the details into a revolutionary socialist perspective.

In the 1950s and 1960s, the Soviets suppressed national and civil liberties in the countries under the "protection" of the "revolutionary homeland". Rebellions broke out in Hungary and Czechoslovakia, and there was a renaissance of the concept and topic of revolution. It was no longer an issue for the proletariat but became the province of suppressed minorities such as students, blacks, and the countries of the Third World. The New Left tried to renew "true communism"; for this purpose, Maoists. Trotskyites, and others made use of the jargon of the universal anticapitalist revolution in the style of the Third World. They claimed that the idea of a society's "ripeness for revolution" was a bourgeois invention and that a well organized group could radically change social conditions in a "revolution here and now". They adopted the notion of Lukács, Marcuse, and the Frankfurt school that the capitalist society is an indivisible whole and can only change as such. The idea of a total revolution that requires destroying all the existing institutions and ruling elites came from their dynamist, nihilist orientation to the present as detached from the past and the future. The Post–Cold War World. The 1990s are witness to the postrevolutionary age of Marxism.[36] The Soviet Union had disintegrated, giving up its revolutionary communist ideology, its nationalist imperialism, and its Eastern European satellites. The creator of this counterrevolution was Gorbachev, who followed the lesson taught by Alexis de Tocqueville in the nineteenth century—that a totalitarian revolution that begins to conduct reforms presages its own downfall. The idea of the revolution in Marxism thus returns to its starting point—from practice to theory.

Historiography as a Strategy

Marx was a philosopher, a student of economics, and a political strategist.[37] All three dimensions were to be found in his historical articles examining a hundred years of French history. He was not interested in historical facts as such but in their place in the scheme of history and in their function in the rules of the game that he fixed: whether history confirmed or disproved the theory of dialectical materialism, as it were. As a strategist, he placed his readers among the happenings and characters of history and embellished, warned, blazed trails, drew conclusions, read historical texts to his readers. As an intellectual, Marx tried to find a correlation between the "laws" of history and his own desire to move history forward.

There were four historical stations in Marx's French journey: the French Revolution in 1789, the February Revolution in 1848, Louis Napoleon's coup d'état, and the Paris Commune in 1871. In Marx's historical writings, France was regarded as a laboratory of historical materialism. Explaining Marx's reasons for this choice, Friedrich Engels analyzed in his introduction that France, more than any other country, is the place where the class war has broken out continually until the final resolution, and thus one finds there, in even the most recent phenomena, the same political manifestations in a changing form.[38]

But here, too, Engels was not exact in his interpretation of Marx. Marx did not see France as an arena of class warfare. French history served him, on the contrary, as negative historical proof of a lack of class consciousness in France.

Because the history of France was particularly fascinating in Marx's opinion, he drew his image of a general revolution from the French model. The conclusion he arrived at was not a congruence between the image and the model but a range of possibilities between them. Events in France served as revolutionary experience and instruction for the future. On the way to the hoped-for revolution one must gain revolutionary experience and discard all illusions in order to reach the goal.

The French revolutions were interconnected so that each one reiterated the lessons of the last one. The French revolutionary tradition may be compared to a torch passed from generation to generation:

> The tradition of all past generations weighs like an alp upon the brain of the living. At the very time when men appear engaged in revolutionizing things and themselves, in bringing about what never was before, at such very epochs of revolutionary crisis do they anxiously conjure up into their service the spirits of the past, assume their names, their battle cries, their costumes to enact a new historic scene in such time-honored disguise and with such borrowed language.[39]

Although the general revolution, the class revolution, must absorb the lessons of the past, it must direct its gaze to the future: "The social revolution of the nineteenth century cannot draw its poetry from the past, it can draw that only from the future".[40]

Modernity exists within a consciousness of historical time:

> Former revolutions require historic reminiscences in order to intoxicate themselves with their own issues. The revolution of the nineteenth century must let the dead bury their dead in order to reach its issue. With the

former, the phrase surpasses the substance; with this one, the substance surpasses the phrase.[41]

The great lesson of history is that one must distinguish between sterile political revolutions and social revolutions that can alter the cause of oppression or, in other words, the economy.

The modernity of the French Revolution resulted from the new way of thinking it brought to the world, its images, the revolutionary self-awareness, the possibilities it created: "The French Revolution brought to the world a concept different from all the concepts of the old world-order. This concept, if developed in a deductive way, is the concept of a new world-order".

The French Revolution was a starting point as well as an intersection of modernity and enlightenment. Modernity proclaimed its political birth in the French Revolution. Now, for the first time, human beings sought to mold their political and social lives in accordance with new principles that did not depend on the legacy of the past. The bourgeoisie, the standard-bearer of the revolution, began a discourse concerning man or the "citizen", free from the burden of history, who took his fate into his own hands.

The revolution was a proclamation of the birth of modern humankind and the inception of modern politics. Modern politics meant public decision making, elections, persuasion, public opinion, criticism. The concepts of democracy, revolution, and citizenship were based on a perception of time different from that which had been accepted until then. The idea was that people should organize themselves in the present with an eye to the future and create their own world.

The Enlightenment, of which the French Revolution was one of the consequences, was generally speaking a way of thinking that based the essential rights of modern persons on the laws of nature and not on the legacy of the past, faith, status, or determinism. In place of a hierarchy of classes and hence a hierarchy of rights, to which people were bound by the accident of birth and which determined the course of their lives, one had the concept of an enlightened humanity. It was no longer an arbitrary, alienated, disunited rabble but was animated by a revolutionary consciousness that all people are born in the image of nature and have self-evident rights of liberty and equality, rights not dependent on sacred scriptures, wealth, or allegiance. This universal concept of humankind was the main achievement of the Enlightenment.

The first test faced by the Enlightenment was the French Revolution. In its first stage, the revolution translated the enlightened discourse of "liberty, equality, fraternity" quite literally into the legal concepts of the Declaration of the Rights of Man and the Citizen, the deposition but not execution of the king, the cancelation of the privileges of the monarchy, the nobility, and the Church, the separation of church and state, a stage-by-stage democratization and progressive instruction in citizenship. That was in the year 1789. However, the modern revolutionary idea soon became a rebellion against the principles of the Enlightenment. In the second stage, the *terreur* of 1793 subordinated the means to the revolutionary end. All of a sudden, the enlightened achievements of the modern revolution disappeared, and anarchy was followed by tyranny. The revolution was the first historical lesson in the fraught relationship between enlightenment and modernity. This was one of the reasons for Marx's attraction to the hundred years of French history, a sort of field of dialectical experimentation in enlightenment and modernity.

France is a classic historical model for every historian. The rapid political metamorphoses, the frequent changes of regime, the changes of myths and symbols, the revolutions of different kinds with their varied development, and, above all, the revolutionary consciousness and the universal aspirations all make it a litmus test for a study of different philosophies of history.

Marx, a historian of a special kind, whose chief intention was to serve as a political strategist who subordinated political facts to his ideological diagnoses, found France a good field for his prognostications. Modern French history alternated between monarchy, republic, and empire and moved back and forth, but Marx's preoccupation with a general social revolution remained constant. The interrelationship between the French revolutionary tradition and a general revolution was described by Marx as follows: the French experience has been dominant in the whole of European history since 1789, and it is from there that the signal has again gone out for a general revolution.

De Tocqueville was quite right in depicting the French model as the vanguard of a general religious revolution:

> The French Revolution always sought out what was least particular and, so to speak, most natural in regard to social state and government. That is why it was able to make itself comprehensible to all, and why it could be imitated in a hundred places at once. Since it appeared to aim at the regeneration of the human race even more than at the reform of France, it kindled a passion that not even the most violent political revolutions had ever aroused before. It inspired proselytism and propaganda and therefore came to resemble a religious revolution, which was what contemporaries found so frightening about it. Or, rather, it itself became a new kind of religion—an imperfect religion, to be sure, without God, cult, or afterlife—yet a religion that, like Islam, inundated the earth with its soldiers, apostles, and martyrs.[42]

France was the standard-bearer of modern revolution. The status of enlightened individuals in modern times, their rights gained as a result of a universal conception of mankind, the pioneering character of the revolution, its crossing of national boundaries, first through missionizing with words and then by missionizing with swords—all this made the French Revolution the vanguard of modern politics for both Marx and the Marxists.

Marx and Marxism typify the interrelationship between enlightenment and modernity. In modernity, said Marx, man creates his own history, but he has to mold it in a different way than in the past. Marx's project of enlightenment contained a historical dialectic in which liberty was achieved through a continual progress in the course of which the workers appropriate the means of production and found an egalitarian society. This enlightened society would be based on class equality and not on capitalist bias or historical privileges, on a nationalization of the means of production and not on their concentration in the hands of a few, on an economic rationale that recognizes the importance of work and property, on a rejection of private capital, profit derived from surplus value, a fetishism of goods, and the alienation of humans from nature, work, and fellow humans.[43] After an intermediate stage of dictatorship of the proletariat, the workers would set up a society that is classless, egalitarian, modern, and enlightened. In Marx's vision, enlightenment and modernity went hand in hand.

The French Revolution: Completion and a Breakthrough

The dialectical relationships between existence and consciousness in Marx were examined in the mirror of the French Revolution. In his youth, Marx accepted Hegel's claim that changes of situation are prepared by philosophy.[44] This point of view was not in accordance with Marx's famous dictum in his "Contribution to the Critique of Political Economy" (1859): "It is not the consciousness of men that determines their existence, but their social existence that determines their consciousness".[45] Because consciousness derives from existence, the whole determines the part: that is, existence determines the consciousness. To this, said Marx, one may add that someone's social existence obviously determines his or her relationship to the surrounding world. Consciousness and existence are interactive.[46] From the moment the consciousness operates in service of the praxis of revolution, it changes existence, but, on the other hand, a revolutionary class immediately creates the existence of a revolutionary consciousness.[47] Because the preindustrial French society of 1789 had not yet created classes aware of their own existence, it was impossible to have a class revolution, but as soon as the proletariat became conscious of itself, it endangered the existence of the bourgeoisie.[48]

In the absence of a suitable socioeconomic situation for a class revolution, a political revolution was the only practical possibility. Marx therefore thought that the modernization and industrialization of France should be continued on the capitalist model, but, simultaneously, social consciousness should be increased not on the basis of the "German ideology" but in accordance with the practical criticism of the French, who are not content with thinking but seek action.[49] The political revolution is a stage on the way to the class revolution. Only when existence and consciousness permit a revolutionary situation would the revolution be possible, but meanwhile the political revolution reflected the limited outlook of "the masses of French socialists who sought to detach the world from its institutions with the magic formula: liberty, equality, fraternity". In his article, "Towards a Critique of Hegel's Philosophy of Judgement" (1843–1844), Marx stressed the importance of consciousness for existence and the importance of understanding existence to effect change: "It is not enough for thought to strive for realisation, reality must itself strive towards thought".[50]

Marx thought that, in founding the modern state, the French Revolution began a process that gave sole autonomy to the state with its centralization and bureaucracy, moved the center of gravity from society to the state, and separated the political state from the civil society. His conclusion—the opposite of Hegel's—was that only an act that creates a dialectical synthesis between the state (which was to wither away) and society could extricate individuals from their alienation. Marx saw man as first and foremost a social entity, self-created and not alien to nature. In *The Holy Family*, in the chapter "The State and Civil Society in the First Revolution", he elucidated this perception:

> The members of the civil society are not like atoms [. . .] An atom has no needs, is self-sufficient [. . .] Each individual has to find an affinity owing to the fact that he becomes at one and the same time a mediator between the needs of his neighbor and the objects of this need.[51]

As this is the case, the natural necessity, the essential traits of humankind, its interest are what sustains the members of civil society. The life of civil society, not the life of the state, is their true affinity.

De Tocqueville, in his books on the United States and on France, preceded Marx in his analysis of the fragmentation of humankind in the modern state. While De Tocqueville feared the alienating individualism to be found in the democratic-egalitarian age, Marx traced the source of individualism to the dislocation of civil society and the change to a political state:

> The political revolution which overthrew this sovereign power and raised state affairs to become affairs of the people, which constituted the political state as a matter of general concern, that is, as a real state, necessarily smashed all estates, corporations, guilds, and privileges, since they were all manifestations of the separation of the people from the community. The political revolution thereby abolished the political character of civil society. It broke up civil society into its simple component parts; on the one hand, the individuals; on the other hand, the material and spiritual elements constituting the content of the life and social position of these individuals.[52]

And who was this egoistic man, the product of the dislocated society? Marx answered: "Feudal society was resolved into its basic element—man, but man as he really formed its basis—egoistic man. This man, the member of civil society, is thus the basis, the precondition, of the political state. He is recognized as such by this state in the rights of man".[53] In Marx's terminology, the whole, rational man, on the other hand, adapts his requirements and chooses to be in society because he has passed the stage in which he regarded himself as an individual. The human consciousness is not exclusive: stored within it are social structures that a person sees as an inseparable part of his intellectual makeup. Estrangement takes place when a man lives in conflict with his neighbor as a result of being a stranger to himself. The greatest estrangement is that between man and society, for then the estrangement reflects the idea that the society is spurious.

There are two sides to man, the individual and the social, which logically speaking are contradictory, but in reality a dialectical synthesis between them is possible. The contradiction exists in a situation of estrangement, and one cannot know which causes which: private property or alienated labor. The relationship between cause and effect is one of interaction that makes alienation in capitalist society and a capitalist state an inescapable and insoluble problem unless there is a basic change in the society: that is, a class revolution.[54]

One must therefore approve of the political revolution of 1789, which accelerated processes that, according to Marx, prepared the arrival of the class revolution. But only a correct analysis of the French Revolution could benefit the consciousness and help in implementing the revolution. Marx thought that the political revolution was a revolution of the civil society. Medieval society gave an undesirable political character to property, the family, and the form of labor in the seigneurial-feudal system. This increased the gap between the political aspect and the desired social aspect. Then the French Revolution came along and completed the rupture. It fixed the different political functions of the various societies within the society. The state became the supreme arbiter between the conflicting political interests in the society. The victorious political interest became identical to the state and loved to honor it. That was the origin of the bourgeois state whose institutional birth was in the French Revolution.

A correct historical consciousness is an essential precondition to a revolutionary praxis. This principle, said Marx, was not understood by the leaders of the French Revolution: "Robespierre, Saint-Just and their party fell because they confused the ancient, realistic-democratic commonweal based on real slavery with the modern spiritualistic-democratic representative state, which is based on emancipated slavery, bourgeois society".[55] The idealization of a certain historical stage or event does not contribute to a correct historical understanding and leads to sterile attempts at artificial revival. What was the mistake of the Jacobins? In Greece and Rome, the distinction between civil society and the state did not yet exist, and they could therefore exist side by side. In modern society, there was an opposition between civil society and the state, and this was impossible. In his article, "The Class Struggles in France", Marx quoted Jean Sismondi's famous saying: "The Roman proletariat lived at the expense of society and modern society lives at the expense of the proletariat". All attempts to compare the socioeconomic conditions in Rome with those in modern and revolutionary France were doomed to failure.

Marx's observation that "the revolution of 1789 to 1848 draped itself alternately as the Roman Republic and the Roman Empire",[56] appeared in his article, "The Eighteenth Brumaire of Louis Bonaparte", in which there was a psychological analysis that claimed that traumas of the past pursue the revolutionaries of the present like a nightmare, and in times of crisis they feel the need for inspiration, encouragement, and guidance from figures of the past. They adopt the original accessories of these heroes, their characteristics, their voices, their images: "the heroes as well as the parties and the masses of the old French Revolution, performed the task of their time in Roman costume and with Roman phrases, the task of unchaining and setting up modern bourgeois society. The first ones knocked the feudal basis to pieces and mowed off the feudal heads which had grown on it".[57] This forced imitation of the past revealed the Roman model as a historical anachronism. Marx's verdict was that the artificial revival was a farce while its older sister was a tragedy. This applied to Robespierre's and Saint-Just's cult of "virtue". Not only was a return to the past not possible, but there was an essential contradiction between the vision of the revolution and its implementation.

Marx totally rejected the attempt of the revolutionaries of 1789 to revive the Roman model and denied Saint-Just's belief that "the revolution has to be Roman". One could not proclaim the rights of man—which could not be exercised in the Roman world—as Saint-Just did at a time when the socioeconomic conditions were quite different from those in ancient Rome, and imagine it was something Roman. This frozen romanticism held up historical progress and thus also delayed the coming of the revolution. The French Revolution resembled those that imitated it in the following hundred years inasmuch as it looked as though mesmerized at the Roman myth as a model of "liberty, justice and virtue".[58]

The French Revolution was a political revolution that was the expression of a subjective will and not a socioeconomic metamorphosis. The preindustrial condition of France held back the creativity of the working class. Due to its lack of class consciousness and in the absence of suitable economic conditions, political terror was the sole instrument of the French Revolution, which sought by this means to subject society politically to the state. How did Marx distinguish between a political revolution and a social, class, or proletarian one? In the introduction to his article "A Critique of Political Economy", he described the nature of this distinction:

> The changes in the economic foundation lead sooner or later to the transformation of the whole immense superstructure. In studying such transformations it is always necessary to distinguish between the material transformation of the economic conditions of production, which can be determined with the precision of natural science, and the legal, political, religious, artistic or philosophic.[59]

In the French Revolution, there was no contradiction between the productive forces and the relationships of production. It was a political-bourgeois revolution of a civil society that was totally separated from the political state.

This political revolution was therefore a structural stage that prepared a social revolution, and that was its importance. But Marx was angry at the social presumption of the revolutionaries of 1789 who made declarations they could not carry out when they had neither the economic conditions nor the political instruments that would enable them to do so. This false view of history was harmful to the revolution because terror as a political instrument for achieving social ends was ineffective and finally turned on its makers. The basic error of the Jacobins was their use of terror instead of an economic understanding of history: "Terror's wish to sacrifice it to an ancient form of political life"[60] and "the French terror [were] nothing but a plebeian formula to neutralize the enemies of the bourgeoisie". The success of the Jacobins in politicizing civil society was inconsistent with their desire to impose their political will on the economic facts. Political means like terror testify, rather, to the weakness and neurotic fears of those who used them and doomed their attempt to change the socioeconomic basis of society to failure.

Marx engaged in an imaginary disputation with Rousseau. He obviously could not accept the latter's distinction between "the general will" and "the will of all", a distinction that in his opinion was meaningless and missed the main point, which was a correct economic understanding of social processes in history. The misleading "general will", known only to a small revolutionary cadre who led the revolutionary majority, was promoted by Marx's literary partner, Engels. In his analysis of the 1848 revolution in his introduction to "The Class Struggles in France", Engels asked, was it not a situation in which the revolution was likely to succeed although led by a minority, but this time not for the benefit of a minority but overwhelmingly in the interests of the majority?[61] Later in our discussion, we shall see Marx's opposition to any Jacobin putsch aimed at changing a historical situation: the failure of the revolt of 1848 led to a sober economic analysis of the situation at that time. The attempt at a Commune in 1871 again ignited for a moment the revolutionary myth but served Marx mainly as a desirable model for the relationship between society and the state.

France was ready for a social-class revolution, and so the failure of the 1848 revolution was a double one. First, the February revolution, like the 1789 revolution, mistakenly attempted to use a political upheaval to change an economic situation. Secondly, despite its failure, it did not learn from the French Revolution and ended with a modern Bonapartism.

Marx considered the view of man as an exclusively political being to be incomplete and therefore mistaken. A revolution of parties, as in the French Revolution, was a political revolution. In the opposite view, humankind was a complete political, social, and economic entity and consequently required a total revolution, which is to say a class revolution that would completely transform the socioeconomic basis of life. In his article, "The German Ideology", Marx spoke of the common failure of all political revolutions in perpetuating the old economic basis of life and said that its replacement, the social revolution, was the only kind that could change the distribution of labor and correct the distorted relationships of production on which the political superstructure depended. Here Marx encountered the problematics revealed by Isaiah Berlin: the fear of conditioning humankind or conditioning the environment. Berlin thought that the people who carried out the October Revolution in Russia falsified Marx's original intention, which was to change the social conditions that diminish the quality of people but not to change them.[62] But in Marx himself one can find the origins of an outlook that tries to condition man: "Both for the production on a mass scale of this communist consciousness, and for the success of the cause itself, the alteration of men on a mass scale is necessary, an alteration which can only take place in a practical movement, a revolution; the revolution is necessary".[63]

There were many aspects to revolution. Marx maintained that "revolutions are the axes of history". Political revolutions, which are essentially limited, permit the coming of the class revolution, which is the only kind that can restore to humankind its image, distorted by alienating social and economic conditions. The legitimacy Marx gave to political revolution was based on two assumptions, one being that it institutionalized historical processes and brought them to completion and so prepared the next step on the path of progress. The other was that only a correct understanding of the limits of political revolution could heighten historical consciousness and prepare a class revolution.

A constant feature of the French Revolution was its radicalization, its movement toward ever greater extremity. Marx revealed the way in which a new party expropriated those more moderate than itself, and the Jacobins took the place of the Constitutionals and the Girondists, or as he claimed, this is how the revolution developed in a progressive manner.[64] The processes initiated by the French Revolution were developed, improved, and institutionalized in the time of Napoleon, the restoration, and the July monarchy.

> The first French Revolution, with its task of breaking all separate local, territorial, urban and provincial powers in order to create the civil unity of the nation, was bound to develop what the absolute monarchy had begun: the centralisation, but at the same time the extent, the attributes and the agents of governmental power. Napoleon perfected this state machinery. The Legitimist monarchy and the July monarchy added nothing but a greater division of labour.[65]

In his book, *The Ancien Régime and the Revolution*, De Tocqueville located the origins of centralization in the absolute monarchy. Marx, on the other hand, traced the development of the power of the state from the revolution to the mid-nineteenth century: "Every common interest was straightway severed from society, counterposed to it as a higher, general interest, snatched from the activity of society's members themselves and made an object of government activity". It transpired that the revolutions that boasted of being the standard-bearers of radicalism and progress gave greater power to the state mechanism: "All the upheavals perfected this mechanism instead of destroying it".[66] The bureaucracy, which was a political instrument of bourgeois government, was increasingly improved until, in the days of Louis Bonaparte, it became an end in itself:

> In the days of the absolute monarchy, in the time of the first revolution and in the time of Napoleon, the bureaucracy was merely a means to support the class-regime of the bourgeoisie, a tool of the ruling class. Only in the days of Louis Bonaparte did it seem that the state became completely independent.[67]

The perfection of the bureaucratic institutions was a result of the shift in the point of gravity from society to the state. The feudal connections had gone, the bourgeoisie had begun its rule. The liberal bourgeoisie was the basis that Louis Napoleon depended on in his revolution: "What on the eighteenth Brumaire became the spoil of [Louis] Napoleon was not the revolutionary movement itself but the liberal bourgeoisie".

The revolutionary terror came to an end with Napoleon and gave way to the exclusive power of the modern state. With his keen political instincts, he understood that the modern age regarded the state and the nation as ends in themselves, and he brought "the terror to an end by replacing perpetual revolution with perpetual war". "He fed the egoism of the French nation to complete satiety".[68] But the political consciousness of his rivals increased in the course of time, and the illusions were dispelled one by one:

> Just as the liberal bourgeoisie was opposed once more by revolutionary terror in the person of Napoleon, so it was opposed once more by counter-revolution in the Restoration in the person of the Bourbons. Finally, in 1830 the bourgeoisie put into effect its wishes of the year 1789, with the only difference that its political enlightenment was now completed, that it no longer considered the constitutional representative state as a means for achieving the ideal of the state, the welfare of the world and universal human aims but, on the contrary, had acknowledged it as the official expression of its own exclusive power and the political recognition of its own special interests.[69]

The 1789 revolution did not extol French uniqueness, and its message was a universal one. It did not proclaim French rights but general bourgeois rights. Although its proclamations were ineffective as it lacked the tools and conditions to implement them, its power lay in destroying traditional partitions through a modern consciousness. The French Revolution was the vanguard of a general revolution. Its buds sprouted in France, but its fruits nourished a general revolution that was still to come: "The life-history of the French Revolution that began in 1789 had not yet ended in the year 1830, which in one of its moments scored a victory which was now enriched with a sense of its social significance".[70]

The Cunning of Power of Louis Napoleon

The burden of history weighs on all generations:

> Men make their own history, but they do not make it just as they please; they do not make it under circumstances chosen by themselves, but under circumstances directly encountered, given and transmitted from the past. The tradition of all the dead generations weighs like a nightmare on the brain of the living.[71]

These words of Marx reflect a flexible deterministic approach, as in "all is foreknown, yet freewill is given". Historical figures are caught in circumstances fixed in former times, and thus their deeds are like marginal notes to decisions hewn in the rock of history.

The source of Marx's approach, which diminishes the importance of the personal element in history, was his view that socioeconomic facts are all-important. This view would seem to be in contradiction to the starting point of Marxism, which is that humans are beings who create themselves, mold nature and determine their own history. Did Marx see an interrelationship between social conditions and historical figures? On the one hand, only the class war in France, circumstances and relationships, enabled a mediocre and grotesque personality to play the part of a hero, and, on the other, this "grotesque personality" ruled France for two decades. In the final summing-up, it was not a transient episode but a constructive stage in the history of France.[72] Louis Bonaparte undoubtedly made a manipulative use of the Napoleonic myth, but the moment he succeeded in institutionalizing himself in French history, others came and imitated the imitation. As soon as Bonaparte ceased being a caricature, he became a model to imitate. When the "Napoleonic ideas" had been institutionalized as a postfascist phenomenon, they served as a historical precedent for fascist phenomena in the twentieth century. At first, Louis Bonaparte treated history as a comedy, but the robot rose against its maker:

> Only when he has eliminated his solemn opponent, when he himself now takes his imperial role seriously and under the Napoleonic mask imagines he is the real Napoleon, does he become the victim of his own conception of the world, the serious buffoon who no longer takes world history for a comedy but his comedy for world history.[73]

Why did the peasantry bring Louis Bonaparte to power on the 10th of December 1848? Marx thought that a peasant uprising was behind the emperor. The peasantry was central to his victory, and on the periphery there was the proletariat, the *Lumpenproletariat*, all kinds of bourgeois, and the army. Louis Bonaparte was the common denominator of the opposition to the "bourgeois republic". To the peasants, this name—Napoleon—did not represent a person but a program. Only Napoleon as a symbol, as a myth of Napoleonic imperialism, was able through a kind of revolution of the peasantry to defeat the "republic of the rich". But when the time came that the name lost its fascination, Louis Bonaparte still believed that the source of his power was the magic of his name and his perpetual caricatural imitation of Napoleon.[74]

The source of Louis Bonaparte's power at the time he took office was his neutral position between the monarchist hawks and his campaign against anarchy, which endangered the bourgeois order. Marx said that in the struggle of the "party of order" against the people, the former had to augment the power of the executive authority, or, that is to say, the power of Louis Bonaparte. "By so doing, it encouraged Bonaparte's dynastic ambitions, and increased the chances of imposing by violence a legal solution in the day of decision".[75] The danger of anarchy that threatened bourgeois society if the status quo was altered paradoxically strengthened the authority of the president. The bourgeoisie was afraid of political chaos:

> stunned by rumours of coups d'état and the restoration of universal suffrage, by the struggle between parliament and the executive power, by the Fronde between Orleanists and Legitimists, by the communist conspiracies in the south of France, by alleged Jacqueries in the departments of Nièvre and Cher, by the advertisements of the different candidates for the presidency, by the cheapjack slogans of the journals, by the threats of the republicans [...] the bourgeois madly snorts at his parliamentary republic: "Rather an end with terror than terror without end.[76]

The political rebellion came down into the streets. It only had to be declared: "If there was ever an event that cast its shadow in front of it long before it occurred, it was [Louis] Napoleon's political upheaval". The upheaval was inevitable, and Louis Bonaparte knew how to take advantage of the situation and make it serve his purposes. This is Marx on Louis Napoleon's rise to power:

> In November 1849, Bonaparte was content with a non-parliamentary ministry, in January 1851 he was content with an extra-parliamentary ministry, on the 11th of April, he felt himself strong enough to set up an anti-parliamentary ministry [...]. This ascending ladder of ministries was the thermometer by which parliament could ascertain the decreasing temperature of its life.[77]

Bonaparte's victory over the legislature was called by Marx "the victory of force without rhetoric over the power of rhetoric".[78] Naked force overcame rhetoric, but the cunning of history gave the power to cunning: "It seemed that France escaped from class despotism only in order to go backwards and come under the yoke of a single person, and then only under the yoke of the authority of someone without authority". Bonaparte, who was full of contradictions, represented the peasantry and the proletariat against the bourgeoisie, "saw himself as the representative of the middle class, [. . .] and wanted to be seen as the patriarchal benefactor of all classes, but he could not give to one class without taking from another". According to Marx, Louis Bonaparte really represented only himself. His cunning navigated between the rival camps: "This role replete with contradictions of the man explains the contradictions of his rule".[79]

The article, "The Eighteenth Brumaire of Louis Bonaparte", written in 1851–1852, was intended to describe Louis Bonaparte's road to power via a coup d'état. He disproved Marx's prediction that the days of his rule were numbered because the cunning of power could not hold out in the face of the economic situation and the social consciousness. The Louis Bonaparte phenomenon frustrated Marx for the simple reason that it did not correspond to the Marxist historical model that based everything on historical economic situations. Although Louis Bonaparte represented the antithesis of Marxism, he remained in office for two decades. Marx summed up his personality as follows:

> Driven by the contradictory demands of his situation, and being at the same time, like a juggler, under the necessity of keeping the public gaze on himself, as Napoleon's successor, by springing constant surprises—that is to say, under the necessity of arranging a coup d'état in miniature every day—Bonaparte throws the whole bourgeois economy into confusion, violates everything that seemed inviolable to the Revolution of 1848, makes some tolerant of revolution and makes others lust for it, and produces anarchy in the name of order, while at the same time stripping the entire state machinery of its halo, profaning it and making it at once loathsome and ridiculous.[80]

This analysis shows Marx to be a doctrinaire who reduced all the facts to a single explanation rather than a historian who sought to trace underground currents and understand complex historical events.

According to Marx, the Bonapartist regime was based on five "Napoleonic ideas": the "Napoleonic property form", the strengthening of the material order and the state apparatus, the strengthening of the bureaucracy, the clergy, and the ascendancy of the army.

What was the "Napoleonic property form"? Louis Napoleon, who gave the farmers land, changed their status from feudal peasants to small landowners. But as agriculture sank into debt and the agricultural situation deteriorated, "[t]he Napoleonic property form, which at the beginning of the nineteenth century was necessary for the liberation and enrichment of the French rural population, in the course of the century developed into a cause of their enslavement and impoverishment".[81] Marx thought that the decline of the French peasantry was due to this enslavement to property.

The Napoleonic "material order" was intended to protect the enslavement of the peasantry to property, and, as a result, the peasantry exchanged one master for another: "In place of the feudal order which took interest, in place of the feudal tax on the land, one had the mortgage; in place of the aristocratic acquisition of land, one had bourgeois capital". Here a comment by Marcuse is fitting: "The freedom to choose between masters does not remove the masters from the world, nor the slaves".[82] The preservation of this new enslavement required the enforcement of a strong system of government.

The third idea was the necessity of strengthening the bureaucracy, with its creation of an artificial class, the clerical, for which the rehabilitation of the state was its daily bread. The small landowner was the basis for a bureaucracy by creating a uniform social stratum. It was a suitable infrastructure for a centralized form of government that eliminated the intermediate levels between the center and the periphery that existed in the aristocratic system. The bureaucracy was a stabilizing element in the Bonapartist regime.

The fourth Napoleonic idea was the role of the clergy: "Another '*idée napoléonienne*' is the domination of the priests as an instrument of government".[83] The fifth and last principle was the ascendancy of the army not for use against hostile countries but "for persecuting and hunting the peasants on behalf of the regime". Louis Bonaparte had a good understanding of the military mentality, and he greatly strengthened the military orders "to buy the soldiers with garlic sausages".[84]

Marx described these "Napoleonic ideas" as "hallucinations of its death struggle, words that are transformed into phrases, spirits transformed into ghosts".[85] He regarded them as mere tactics and nothing more, and did not realize in 1851 that they would be implemented in France for a whole generation and would serve as a precedent and an example for other regimes on the continent. Marx gave a simplistic account of the Bonapartist phenomenon, but it should not be seen as a fortuitous occurrence resulting from the social situation and interparty squabbles. A combination of circumstances in 1848 did in fact cause the rise of Louis Bonaparte but is not sufficient to explain the consolidation of his regime.

According to Marx, Louis Bonaparte understood the modern phenomenon of the masses. He realized that "on the 13th of June 1849, the official leaders of the various semi-revolutionary parties were decapitated, and the masses obtained their heads". In appealing directly to the people over the heads of the legislature for a renewal of voting rights and in campaigning among the masses in France, he showed that he understood the importance of direct contact with the masses, of charisma as a replacement for the party system, of a mobilizing personal myth.

In the initial period of his rule, according to Marx, the state encircled and directed civil society and overshadowed it.[86] Civil society was paralyzed, the citizens were passive, and such were the consequences of totally centralized government. This Tocquevillian idea reappeared with Marx, and we shall later see how the Marxistically inclined Paris Commune dealt with this problem. Here the bourgeoisie was faced with a paradox: its material interests made a large state apparatus necessary and its political interests necessitated social repression. On the one hand, the bourgeoisie was compelled to destroy the advantages it derived from the parliamentary system, and on the other hand, it had to provide the executive, which opposed it, with invincible power. Louis Bonaparte understood the situation perfectly and exploited it in order to build himself up as the representative of the executive and increase the authority of the central government as the reflection of the omnipotent state.

The state mechanism was strengthened in the time of Louis Napoleon. The government, which wished to subject everything to its direct control, needed an army of officials in order to carry out its administrative centralization policies. Marx used Louis Bonaparte's coup d'état as a means of illustrating certain developments in modern society. His analysis of the Bonaparte phenomenon in "The Class Struggles in France" and above all in "The Eighteenth Brumaire of Louis Bonaparte" revealed tendencies that appeared in a developed form at the beginning of the twentieth century in thought, in political movements, and in the fascist regime.

The Paris Commune: Myth in the Service of Revolution

In Marxist historiography, the Paris Commune (1871) is regarded as the first revolutionary attempt to change the class structure rather than be satisfied with a political reversal. Both the political Jacobin element and the economic Proudhonist element in the French revolutionary tradition had now disappeared. The vision of a "socialist republic" carried over from the February Revolution became a living reality a generation later.

In his introduction to Marx's pamphlet, *The Civil War in France*, Engels wrote: "Do you want to see the image of that dictatorship? Cast your eyes on the Paris Commune: that was a dictatorship of the proletariat!"[87] And was Marx of the same opinion? In the pamphlet we have mentioned, which focused on the meaning of the Paris Commune for the modern world, the expression "dictatorship of the proletariat" did not appear. Only in one place did Marx describe the Commune as a government of the working class that intended to implement communism. The Commune wished to turn capital, land, and the means of production, which were vehicles for the oppression of labor and chains on the hands of the workers, into vehicles for liberating labor and imposing equal conditions. The temporary nature of the dictatorship was explained by the assertion that it was merely a stage preceding the disappearance of classes.

In Marx's account of the Commune, there is sometimes a confusion between an attempt to trace the events historically and their representation as a worthy revolutionary model, between the historical Commune and the ideal Commune. Marx saw the workers who raised the standard of the Commune as the envoys and local representatives of the people of Paris in general elections. This new political mechanism in no way resembled the political structures of the past: "The Commune was to be a working, not a parliamentary, body, executive and legislative at the same time".[88] One may ask whether Marx intended to replace a centralized structure with a worse centralized structure. Centralization, which until then had been solely a legacy of the bourgeois state, now passed into the hands of the Commune. The amalgamation of the three powers in the Commune, whose authority was unlimited, was an attempt to create a centralized political body that left the state-society dichotomy, which had been dislocated earlier, as it was.

The state mechanism was described by Marx as "a machine for the requirements of class rule". When speaking of the Commune's demand to take hold of the reins of government and become master of its fate, Marx thought that the proletariat was not yet sufficiently mature to use the state mechanism for its own purposes. The agents of the former regime—the professional soldiers, the police, the officials, the priests, and the judges—whose power descended from the age of absolute monarchy, were intended to preserve a hierarchical distribution of labor and to support bourgeois society in its struggle against feudalism.

The privileges of the landowners and nobility, the provincial laws, the monopolies of cities and guilds—all these held up the development of a modern state. The French Revolution destroyed the medieval elements that mediated between civil society and the political superstructure and in so doing institutionalized the modern state. The Napoleonic empire perfected the state mechanism, and the revolutions that came afterward strengthened all the more the property owners who were the rulers and formers of opinion. These developed a positive correlation between the political authorities and capital:

> At the same pace at which the progress of modern industry developed, widened, intensified the class antagonism between capital and labour, the State power assumed more and more the character of the national power of capital over labour, of a public force organized for social enslavement, of an engine of class despotism. After every revolution marking a progressive phase in the class struggle, the purely repressive character of the State power stands out in bolder and bolder relief.[89]

In his introduction to "The Civil War in France", Engels explained the dialectics of the modern state and came to the conclusion that the political robot rose against its maker (society). Society forged itself instruments to protect its concerns, the chief of which was government. Particular interests made "servants of society into masters of society".[90] The general interest of the society was exchanged for the partial interest of those in power: the state rose against the society that had created it.

According to Marx, the Commune wished to change this state of affairs. The agents of the old regime—the army, the police, the bureaucracy, the Church and the educational authorities—were divested of their political character in the period of the Commune. The regular army was replaced by the proletarian National Guard, the political functions of the police were invalidated, and it became a tool in the service of the Commune. The same applied to the bureaucrats: the Church was separated from the state, and its assets were impounded; judges had to be elected, were subject to dismissal, and were responsible to those who appointed them. Once again, the ideologist had overcome the intellectual in Marx. All these bodies were clearly not divested of their political character. If, for example, the army and police had derived their legitimacy from the state in the past, now they were responsible to the Commune.

The Commune sought to reveal the state to be a class institution that placed the right of self-administration, public initiative, and the means of production in the hands of a small number of wielders of power, but as soon as it demanded universal suffrage, the self-administration of workers, a minimum wage for workers, and a maximum wage for officials, the liberation of the peasantry, and other social reforms, it did it, of course, through the centralized and coercive political mechanism. The dictatorship it set up as an intermediate stage toward a change in the structure of society had the same power basis as the system they wished to get rid of, but perhaps because of the propagandist nature of the article or perhaps for more doctrinal reasons connected with his systematic ideological way of thinking, Marx refrained from adding qualifying shades to the picture he painted in black and white.

The French revolutions of the nineteenth century laid stress on the contents of the class-state. The 1830 revolution shifted the power from the landowners to the capitalists, the February revolution gave it to the bourgeois republicans, and the "party of order" in the parliamentary republic gave unlimited powers to Louis Bonaparte. The proletariat lost either way: someone said that the Louis Bonaparte regime was "a state that distinguished less than any other between sections of the ruling class". The common denominator of the different factions was the state as a tool to suppress the proletariat, "national war-engine of capital against labour".[91]

The Commune wished to change all this, "to restore to the body of society all the power and vigor that was drained from it until now by that parasitic growth, the 'state', which was nurtured by society and which hindered its freedom of movement".[92] But it refrained, rightly in Engels's opinion, from carrying out the revolution with the political tools created by the bourgeoisie, from operating with the mechanism of the old state. The proletariat had to destroy that mechanism and create political tools suited to the modern age, for a return to the medieval social system would be an anachronism. The institutions of society that sprang up from below had to be recreated and the powers of the provinces, the local communes, and the villages revived.

Marx made the historical Paris Commune into a myth in the service of world revolution. The ideal commune was revealed as the model of the new society:

> Working men's Paris, with its Commune, will be for ever celebrated as the glorious harbinger of a new society. Its martyrs are enshrined in the great heart of the working class. Its exterminators history has already nailed to that eternal pillory from which all the prayers of their priests will not avail to redeem them.[93]

Paris was the spearhead of the revolution. Just as Marx saw the French revolutionary tradition as an empirical laboratory that provided a cumulative historical training for a general revolution, so he saw Paris as a concentration of

France. The opponents of the revolution also believed it was "the destiny of Paris in every historical crisis to represent the whole of France". The belief of the anarchists, the revolutionaries, and the Prussians that the fate of France depended on its capital demonstrated the mythical importance of Paris in the revolutionary consciousness.

Paris was the proletariat and the capital of the revolution: "Paris armed was the Revolution armed. A victory of Paris over the Prussian aggressor would have been a victory of the French workman over the French capitalist and his State parasites".[94] In Marx's opinion, Paris in 1870 represented the revolutionary proletariat, although that very same city had in the past been the site of a counterrevolution, like a traffic light in which a change of color signifies a change of regime. Revolutionary Paris was a stumbling-block to the representatives of the landowners; the revolution of the 4th of September 1870 was a declaration of war against the bourgeoisie and a protestation against the political regime of the Second Empire. The bourgeoisie under the leadership of Thiers by means of laws intended to destroy trade and industry, shut down newspapers, renew the siege, and move the site of the National Assembly to Versailles.[95]

In view of the threats of the monarchist Bordeaux assembly, "an assembly of Junkers and illiterates", the workers of Paris were faced with a choice: either to lay down their arms and acknowledge the illegality of the revolution or to continue the revolutionary movement and totally destroy the social fabric of the old regime. The workers of Paris, wrote Marx, did not want a civil war imposed on them, but their refusal to return the cannons of the National Guard to Thiers was a pretext for the liquidation of the revolution of the 4th of September. Marx made an ideology out of the Commune: he said that from the 18th of March 1871, when the workers of Paris seized power and the central committee was declared a provisional government until the convening of the assembly at Versailles, the Paris Commune did not commit any acts of violence except for those forced upon it.

The mythical treatment of the Paris Commune reached its height in a metaphorical contrast drawn by Marx: "Paris all truth, Versailles all lie".[96] In the short period of its activity, "the Commune made a great change in the image of Paris". It cleared the streets of lawlessness while Versailles mobilized the old world: it was "a convocation of evil spirits, remnants of all the regimes which have passed away [. . .], searching for prey in the corpse of the nation". Paris was not only a capital city where the institutions of government were situated but the mythical ideal of a modern urban society, just as Versailles symbolized the past. The bloodbath in Paris and the defeat of the Commune meant "not only the annihilation of the revolution but the annihilation of France, whose head had been cut off".[97] In his defeat, the standard-bearer represented the failure of the revolution.

Marx regarded the Commune as an economic prototype, a political model, and a universal ideal. As an economic prototype, Marx wrote that the Paris Commune was intended to be a model for all the large centers of production in France, to instruct all the provinces in France in setting up communes, and to promote workers' self-administration.⁹⁸ As a political model, "the Commune was to be the political form of even the smallest country hamlet".⁹⁹ The rural communities would manage their affairs through meetings of delegates in the capital of the province, and these assemblies would send delegates to the national headquarters in Paris. As a universal ideal, "If the Commune was thus the true representative of all [. . .] working men's Government, as the bold champion of the emancipation of labor, emphatically international. [. . .] the Commune annexed to France the working people all over the world".¹⁰⁰ Unlike the Second Empire, which pretended to be cosmopolitan, the Commune chose a German as its Minister of Labor, honored Poland in its struggle, and tore down the column in the Place Vendôme, a symbol of the outbreak of the war.

Marx exploited the slaughter of workers in Paris for the purposes of the revolutionary myth. He regarded the massacre of June 1848 as nothing compared to the massacre of 1871, which he considered an unprecedented bloodbath in the annals of class warfare. He believed that the only parallel to the intensity of this massacre and the desire for revenge that it engendered was to be found in the bloody history of the Roman Empire, but the Romans did not reach the heights of civilization with machine guns. Humankind, for Marx, was a product of history. It was formed by the social and economic conditions which it itself had created. Civilization did not necessarily mean enlightenment, and modernity had no need of enlightenment.

Marx was of the opinion that it was modern nationalism that destroyed the experiment of the Commune. In the events of 1871, the ruling class conspired to defeat the revolution by fomenting a civil war under the protection of a foreign invader. The ruling classes and the Prussians made an alliance against the workers. After the most terrible war of modern times, Marx wrote, the victorious army and the defeated army came together to kill and destroy the proletariat.¹⁰¹ Bismarck saw the defeat of the Commune as the last word of modern society, and Marx regarded it as historical evidence of the decadence of the old bourgeois society. Both of them spoke on behalf of modernity, but their differing interpretations demonstrated once again that ideology is the product of a philosophy of history.

The revolutionary transitional stage was a totalitarian reality in the seventy years of Bolshevism. Kautsky accused Lenin and the Bolsheviks of practicing political self-preservation by means of terror. The dictatorship of the proletariat, which Marx considered a post-revolutionary intermediate stage, became the dictatorship of a party. There was an unrestrained use of revolutionary means whose purpose was to create a concentration of power through a combination of bureaucracy, violence, terror, and military might. The theoretical threat became a historical reality.

Notes

1 Marx, "The Difference Between the Democritean and Epicurean Philosophy of Nature", in Karl Marx and Friedrich Engels, eds., *Collected Works*, (ed.) by the Institute of Marxism Leninism, 50 vols., Moscow and New York 1975, 30–31.

2. Marx, *Capital: Critique of Political Economy*, 1 vol., London 1982, 799.
3. William Clare Roberts, *Marx's Inferno: The Political Theory of Capital*, Princeton, NJ 2018; David Harvey, *Marx, Capital, and the Madness of Economic Reason*, Oxford 2017.
4. Leonard P. Wessel, *Prometheus Bound: The Mythic Structure of Karl Marx's Scientific Thinking*, London 1984.
5. Terrell Carver, ed., *The Cambridge Companion to Marx*, Cambridge 1991.
6. Joseph A. Schumpeter, *Capitalism, Socialism, and Democracy*, New York 2008.
7. Alexander Grey, *The Socialist Tradition*, London 1946.
8. Frank E. Manuel and Fritzie P. Manuel, *Utopian Thought in the Western World*, Cambridge, MA 1979.
9. Maurice Dommanget, *Babeuf et les Problemes du Babouvisme*, Paris 1963.
10. Lewis Mumford, *The Story of Utopias, Ideal Commonwealth and Social Myths*, Philadelphia 1972.
11. George Douglas Howard Cole, *History of the Socialist Thought*, 5 vols., London 1954–1960.
12. Sidney Webb, *Socialism in England*, Trieste 2017.
13. Roger Wells, *Insurrection: The British Empire 1795–1803*, Gloucester, MA 1986.
14. Bernard Shaw, *Fabian Essays in Socialism*, Scotts Valley, CA 2017.
15. Jonathan Sterinberng, *Bismarck: A Life*, Oxford 2013.
16. Karl Kautsky, *Communism vs. Social Democracy*, New York 1946.
17. Edward Hallett Carr, *A History of Soviet Russia*, 7 vols., New York 1950.
18. Friedrich Engels, *Selected Works*, 3 vols., New York 1950, 153.
19. Karl Marx, "The German Ideology", *Marx and Engels Collected Works*, vol. 5, London 2010, 19–540.
20. Terrell Carver and James Farr, eds., *The Cambridge Companion to the Communist Manifesto*, Cambridge 2015.
21. Georgi V. Plekhanov, *Fundamental Problems of Marxism*, London 1969.
22. Silvio Pons, *The Cambridge History of Communism*, Cambridge 2017.
23. Karl Kautsky, *The Dictatorship of the Proletariat*, Ann Arbor, MI 1919.
24. Antonio Labriola, *Essays on the Materialist Conception of History*, Chicago 1904; Antonio Gramsci, *Selections from Political Writings*, London 1910–1920; Lucien Goldman, *Marxisme et sciences humaines*, Paris 1970.
25. Vladimir Lenin, "What Is to Be done?" *Collected Works*, vol. 5, Moscow 1964–1970.
26. Leon Trotsky, *Out Political Tasks*, London 1980; idem, *The Permanent Revolution and the Results and Prospects*, New York 1962.
27. Joseph Stalin, "The Foundations of Leninism", in B. Franklin, ed., *The Essential Stalin*, London 1924.
28. Rosa Luxemburg, *The Russian Revolution*, Ann Arbor, MI 1961.
29. Mikhail Agursky, *The Third Rome—National Bolshevism in the USSR*, London 1987.
30. Otto Bauer, *Die Nationalitatenfrage und die Sozialdemokratie*, Vienna 1907; Karl Lerner, *Der Kampt der Osterreichischen Nationen um den Staat*, Leipzig 1924.
31. Ronald W. Clark, *Lenin*, New York 1988.
32. Philip Longworth, *The Making of Eastern Europe*, New York 1987.
33. John K. Fairbank and Albert Feuerwerker, eds., *The Cambridge History of China*, vol. 13, *Republican China 1912–1949*, Part 2, Cambridge 1998.
34. Mao Tse-Tung, *On New Democracy*, Oregon 2003.
35. György Lukács, *History and Class Consciousness*, London 1971.
36. Russell Jacoby, *Dialectic of Defeat: Contours of Western Marxism*, Cambridge 2002.
37. David McLellan, *Karl Marx: A Biography*, Basingstoke 2006; Jonathan Sperber, *Karl Marx: A Nineteenth-Century Life*, New York 2014.
38. Engels, "Introduction to the Third Edition of Karl Marx (1885)", in *Der achtzehnte Brumaire des Louis Napoleon*, New York 1852.

39 Marx, *The Eighteenth Brumaire of Louis Bonaparte*, trans., D. L. Hughley, New York 2005, 1.
40 Ibid., 3.
41 Ibid., 4.
42 De Tocqueville, *The Ancien Régime and the French Revolution*, Cambridge 2011, 21.
43 Amy Wendling, *Karl Marx on Technology and Alienation*, Basingstoke 2009.
44 Georg Wilhelm Friedrich Hegel, "Hegel to Niethammer: Bamberg, October 28, 1808," in Clark Butler and Christiane Seiler, trans., *Hegel: The Letters*, Bloomington, IN 1984, 178–182; David Leopold, *The Young Karl Marx: German Philosophy, Modern Politics, and Human Flourishing*, Cambridge 2009.
45 Marx, "Preface", *Marx and Engels Collected Works*, vol. 29, London 2010, 263.
46 Marx, *Rheinische Zeitung*, 14th in July 1842, 97–98.
47 Marx, "Critique of Modern German Philosophy According to Its Representatives Feuerbach, B. Bauer and Stirner", *Marx and Engels Collected Works*, vol. 5, 60.
48 Marx, "The Eighteenth Brumaire of Louis Bonaparte", *Marx and Engels Collected Works*, vol. 11, 99–181.
49 Marx and Engels, "The Holy Family, or Critique of Critical Criticism", *Marx and Engels Collected Works*, vol. 4, 5–211.
50 Marx, "Contribution to the Critique of Hegel's Philosophy of Law", *Marx and Engels Collected Works*, vol. 3, 183.
51 Marx and Engels, "The Holy Family, or Critique of Critical Criticism", *Marx and Engels Collected Works*, vol. 4, 120.
52 Marx, "On the Jewish Question", *Marx and Engels Collected Works*, vol. 3, 166.
53 Ibid.
54 Jan Kandiyali, *Reassessing Marx's Social and Political Philosophy: Freedom, Recognition, and Human Flourishing*, London 2018.
55 Marx and Engels, "The Holy Family, or Critique of Critical Criticism", 122.
56 Marx, "The Eighteenth Brumaire of Louis Bonaparte", *Marx and Engels Collected Works*, 104.
57 Ibid.
58 Marx and Engels, "The Holy Family, or Critique of Critical Criticism", 121.
59 Marx, "Outlines of the Critique of Political Economy (Rough Draft of 1857–58) [Second Instalment]", *Marx and Engels Collected Works*, vol. 29, 263.
60 Marx and Engels, "The Holy Family, or Critique of Critical Criticism", 122.
61 Engels, "Introduction to Marx's The Class Struggles in France, 1848 to 1850", *Marx and Engels Collected Works*, vol. 10.
62 Isaiah Berlin, *Liberty: Incorporating Four Essays on Liberty*, Oxford 2002.
63 Marx, "Critique of Modern German Philosophy According to Its Representatives Feuerbach, B. Bauer and Stirner", 52–53.
64 Marx, "The Eighteenth Brumaire of Louis Bonaparte".
65 Ibid., 185–186.
66 Ibid., 186.
67 Ibid.
68 Marx and Engels, "The Holy Family, or Critique of Critical Criticism", 123.
69 Ibid., 124.
70 Ibid.
71 Marx, "The Eighteenth Brumaire of Louis Bonaparte", 103.
72 Ibid.
73 Ibid., 149–150.
74 Marx, "The Class Struggles in France, 1848 to 1850", *Marx and Engels Collected Works*, vol. 10, 82.
75 Ibid.
76 Marx, "The Eighteenth Brumaire of Louis Bonaparte", 175–176.
77 Ibid., 172.

78 Ibid., 186.
79 Ibid., 195.
80 Ibid., 198.
81 Ibid., 183.
82 Herbert Marcuse, "The End of Utopia", in *Five Lectures: Psychoanalysis, Politics, and Utopia*, Boston 1970, 143.
83 Marx, "The Eighteenth Brumaire of Louis Bonaparte", 192.
84 Marx, "The Class Struggles in France, 1848 to 1850", 143.
85 Marx, "The Eighteenth Brumaire of Louis Bonaparte", 193.
86 Ibid.
87 Engels, "Introduction to 'The Civil War in France'", *Marx and Engels Collected Works*, vol. 27, 191.
88 Marx, "The Civil War in France", 331.
89 Ibid., 379.
90 Engels, "Introduction to 'The Civil War in France'", 190.
91 Marx, "The Civil War in France", 330.
92 Ibid., 493.
93 Ibid., 355.
94 Marx, "The Civil War in France", *Marx and Engels Collected Works*, vol. 22, 311.
95 Ibid.
96 Ibid., 349.
97 Ibid., 345.
98 Ibid.
99 Ibid., 332.
100 Ibid., 338.
101 Ibid.

B. The Lenin Revolution and the Question of Nationality

Leninism and Nationalism

The seventy years of Bolshevism in Russia are a historical testimony to the enslavement of the proletarian Prometheus in a poor, armed, isolated land. How would Marx have seen the Bolshevik Revolution? It is likely that he would have condemned the failed experiment of a communist revolution before its time in a single country. It is likely that he would have been critical of the Bolshevik revolutionaries who had not learned the lessons of the failure of the political revolutions in nineteenth-century France. He would have foreseen that the rapid forced modernization of a country that was not modern would lead to the subordination of historical reality to a theoretical model. The original sin was the hubris of October 1917, the attempt to bind an entire country to an ideological experiment that turned into the rule of a party.

A Bolshevik elite sought to literally translate a theory of historical development into revolutionary practice. It combined elements of Marxism with the special conditions of Russia: rapid industrialization, Russification of the population, party dictatorship, class terror as a transitional stage from capitalism to socialism, indoctrination of the educational system, collectivization of agriculture, conditioning and annihilation of the peasants. Communism in one country justified all revolutionary measures.[1] In contrast to the theoretical character of Marxism, the revolutionary Bolshevik doctrine had a political existence expressed in a party, armed forces, and a police. The revolution concentrated its efforts on destroying of the remnants of the bourgeois class and on laying the foundations of a communist society. Unlike Kautsky, who claimed that a communist society would come into being with the collapse of the capitalist system, the Bolsheviks thought that Russian communism was a transitional revolutionary stage, and in 1917 Russia was ready to bring it about.

The revolutionary transitional stage was a totalitarian fact in the seventy years of Bolshevism. Kautsky accused Lenin and the Bolsheviks of practicing political self-preservation by means of terror. The dictatorship of the proletariat, which Marx considered a postrevolutionary intermediate stage, became the dictatorship of a party. There was an unrestrained use of revolutionary means whose purpose was to create a concentration of power through a combination of bureaucracy, violence, terror, and military might. The theoretical threat became a historical reality.[2]

Lenin, the personification of Bolshevism, was the undisputed leader of the most radical wing of Russian Marxism.[3] In 1917, he founded a new state, the center of world revolution, the "third Rome of world radicalism", as the historian Michael Agursky called it.[4] The international gospel, however, was a self-testimony on the part of Lenin, and it soon became national. Because he saw Russia as the theater of his project, his revolutionary motivation turned out to be a nationalism. It is a common mistake to ascribe to Stalin the nationalization of the Soviet system.[5] Bolshevism as a political movement became national long before the revolution, and this process was due to three factors: the national legacy of Russian socialism adopted by Lenin; the rivalry with the West and especially the socialist West, which claimed primacy in the new socialist world, while Lenin sought this position for Russia; and the German-Russian confrontation, which shaped the political development of Russia.

The national question and the theoretical Marxist question were contradictory. One meant exclusivity and isolation, and the other meant unity and equality. Both of them were the revolutionary offspring of modernism. That is why it is worthwhile lingering at the national-Marxist intersection of an intellectual like Lenin. Communism fostered Russian nationalism for some seventy years, and it was Lenin who formed its intellectual structure. One must trace his words and deeds with regard to nationalism, seeing the Marxist viewpoint against the background of the First World War, and in this way pick out a few points in the progress of modernity in a nonmodern country.

Lenin received a cosmopolitan education from his tutor and his mother, who gave him a grounding in the German, French, and English languages. His primary education was completed by Fyodor Kerensky, the father of Alexander Kerensky, one of the leaders of the 1917 revolution. His revolutionary outlook was quickened with the execution of his brother when he was seventeen years old. In his five years of exile, 1900–1905, he imbibed the intellectual influence of the Western-European world. These biographical circumstances and his position as a son of the Greater Russian people formed his relationship with the national question.[6] Although the national question was not central to his outlook, the special problems of Russia on the one hand and the search for a Marxist-international solution on the other formed his approach to nationalism.

In Stalin,[7] Bauer, Borochov, and Kautsky, one can find precise definitions of a nation and of the national problem, but Lenin consistently in all his articles refrained from defining the nation and nationhood and from providing a basic description of the national question as he understood it. Marxism viewed nationalism from a viewpoint of historical relativism: independent national states were obviously part of the bourgeois revolution and a necessary precondition to the victory of democracy. The basic economic assumption was that in order to dominate the production of commodities, the bourgeoisie needed to control the local markets in united territories, political unities whose inhabitants spoke a single language. The creation of "bourgeois" nations was thus seen as a progressive step from the historical point of view.

Nationhood was seen by Lenin as a passing phenomenon. Nationalism was created by capitalism, and when capitalism was overtaken by socialism, nationalism would also disappear.[8] At the same time, the national question was an urgent one for Lenin, requiring an analysis of the situation and proposals for a solution, and his solution was that every people has the right to self-determination and to secede from a larger entity.[9] Idealism and patriotism were interwoven in the national question. There were three reasons why Lenin refrained from defining nationhood: first, he had no intention of defining temporary situations because in so doing one contributes to their perpetuation. Second, an objective definition is impossible because one is dealing with different periods and places. The Swiss nation is essentially different from the Latvian nation and the latter is different from the Chinese. And the third reason was that nations are divided into three categories: the capitalist nations of Western Europe, Japan, and the United States, the countries of Eastern Europe, including Russia and Austria, and the semi-colonial peoples.[10] Each of these groups has its own characteristics, and there can therefore be no comprehensive definition.[11] Those who seek precise definitions think that the most important and competent commentator on the national question in the Bolshevik Party was Stalin, who under the leadership of Lenin clearly defined a people and a nation. Hence, in their opinion, the definitions of Lenin and Stalin were the same.

Stalin thought that the national question had two aspects: one, political liberation from the shackles of imperialism and the founding of an independent national state, and the other, the convergence of nations through a world market and a world economy. Imperialism, thought Stalin, had these two contrary tendencies because imperialism could not exist without colonialist exploitation, but in communism these are two sides of the same coin. Stalin's solutions undoubtedly derived from the basic ideas of Lenin. Stalin defined a nation as "a fixed partnership of people that has existed for a long period and is founded on the basis of a common language, territory, economic life and the specific character of a common culture".[12] With regard to the origin of Stalin's definition, Lenin agreed that a nation is a fixed partnership of people that has existed for a long period, and that "the basis of a common language and history is the chief component of a nation's existence".[13] Economic factors require the existence of nations, and his conclusion was that "every national movement is the result of a world economic struggle as a national phenomenon".[14] The parallel drawn by Lenin differed from Bauer's and Kautsky's definitions of "cultural partnership", and his analysis rejected the mystical qualities ascribed to nations, giving them a "psychic" character. Once again, Lenin is revealed as a Marxist who consistently adhered to dialectical materialism.

The problem that has troubled Marxist thinkers with regard to the national question is the matter of territory. In Marx, it is the difference between the final territorial solution (his call to the workers of the world to unite and his claim that workers have no motherland) and his pragmatic declarations concerning various national problems. For instance, Marx's opposition to granting the right of self-determination to the Slavic countries and his call for the annexation of Schleswig-Holstein to Prussia, and his call for the separation of Poland and Ireland from Russia and Britain. In other words, the territorial problem was pragmatic and not ideological. At a later stage, in his opinion, the problem would be automatically solved by the disappearance of the state.

Following Marx, Stalin distinguished between the national movements of "reactionary" peoples (such as the Czechs and Southern Slavs), who represented "ancient Russian positions", and those of "revolutionary peoples" that fought against despotism.[15] The Austrian, Karl Renner, said that the territorial framework was marginal to a solution of the national problem because it failed to define national identity. What defined it was "the shared culture, language, historical memory and life-style through which the individual sees himself as part of a national body". Otto Bauer agreed, adding that "a nation is a partnership that grows out of a shared destiny", and thus economic conditions or a territory are not sufficient to form a nation. One needs a tradition, cultural values, and a common destiny, and a territorial solution would therefore be a federation of national units under a shared leadership like a United States of Europe.[16]

Lenin, as we said, distinguished between peoples by means of language and territory. A dominant people granting self-determination to an oppressed one would pave the way for other peoples. For example, because the Finns have their own language and inhabit a certain territory, their demand for self-determination is legitimate and their struggle for freedom is the struggle of the whole Russian people.[17] Lenin laid down terms for an administrative distribution of territories: the criteria for a separate territory were the economic situation and the national demographic composition.[18] The division of the land would be decided by the vote of the inhabitants, and its legality would be determined by the principle of equal rights and by the ballot. Each region would have local self-administration in its territory and would enjoy an autonomous character. These self-administrative bodies, which would be autonomous legislative councils, would decide on the language that the state or the provincial establishment would use.

Territory was the basis of a people's existence, but there was no need to grant self-determination to all peoples or independence to all territories. Each act of this kind would be determined by the economic conditions in the country concerned. For instance, there should be a federation of peoples in the Balkan countries, which would liberate the peasantry from the yoke of the local feudal rulers and would liquidate the landowners.[19] The situation created in the Balkans by a lack of capitalist development and consequently the lack of a proletariat was, according to Lenin, one example out of many.

In the case of Russia, Lenin proposed that Poland and Finland should be granted the right of self-determination and secession, but in his correspondence with the communists of Azerbaijan, Georgia, Armenia, and Dagestan, he called for a united front against the desire for secession and brandished the

Bolshevik slogan of territorial unity under the Soviet banner.[20] Lenin regarded a desire for conquest or a lust for territory as imperialism or chauvinism, but the explanation of his ambiguous position was that he was a member of the dominant Greater Russian people.

As we have seen, the cornerstone of Lenin's solution to the national problem, from the beginning of his political career, was the peoples' demand for self-determination and freedom to break away from a larger entity. This demand went together with the need for a popular army, for election of officials by the people, and for separation of church and state.[21] In the Leninist discourse, the meaning of self-determination was the political separation of a people from another people that opposes it in a given territory.[22] This demand can come from any people that feels itself to be oppressed, and it must be made through a democratic process such as a plebiscite or elections. This may seem to be a bourgeois requirement, but Lenin, in a typical dialectic, was interested in bringing the democratic bourgeoisie to power.[23] Proletarian support of a bourgeois regime was not motivated by love of the bourgeoisie but by foresight: the democratic bourgeoisie would advance the proletariat with its actions and would bring it to power in turn. But there was a difference between the demand for self-determination of the capitalist bourgeoisie and the demand for self-determination of the proletariat, which saw itself as a candidate.[24]

What was the task of the proletariat in the national question? Lenin thought it was a dual one: first, to suppress nationalism of any kind whatsoever, and especially Greater Russian nationalism, and second, to grant full equality of rights to all peoples, including political rights such of those of self-determination and secession.[25] Nationalism, in his opinion, was essentially negative because by definition it was interested in oppressing other peoples, and the task of the proletariat was to combat every form of nationalism. Self-determination was an essentially bourgeois objective that had to be encouraged in a long-term perspective until the time was ripe for the socialist revolution. Internationalism and the withering-away of the state in the communist stage of history would completely eliminate the demand for nationhood.

In the introduction to his "Critique of Political Economy" (1859), Marx made the famous assertion that social life determines human consciousness. Lenin deduced from this, concerning the relationship to the cultural processes of various nations, that the cultural problem is secondary to the economic problem. He supported state education and the equality of all languages. Carl Renner and Otto Bauer favored a federation of peoples with a comprehensive cultural approach. Lenin regarded this position as "national culture", which was essentially bourgeois and reactionary, because the proletariat saw itself as constituting an international democratic culture and an international class.[26] Nationalism was by its very nature the oppression of another culture.

Where education was concerned, Lenin wanted to expose the nakedness of national culture. Placing all the schools in a single territory would not be possible because it would create a policy of discrimination between one school and another. In the Southern United States, for example, education was essentially antiblack, while in the North it was more or less egalitarian. Another example was that of Salzburg in Austria, where only three children were in a school because they were of a different nationality. Lenin thought that, from a democratic point of view, the preference for one form of education or another is a necessity and that, from the point of view of the proletariat, workers' education must be international, not local,[27] because "the workers of the world will create their own international culture". Cultural autonomy in his opinion would divide up the workers into many different areas and industries; hence his opposition to this kind of autonomy. Education in schools depended on the economic situation, and thus "splitting them up by providing a national education is a chauvinistic approach: cultural life is an inseparable part of economic life".[28] Economics determine the education of the masses, not the opposite.

According to Lenin, the solution to the problem of education in Russia was the creation of regional educational councils that would correspond to the cultural and educational needs of the population. As a mixed demographic cultural unit, there should not be fewer than twenty members in a council, which would demonstrate its importance. In the councils, there should be absolute equality between one language and another and between one form of education and another, whether from an administrative or from an educational point of view.[29] Lenin attacked those who saw cultural mixtures or mixtures of languages as something artificial. Languages would be matched to economic requirements and commercial interests, and the people would always favor these interests over combinations of languages that have no economic use. Lenin gave Switzerland and Finland as cogent examples of a diversity of languages in relation to the number of inhabitants.[30] A Russification of language was thus contrary to his view that "an equality of languages is an inseparable part of social-democratic doctrine, and this doctrine is part of civic equality".[31] In practical terms, Lenin called for the languages to be determined in every area by a local self-administrative body and autonomous legislative councils. These bodies would be directed by the state and the provincial or legal establishment, but every national minority would have the right to decide on its language on a basis of equality.[32]

Lenin's position with regard to education, culture, and language was ambivalent. On the one hand, he opposed the Russification of language and favored giving every people full freedom to speak and write in its own, and on the other hand he favored a single education for all and a prohibition of separate national forms of education. Despite Lenin's declaration of the founding of a single governmental educational system and the annulment of the educational programs of the former czarist educational system, a chain of national schools arose among all the territorial peoples and, in the 1920s, among the extraterritorial peoples as well.

The Infantile Disorders of Nationhood in History

Lenin thought that in history nationalism only began with the final victory of capitalism over feudalism. The defeat of feudalism made possible the creation of national movements, and modern capitalism found complete fulfillment only in the framework of the nation-state. It was economic factors from the time of the French Revolution onward that determined that the path of nationalism led to the nation-state.[33]

In most Western countries, said Lenin, there was a bourgeois-democratic state in the years 1789–1817, but in multinational states like Russia and Austria, the change to a bourgeois-democratic regime was not yet completed. One could speak of two periods in the capitalist era: that of the disappearance of feudalism of every kind and the rise of capitalism and that of the rise of classic capitalist states and the development of the confrontation between the bourgeoisie and the proletariat, "a period that can be called the period of capitalist decline. In the first period, the nation-states were created, and in the second the states developed the power of capitalism".[34]

What caused the formation of capitalism, and, as a result, the rise of nations and nationalism? Its domination of the production of goods caused the bourgeoisie to take over the home market and establish a political-territorial unity and an economic basis for the nationalist movement. Language accelerated the communication between the various sections of the population and made possible a direct connection between the person of means and the market and between the buyer and the seller. As a result, every national movement encouraged the use of a single language with the same requirements, which were governed by capitalist demands.[35]

Nationalism took its first steps "as a result of a struggle against the repression of a nation which produced the desire for a state". The next stage was a rapid growth of connections between states that broke asunder the chains of nationhood and created an international unity of capital, economic life, politics, science, and so on.[36] This gave rise to two historical developments: one was the awakening of national life and the nationalist movement, the subjugation of oppressed peoples, and the creation of nation-states, and the other was the acceleration of the development of international relations through a unification of economic, political, and cultural life.[37] What was the role of the proletariat in these processes? Lenin's answer was "to help the bourgeoisie get rid of feudal servitude, suppression of the people and national and linguistic privileges".

National development was the handiwork of the bourgeoisie. The first stage, the universal right to self-determination, led to the second, the unification of the peoples as a capitalist requirement. Modern capitalism reached fulfillment in the nation-state. The proletariat needed to encourage national development, which caused the suppression of the privileges of one people at the expense of another and eventually led to the development of the means of production, which hastened the arrival of socialism as a transitional stage and internationalism as a final stage.

Lenin judged world populations according to two criteria:[38] homogeneous versus heterogeneous populations, and politically free countries versus ones that are politically dependent. Lenin's idea was that in every block of states where the population was more or less homogeneous, like the countries of Western Europe, the United States and Japan, there was hardly any national repression.

The countries of Western Europe, which had a homogeneous population, could be divided into three groups: countries without a national minority like Italy, Holland, Portugal, Sweden, Norway, Spain, and Denmark; countries with a small national minority like Germany, Britain, and France; and countries with large national minorities like Switzerland and Belgium. In the blocs of states where the population was homogeneous, the peoples were equal before the law. Out of twelve such states, in which there were 272 million souls, only four percent were repressed. The capitalist countries consequently had widespread economic development, political freedom, and a very high cultural level. On the other hand, in countries like Austria, Turkey, Russia, and the six Baltic states, there was national repression due to a heterogeneous population and a lack of national equality.

Lenin's analysis led him to certain conclusions with regard to Russia. Because fifty-seven percent of the non-Russian population was repressed, he proposed adopting the solutions of Marx and Engels and adapting them to the Russian situation, at the same time recognizing that "no people or language is privileged".[39] The political solution lay in his obligation to grant peoples freedom of self-determination and the possibility of political and cultural separation. As one commentator said, "It seems that the right to self-determination is the magic key to the solution of the national problem".[40]

Lenin retained a theoretical consistency throughout his political career. There was only a change in the forms of expression in different times and places. In 1903, against the background of the declaration of the Armenian Social-Democratic League, a declaration that concerned the solution to the national problem in general and the Armenian one in particular, Lenin stated that every man has the right to self-determination expressed in a comprehensive development of regional administration that would protect heterogeneous elements.[41] Later that year, he made a similar declaration, recognizing "the right to self-determination of all the peoples that constitute the state". He added, "We will not kill ourselves in this struggle because we social-democrats, the party of the proletariat, support the proletariat of every people above all, more than we support the struggle for the self-determination of peoples".[42] The tactic was thus consistent: the right to self-determination or secession was a transitional stage to socialism or the withering-away of the state: "The aim of socialism is not only splitting up humanity into small states, the elimination of isolationism between states, or bringing peoples close to each other. The aim is to fuse them. Just as humanity will not achieve the elimination of classes without the dictatorship of the oppressed in the transitional stage, so it will not achieve the inevitable fusion of all oppressed peoples—proletarian liberty".[43]

In his article, "Left-wing Communism, An Infantile Disorder", Lenin stated that "as long as there are national and political differences between peoples and countries, and these differences are of long duration, even after the establishment of the dictatorship of the proletariat there must be a tactical international union of the communist workers of all countries, not a rejection of national differences".[44] Lenin, unlike Marx, was sure that the question of the state was one of the immediate objectives of the proletarian struggle. The state itself was revealed as a weapon in the class struggle, one of the weapons wielded by the government for the preservation of a class.[45] That was the reason Lenin wanted a national solution as a tactic appropriate to the time and place. Hence Lenin's relative approach to the political context, and in this he followed his doctrinal master: "According to Marx, the solution to the national problem depends on an individual judgement of each particular case".[46] Examples of this are the solutions proposed by Marx to the problem of Poland, his opposition to the self-determination of the Slavic peoples, and his recommendation for Ireland to secede from England and later rejoin it in a federation. Lenin said: "In these days [1916], the national problem must be seen differently. Today there are five major powers in the world which oppress other peoples, a fact which requires a reassessment".[47]

In 1913, three years before this declaration, Lenin added to his usual statement in favor of the "self-determination of all peoples" the principle of "the right of secession".[48] Every state can secede from the country it is part of if it so desires. In May 1917, he declared that it was the right of every people in the Russian state to break away from it and create a free country. The republic of the Russian people had to liberate the other peoples not by violence but by agreement. However, two years later, in 1919, after he had been in power for about a year and a half, Lenin qualified this position by saying "the right of secession is dependent on the historical status and level of historical development of a people from the middle ages to bourgeois democracy and from the bourgeoisie to the soviets or the democracy of the proletariat".[49] A sense of historical relativity allows us to understand the reason for this statement, which was made from a position of power.

An example of Lenin's solution to the national problem was that arrived at in the case of Norway and Sweden. In his opinion, it was a desirable solution because it satisfied both the right of secession and the principle of self-determination. The democratic plebiscite in Norway in 1905 that decided the question of the secession of the Norwegian people from the Swedish people and the establishment of a Norwegian state could be the criterion for a solution of any national problem.[50] The three components of a solution were the following:

> 1. The right to self-determination. 2. The right of secession. 3. A guarantee of the rights of a national minority derived from the principle of absolute equality, which means not granting any state additional rights and granting full and equal rights to national minorities.[51]

And what was the role of the proletariat with regard to these principles? According to Lenin, "Only the proletariat can in our time bring true liberty to all nations and bring about the unification of the workers of all nations". The proletariat would make certain that no people or language would be privileged "on even the lowest level of oppression or injustice towards a national minority". Such were the principles of a democratic working class.[52] The party of the social-democratic proletariat would also declare "the right of all peoples to self-determination, and would stand for full democracy, equal rights for all inhabitants without regard for sex, language, race, nationality or religion".[53] The Leninist solution sought to be pragmatic and adaptable to any nation.

Socialist ideology aims not only at ending the division of humankind into small states and suppressing national particularism but at creating a convergence between peoples and a fusion between them. This would take place in two stages: a period of liberation and a period of amalgamation. This theory, which Lenin arrived at after the summer of 1913, resulted from a development of the principle of self-determination.[54] Lenin specifically stated that one should not grant a self-determination that provided only national rights but one that also provided political rights: in other words, total independence. A fusion of peoples would take place in conditions created by a democracy in which there would be total equality between peoples and in which every state would have the right to self-determination and political secession. After democracy, which divides humanity, socialism would end the division into small states, bring them close to one another, and even unite them.

Thus, national separation is not required in the first stage of socialism, but a large centralized state. This would come about through a plebiscite or some other democratic process and would be an important historical development because it would advance the socialist unification of the entire world.[55] This large centralized state could not be Russia because it lacked the historical conditions required by every Marxist: it was not democratic, it did not have a socialist foundation, and it was based on despotism and bureaucracy.

To the question of how the socialist revolution would be carried out in practice, Lenin replied that such a revolution was likely to happen in the wake of large demonstrations, famines, riots, or a military uprising. Any of these occurrences or all of them together could provoke a political crisis. Political crises would result in plebiscites or elections, which would accelerate the struggle among the peoples and cause them to break away from the oppressing state. This analysis would be put to the test when a socialist regime replaces the capitalist one.

In the capitalist stage, however, there are oppressing and oppressed states, in which the classes have not yet disappeared. The proletariat would bring salvation when it eliminated the classes. The tactics used by the proletariat would combine a fight for the legitimate rights of the worker with a complete unification of the workers of all nations in education, trade unions, and politics. The struggle for the legitimate rights of all peoples does not grant privileges to any bourgeois nation, for that could weaken the international solidarity of the working class and divide the workers. This unification of the workers, initially based on a dictatorship of the oppressed classes, would aim at a total integration of the world proletariat and of the nations of the world and would be implemented in the transitional stage of national equality.

Lenin called for the Russian social democrats and for all the parties that represented the proletariat to unite in the interests of a free Russia or, in other words, to be more active in recognizing the right of the non-Russian peoples to self-determination. He did not change his slogans when he came to power, but when the Ukrainians asked for independence, he said that their policy was petty-bourgeois: "We are internationalists; we support the union of all the workers of the world and its peasantry, and we are therefore first and foremost in favor of a unification of the Ukrainian proletariat and peasantry and the Russian one [. . .] The demand of the Ukrainian communists reflects a petty-bourgeois policy".[56] Thus, Lenin chose a solution that was in contradiction to his teaching and that placed it in doubt. Was not the Ukrainian demand for independence an action that Lenin had constantly supported, an action covered by the right of every people to self-determination and to decide on the borders of the state according to the will of the inhabitants and its right of total freedom to secede?[57] Did he not attack the Polish Social-Democratic Party, which opposed the secession of Poland from Russia on the grounds that the freedom to unite depended on the freedom to secede, and one could not exist without the other?

In his vision of the future fusion of the peoples, Lenin's support for the self-determination and freedom of secession of all peoples was purely tactical, because in his opinion, "the creation of a nationality in the capitalist era is a bourgeois action, and it will therefore disappear with the destruction of capitalism". Consequently, national sentiment is no guarantee of freedom. Nationalism is a phenomenon that will pass away with the victory of socialism. Until that time, the proletariat will seek to grant all peoples the democratic possibility of choosing its future as an independent state, while the overriding intention is the creation of a large centralized democratic state. The fusion of the peoples is the final stage, when the division of mankind into small counties is eliminated and all national differences are annulled.[58]

1914: "From an Imperialist War to a Socialist War"

"Imperialism, the Highest Stage of Capitalism" is considered one of the most revolutionary essays in the history of political thought in general and of Marxist theory in particular.[59] In this essay, the First World War was seen as an imperialist war in which the participants were imperialist nations: "This imperialist war is a direct continuation and culmination of capitalism, for it is a war for the privileges of the peoples of the great powers, and a war for the redistribution of the positions of the great powers in their rule over other peoples".[60]

Imperialism, said Lenin, has five basic characteristics: (1) a situation in which the concentration of wealth and production has reached such an advanced stage that there are monopolies that play a decisive role in economic life; (2) a merger of bank capital and industrial capital, and the creation of a financial oligarchy on the basis of this "financial capital"; (3) a situation in which the exportation of capital as distinct from the exportation of goods is of special importance; (4).a situation in which there is a creation of international capitalist monopolies that divide up the world between them; (5) a territorial division of the world among the main capitalist powers.

The First World War was unavoidable, and, in Lenin's opinion, the bourgeois governments in Europe prepared it for decades. The arms race, the rivalry for markets, the development of capitalism in the developed countries to a new imperialist level, the dynastic interests of the Eastern European monarchies, the dimming of the class consciousness of the proletariat, the desire to impose national divisions on the workers—all this inevitably led to a world war between two groups of belligerent nations.[61] At the head of one group stood Germany, and at the head of the other group stood Britain and France. Lenin explained the significance of this modern war in caustic terms:

> The plundering of territories and the subjugation of nations, the destruction of the rival nation, the distraction of the working masses from the internal crises in Russia, Germany, Britain and the United States, the imposition of national division and stultification on the workers, the destruction of their vanguard in order to weaken the revolutionary movement of the proletariat—that is the only true content, that is the reality and that is the meaning of war in our time.[62]

According to Lenin, the German bourgeoisie hoodwinked the proletariat in their country by saying that it was defending the motherland, freedom, and culture, that it was liberating oppressed peoples and sought to uproot reactionary czarism. But in reality the German bourgeoisie and the Junker aristocracy had always been faithful allies of the czars and enemies of the Russian workers and peasants. Under the cover of the war, the German bourgeoisie and Junkers directed their efforts in support of the czarist regime and against the revolution in Russia. Germany, said Lenin, attacked Serbia in order to suppress the national revolution of the Southern Serbs and at the same time turned its armed forces against countries with greater freedom, Britain and France, in order to forestall its imperialist rivals.

This was opposed by Britain and France, whose real objective was to acquire the German colonies and weaken a competing nation that was economically highly developed. They prepared the armies of the czarist regime—"the most reactionary and barbaric monarchy in Europe"—to attack Germany. Within the framework of this process, the "advanced" democratic nations helped the czarist regime to oppress Poland and the Ukraine and to crush the Bolshevik Revolution in Russia more effectively.

The three congresses of the Second International warned of an imminent European imperialist war.[63] Lenin said that the Basel resolution of 1912 located the imperialist conflicts of 1914. In his opinion, the two groups of imperialist states were not essentially different, but in order to mislead the proletariat in their countries and divert their attention from the real war, the class war—that is, the war of the people against the bourgeoisie in "their" countries and in the "foreign" countries—they made false rhetorical declarations about patriotism.[64] They tried in this way to arouse enthusiasm for a national war and foster the illusion of fighting for victory over the adversary. They claimed to liberate nations, but their actions were totally imperialistic.

Lenin related to the First World War in a way that could be described as "Let them fight it out!", but he nevertheless was not opposed to the war in principle and was contemptuous of the pacifism of capital and the pillage and oppression of foreign colonies and states. His strategy was to keep aloof from the imperialist game, which accounts for his negative attitude to the First World War: "Imperialism is the growth of capital to the point where it exceeds the framework of national states, the extension of national oppression and placing it on a new historical foundation". The First World War embodied this "new historical foundation".

In his article "The Junius Pamphlet" of August 1916, Lenin denied the "myth of the liberating national character of the war", saying that the war was essentially imperialist and not national.[65] The basic assumption in Marxist dialectics is that all boundaries in nature and society are elastic: there is nothing that cannot in certain conditions become its opposite. A national war can become imperialist and the contrary. The wars of the French Revolution began as national wars, but when Napoleon created a French empire by subjugating national states, the French wars became imperialistic. They in turn gave rise to national wars of liberation against the Napoleonic empire.

Lenin had difficulty in understanding how the World War could be a national war, for the class that represented dialectical development was the proletariat, which objectively aimed at turning the war into a civil war against the bourgeoisie. In certain conditions, Lenin wrote, there could be a situation in which there would be a national war in Europe, if the proletariat in Europe were ineffective for twenty years, if the present war ended in victories like those of Napoleon and the subjugation of many nation-states, if the imperialism outside Europe continued for twenty more years without becoming socialist.

The only national element in the war was represented by Serbia's struggle against Austria. If that was isolated and not connected to the general European war, all socialists, according to Lenin, would have wanted the victory for Serbia. But there was no national basis to the Serbian-Austrian War, and it had no real significance in the present war:

> If Germany wins, she will throttle Belgium, one more part of Poland, perhaps part of France, etc. If Russia wins, she will throttle Galicia, one more part of Poland, Armenia, etc. If the war ends in a "draw", the old national oppression will remain. To Serbia, i.e., to perhaps one per cent or so of the participants in the present war, the war is a "continuation of the politics" of the bourgeois liberation movement. To the other ninety-nine per cent, the war is a continuation of the politics of imperialism, i.e., of the decrepit bourgeoisie, which is capable only of raping nations, not freeing them.[66]

Lenin distinguished between the imperialist bourgeoisie, reactionary with regard to the dialectic of historical development, and the liberating, progressive bourgeoisie that fought against feudalism and absolutism. In his controversy with Lenin, Kautsky claimed that, from the beginning of the war, the political connections that had developed in the course of history between one people and another and one class and another had been discontinued and that there was a completely new situation in which attacking peoples faced defensive peoples. In that situation, the national interest was paramount.

Lenin replied that the wars he had mentioned had continued the policies of bourgeois national movements, and as such they were positive accelerators of revolution. This principle did not apply to the imperialist bourgeoisie represented by the two groups fighting in the First World War, whose sole purpose was to oppress peoples, retain colonies, and gain possessions. The common belief during the war that: "national wars are no longer possible" was mistaken, for two reasons: theoretically, because it was a training in indifference to national movements, and politically because that indifference becomes chauvinism when the peoples of the great European nations declare the impossibility of national wars. National wars against imperialist powers were not only possible and likely to happen but were progressive and revolutionary.

Lenin's attitude to colonies was colored by his distinction between national and imperialist wars. In the imperialist era, national wars by colonies or semi-colonies are part of the situation and even necessary. Movements of national liberation increase, and the political struggles of colonies against imperialism take the form of national wars that foment imperialist wars between powers. For example, the Seven Years' War, which Britain and France fought over colonies, was an imperialist war in all respects. The British colonies in America that fought for national liberation from Britain and from France and Spain, which still controlled parts of the country, also had an imperialist aspect. It was an example of a war of national liberation in which imperialist rivalry was an auxiliary factor, unlike the situation in 1914. One should not rule out the possibility of national wars in Europe in the imperialist era such as those of small countries against imperialist powers or of national movements in Eastern Europe.

National rebellions and crises of imperialism were bound up with the First World War. The British suppressed the Indian troops that rebelled in Singapore, In French Annam and in the Cameroons, the Germans attempted to revolt, in Europe the British suppressed the rebellion of the Irish with the death sentence, and the Austrian government sentenced the representatives of the Czech Sejm to death for treason.[67] Although Lenin saw the "first world" as imperialist and not national, there could not in his opinion be a social revolution without rebellions in the colonies, without the revolutionary participation of a few of the bourgeois, without a general mass movement against property owners, the Church, the monarchy, and the state.

Lenin's conclusion was that social democracy has to reveal the true significance of the war and ruthlessly expose the lie and rhetoric of 'patriotism' put out by the ruling classes and property owners to justify the war. The aim of the social-democratic parties in Europe should be "turning a war of the nations into civil war is the only socialist activity in the era of an imperialist armed conflict of the bourgeoisie of all nations".[68]

The Second International (1889–1914), founded when Lenin was nineteen years old, brought together all the social-democratic parties that recognized the centrality of class warfare. This vague formula applied to the Russian one, which called for the overthrow of the capitalist system in a revolution and the building of socialism through the institution of a dictatorship of the proletariat. It also embraced parties with a reformist platform, like the Social-Democratic Party in Germany, which saw class warfare as a peaceful transition and supported parliamentary reform toward socialism. The revolution, however, was empty rhetoric devoid of content. Most of the socialists were shown not to be ready for the revolutionary situation that the war had brought about. Although the Russian Social-Democratic Party was small and illegal and political migrants served in it as delegates to the international congress, it was the leader of a flank of the Second International and sought real content instead of lip service to revolutionary Marxist rhetoric. Hence its struggle to establish a new type of revolutionary party in Russia.

Lenin denounced most of the leaders of the Second International, for exchanging socialism for nationalism. The leaders of internationalism called on the working class to support the belligerent governments, to vote in the parliaments for budgetary allocations for the war, to support the war, and to infiltrate the bourgeois institutions of the fighting countries. This position of the leaders of the social-democratic parties prevented the labor parties in these countries from rebelling against the bourgeois governments. Lenin wrote in his article "The War and Russian Social Democracy" (October 1914): "It is with feelings of most bitter disappointment that we must point out the fact that the social-democratic parties of the chief countries of western Europe have failed to do their duty, and the conduct of these parties borders on betrayal of socialism".[69] In his opinion, the support of the war by the socialist parties, and especially the German and Austrian social democrats, even harmed the Russian Revolution: the war helped the czar in his fight against Russian democracy and the working class because France and Britain financed the aims of czarism. In his article, "The Collapse of the Second International"[70] (summer 1915), Lenin spoke of the connection between social chauvinism and opportunism. By the term "social chauvinism", Lenin meant the idea of defending the motherland in the present imperialist war, justifying the alliance of the socialists with the bourgeoisie and with the governments of the countries participating in the war, and the failure of the socialists to advocate and promulgate revolutionary proletarian action against the bourgeoisie.[71]

Lenin was not a thinker who considered the writings of Marx and Engels the words of the living God. As in his attitude to the question of the peasants, a key question for the success of the revolution, he knew how to interpret the main lines set out by Marx and Engels. In his opinion, "opportunism in the present war is accompanied by social chauvinism", and its aim was inter-class collaboration.[72] The great aim of the Second International of "uniting all the workers of the world" foundered on the rocks of the First World War. The division of the labor movement in the hour of testing into its separate national parts was a severe blow to the Marxist-internationalist idea. Lenin was not willing to accept this defeat, which was also a defeat for him personally, and he found ideological pretexts for the collapse of the 1914 International. The Western socialists were accused of exchanging socialist revolution for "bourgeois republicanism", of rejecting class warfare, and of abandoning the basic idea of socialism—that workers have no motherland. The idea that nationalism could overpower the revolution and that the particular could defeat the universal was hard for him to take.

Revolution and Nationalism

From 1914 onward, it was clear that there could not be a formal pan-European framework that would bring together members of different peoples with the same ideology. The question remained how, nevertheless, there could be a broad supranational framework for advocates of Marxist teachings. Lenin chose to narrow the framework, providing it was clearly defined, effective, and stood the test of time. The Comintern, the Third International, founded in March 1919 as an association of world communist parties, was an attempt to create a formal framework for people with the same ideas. The Russian Revolution failed in its objective of being the vanguard of a world revolution that had been long in coming. Years later, the Warsaw Pact was another example of a vision of unity that failed and likewise had to come to terms with the depressing postrevolutionary situation after the Second World War.[73] The collapse of the Second International was a slap in the face for Lenin's faith in international cooperation among the workers of Europe who had cast off their national chains. His despair of the possibility of healing the breach with the revisionists and his attitude to "treacherous opportunists" were reflections of short-term policies and the abandonment of world revolution.

One of Lenin's well-known sayings reflected the breakup of the camp: "To a Marxist, it is obvious that a revolution cannot happen without a revolutionary situation, but not every revolutionary situation brings about a revolution".[74] A revolutionary situation has three elements: a crisis in the authority of the ruling class, an inability of the ruling class to retain its power, increasing bitterness of the oppressed classes, and consequently greater activity of the masses. In a revolutionary situation, all these elements come together for a short period. Did the First World War among the various "imperialist" nations contain a "revolution situation" within it, as the 1905 revolution was thought to have done? Lenin believed that it did: there was a political and economic crisis throughout Europe, the political regime was being undermined and the war spread; together with a deepening of the distress and bitterness of the oppressed classes, the war profits of "capitalist groups" increased immeasurably. The longer the war lasted, the more glaring the contrasts became.

The failure of the 1848 uprising taught Marx a lesson: when the social conditions for a class revolution are not yet ripe, there can only be a political revolution. Like his master, Lenin thought that "the experience of war causes a torpor of the senses and cleavages of the soul in some, but it opens the eyes of others and galvanizes them".[75] By and large, Lenin believed that in most of the advanced countries and in most of the great European powers, a revolutionary situation existed, but "how long will it last, and how much worse will this revolutionary situation become? Will it bring about a revolution? We don't know".[76]

Lenin was not a determinist, nor was he a chronicler. His aim was to activate the revolution, and one of the ways of doing it was to intensify the class consciousness of a revolutionary cadre that could guide the masses. Hence the importance he attached to understanding the significance of historical events, and the matter on the agenda at that time was the war. Was the war a progressive factor that accelerated a revolutionary situation? Would the warring sides share the fruits of victory and world markets, or would the winner of the confrontation be some other factor? What would the gains and losses amount to? As a clear-sighted politician, Lenin knew that these questions affected his political objectives: "Opening the eyes of the masses to the reality of the revolutionary situation, awakening the revolutionary consciousness and revolutionary power of the proletariat, helping it to take revolutionary action".[77]

The situation was not static, and therefore the revolution would not break out at the same time in all places: "Capitalism is not so harmoniously built that the various sources of rebellion can immediately merge of their own accord, without reverses and defeats. On the other hand, the very fact that revolts do break out at different times, in different places, and are of different kinds, guarantees wide scope and depth to the general movement".[78] This statement in Lenin's article "The Irish Rebellion of 1916" relates to the failure of that rebellion. In his opinion, the imperialist nations exploited the breaches in the rival camp. The Germans exploited the Irish rebellion, and the French exploited the Czech independence movement. He observed, "We would be very poor revolutionaries if, in the great war for the liberation of the proletariat for socialism, we did not exploit every popular movement caused by particular fissures in imperialism to create a worsening and broadening of the crisis".[79] Once again, Lenin miscalculated: although national rebellions in imperialist countries helped the revolution and broadened its scope, "the misfortune of the Irish was that their rebellion came too early, before the European revolt of the proletariat was ready".

The success of the revolution in Russia was also the failure of the Marxist revolutionary model: the success of the revolution in one place put an end to the spread of world revolution. The intervention of the Entente Powers in financing the "Whites" in the civil war in Russia (1919–1920) and their direct support for them and activities on their behalf did not succeed in nullifying the achievements of the Bolshevik Revolution, but they prevented the spread of the revolution to Europe. The historian Christopher Hill's opinion that "all the great revolutions had international consequences" was also held by Marx himself and by the Russian revolutionaries who saw their activities as part of an international process and did not want them to be judged only by the results in their own countries. The First World War, which created a revolutionary situation, could in the final analysis have resulted in a revolution of the proletariat. Not every revolutionary situation brings about a revolution, but there cannot be a revolution without a revolutionary situation. Lenin was convinced that all peoples would reach socialism, but they would not all reach it by the same route.

On the 8th of November 1917, just after the October revolution, Lenin and the revolutionary leaders approached the two sides in the First World War and proposed making peace "without annexations or indemnities", a peace based on "the principle of national self-determination". When the Bolsheviks came to power, they had no alternative to making peace.[80] There was no theoretical objection to "revolutionary self-defence", and the practical difficulties in continuing the revolution were tremendous. The army was disintegrating, and the soldiers and peasants hastened back to their villages to participate in the distribution of land. The Bolsheviks immediately declared the right of oppressed peoples to secede from Russia, publishing and denouncing the secret pacts between the sides, and, in all the belligerent states, the communists pressed for them to enter into negotiations for a comprehensive peace.

The conditions of the Soviet government for entering into negotiations included a demand for the self-determination of all the belligerent parties in the spirit of President Woodrow Wilson's fourteen points.[81] The Entente rejected the Bolsheviks' demand, and the stream of supplies that the Western allies sent to Russia halted. In August 1918, Lenin responded: "The Russian capitalists are holding out their hand to the British and French capitalists and property-owners". On the 2nd of December, the first meeting between the Soviet peace delegation and the delegation of the Central Powers took place at Brest-Litovsk, and two weeks later a cease-fire agreement was signed. The Soviet delegation exploited this stage observed by many people in Europe, and Trotsky called on the peoples of all the belligerent states to overthrow their governments and make a comprehensive peace. Unlike Trotsky, who wanted to continue negotiating and to spread revolutionary propaganda, Hoffmann, the German delegate, demanded a quick peace and the severance of Poland, Lithuania, and most of Latvia and western White Russia from Russia. The appearance of a Ukrainian peace delegation demanding self-determination only made matters worse. Trotsky rushed to Petrograd to reach a decision: peace or war.[82]

On the twentieth of January 1918, Lenin published his "Hypotheses" (thesis), in which he asked for "peace at any price", "peace no matter what", in order to obtain "the breathing-space of a lull". As against this, the left-wing social revolutionaries and the left-wing communists under the leadership of Bukharin demanded "revolutionary war". Trotsky adopted an intermediate position, "neither peace nor war". At the end of February, British forces began to arrive in Murmansk, and Lenin decided that Russia had to make a separate peace, fearing that the British and Germans would reach an agreement at Russia's expense. Lenin wished to overcome the stubborn opposition of Trotsky and others who, intoxicated with the victory of the revolution, were willing to risk everything and rely on revolutions taking place soon in Western Europe. Lenin insisted that the primary duty of the party was to preserve the existence of the Soviet republic in Russia and thought that foreign policy could not be based on conjectures concerning world revolution. Lenin made his party accept his choice while he took the most disagreeable step that had ever been required:

> If you're not willing to adapt yourself, if you don't have it in you to grovel in the dust, you're just a bloated skin-bag! I'm proposing this not because the thing is particularly pleasant for me, but because no other path is open to us, because it doesn't seem that history is forthcoming enough to stir up revolution everywhere at once.

Taking advantage of the indecisiveness in Russia, the Germans steadily advanced and went on the attack from the Black Sea to the Baltic with a force of thirty divisions, fifteen of them moving in the direction of Petrograd. Lenin came to the conclusion that Russia had to agree to peace at any price, exploit the lull for an economic and military recovery, and expect a revolution in Germany. Lenin's policy was finally accepted, but, before that happened, many territories were lost that would not have been taken if Trotsky's policy of creating facts on the ground had not been followed. Despite the Soviet government's announcement of its readiness to accept the German terms, Germany toughened its conditions: Estonia, Latvia, Lithuania, White Russia up to the Dnieper, the Ukraine, and Crimea were taken from Russia, and Germany undertook to decide "their fate in the future". Russia agreed to recognize the independence of the Ukraine and Finland and to disarm.

By the treaty of Brest-Litovsk, Russia lost a quarter of its territory, a third of its population, and two-thirds of its coal and iron, but meanwhile the Red Army had been created. "Because of this 'robbers' peace", Lenin said to Bruce Lockhart, Germany had to have more armed forces in the east.[83] Passive resistance, he said, is a more effective weapon than an army that is unable to fight. "We are giving up territory in order to gain time", he said, and in the newspaper *Pravda*, he wrote that it was a cease-fire, not a peace. Lenin signed the treaty but refused to read the text. In the Brest-Litovsk episode, he acted more coolheadedly than Trotsky, and already in 1916 he realized that socialism could not be victorious in all countries simultaneously.

Lenin was revealed as a consistent thinker and a pragmatic politician who did not adhere to abstract principles with regard to revolution.[84] He supported a general strategy of keeping his country out of the First World War, the arena of the "struggle of the imperialist nations". The propaganda that issued from Brest-Litovsk called on the peoples of Europe to dissociate themselves from the militaristic policies of their governments, and in 1918, the war came to an end. While seizing power and institutionalizing the revolution, Lenin carried on a stormy controversy with his friends in the party with regard for the necessity for peace and was successful. Throughout all this time, he showed political insight and combined ideological extremism with a capacity to adapt.[85]

Implementation is a test for every Marxist thinker and leader. How can one realize the Marxist vision, a total doctrine that, as Lenin said, is like a rock that cannot be split? For Lenin, the test was to find a path between the theory and practical politics. His leadership was tested in four spheres: the timing of the revolution and its institutionalization, the war, the problem of the peasantry, and the question of peace. Lenin's approach to the national question was to realize in stages the vision of a universal classless society and at the same time to implement Engels's idea of the withering-away of the state. Did the Soviet state, which arose under Lenin's influence and political leadership, solve the problems to which he sought a solution in the twenty years that preceded it? Poland, Finland, and the Baltic states did indeed achieve political independence, but large peoples—the Ukrainians, the White Russians, and the Trans-Caucasians—did not benefit from the principle of self-determination despite Lenin's declarations. They were gradually annexed to the Soviet state.

From the time of the effervescence of April 1917, Lenin changed direction. He accepted Trotsky's doctrine of revolution in stages and was a renegade when he came to power with regard to a pragmatic solution to the national question. He was faced with many problems: the struggle within the party, the World War, the institutionalization of Marxism, the civil war, and the threat from the Western powers. The truth of Lenin's assertion that the quality of national independence is shown in its deeds was demonstrated in the years immediately following the Bolshevik Revolution. After the 1930s, the Soviet Union coalesced as a multinational state until Michael Gorbachev began to move in a direction from which there was no return.

Notes

1. Sheila Fitzpatrick, ed., *Cultural Revolution in Russia*, Bloomington 1978; idem, ed., *The Russian Revolution*, New York 1982.
2. Hal Draper, "The Dictatorship of the Proletariat", in *From Marx to Lenin*, New York 1987.
3. Victor Sebestyen, *Lenin: The Man, the Dictator, and the Master of Terror*, New York 2017; Christopher Read, *Lenin: A Revolutionary Life*, London 2005.
4. Mikhail Agursky, *The Third Rome—National Bolshevism in the USSR*, London 1987.
5. Robert Vincent Daniels, *Trotsky, Stalin and Socialism*, Boulder, CO 1991.
6. Dmitri Volkogonov, *Lenin: A New Biography*, New York 1994.
7. Joseph Stalin, "The Foundations of Leninism", Reptd., in B. Franklin, ed., *The Essential Stalin*, London 1924; Joseph Stalin, "Lenin as the Organizer and Leader of the Russian Communist Party", in Lenin, ed., *Selected Works*, vol. 1, Moscow 1950.
8. Alfred D. Low, *Lenin on the Question of Nationality*, New York 1958, 28.
9. Hans Kohn, *Nationalism in the Soviet Union*, New York 1934, 42.
10. Vladimir I. Lenin, *Collected Works*, 45 vols., vol. 29, Moscow 1964–1970, 150–152.
11. Ibid., 151–152.
12. Stalin, *The Foundations of Leninism*, 33.
13. Lenin, vol. 7, 101.
14. Lenin, vol. 19, 72.

15 Ronald Grigor Suny and Terry Martin, eds., *A State of Nations: Empire and Nation-Making in the Age of Lenin and Stalin*, Oxford 2001.
16 Otto Bauer, *Die Nationalitatenfrage und die Sozialdemokratie*, Vienna 1907.
17 Lenin, vol. 16, 81.
18 Ibid., vol. 20, 281.
19 Ibid., vol. 19, 39.
20 Ibid., vol. 32, 319.
21 Ibid., vol. 22, 358.
22 Ibid., 146.
23 Low, *Lenin on the Question of Nationality*.
24 Lenin, vol. 18, 443.
25 Ibid., vol. 20, 45.
26 Ibid., vol. 21, 25.
27 Ibid., vol. 20, 224.
28 Ibid., vol. 21, 36–37.
29 Ibid., vol. 20, 218–284.
30 Ibid., vol. 21, 20.
31 Ibid., vol. 7, 282.
32 Ibid., vol. 20, 281.
33 Ibid., vol. 18, 440.
34 Ibid., vol. 20, 401.
35 Ibid, 396.
36 Ibid., vol. 18, 139.
37 Ibid., vol. 20, 27.
38 Ibid., vol. 23, 273.
39 Ibid., vol. 19, 87.
40 Low, *Lenin on the Question of Nationality*, 119.
41 Lenin, vol. 6, 328.
42 Ibid, 454.
43 Lenin, vol. 31, " 'Left-Wing' Communism: An Infantile Disorder", 17–118.
44 Ibid.
45 Georg Lukacs, *Lenin: A Study on the Unity of His Thought*, trans. Nicholas Jacobs, London 1970, 60–61.
46 Lenin, vol. 22, 343–339.
47 Ibid., vol. 22, 341.
48 Ibid., vol. 19, 88.
49 Ibid., vol. 29, 129.
50 Ibid.
51 Lenin, vol. 20, 425.
52 Ibid., vol. 20, 42.
53 Ibid., vol. 19, 495.
54 Low, *Lenin on the Question of Nationality*, 95.
55 Lenin, vol. 22, 22.
56 Ibid., vol. 30, 194.
57 Ibid., vol. 25, 92.
58 Ibid., vol. 1, 73.
59 Ibid., vol. 22, 185–300.
60 Ibid., 225.
61 Stanley W. Page, *The Geopolitics of Leninism*, New York 1982; Mikhail Pokrovsky, *Russia in World History*, ed., R. Szporluk, Ann Arbor 1970.
62 Lenin, vol. 21, 27.
63 The seventh congress in Stuttgart, August 1907, defined the wars among commercial countries as wars over "world markets". The eighth congress, convened in Copenhagen, August 1910, and the unconventional congress in Basel, 1912,

emphasized the danger in European wars and amplified the imperial essence of the war to come.

64 Lenin, vol. 21, 221–222.
65 Ibid., vol. 22, 308–309.
66 Ibid., vol. 21, 235–236.
67 Ibid., vol. 22, 353.
68 Ibid., vol. 21, 34.
69 Ibid., vol. 21, 27–28
70 Ibid., "The Collapse of the Second International", vol. 21, 309.
71 Ibid.
72 Philip Longworth, *The Making of Eastern Europe*, New York 1959.
73 Lenin, "The Collapse of the Second International".
74 Ibid.
75 Ibid., 184–185.
76 Ibid.
77 Lenin, vol. 22, 358.
78 Ibid., 337.
79 John W. Wheeler-Bennett, *Brest-Litovsk: The Forgotten Peace, March 1918*, New York 1971.
80 Robert D. Warth, *Leon Trotsky*, Boston 1977; Curtis Stokes., *The Evolution of Trotsky's Theory of Revolution*, Washington, DC 1982; Trotsky, "The Russian in Lenin", *Current History*, 19 (1923–1924), 1025.
81 Arthur Herman, *1917: Lenin, Wilson, and the Birth of the New World Disorder*, New York 2018.
82 Piero Melograni, *Lenin and the Myth of World Revolution: Ideology and Reasons of State, 1917–1920*, Amherst, NY 1989.
83 Yuri Felshtinsky, *Lenin, Trotsky, Germany and the Treaty of Brest-Litovsk: The Collapse of the World Revolution, November 1917–November 1918*, Milford 2012.
84 Rolf. H. W. Theen, *Lenin: Genesis and Development of a Revolutionary*, Princeton, NJ 2014.
85 T. H. Rigby, *Lenin's Government: Sovnarkom 1917–1922*, Cambridge 2008.

4 Anarchism, Nihilism, Racism

A. Anarchism: "We Made a Revolution Without an Idea"

Anarchism is a philosophical concept, a political belief, and a social movement with the goal of a stateless society, free of legal, political, or economic rule, which can be attained only through ceaseless revolutionary actions. Anarchists believe in revolutionary social change but are wary of organized political revolutions for fear that they may merely replace one authoritarian system by another. Anarchism's philosophical point of departure is that human beings are basically good and that, if they are freed from compulsory laws, arbitrary rule and centralized economies, they will create humane harmony and social solidarity.[1]

The philosophy of anarchism is quite ancient. It ranges from the biblical prophet Samuel's criticism of the monarchy, through the Greek Stoic philosopher Zeno's critique of the Platonic Republic, to the medieval Christian sects that fought both political and papal rule. However, anarchism is known mainly as a modern movement, beginning during the French Revolution. The Girondins reviled their radical foes, the Jacobins, with the title "anarchists" because of their desire to continue the revolution even after Louis XVI had been deposed. The bourgeois revolution actually opposed two typical anarchist demands: decentralization and the abandonment of property. The revolution, which had begun as a rebellion against the monarchist, feudal, ecclesiastical status quo, ended up with a centralized government that established the power of the bourgeois.[2]

The French Revolution provided images, legends, and myths for the anarchist tradition of the nineteenth and twentieth centuries, supporting the idea that political and social structures are destructible, that monarchies and aristocracies can be removed with a wave of the hand, and that no constitutional structure is eternal if it is confronted by a series of violent acts.

The anarchist tradition held up for emulation the Sans-Culottes, who had acted against the Girondins, the Jacobins, and the revolutionary dictatorship in 1793. Jacques Rous, the leader of the most violent group, the Enrages, contributed to later anarchist practice with his example of how social justice can be represented by the direct action of the masses in the streets. He and Herbert despaired of Robespierre and executed him with a guillotine that they themselves helped set up. In 1793, William Godwin in England published a book that was the first modern formulation of anarchism. He presented an anarchist model of small autonomous communities that share their property in a communal way. The abolishment of tyranny and of accumulated property would not take place through revolutionary action or social reform but by spreading the idea of justice and using enlightened methods to persuade individuals of the necessity of free arrangements.

Anarchism inherited several elements of the French Revolution: terror as a form of political activity, republican virtue as a form of political education, and conspiracy as a lifestyle. Gracchus Babeuf's "Conspiration des Equax" of 1793 served as a mythic model for the nineteenth-century anarchists. The means Babeuf advocated and his call for the elimination of private property were anarchistic, but he believed in a strong state—a dictatorship—and the nationalization of the means of production.[3] This was typical of the dialectics of many ideas of the French Revolution, which were anarchistic at first yet turned statist and centralist as they succeeded and became established.

After Babeuf, Filippo Buonarotti was the prototype of the professional saboteur. He founded secret societies in Switzerland and Belgium, as well as in France after the 1830 revolution. Babeuf, Buonarotti, and Louis Auguste Blanqui—who spent forty of his seventy-six years in prison—were depicted by later generations as the personification of revolution in the nineteenth century.[4]

According to James Joll, a historian of anarchism, three myths of the French Revolution became an integral part of anarchist belief: that a violent revolution is possible; that the next revolution would be a truly social one and would not merely replace one ruling class by another; and that this future revolution would arrive only when a revolutionary conspiracy of devoted anarchists would arise from the existing society. From this point on, revolutions would be made not only in philosophical essays but also in the streets.[5]

While the Enrages, Babeuf, and Buonarotti provided examples of the violent revolutionary climate of anarchist terror, utopian socialists from Charles Fourier to Saint-Simon and Godwin discussed the future of society. Their ideal visions of a new world and their image of a rational, peace-loving sort of anarchist became part of the philosophy from which modern anarchism arose. The futurist communities of Fourier, the *phalansteries*, typified the element of cooperation.[6] Saint-Simon criticized the revolutionaries for merely improving the mechanism of the state.[7]

A revolutionary philosophy justifying radical change was proposed by the Young Hegelians. In the revolutionary dialectics they developed, all conflict, both political and class based, contributes to a new synthesis of history. Max Stirner, following Feuerbach, claimed that the state would be replaced by a union of egoists and recommended violent means for realizing individual rights. The conclusion of another Young Hegelian, Karl Marx, was that the class war would end in the dictatorship of the proletariat, while Proudhon reached anarchist conclusions instead.[8]

It was Proudhon who provided the crucial motivation for modern anarchism. In 1840, he adopted the term "anarchism" in his essay "What is property?" He did not believe that all rule should be abolished, advocating instead political federalism and economic "mutualism", which would restrict the authority of the central mechanisms of power through free local organizations.[9] The ideal society requires two nonviolent revolutions: one against the present economic order and the other against the present political order. Instead of a mass revolution, there must be a revolution of cells (tiny groups). At the time of the bourgeois revolutions of 1848 in Paris, Berlin, and Vienna, Proudhon concluded, "We made a revolution without an idea".

Wilhelm Weitling, in his book *Guarantees of Harmony and Freedom*, combined the idea of the inevitable revolution with anarchist and Christian beliefs.[10] As a revolutionary of the 1840s, he influenced the anarchists directly. Bakunin, whom he met in Switzerland, was impressed by Weitling's book, in which he wrote that revolutions would arise "either through harsh physical force or through spiritual power, or both. The revolutions will no longer be bloody". Bakunin thought that true revolutions are made by those who have nothing to lose. He claimed that the new ethics of revolution "can only be effectively taught among the bewildered masses swarming in our great cities and plunged into the utmost boundless misery".

Most anarchists consider themselves socialists, but since they also conceive of themselves as revolutionaries, they refuse to act through parliamentary legislation or social reform. Anarchism appeared as an organized movement in Western Europe in the 1850s and 1860s. The First International, which was founded in 1864, served as a battlefield in the conflict between Marxist and anarchist groups. In 1883, the anarchists founded their own International, and its first congress was held in Amsterdam in 1907.

Kropotkin opposed the capitalist regime, advocating the founding of free communist cells that would coordinate the means of production and consumption.[11] This combination of anarchism and communism supported economic decentralization, which was supposed to come after the state would totally disappear in a popular revolution. From the 1880s, anarchism became more and more communistic. The Russian writer Leo Tolstoy, on the other hand, completely rejected communism, which he believed to be based on centralism, just as he rejected revolution and violence. Tolstoy's variety of anarchism was a combination of a spiritual revolution and noncooperation with state institutions—the army, the courts, and the administration. Henry David Thoreau in the nineteenth century and Mahatma Gandhi in the twentieth also favored civil disobedience over violent revolution.

In the 1880s, a crisis in Marxism led to three new directions: Eduard Bernstein's parliamentary revisionism, Vladimir Lenin's party cadre system, and George Sorel's revolutionary violence. Sorel, a French theoretician who combined individualistic anarchism with organized revolutionary syndicalism in both France and Italy, rejected the idea of a political revolution. Instead, he advocated a permanent rebellion in the form of a proletarian general strike. He believed that revolutions stem from power and necessitate terror, while rebellions stem from freedom and necessitate violence. This philosophy of violence infiltrated the foundations of the revolutionary syndicalism advocated by fascism at the beginning of its career.

In the late nineteenth and early twentieth centuries, anarchists preached terror and the assassination of government representatives. Direct violent action replaced political and social revolution. This philosophy led to the assassination of French President M. F. Sadi Carnot in 1894, Empress Elizabeth of Austria in 1898, King Humbert I of Italy in 1900, and American President William McKinley in 1901, as well as assassinations of other figures in parliaments and public institutions.

It is thus not surprising that anarchists got the image of terrorists, although actually most anarchists were not terrorists. Anarchists' activities covered a wide range from direct action, sabotage, political strikes, and general strikes to civil disobedience, pacifism, antiparliamentarianism, and antipatriotism. Anarchic terrorism flourished in an atmosphere of radical nationalism, a society of minorities, and economic exploitation. The anarchists generally refused to organize themselves into political parties, and anarchism never became an organized mass movement like socialism. The essence of anarchism opposes organization. To spread their ideas, the anarchists made use of propaganda, demonstrations, manifestos, and strikes, mainly in workers' unions. Anarchists and communists often strode arm in arm in revolutions and civil wars, but the Soviet revolution considered anarchism counterrevolutionary. Anarchist quarters in Moscow were shelled in April 1918 on orders from Trotsky, the anarchist leaders were imprisoned, and their activities were suppressed. Plump De Rivera's Spain also suppressed anarchist organizations, such as the Federacion Anarquista Iberica and Confederacion Nacional del Trabajo.

Anarchists and communists both sided with the Republicans against General Francisco Franco in the Spanish Civil War of 1936–1939, but the hostility between them led to the dissolution of their alliance, the repression of the anarchists, and Franco's victory. In France and Italy, the anarchists left their stamp on revolutionary syndicalism. Anarchist unions such as the Unione Anarchica Italiana and Unione Sindicale Italiana were made illegal in the Mussolini period.

Unlike European anarchism, which was associated in one way or another with revolution, American anarchism was not associated with revolution at all. From prominent figures such as Emma Goldman and Alexander Berkman, who returned disappointed from visits to the land of the Bolshevik Revolution, to the radical students' movements in the 1960s, the American version of protest movements was always more liberal than anarchist.[12]

Notes

1 Alan Ritter, *Anarchism: A Theoretical Analysis*, Cambridge 2010; Benjamin Franks, Nathan Jun, and Leonard Williams, eds., *Anarchism: A Conceptual Approach*, London 2018.
2 John A. Simmons, *On the Edge of Anarchy: Locke, Consent, and the Limits of Society*, Princeton, NJ 2014; Peter T. Lesson, *Anarchy Unbound: Why Self-Governance Works Better Than You Think*, Cambridge 2014.

3 David Thomson, *The Babeuf Plot*, London 1947.
4 Alan Barrie Spitzer, *The Revolutionary Theories of Louis Auguste Blanqui*, New York 1957.
5 James Joll, *The Anarchists*, Cambridge, MA 1980, 25–42.
6 Charles Gide, *Selections from the Works of Fourier*, London 1901.
7 Frank E. Manuel, *The New World of Henri Saint-Simon*, Cambridge, MA 1956.
8 Pierre Joseph Proudhon, *La Revolution sociale demontree par le coup d'etat du Deux Decembre*, Paris 1852.
9 Idem, *Qu'est-ce que la propriete?* Paris 1840.
10 Wilhem Weitling, *Garantien der Harmonie und Freiheit*, Berlin 1908.
11 Petr Kropotkin, *Law and Authority*, London 1900.
12 Candace Falk and Barry Pateman, eds., *Emma Goldman: A Documentary History of the American Years*, vol. 3, Stanford 2012; James C. Scott, *Two Cheers for Anarchism: Six Pieces on Autonomy, Dignity, and Meaningful Work and Play*, Princeton, NJ 2012.

B. From Bakunin to Nechayev: The "Jesuit Order"

The fathers of modern anarchism were Mikhail Bakunin (1814–1876) and Prince Peter Kropotkin (1842–1921). Bakunin gave anarchism a collectivist direction, claiming that the revolution must be a spontaneous mass rebellion rather than an act of a political leadership with armed forces. A military revolution would lead to a class dictatorship, an organized oligarchy, and a strong state. Repression from above must be countered by terror from below—that is, propaganda through action.

In his observations on man, society, and liberty (1871), Mikhael Bakunin claimed that man becomes conscious of himself and his humanity only in society and only by the collective action of the whole society. According to Bakunin, release from the constraints of nature comes from work in partnership, and without economic liberation there can be no intellectual or moral liberation. Release from the limitations of nature is possible only through education and study, but one should remember that these are social attributes. In a state of liberty, a man is known to his neighbors and relates to those around him as human beings. Liberty is not isolation but dialogue, not separation from mankind but affinity. The freedom of the individual is the reflection of his or her humanity in the consciousness of other humans who are free and equal to themselves.[1]

Is the critical contemporary reading in the post-totalitarian era of some of Bakunin's writings a niggardly objection to Bakunin's tiresome use of the word "liberty", for example, or is it because his writings were naive, pretotalitarian, unable to envisage where this linguistic expression would lead to in Russia fifty years later?[2] Was it "puerile prattle", "insidious Hegelian verbiage", as Isaiah Berlin derisively called it, or "one of the completest embodiments in history of the spirit of liberty", as it was termed by the historian E. H. Carr?[3] Bakunin, the "father of terror", was a many-sided personality who can be seen as the embodiment of the confusions, weaknesses, and virtues of the generation of revolutionary intelligentsia at the end of the nineteenth century and the beginning of the twentieth. And perhaps the historian was right who said that very few intellectuals demanded freedom with the fervor shown by Bakunin.[4] Was Bakunin intellectually responsible for the phenomenon that Michael Confino called "violence within violence"? For Alexander Herzen and Ivan Turgenev, thinkers of Bakunin's generation, he was an example of a self-questioning intellectual who therefore, like others in Russia, was in the final analysis ineffectual.[5] Herzen wrote that he was capable of becoming anything—propagandist, tribune, preacher, leader of a party, the leader of a faction, the leader of a heretical movement—but if he lived in Russia, Columbus would have not have had a ship and would not have discovered America.[6]

The Jacobin discrepancy ran like a thread through the rebellious revolutionary tradition: the striving for absolute liberty from authority on the one hand and the tendency to revolutionary despotism on the other. It was characteristic of anarchism in general and of Bakunin in particular. Herzen and Turgenev rightly saw that the contradictions in anarchism were not due to lack of method or the absence of a coherent theory but to a desire for comprehensiveness. It was the ancient messianic vision that strove for harmony and social unity at any price. This could derive from the radical scheme of Hegelian idealism or from the millennarian passion that motivated Marx, but in the case of Bakunin it was due to a personal obsession. Bakunin had a tendency to intellectual construction and extreme abstraction that caused him to subordinate reality to his ideas. He said of himself that after he left Russia as a young man, he laid his thoughts aside and was reborn as a man of instinct and action, but Belinsky was right on target when he said: "He likes ideas and not people; he wants to rule [. . .], not to love".[7]

Intellectuals estranged from their societies, which they find authoritarian, develop an uncompromising hostility toward them and sometimes dream of their total destruction. The alienated intellectual believes that the destruction will usher in a golden age in which all the contradictions in human existence will be resolved.[8] The ideal of absolute liberty that would come about through the destruction attracted many intellectuals, especially those of the early populist branches of Russian socialism. It was a short step from a radical striving for liberty to a comprehensive vision of violence. Bakunin did not regard liberty as a necessity in a situation in which there was no alternative but a creative, cleansing value in itself. There cannot be a revolution without acts of violence, which stem from creativity. It is a redemptive destruction, a destruction that creates new worlds and endows them with the breath of life.

In his religious passion, Bakunin studied all philosophical systems. The starting point of his philosophizing was the idea that "the battle between the Devil and God is transferred from the inner life to the outer reality and embraces the whole of history as the realization of two principles: good and evil, the state and revolution, revolution and counter-revolution". The scholar of anarchism, Ze'ev Iviansky, wrote of Bakunin's vacillation between "the ideal of the state" and "the ideal of Sodom" in which "Satan fights against God".[9] Bakunin applied religious concepts to revolution: "I look for God in humanity, and from now on I look for God in revolution".[10]

The Jesuit order, with its resolution, asceticism, preaching, and action, was a model for the anarchists.[11] Bakunin supported a secret society of revolutionary groups, "a popular order of brotherhood for the whole of Russia consisting of forty to fifty people". The revolutionary order had a religious impulse and drew in others: "This is a new religion through its power to attract people and be a collective redemptive force". Alexis De Tocqueville, looking at the modern revolutionary intellectual who wishes to mend the world through preaching and propaganda, discerned the messianic vision behind this revolutionary fired with missionary zeal. He conceived of humanity in the abstract, not people of flesh and blood. The drive for conversion created a propaganda, and this led to a religious revolution, "a new religion, a religion full of deficiencies: a religion without a god, without a ritual, and without a hereafter. Yet, nevertheless, this religion, like Islam, has covered the earth with its armies, representatives and saints". Although Bakunin was an outstanding example of the idea of redemption, his young colleague and partner Sergei Nechayev (1847–1882) took it to its ultimate conclusion. Bakunin's follower, Nechayev, came to more nihilistic radicalism: all means are legitimate for destroying corrupted states. Natalia Herzen, the wife of Alexander, early recognized the redemptive syndrome in Nechayev, and Bakunin wrote on the 16th of June 1870: "I cannot think of anyone who could continue our redemptive project better than Nechayev".[12]

In 1869, Bakunin met Nechayev for the first time in Geneva. He was twenty-two years old, and said that he had escaped from prison in Russia. Who was this "fanatical young man who does not believe in God, a strong character who doesn't talk much?" asked Bakunin in a letter to a Swiss friend. Nechayev was born in 1847 in the textile-manufacturing town of Ivanovo. He grew up in a revolutionary atmosphere of secret societies that vied with one another to be the most extreme. After the first revolutionary society in Russia Land and Liberty, Young Russia was founded, a small group of violent Jacobins opposed to all liberal reforms. In a manifesto they drew up, they called for a "bloody and merciless" peasant revolution, a revolution that would completely destroy the existing order. Two years later, in 1864, the student Nicholas Ishutin founded the terrorist organization, Hell. This was the hard core of a secret society called "The Organization", an ascetic group of students who abandoned their studies and devoted themselves to revolutionary activities among the workers of the town.

Nechayev arrived in Moscow a few weeks after the attempt on the life of the czar on the 4th of April 1866 by Dmitry Karakosov, a member of the Organization. Another attempt about a year later made the government exert pressure on the students. In that violent atmosphere, Nechayev's consciousness became more acute, and he lent a willing ear to Bakunin's call to the students to abandon their studies and organize themselves for rebellion. Piotr Tkachev, the central figure of the Russian Jacobin movement, and seven other students, founded a revolutionary committee and drew up a "Program of Revolutionary Action". A Blanquist orientation in the manifesto was revealed in its appointment of a revolutionary elite who would decide on the structure of the state and in the intention of carrying out a social revolution facilitated by a political insurrection. In order to do this, a new kind of "revolutionary type" had to be created who would dedicate himself to the revolutionary struggle and make contact with similar movements abroad. The groups were scattered, the members changed their locations, and they were not corrupted by power. The experts in the group wrote a "Catechism" whose regulations would be binding on the members, would determine the actions of the organization, and would outline the future state. The revolutionary would have loyalty only to the revolution: "Those who join the organization are committed to renounce all positions, all business and all family ties".[13] The propaganda would at first be centered in the towns, would spread to the cities in the autumn of 1864, and would prepare the people for revolution in the spring of 1870. Both the government and the revolutionaries expected an outbreak of violence at that time.

Most of the Russian radicals of the 1860s came from the upper classes, and compassion was a major factor in their activities on behalf of the lower classes. Nechayev was the first radical to come from the margins of society, and his friends were aghast at his lack of compassion, his hatred and contempt—the chief motivations of his revolutionary spirit. The revolutionary Vera Zasulish declared that his hatred "was not only directed against the government and the exploiters, but against the whole of society and its social foundations, [. . .] against the rich and the poor, the conservatives, the liberals, and the radicals". The principles of the terrorist organization Hell were internalized by Nechayev: he had come to the conclusion that the end justified the means.

At their meeting in Geneva, Bakunin convinced Nechayev that his organization, which he said contained thousands of revolutionaries scattered throughout Russia, would set in motion the peasant revolution that would break out in the following spring. Herzen was suspicious of Nechayev from the start, but Bakunin considered him a hero. Three revolutionaries—Bakunin, Nechayev, and Ugariov—drew up the manifesto, "Catechism of a Revolutionary", and intended to distribute it to all the local groups in Russia. Never until that time had there been such a hymn of praise to violence and such an intellectual justification of terror. The manifesto called for a relentless terror to be waged in a continual struggle with the state, its institutions, and its representatives. Anyone who rejected the values of contemporary society could join the revolutionary struggle, but the purest embodiment of the revolution was to be found in thieves and robbers:

> Brigandry is one of the most respected elements in the life of the people in Russia [. . .] The brigand is the only true revolutionary in Russia, without empty verbiage and rhetoric. The popular revolution proves to be a combined revolt of the brigands and peasants. The world of the brigands, and that alone, is always in harmony with the revolution. One has to turn towards that world if one wishes to plan serious projects in Russia and to carry out a popular revolution.[14]
>
> The revolutionary hates the present social morality and is contemptuous of all its forms [. . .] All that contributes to the victory of the revolution is moral, and all that hinders the revolution is criminal and immoral [. . .] One must suppress all feelings of friendship, kinship, gratitude, even

honor, out of desire for revolution [. . .] The revolutionary has no private interests [. . .] or property [. . .] Day and night, the revolutionary has only one thought—destruction, relentless destruction.[15]

We know of no activity except for the activity of destruction, but we acknowledge that the forms of these activities are very varied: poison, knives, hanging, etc. In this struggle, the revolution sanctifies everything. Our program is a negative project which is special to us and has no limits—total destruction.[16]

Before he returned to Russia, Bakunin appointed Nechayev the representative of the Russian branch of the "world revolutionary alliance". In Moscow, Nechayev founded a new secret society, The People's Vengeance, based on cells of five members, and their aim was to prepare the people for revolution. The group consisted of a few dozen members. Nechayev demanded total discipline in the name of the alliance, and when a member of the group, a student called Ivanov, was suspected of treachery in November 1869, Nechayev persuaded three members to murder him. His corpse was discovered by the authorities, hundreds of activists were arrested, the People's Vengeance group was broken up, and Nechayev had once again to escape from Russia. In Geneva, he continued to disseminate the myth of the Russian revolutionary committee, and with the help of Bakunin he began to represent himself as a persecuted martyr. His deviant ways, his satanic character, and his betrayals made him loathsome in European socialist circles, which helped Marx to exclude Bakunin from the International. For the next two years, Nechayev was active in London, Paris, and Zurich, but the Russian immigrants kept their distance from him. He was arrested, deported to Russia, and given a life sentence, and he persuaded his warders to change their beliefs to socialism. He died in 1882, ten years after he was imprisoned.

Nechayev would have been marginal in Russian history if he had not been connected with Bakunin, with whom he wrote the "Catechism of a Revolutionary".[17] When the manifesto was read out at his trial, a storm broke out in the room: there was no precedent for a justification of violence against fellow revolutionaries. A new type of revolutionary had come into being who called for revolution to be the sole value. This kind of revolutionary radicalism scorned the traditional values of revolutionary brotherhood and love for the oppressed masses. "Nechayevism"—hymns of praise to revolutionary violence that turned into murderous nihilism—provided inspiration for Dostoevsky's novel *The Devils*. The hero Stavrogin was talking to Verkhovensky (a stand-in for Nechayev):

> Can you count on the fingers of your hand the people who could be accepted as members of your group? There is only bureaucracy and sentimentality here—in short, there is only a certain amount of cement. But there is one thing that is infinitely better: persuade four members of the group to murder a fifth member on the pretext that he is an informer, and immediately, by means of the shedding of blood, you will bind them to you with an unbreakable bond. They will be your slaves.

Dostoevsky and Albert Camus saw the "Catechism of a Revolutionary" as the inevitable product of the religion of Prometheus, a religion that was dominant in modern radical thought. In that religion, humanity is God. "Nechayevism" came to the conclusion that the present humanity had to be sacrificed for the sake of a future humanity. The formula was simple: the further away the ideal was from the reality, the more violence is needed now for the sake of future liberty.

Those who, like Dostoevsky, believed that the idealism of the fathers of Russian radicalism gave birth to political nihilism in their sons, found overwhelming proof in the biographies of Bakunin and Nechayev. Camus saw the moral relativism of the "Catechism" as the continuation of German historicism. If the "spirit" can be realized only at the end of history, values such as wisdom, justice, and truth are not inherent in man but are goals to be achieved through a historical process. Accordingly, they cannot serve as criteria of moral judgment in the present, as morality becomes irrelevant. One is left with the cynical view that man's sole duty is to identify with the forces helping the victory of the cause in the stage of history in which one lives. Bakunin brought this relative approach, in which reality was judged by its place in an abstract historical model, to a head. He viewed history as a battle between revolution and counterrevolution, and his conclusion was that revelation justified anything done in its name.

Notes

1. For the development of Bakunin's attitude toward liberty, see Mark Leier, *Bakunin: The Creative Passion: A Biography*, New York 2006.
2. Sam Dolgoff, ed., *Bakunin on Anarchy*, London 2013.
3. Isaiah Berlin, "Herzen and Bakunin on Individual Liberty", in *Russian Thinkers*, London 1994; Edward Hallett Carr, *Michael Bakunin*, New York 1975, 440.
4. Aileen Kelly, *Mikhail Bakunin—A Study in the Psychology and Politics of Utopianism*, New Haven, CT 1987.
5. Angaut, Jean-Christophe. "Revolution and the Slav Question : 1848 and Mikhail Bakunin", in Douglas Moggach and Gareth Stedman Jones, eds., *The 1848 Revolutions and European Political Thought*, Cambridge 2018.
6. Isaiah Berlin, *Karl Marx: His Life and Environment*, Oxford 1996.
7. Carr, *Michael Bakunin*, 12.
8. Tom Stoppard, *The Coast of Utopia*, New York 2002.
9. Ze'ev Iviansky, "Individual Terror: Concept and Typology", *Journal of Contemporary History*, 12:1 (January 1977): 43–63.
10. Evgenii Lampert, *Studies in Rebellion*, London 1957, 134.
11. Noam Chomsky, *On Anarchism*, New York 2013.
12. Iviansky, "Individual Terror: Concept and Typology".
13. Franco Venturi, *Roots of Revolution*, London 1969, 592.
14. Ibid, 601.
15. Carr, *Michael Bakunin*, 379–380.
16. Venturi, *Roots of Revolution*, 605.
17. Michael Confino, *Violence dans la Violence*, Paris 1973.

C. Herbert Marcuse: The Messiah of Criticism

Herbert Marcuse (1898–1979) drew attention to the conditioning of the Promethean communications media in the second half of the twentieth century. Revolutionaries sought to change the world in various ways, but he held that first one had to interpret it. Marcuse thought that a correct interpretation of the social reality was a necessary precondition for changing it. With him, the intellectual came before the revolution, or, in other words, critical interpretation was a revolutionary instrument in his hands—an approach that revealed a domesticated Prometheus who was an inseparable part of the one-dimensional society.

Before he was praised in the universities of Berkeley and Berlin as "the students' Marx" for his book *One-Dimensional Man* (1964), Marcuse wrote, in his article "Philosophy and Critical Theory" (1935), that the "transformation of a given status is not, of course, the business of philosophy. The philosopher can only participate in social struggles insofar as he is not a professional philosopher".[1] By those who "participate in social struggles", he meant intellectuals such as the members of the Frankfurt School. They were outstanding in critical theory, whose purpose, in his opinion, is "the liberation of mankind, which binds it to certain ancient truths". The philosopher was exempted from consideration of these "ancient truths": the intellectual was bound by them.

More than two generations before the advent of "political correctness", Marcuse warned of a one-dimensional language and reality.[2] A whole series of words had gone out of use, and a new conformist series had replaced them. In a subtle way, beneath the surface, normal language had become the vehicle of an ideology that served a certain society, embalmed practical and theoretical criticism in linguistic technicality, made it subject to a powerful clique within the establishment and enshrined it in technical terms comprehensible only to the initiated. When a concept was subjected to this process, it was immunized against contradiction.

This self-confirming practice pervaded the current discourse of present-day politics. The area of discussion was often fixed within arbitrary theoretical limits, and its language was culled from a complex variety of sources. A language that excludes nonconformist elements necessarily produces a poor reality. In the postindustrial society, said Marcuse, many formulas and expressions such as "free enterprise", "free elections", and the "free individual" were immunized against criticism, just as in the communist world there were expressions exempt from criticism such as "class solidarity", "building socialism", and "liquidation of the hostile classes". On both sides, discussion outside the accepted limits was viewed as heretical or hostile propaganda.

With Marcuse, one cannot separate the sociologist from the intellectual. The exposure of the repressed elements of society and the revelation of its true nature were *ipso facto* essential stages in the repair of the human being and the repair of society. Theory and criticism, in his opinion, were a necessary precondition to fixing the world.

Marcuse was the last Mohican of the Frankfurt School, which sought to create a critical theory on the basis of Marx and Freud (how a critique can be created out of these two schools of thought is another question). When the Nazis came to power, he immigrated to the United States and continued his researches under the patronage of the CIA. In his book *Reason and Revolution* (1941), he described philosophy in Hegelian terms as having a critical task. In *Eros and Civilization* (1955), he depicted alienation in capitalist society in Freudian terms: the "pleasure principle" repressed by the "reality principle". In *Soviet Marxism* (1958), he criticized the distortion of Marxism in the Soviet Union, which was a one-dimensional regime.[3] In the 1960s, the New Left called Marcuse "a modern prophet" for his book, *One-Dimensional* Man (1964).

In *One-Dimensional Man*, Marcuse revealed accepted forms of liberty to be subtle forms of subjugation. The forces governing the world of discourse determine the reality of discussion. This constitutes the celebrated Orwellian terminology ("war is peace") whereby a party protecting the capitalist way of life is called "the socialist party", a despotic regime is called a "democratic government", and rigged elections are called "free" ones. A "thing denoting its opposite" that was once regarded as unacceptable according to the rules of logic had now become a form of manipulation. The "clean bomb" is a notable example.

A discourse that closes the door on all discussion not in accordance with its concepts is repressive and imposes on the listener a biased point of view. The consequences—immunity to paradox, identification of the object with its role, the summarizing of a concept through familiar images—reveal the language to be a sacred tongue insulated against criticism.[4] Functional language that has undergone a process of homogenization becomes anticritical. The task of the intellectual is therefore to take apart the conceptual structure of society, to point to its contradictions, to indicate suitable replacements, to redeem language from meanings that have been emasculated. In other words, the things one sees from here one does not see from there.

In the course of its development, dialectical thought has become a kind of understanding of reality with its tensions and contradictions. Thus, various aspects of historical reality have been brought into confrontation. The possibility of achieving power seemed to be a practical possibility, a future historical realization, but the suppression of a certain dimension and its elimination is not an academic matter but a political concern. Marcuse followed Hegel: reason refuses to accept a given reality as it appears. An intellectual who adopts the weapon of reason interprets reality in a multidimensional way. This is not the only possible reality. Beyond its limits, a better reality is observed.

In explaining himself, Marcuse went as far back as the dispute in Greek philosophy between the dialectical logic of Plato and the formal logic of Aristotle. In classical thought, reason was the means to distinguish between truth and falsehood, between the genuine and the factitious. Logic reveals what really exists as against what appears to exist. The conclusion to be drawn is that if we can learn to know what really exists, we will act in accordance with the truth.[5] For a true contemplation of reality, two key concepts are relevant: *logos* and *eros*. Both logical knowledge and erotic knowledge release us from the grip of institutionalized, temporary, and conditioned reality.

According to Marcuse, the history of the human race is a history of repression, and its logic is a logic of repression. The thinking of formal logic cleanses institutionalized reality of its negative quality. With the obliteration of the negativity, the discrepancy between the actual and the desirable is also canceled out, and the many-sided reality consequently becomes one-dimensional. One-dimensional thought rejects an opposing logic that contradicts the prevailing way of thinking.

As a Marxist intellectual, Marcuse saw the development of man's repressive tendencies as consistent with technological determinism. Advanced forms of technology are advanced forms of repression. A person's repression of fellow persons has been constant from the beginning of history to the technological era. An individual's personal dependence in industrial society—the worker on theemployer, the tenant on the landowner—has now come to an end and is superseded by a dependence on an objective order of things: economic laws, the laws of supply and demand. The paradox is that the system of production that overcomes the struggle for existence and is spread throughout the world destroys the lives of those who set it up.

Something was wrong in the rationality of the system, and consequently a new social structure was created. The former negating forces were integrated into the existing order and made yesterday's opposition part of the oppressing order of today.[6] What was new was the weakening of the opposition between the culture and the social reality by means of the annihilation of the foreign elements and of the transcendental elements of the general culture, which are a part of reality. The liquidation of the two-dimensional reality was not effected through the destruction and invalidation of cultural values but by the opposite: by incorporating them and including them wholesale in the existing system. Their presence and reproduction make them an instrument of social unification.

The present ideology of justice and order is part of the institutional system. Thus, ways of thinking and acting in the one-dimensional world are immunized against any rationalism other than institutionalized rationalism. We know that progress brings destruction in its wake, death is the price of life, and labor is the precondition of peace of mind. How did this work in the case of Marcuse? What were the roots of that development?

If, in the first half of the nineteenth century, two classes confronted one another in society, the bourgeois and the proletariat, capitalist development changed their situation in such a way that they were no longer agents of historical change.[7] The former adversaries were now united in the preservation and improvement of the status quo. This development explains why a critical consciousness is so important. It has to expose the union of an ever increasing power of production with an ever increasing power of destruction, the nuclear threat, the capitulation of thought to the pressure of the authorities, the continued existence of poverty and want side by side with unprecedented wealth and abundance. In fact, said Marcuse, the rationality of industrial society that produces the growth and efficiency is really irrational. There is a meaning to the distinction between a true and a deceptive consciousness, between the real and the ephemeral.

Is technology neutral? Marx answered negatively: "The hand-mill gives you society with the feudal lord, the steam-mill gives you society with the industrial capitalist". Consequently, it is not the medium—technology—that is the message but the method of production it engenders. Marcuse, like Marx, thought that the scientific dominance in our days has an instrumental character. Modern technology gives clear authorization to the rule of a class and provides a rationalization for human repression. The despotism of technology shows how impossible it is, technically speaking, for a humans to be independent or to determine the course of their lives. Technological repression is political repression. Thus, the "rational society" undermines the concept of reason.[8]

Industrial society is a political phenomenon that shapes the world of the imagination, the way people behave, and spiritual and material culture. Through technology, politics, culture, and economics are blended in a dominant system that invalidates all alternatives. Technological rationality becomes political rationality.[9] It is paradoxical that in the free world, the society of private enterprise is totalitarian with regard to its technical organization, advertising, and mass media. Individuals cannot escape from the great mechanism of the technological society. They are slaves to this mechanism, need what advertising offers, and think whatever the media tell them. The individual is conditioned by a subtle totalitarianism and does not know it.

One can no longer distinguish between technology itself and its uses. In industrial society, the productive mechanism, the distribution, and the automation tend to be so totalitarian that they determine the needs and aspirations of the individual. In this way, society obliterates the difference between the needs of the individual and those of society. Technology helps to create new forms, more pleasant and effective, of social supervision and control. There is a manipulation of human needs on behalf of protected interests.

In the technological society, which is increasingly capable of supplying the needs of the individual through the way in which it was organized, independent thought and the right to make political choices no longer allow for criticism. From this point of view, there was no difference, in Marcuse's opinion, between an authoritarian and a nonauthoritarian regime.[10] Freedom of thought, speech, and conscience were once critical ideas that could transform a material and spiritual culture into one that was more rational and productive. From the time these rights and liberties were institutionalized, their fate was sealed: "realization destroys the basic foundations".

The difference between the postindustrial society and its predecessor, the industrial, was the disappearance of the historical forces that contained the possibility of achieving new forms of life. Here again one sees the rational character of the society's irrationality. It is very difficult to speak of alienation in view of the productivity and effectiveness of that society, its capacity to increase and distribute amenities of comfort. When individuals identify with an existence imposed on them from the outside, that identification is not an illusion but a reality. It is an objectification of alienation.

The social reality reflects the ideology, but, here, the ideology embodies the process of production. An indoctrination of products, convictions, and habits binds the customer to the producer in a pleasant and agreeable way. It becomes a way of life. Thus, a one-dimensional model of thought and behavior comes into being, and ideas, ambitions, and objectives outside the spheres of institutionalized speech and action are totally rejected.

The affluent society contracts the political horizons. It becomes a society of adjustment and total mobilization (concepts that Marcuse uncritically adopted from Ernst Jünger).[11] The chief aims of this society are the concentration of the national economy on the needs of the corporations, for whom the government is a spokesman and arbiter; the integration of the economy into the international system of military alliances, financial arrangements, technical assistance, and development projects; the amalgamation of blue-collar and white-collar workers; a coordination between the leadership of industry and that of the trade unions; the unification of the leisure activities of the different social classes; the collaboration of the academic world with the national policies; the penetration of public opinion into the homes of the individual and the family; and greater power for the mass media, which project a false reality.

According to Marcuse, one must distinguish between real needs and false ones. False needs are those that perpetuate labor, aggressiveness, distress. Most needs that we have—the need to be entertained, to act in response to advertising, to love and hate what is loved and hated by others—are false. Consequently, there can be no release without a consciousness of repression. Marcuse spoke of spiritual repression, quite different from the one the fathers of socialism spoke of.[12] If Marx spoke about the fetishism of goods, Marcuse spoke about the fetishism of people. The individual enters an artificial race imposed upon him by society but finds satisfaction in that race. The human in the affluent society thinks that happiness is an abundance of comforts. All spiritual concepts have taken on a materialistic hue.

"The slaves of advanced industrial civilization", according to Marcuse, are slaves who have passed through a process of sublimation, but they are slaves nevertheless because "what determines slavery is not obedience, nor the difficulty of the work, but being a human instrument and merely a means".[13] With regard to this, Alexis De Tocqueville wrote, a hundred and fifty years before Marcuse, "The princes gave a bodily form to violence: the republics today give it a spiritual form, the form of man's desire to be enslaved". People have become receptacles that have passed through a preconditioning. If the technician and his employer enjoy the same television program and take their vacations in the same place, if the salesperson is dressed and made up like her employer's daughter, if the worker drives a Cadillac, if they all read the same newspaper, this amalgamation and assimilation do not represent a disappearance of classes but a blurring of consciousness.

In a society in which the free press censors itself, in a society in which there appears to be a free competition between different products, the freedom to choose between masters does not take the masters out of the world, or the slaves.[14] The freedom to choose among a great variety of products and services is not liberty. Control of the individual's body and soul by the products is so effective that one cannot distinguish between the media's function of communicating knowledge and their manipulations or between work performed for state security and work done to bring profits to giant companies.

Unlike in the past, the technological means of supervision and control appear to be the embodiment of reason. This new "reason" apparently works for the benefit of all groups in society to such a degree that any opposition to it appears to be quite unreasonable, and any action against it is impossible. It is not surprising if the means of supervision and control are so internalized that the individual is unable to protest. The alienated individual is isolated in his alienated existence. Indoctrination no longer takes the form of advertising: it is a better lifestyle, a great improvement on anything that went before, and as such it is opposed to changes in quality and works against them. Many of the concepts that disturb us cancel themselves out when it is demonstrated that they cannot be proved. The rule of the one-dimensional reality does not exclude spiritual concerns but adopts them within a scheme of values that take the form of Zen Buddhism, existentialism, beatnikism—and Marcuse, in the spirit of the period, would no doubt have added, certain aspects of post-modernism, which are forms of virtual protest. These can be seen as the ritualistic aspect of the status quo, which ingests them without any difficulty.

Society is passing through a process of change of sociological form. Unlike Marx's image of the worker, modern workers are part of the technological community. They are devoted to their machines, which increases their sense of solidarity and harnesses them to their work. The stratification of their sphere of occupation reveals qualities of adaptation and harmonization, and the power of the blue-collar worker is reduced in relation to the white-collar worker. The machine, not the output of the individual, determines productivity. These changes in the character of work and the means of production alter the position of the worker: one sees an eagerness on the part of the worker to participate in solving problems of production. Industrial society becomes a regime of conditioned pluralism in which the institutions compete to see which can better exercise the system's control of the individual. The question is therefore, "Does not this form of pluralism signify the end of pluralism?"

Marcuse combined Marx and Freud: humans have the right to express their sexuality to the full in their daily work and in their work relationships. The socialization process, however, effects a de-eroticization, a taming of libido. Sex becomes legal tender. This "achievement" is due to mass production and the possibility of obtaining good clothes, beauty treatments available to all, functionality that has become "artistic", the wide-open character of shops and offices, their transparent glass doors, the lowering of counters in offices, the removal of wooden partitions. The mobilization of libido explains the wish to join the system,[15] the absence of fear, and the predetermined coordination between the needs of the individual and the aspirations that social norms require of him. The suppression of desire appears to be reflected in a social satisfaction that diminishes protest and rebellion.

A sphere of debate in which contraries are reconciled is possible today due to the unification of areas of life between which there was formerly a polar opposition. This unification is reflected in linguistic combinations: "The workers wish to achieve harmony in the production of various missiles". How can "workers", "the production of missiles", and "harmony" go together? The thing is possible through a kind of Orwellian "newspeak" and a reduction of thought and vocabulary as envisaged by Arthur Koestler.[16]

Critical thought is the great refusal. To be rational means to negate. The impoverishment of thought, the contraction of language, the circumscription of philosophy—all this makes one think that there are no real alternatives. Realism makes reason exclusive simply because it is realistic. Any other way of thinking is "poetic truth" or "metaphysical truth". In a one-dimensional society, the ideology is the philosophy, the sphere of questions becomes the sphere of answers. Institutionalized speech becomes a manipulation. Consequently, consciousness is both the tool and the essence of criticism, and that is the great task of philosophy.

Does the Orwellian vision of the one-dimensional society, as seen by Marcuse, fill out the picture painted by De Tocqueville in the nineteenth century?[17] The figure of Marcuse is radical, deterministic, and often unbelievable in its one-dimensionality, but the main lines of his analysis give us an awareness of the silencing of criticism, the neutralization of opposition, the death of utopia, the similarity of opposites, and, in short, the taming of the Promethean passion. One question remains with regard to Marcuse. How did he himself manage to elude the totalitarian pattern of thought that overtook the whole society? How did the one-dimensionality pass over him? Did he fulfill the requirement he already expressed in 1935 that critical theory is also critical toward itself and also deals with social matters?

The irony of reason is that the fall of the Soviet Union and its satellites—a poor model of a one-dimensional society—came about through the existence of another one-dimensional society, richer than itself. It was the critical consciousness emanating from the televisions of the one-dimensional capitalist society that in the final reckoning brought down the wall.

Notes

1 Herbert Marcuse, "Philosophy and Political Theory", *Times*, 44 (Spring 1993), 88.
2 Marcuse, *One-Dimensional Man: Studies in the Ideology of Advanced Industrial Society*, London 2002.
3 Marcuse, *Soviet Marxism*, London 1958; idem, *Reason and Revolution: Hegel and the Rise of Social Theory*, London 1986; idem, *Hegel's Ontology and the Theory of Historicity*, Cambridge, MA 1989.
4 Marcuse, *One-Dimensional Man*, 87–127.
5 Ibid., 129.
6 Ibid., 147–150.
7 George Kateb, "The Political Thought of H. Marcuse", *Commentary* (1970): 18–63.
8 Morton Schoolman, *The Imaginary Witness: The Critical Spirit of Herbert Marcuse*, London 1980.
9 Marcuse, *The One-Dimensional Man*, 160–161.
10 Marcuse, *Negations: Essays in Critical Theory,* trans., J. Shapiro, Boston 1968.
11 John Orr, "German Social Theory and the Hidden Face of Technology", *European Journal of Sociology*, XV:2 (1974): 312–336.
12 Marcuse, *An Essay on Liberation*, Boston 1971.
13 Marc Ferro, *October 1917: A Social History of the Russian Revolution*, III, London 1980, 600.
14 Marcuse, *The One-Dimensional Man*, 4–5.
15 Ibid., 84–85.
16 Alasdair MacIntyre, *Marcuse*, New York 1970.
17 De Tocqueville, *Democracy in America*, trans., James T. Schleifer, Indianapolis, IN 2010a.

D. Baader–Meinhoff: A Crusade of Violence

In February 1973, Jean-Paul Sartre declared in an interview in the German weekly *Der Spiegel*: "I am very interested in the Baader-Meinhoff group. I believe it is a true revolutionary group, but I have a feeling that it began a little too early".[1] On reading this, Klaus Croissant, Andreas Baader's lawyer, turned to Sartre and asked him to join the protest against the terms of imprisonment of the members of the terror group. On the 4th of December 1974, after many entreaties, the German prison authorities allowed the French intellectual to visit the terrorist in his cell for half an hour. In the press conference that ensued, Sartre declared that "Baader is held in a cell for a small boy in which the only sounds one hears are the footsteps of the warders three times a day". Sartre attacked the West German government for applying different norms to different political prisoners and curtailing the rights of a prisoner who was "a person with all the qualities of a free man". Andreas Baader was disappointed by the visit: "I thought I had found a friend in you, but you are just another judge".[2] What motivated the intellectual to visit the student? Was this another case of the empathy among the French for "authentic violence"?

When the journalist Michelle Ray was invited by the members of the Red Army Faction (Rote Armee Faktion, RAF) to report on the members of the group and their objectives in her journal, the first rumor they wished to disprove was that they were anarchists.[3] Her hosts—Andreas Baader, Gudrun Ensslin, and Ulrike Meinhoff—explained to her their radical outlook, which supported an intensification of social opposition to the affluent West German society. The undermining of the German people's deceptive state of mind would, they thought, undoubtedly lead to a hoped-for revolution.

In 1968, student rebellions broke out in German campuses, especially in Frankfurt and West Berlin. Lecturers, jurists, and intellectuals joined the youngsters in protest against the founding generation. Outstanding among them was the lawyer Hans Mahler who left his family for the sake of revolution and made his name by accusing the police of killing the student Benno Ohnesorg when the Persian Shah was visiting Berlin. Andreas Baader, a terrorist with personal charisma, and his girlfriend Gudrun Ensslin with whom he went to live in Frankfurt, were important members of the group. They had an aggressive attitude toward the Association of German Socialist Students (the SDS) and toward Rudy Dutschke, the leader of the students from Berlin. Unlike the students, whom she said were "all talk", Ensslin demanded active terror.

The terror group's opening shot took place in April 1968. The group won public sympathy shown in a sympathetic press, the collection of contributions, and legal protection. When Andreas and Gudrun were arrested and brought to trial, Ensslin declared that she was not obligated to the German legal system because she had engaged in a political, not a criminal action. Her deeds, she said, were not liable to judgment. Baader, for his part, claimed that social coercion demanded a struggle, and because this was the law court of a class, there was no possibility that it would give him a just verdict. Ensslin's psychologist, Dr. Reinhard Redhardt, said of her that she is capable of hating from the depths of her soul. She is filled with fanaticism like a medieval crusader. He was right. This new crusader zeal was not so different from the Jesuit zeal of Bakunin.

In 1969, there began a radicalization of the group. Its propaganda demanded the use of weapons, and these were acquired from neo-Nazi groups. The members of the group adopted urban guerrilla tactics as advocated by the Brazilian revolutionary Carlos Marighella, who replaced the party system with a dedicated band of people. According to this school of thought, they had to consider themselves soldiers. They did their training with other terror groups, especially in training camps in the Middle East. They went in for setting fire to businesses, hijacking airplanes, kidnapping public figures, robbing banks, blowing up public institutions and factories, and attacking and killing police officers and foreign army personnel.[4]

The main intellectual figure of the group was Ulrike Meinhoff. She was born in 1934, when the Nazis came to power. As a student of education and psychology in conservative Marburg, she knew Werner Link, who taught political science and was influenced by the East German Marxism of his teacher Wolfgang Abendroth. She consequently turned to the New Left when she learned from them that communism was peace loving and opposed atomic weapons and the arms race. In 1957, she went to the University of Münster in Westphalia, where she made the acquaintance of the political science student Jürgen Seifert, who was active in organizations opposed to arming Germany. She was chosen as the delegate of the press committee of the university's students' league against the use of the atomic bomb. In the committee, she made the acquaintance of Klaus Rainer Röhl, editor of the weekly journal *Konkret*, who was impressed by her "intellectual honesty". In 1958, she was a radical pacifist who dreamed of a Christian peace. In *Das Argument*, a journal she launched, seven issues attacked the arms race. In a controversy with Catholic theologians who supported German self-defense, she wrote: "Have the bishops who stand against freedom-suppressing communism ignored the fact that their viewpoint invalidates the loftiest ideal of liberty, the incontrovertible liberty of freedom of conscience?"

Meinhoff was infatuated with politics. Involved with the new generation of the 1960s and filled with moral fervor against "the bomb", she saw the fight for peace as a moral, not a political issue.[5] The economic miracle produced the affluent German consumer society and resulted in many young people flocking to the universities. Although Meinhoff was an intellectual, she did not come to politics through study of the great political thinkers. She did not go in for study in depth but was drawn to the intellectual controversies of the period.

The editor of *Konkret* made her the first woman editor of his journal, and two years later they got married. The journal, which ran into difficulties because of the withdrawal of the support of the East German Communist Party, changed its position from approval of the erection of the Berlin Wall to one opposed to both the East and West. *Konkret* changed its character, and from a journal with a distribution of 10,000 copies, it became a weekly that was half politics and half sex. In 1964, its distribution reached 100,000 copies, and Meinhoff became a society woman, "the joker of the revolution", as she put it.

At her peak—a mother of twins, the editor of a successful weekly—she left everything and went to live in Berlin at the modern Free University. She abandoned the affluent society and leaped into the intellectual life and revolutionary waters of Berlin. Meinhoff crossed the Rubicon and embarked on propaganda-through-action, thinking that "one cannot change the world by shooting: one can only destroy it".[6] Her radicalism in the years 1967–1968 was expressed, in the manner of left-wing students, in anti-imperialism and hatred of Israel. She declared, "One has to provoke the hidden fascism in society so that everyone can see it". Her friend Peter Rühmkorf, a member of the staff of *Konkret*, was surprised: "The meaning of this was to turn the wheel of history backwards and to invite fascism from the start". In his book *The Misery of Our Intellectuals* (1974), Kurt Sontheimer characterized that generation of German intellectuals as turning sharply from antiauthoritarianism and refusal to accept the yoke of academic authority to a delegitimization of the social institutions and the government.[7] Intellectual theories of "anticoercive power" were held by closed groups supporting violent anarchy.

Meinhoff saw this polarization as all-important and thought that the exposure of the violent mechanism of the one-dimensional society would finally bind the intellectuals to the masses: "We must provoke the fascist police and bring its true character into the open, and then the masses will recognize the justice of our cause, will acknowledge our leadership and support us".[8] In relation to the trial of Baader and Ensslin, she considered setting fire to a business in Frankfurt an example of civil disobedience. She declared that "there is no point in talking and writing. One must engage in action". Meinhoff and Ensslin were quite similar in their character and beliefs: Protestantism, postfascism, radicalism, and romanticism. Following Ensslin, her senior in acts of terror, Meinhoff took part in three operations: bank robberies in Berlin, training in weapons in Jordan, and the liberation of Baader from prison in 1970. *Der Spiegel* gave a detailed account of how Meinhoff released Baader: the two terrorists jumped from the reading room of the prison into the street. It was a metaphor for Meinhoff's leap from an intellectual position in support of propaganda-through-action to that of an anarchist with a revolver. All at once, she cut her connection with bourgeois society, the New Left, the intelligentsia, and the law. The pen was exchanged for the gun.[9]

On the 15th of June 1972, she was arrested and interned with her friends in a prison, Stammheim, which had been specially built for them. It was a time of frustration and despair. Sartre, who visited Baader in prison, did not think it right to visit her. The members of the so-called Second of June movement, who demanded the release of Mahler in exchange for the release of Peter Lorenz, whom they had kidnapped, did not trouble to mention her at all. On the 9th of May 1976, she committed suicide by hanging. She was her own final victim.

The Baader-Meinhoff group was an outstanding example of the Frankist syndrome. In Judaism, there was a remarkable current of nihilism known as "Frankism". Though marginal in extent, it was very significant, and it attracted quite a number of Jewish adherents in eighteenth-century Europe. Frankism had an extraordinary character of formless nihilistic turbulence together with an organized structural system. The false Messiah Jacob Frank declared: "Wherever I go, all will be destroyed, for I have come only to destroy everything". In his court, he set up a uniformed semi-military order subject to an ideology of "redemption through sin", as commanded by its charismatic leader. Gershom Scholem's wonderful articles on the subject reveal the dual face of nothingness and the absolute in Jacob Frank. On the one hand, there was "an atmosphere of anarchy within freedom and universal confusion" and, on the other, "a taste for militarism, [. . .] the transformation of the Sabbetaian faith into a militarism that was both mystical and real".[10]

The roots of the nihilistic-totalitarian phenomenon go back to the gnostics of the second century CE. According to their teachings, one had to liberate oneself from the moral law, which is one of the forms of cosmic enslavement. All was permitted: hence the gnostics' opposition to any order in the world. The commandments "Thou shalt" and "Thou shalt not" were forms of cosmic enslavement, which explains the rebellion against them. The totalitarian-militaristic aspect was revealed in the military character of the gnostics, in their organized violence, and in the dictatorial rule of the priestly Archontics over their followers.

In modern times, the mutual affinity between nothingness and the absolute was translated into political terms by intellectuals who blindly followed totalitarian ideologies and regimes of the right and left. The death camp of Auschwitz and the slave labor camps of the gulags were all sanctified in the name of the absolute: the race, the nation, the class, or the revolution. The sanctification of the nation or the revolution necessitated the destruction of all the old values and the creation of new ones. The totalitarian ideologies were secular religions in all respects: the sacred was not situated beyond the present time and place. It was not in heaven. The new Platonist absolute society could already be set up in this world. The call of heaven was out of reach, and all one was asked to do was to remove impediments.

Totalitarian ideology and violence are the two faces of the absolute. An ideology, as a philosophy of history, creates a framework of mobilizing symbols, values, and ideas, a framework in which the past is used to provide it with justification in the present. Class warfare, for example, is the historical justification for the Marxist ideology, whose absolute is the classless society. Similarly, war between nations is the justification of fascism, and conflict between races is the justification of Nazism. If ideology creates the past, violence imposes itself on the present.[11] In ideology, which gives total sanction to violence, revolution, and war, one can discern a vision of the absolute, a vision that sanctifies all means to its attainment.

Thus, violence and the political absolute are not contradictory: they are two sides of the same coin. Wherever the messianic vision of the absolute is found, one finds a justification of violence. At the entrance to paradise one finds the eternal peace envisaged by Kant, the world brotherhood of workers of Marxism, and the "Third Rome" of Mazzini, in which the nations will dwell together in peace, each under its vine and fig tree. Secular messianism, which sought to realize the absolute here and now by means of political visions of redemption, became the "knavish" messianism of brown and red churches.

The "knavish" messianism did not see itself as a castration, violation, or distortion of rational, secular, humanistic utopias, or of any other kind. The totalitarian ideologies of the left and right saw themselves as the authentic choice of a people, class, elite, or leader. Violence was no longer regarded as a necessary means dependent on circumstances but was recognized as a legitimate tool of totalitarianism that needed it for purposes of internal terror, external war, or perpetual revolution. Violence was a living testimony to the existence of an enemy at home or abroad, an existence that gave permanent justification to the totalitarian regime.

After the Second World War, the world awoke from the illusion of achieving absolute fulfillment in the twinkling of an eye. The Cold War was simply a stage on the way to a realistic détente. The great powers continued to pay lip service to ideology—one as the police force of the free world, the other as the vanguard of world proletarian revolution—but in reality they learned to live with "the day of small things". Negotiation and compromise, apart from specific struggles over rival territories, replaced world-embracing visions.

The totalitarian ideologies and regimes made way for groups for whom the ambition of imposing a new absolute society was several sizes too large. The dream now was to create model fraternities, and ephemeral nihilistic organizations on the right and left sought to be the orders of violence of the 1970s and 1980s. Groups such as Baader-Meinhoff and the Red Brigades on the left and the New Order and Black Order on the right created military hierarchies in their organizations as models for a hoped-for future society.

There was no common denominator between Marx, who believed in a dynamic of economic forces and who ruled out terror, and the Red Brigades, whose members regarded themselves as radical Marxists. There was no common denominator between the traditional conservative, royalist right, and right-wing underground organizations such as the Black Order in Italy. An illustration of this is the fact that twelve Italian terrorist organizations (!) of the left and right claimed responsibility for the attack on the railway station in Bologna in December 1984 in which seventeen people were killed. The attack in Bologna was a point of convergence of violence and nihilism. When the ideological content disappears, violence becomes an end in itself, and this nihilism shows the extreme right and left to be identical.

In modernity, the aspiration to nothingness and the desire for the absolute always strode arm in arm. One never existed without the other. Destruction for destruction's sake cannot exist alone, and it requires a total framework, an organized structure, a military order. The feverish minds of many intellectuals are drawn to this dual desire, which is really one and the same: the desire to destroy all values and to impose them.

Notes

1 Annie Cohen-Solal, *Sartre, 1905–1980*, Paris 1985, 507.
2 Ibid.
3 J. Smith, André Moncourt, and Ward Churchill, eds., "The Red Army Faction", in *A Documentary History, vol. 2: Dancing with Imperialism*, Oakland, CA 2013.
4 Bernhard Blumenau, *The United Nations and Terrorism: Germany, Multilateralism, and Antiterrorism Efforts in the 1970s*, Basingstoke 2014.
5 Jeremy Varon, *Bringing the War Home: The Weather Underground, the Red Army Faction, and Revolutionary Violence in the Sixties and Seventies*, Berkeley, CA 2004.
6 Andre Moncourt, *Daring to Struggle, Failing to Win: The Red Army Factions 1977 Campaign of Desperation*, Oakland, CA 2008.
7 Kurt Sontheimer, *Das Elend Muserer Intellectuellen*, Berlin 1976.
8 Saul Kantzler, *The International Terror: Ideology, Organization, Practice*, Tel-Aviv, 1980, 100.
9 Stefan Aust, *Baader-Meinhof: The Inside Story of the R.A.F.*, trans., Anthea Bell, Oxford 2009.
10 Gershom Scholem, "Redemption Through Sin", in *The Messianic Idea in Judaism and Other Essays*, New York 1995, 78–141.
11 Philip P. Wiener and John Fisher, eds., *Violence and Aggression in the History of Ideas*, New Brunswick, NJ 1974.

E. Nihilism

Only in the revolutions of the twentieth century were the concepts of nihilism as a philosophical category and as a political category joined. Whereas the original Greek concept of *nihil* (nothing, zero) was purely philosophical, modern nihilism has aesthetic, technological, and totalitarian ramifications. Modern nihilism was formulated in 1799 by Friedrich Heinrich Jacobi, who considered nihilism a radical form of idealism.[1] The Romantics turned it into an aesthetic category, and during the course of the nineteenth century, it was considered one of the social and political ramifications of atheism.

Friedrich Nietzsche represents a crossroads: nihilism is no longer identified with a philosophical approach, a literary movement, or a political demand. Instead, it characterizes a whole civilization or a moment in its (modern) history—specifically, the death of God. At this modern consciousness, the "new Man" was born, and he creates his world ex nihilo.[2] Nietzsche's basic assumption that the world is an aesthetic phenomenon places his aesthetics at the center of his revolutionary philosophy. One basic element of Nietzsche's revolution is his philosophic style of exposure as formulated by the genealogy of morals, which sought to destroy all the norms and conventions accepted in the Judeo-Christian world and the classical heritage of the West. Another is his historicist nihilist method, which becomes the starting point for the reorientation of philosophy. Nietzsche's affirmative claims—the will to power, the superman, self-overcoming, and the eternal recurrence—are necessary counterpoints to his nihilism.

Both the Janus-like nihilism and the will-to-power profoundly influenced cultural criticism at the beginning of the twentieth century and provided a model for the "new Man".[3]

When the new Man rebelled against history and the traditional criteria of good and evil, truth and falsehood, he became the midwife of his own world. Modern Man attempted paradoxically to change himself. The French Revolution in the eighteenth century, the ideologies of the nineteenth century, and the political myths of the twentieth century constituted a revolutionary proclamation that human beings were ready to recreate their own humanity, which means to annihilate the "historic man". The criticism of European culture at the end of the nineteenth century was transformed, sometimes directly and sometimes indirectly, into radical political criticism that questioned the basic assumptions of European democracy. In the end, it contributed to the undermining of democracy and the use of totalitarian powers. The ideological development and political history of Europe in the early twentieth century included a unique intellectual trend that characterized its revolutionary state of mind and reflected a nihilist-totalitarian syndrome.

Russian nihilism was born out of the stagnation in governmental reform that followed the emancipation of the serfs in 1861.[4] As the Russian intelligentsia achieved a victory for constitutionalism, its younger generation turned more and more to a conspiratorial populism, the combination of a small elite of freethinking leaders at the head of a massive, axe-wielding peasant revolt. The aim of this revolt would be the destruction not only of the autocracy but of all institutions of society—religion, the family, property—all to be replaced by free and critically thinking individuals coming together on the basis of equality and mutual aid inspired by the example of the Russian village commune. In this sense, nihilism was a Slavophile reaction against the Western-style constitutionalism that underlay the thinking of Alexander Herzen and Nikolai Ogarev—a reaction of the "sons" of the 1860s against the "fathers" of the 1840s and 1850s.

The term "nihilism" was first applied to the attitudes of the young intelligentsia by Turgenev, who used it as a pejorative in his novel, *Fathers and Sons*. For some of its advocates, nihilism was indeed a truly Russian expression of "the passion of the Russian mind; which goes to extremes in all its conclusions [. . .]. Carrying things to extremes is the characteristic element of our history". Russian nihilism, however, was not a belief in nothing, an apathy to existing order, as exemplified by the character of Raskolnikov in Dostoevsky's *Crime and Punishment*. On the contrary, it was a passionate hatred of the existing order and a determination to substitute for it a freer and more universally just society.[5] In the eyes of nihilists, it was Chernyshevsky's *What Is to Be Done?* that portrayed their Rousseauian outlook that humans were meant to be free and equal but are shackled by the imperfections of society. The peculiarly Russian element in nihilism was perhaps its turn to conspiratorial organization and mass political violence as an integral element of its ideology—the only way, in their eyes, of achieving total social reform.

While Chernyshevsky's writings and in particular their advocation of independent social organizations—student communes, artisan associations, peasant unions, and the like—provided an inspiration for the practical activities of the younger intelligentsia, it was the focus on the individual advocated by Dimitri Pisarev and by the editors of the *Russkoe slovo* that captured their imaginations. The nihilists were focused on the strong, uninhibited, and independent thinker. Their ideal was the person capable of survival in the Darwinian survival of the fittest.[6]

Although nihilism was much discussed in the literary criticism of the 1860s and after, it did not give direct birth to any influential organizations. Its emphasis on individualism was too strong for this. Nevertheless, there is a clear root of intellect that leads from the rebellious all-criticizing individualism of the nihilist writers of *Russkoe slovo to* the anarchism of Bakunin's followers and successors. At the same time, nihilism nourished the concept of a revolutionary elite leading the "benighted masses" and thus was one of the cornerstones of Russian Jacobinism as personified in Nechayev, Tkachev, and ultimately Lenin.

Over and above "nihilism" and "totalitarianism" as such, is an additional dialectical phenomenon: the nihilist mentality, whether from inner compulsion or immanent logic, is driven to accept totalitarian patterns of behavior that are characterized by extreme dynamism. The philosophy of activism, violence, and dynamism thus typifies cultural protest and at the same time gives content to political revolts: dynamic nihilism is anchored in the aesthetic absolute of the totalitarian mentality.

Georges Sorel, Filippo Tommaso Marinetti, Vladimir Mayakovsky, Wyndham Lewis, and Ernst Jűnger initiated this nihilist-totalitarian revolution. As cultural critics, they brought about an "intellectual revolution" according to the concept of Stuart Hughes. These "anti-intellectual" intellectuals revolted against the Enlightenment and gave political myth absolute primacy. Glorification of conflict as the structure of reality shaped the new type of authentic man. Modern technology, which they admired, provided the means of making revolutionary order out of chaos and gave them a new Romantic myth serving the politics of violence. This nihilist style was shaped by radical nationalism or mythical socialism or a combination of the two in the form of National Socialism.[7]

In his early book, *The Revolution of Nihilism* (1939), Hermann Rauschning examined National Socialism as a dynamist philosophy without a doctrine.[8] Nazism, in his view, is absolute liberation from the past, action for its own sake, a process of destruction that must develop, according to its own internal logic, into totalitarian tyranny. Thus, by a necessary paradox, "political nihilism" turned into a political religion in three totalitarian regimes—fascism, National Socialism, and Bolshevism. Ernst Bloch, the philosopher of the utopia in the twentieth century, claimed in his book, *The Principle of Hope*, that the nihilistic inspiration common to the totalitarian mentalities of both the radical right and left is "action for its own sake, which can simultaneously lead to the affirmation of Lenin and pave the way for Mussolini".[9] Twelve years after Rauschning's book was published, Albert Camus further developed his thesis in *L'Homme Revolte:* unlimited freedom leads to unlimited despotism.[10] The shortest way to negating everything is affirming everything. The year Camus's book was published, 1951, also saw the publication of J. L. Talmon's *The Rise of Totalitarian Democracy*, which claimed that it is not far from perfection-seeking anarchism to revolutionary centralism.[11] The association between nihilism, totalitarianism, and technology is one of the key issues of the twentieth century. The most extreme manifestation of this association was the Holocaust, when 6 million Jews were annihilated by the Nazi machine.

In spite of the clear distinction that must be made between Nazi Germany and the Soviet Union, we have witnessed the major role played by engineers in these two revolutionary regimes. In both regimes, the engineers were *attracted* not by ideological content but by the totalitarian patterns in the nihilization of the old society and the construction of a new one.

Notes

1 Friedrich Heinrich Jacobi, *Werke III*, Leipzig 1816, 44.
2 See Bernard Beginster, *The Affirmation of Life: Nietzsche on Overcoming Nihilism*, Cambridge MA 2006; Michael Allen Gillespie, *Nihilism Before Nietzsche*, Chicago 1995.
3 David Ohana, *The Dawn of Political Nihilism*, Eastbourne 2012.
4 Fredrick C. Copelston, *Philosophy in Russia—From Herzen to Lenin and Berdyaev*, London 1986.
5 Sean Illing, *Prophets of Nihilism: Nietzsche, Dostoevsky, and Camus*, Washington, DC 2017.
6 Wanda Bannour, *Les nihilistes russes*, Paris 1975.
7 David Ohana, *The Nihilist Order: The Intellectual Roots of Totalitarianism*, Eastbourne 2016.
8 Hermann Rauschning, *The Revolution of Nihilism*, New York 1939.
9 Ernst Bloch, *The Principle of Hope*, trans., N. Placie, S. Placie, and P. Knight, Cambridge, MA 1986, 1945.
10 Albert Camus, *The Rebel*, trans., Antony Bower, New York 1953.
11 Jacob L. Talmon, *The Origins of Totalitarian Democracy*, London 1952.

F. Racism

Western culture is the only one to have created ideologies and theories that are general descriptions of humanity, philosophies of history that relate to peoples in terms of classes, races, or other collective criteria. As such, general theories of race are modern, and reflect above all the historical development of Western culture.[1] For the first time in history, a system of thought claimed to be a scientific explanation. The starting point of this system was a theory about the development of races, the hierarchy between them, and their relative values. Paradoxically, the idea of universality promoted by the Enlightenment from the seventeenth and eighteenth centuries onward was used to give scientific validity to the variety of the human family that was regarded by modernity as a single entity.[2] The racial ideology sprang up in the nineteenth century at the same time as the other comprehensive and world-embracing ideologies and "isms"—socialism, Marxism, liberalism, nationalism, and so on—which the post-modernists today call "meta-narratives".

The first person to create general theories was Aristotle. In his *Politics*, he wrote: "Some people are obviously free by nature, and others are slaves by nature".[3] For the latter, the Greek philosopher thought that slavery was desirable and just. He and the other Greeks regarded non-Greeks as barbarians. Similarly, the early Christians distinguished between believers—themselves—and nonbelievers. The Greeks and Romans distinguished between civilization and barbarism, and the Christians distinguished between the saved and the excommunicated—distinctions that later became rationalizations of racism but that were not in themselves racist.[4]

In various cultures in the ancient world, there was a color consciousness, a sense of superiority, and strong feelings about friends and enemies. People of the Han dynasty in the third century CE described encounters with savages "who were like the monkeys from which they were descended".[5] The Chinese of the Tang dynasty were scornful of the naked inhabitants of the southern islands. In southern India, the invading Aryans considered themselves "natural aristocrats" and viewed the brown-skinned natives of the country as slaves.[6] The members of the Zulu tribes in Africa compared the people of other tribes to wild animals.[7] The Islamic scholar Said al-Andalusi thought Ethiopians stupid and lacking in self-control.[8] Do these examples show that the Indians, Chinese, Zulus, and Muslims were racist?

The Indian caste system is constructed in a gradated manner. Those in the lower castes are regarded as inferior and are forbidden to marry people of the higher castes. In this system, there are social and religious differences, but all the castes belong to the same race. The ancient Chinese, who considered the "middle kingdom" the center of the world, hated foreigners, and for hundreds of years regarded the Europeans as barbarians, but, to the same degree, they were hostile to other Asiatic peoples. They never developed a racial hierarchy among peoples or viewed biological differences as a basis for domination or as an explanation of superiority. The Zulus, the dominant power in South Africa, were ethnocentric and saw their group as the center of the world, but other African peoples thought the same way. The tribal conflicts were color-blind. Still today, the differences between the Hutus and Tutsis in the murderous civil war in Rwanda are not racial.

One must conclude that a distinction must be made between racism on the one hand and tribalism and ethnocentrism on the other.[9] Racism refers to a hierarchy of human groups based on biological characteristics, while tribalism and ethnocentrism are a preference for one's own group to foreigners. The source of the concept of ethnocentrism is the Greek word *ethnos*, meaning "people" or "nation"—ethnic groups with a common family tie or history—but these relationships have nothing to do with race. Nationality, religion, and common traditions are closer to tribalism or ethnocentrism, the roots of which are cultural, than to racism, whose root is biological.

Tribalism and ethnocentrism are universal. All human communities—primitive and advanced, Western and non-Western—have always been narcissistic from the cultural point of view, suspicious of foreigners, and used to seeing others as inferior. Tribalism is a strong allegiance to the group, which we feel in various degrees toward our family, our neighbors, our religion, or our nation.

Tribalism and ethnocentrism accompanied by jealousy, provincialism, and hatred or fear of foreigners is not the same as racism. The conflicts between Serbs and Croats, Sikhs and Hindus, Basques and Spaniards, Protestants and Catholics, English and Irish, Turks and Armenians are unquestionably tribal. They are conflicts derived from ethnic loyalties. These groups that fight one another have the same skin color; they belong to the same race. Many of the great wars in history—the Hundred Years' War, the American Civil War, the slaughter among Hindus and Muslims in India in 1948, and the two world wars in the twentieth century—took place between members of the same race with a common cultural heritage.

The Jews, like others, were also seen in the ancient world as a tribe. Although the Jews were persecuted by the Romans, the Christians were persecuted more. Later, the Christians persecuted the Jews, not on racial grounds but on grounds of religion. Jews who accepted baptism were accepted in the Middle Ages as full members of the Church. One can trace the origins of the secularization of anti-Jewish sentiments in modern times to Spain in the sixteenth century. Jews were accused of not being proper Christians, heretics who practiced Judaism in secret. Accordingly, new laws were enacted not on the basis of the Jews' beliefs but on the basis of their blood. It was a new kind of anti-Semitism: for the first time, European Christians practiced a policy whereby Jewish blood could not be changed through baptism. This was a turning point that marked the change from a religious anti-Semitism to a racial one.[10]

It is the ideology that makes the difference between anti-Semitism and racism. Secular anti-Semitism developed in the nineteenth century at the time of the Dreyfus Affair. Jews were persecuted not because of their beliefs but because of what they were. The Holocaust was the murderous culmination of the process of demonization of the Jews. However, the Jews in Germany belonged to the white race like their oppressors. It was also because they shared the same color of skin that the Nazis cultivated the myth of the Aryan race and created symbols like the yellow badge to distinguish between themselves and the Jews, marked out for discrimination and extermination. Although anti-Semitism and racism were both forms of dehumanization, they took different paths in Western history.

If racism is not universal, does it not perhaps derive, as some scholars have suggested, from an ideology of slavery?[11] Marxist scholars have claimed that racism developed as a convenient means for the Western bourgeoisie to justify the trade in black Africans and their exploitation. And, indeed, it is true that the practice of slavery in the United States facilitated the emergence of racism. It is not difficult to see that the white Americans who instituted the slavery of Africans would develop a doctrine of superiority to justify the practice. Racism is bound up with slavery in that case because the two were interconnected in the United States, but from a historical viewpoint the American experience is too specific to allow universal conclusions to be drawn from it. Two historical conclusions can be drawn: slavery has usually existed without a racial element, and there can also be racism without slavery.[12]

The Europeans at the beginning of the modern age—groups of travelers, soldiers, and missionaries—shaped the consciousness of modern times. Being under the influence of classical and medieval attitudes, they regarded the non-European cultures they encountered in their voyages, wars, and crusades as inferior and primitive. Columbus expected to find "people with tails"[13] in his voyages, and other explorers were of the same opinion. Until the late Middle Ages, China, North Africa, and India were civilizations with political, economic, and military achievements, but in the sixteenth and seventeenth centuries the balance began to change, and with the progress of modernity, Europe became the dominant civilization. Its power was demonstrated in the production of goods, in quality of life, in demographic growth and a decrease in mortality, in the spread of knowledge, and in the military sphere. Science, government, and capitalism led to European hegemony and a sense of superiority over other civilizations.[14]

At the beginning of the modern age, Europe was at the height of political and religious revolutions that not only brought great changes among the people involved but also made great differences between themselves and other cultures. If before the fifteenth century one could speak of medieval Christendom, after Columbus's voyages, the idea of Western civilization with its qualities and defects began to emerge.[15] From the fifteenth to the nineteenth centuries, the West passed a turning point, and a traditional society became a modern one. In the seventeenth and eighteenth centuries, the Enlightenment produced the success of the West but also Western racism.

Many thinkers of the Enlightenment were guilty of racial prejudice. David Hume wrote: "I am apt to suspect the Negroes, and in general all the other species of men [. . .] to be naturally inferior to the whites".[16] Emmanuel Kant said that "the Negroes in Africa have not received from nature an intelligence much above foolishness".[17] Hegel thought that "the negro race is a disgrace to humanity. It finds despotism acceptable, like cannibalism. The essence of humanity is freedom [. . .]. From that point of view, we should drop Africa and never mention it again".[18] Yet the revolutionary element in the thought of these thinkers was the universality of the human race.

The thinker who rebelled against the universality of the Enlightenment was Count Joseph Arthur de Gobineau. In his book *L'Inégalité des races humaines* (The Inequality of the Human Races) (1853–1855), he propounded a pessimistic philosophy of history.[19] He believed that in the modern world there was no longer any race that had preserved its purity. Basing himself on the common Aryan root of Indo-European languages like Sanskrit, Greek, Latin, and German, the French diplomat and scholar concluded that the highest development of mankind was to be found in the Aryans, a special group of Germanic peoples who blended Asiatic and European cultures in a brilliant manner. Gobineau thought there were superior and inferior races, but the racial hierarchy had been disturbed by mixed marriages and the prevalence of democracy and regimes of inferior races that treated inferior races as equal to superior ones.

Gobineau is an example of the usual confusion of concepts from language, biology, and physical and social ethnography to be found in racial doctrines. The term "Indo-European", for example, has a philological sense referring only to the closeness of a group of languages that branch out from one another. There is no scientific basis for the idea that the speakers of these languages belong to the same race. Gobineau's doctrine reached Germany and also influenced the British racist writer Houston Stewart Chamberlain. This intellectual climate finally engendered the worst form of racism of all, the murderous racial doctrine of National Socialism.

The events of the Holocaust and the racist atrocities of the second half of the twentieth century gave birth to skeptical and relativistic cultural attitudes. Today, the paradigm of liberal antiracism is multiculturalism. For the supporters of multiculturalism, Afro-Americans, women, and homosexuals are the collective victims of fanaticism and intolerance based on race, gender, and homophobia. The multiculturalists therefore call for a fight against racism and sexual bigotry.[20]

Multiculturalism grew out of the idea that Western culture is inherently racist because it fosters "white" or "European" values. This "dominant white culture" exercised a cultural repression of minority cultures. In its most comprehensive manifestations, multiculturalism provides a critique of political and cultural institutions and proposes an egalitarian model for minority cultures. It is a political movement based on a rejection of the superiority of Western culture, a doctrine that cultivates the multiplicity and relativity of cultures. The meaning of this relativity is that all cultures are basically equal and that one culture is no better or worse than another.[21]

Anti-racism is sometimes a new and sophisticated form of racism. The "slave revolt" of the Third World represented the West as embodying all the diseases of the human race. Frantz Fanon, a doctor and intellectual who completed his studies in France, called in his book *Les damnés de la terre* (The Wretched of the Earth), which appeared at the end of the colonial era and the Algerian War, for the mask to be stripped from racist colonialism, and he developed a philosophy of oppositional violence. "Hatred, blind hatred, which is as yet an abstraction, is the only wealth" of the natives against whom the racism is directed, wrote Jean-Paul Sartre in his introduction to Fanon's book.[22] Someone who has shown this kind of hatred in our time is Louis Farrakhan, leader of the American Muslim group, Nation of Islam, who accuses the Jews of responsibility for the American slave trade. The Million-Man March he organized in Washington was a call for racial self-sufficiency and the culmination of the indictment of the "white race".

Paradoxically, cultural superiority today seems a totally marginal issue because to some extent we live in a global civilization that is highly influenced by the West. The West has once again slipped in through the back door and made a mockery of the cultural relativity it advocates. Worldwide technology has united many people through Western capitalism. Racism and the "global village" are both products of Western culture.

Notes

1 Dinesh D'Souza, *The End of Racism*, New York 1995.
2 Tzvetan Todorov, *On Human Diversity: Nationalism, Racism, and Exoticism in French Thought*, Cambridge, MA 1993; Stephen Jay Gould, *The Mismeasure of Man*, New York 1981; O. Handlin, *Race and Nationality in American Life*, New York 1957.
3 Aristotle, *The Politics*, New York 1981, 69.
4 Martin Bernal, *Black Athena: The Afroasiatic Roots of Classical Civilization*, New Brunswick 1987.
5 Thomas F. Gossett, *Race: The History of an Idea in America*, Dallas 1963.
6 Nirad C. Chaudhuri, *The Continent of Circe*, Oxford 1966.
7 S. B. Ngcobo, "The Bantu Peoples", in G. H. Calpin, ed., *The South African Way of Life*, New York 1954.
8 Bernard Lewis, *Race and Slavery in the Middle East*, Oxford 1990.
9 V. Reynolds, V. Falger, and I. Vine, *The Sociological Ethnocentrism*, Athens 1987; Claude Lévi-Strauss, "Race and History", in Leo Kuper, ed., *Race, Science and Society*, Paris 1975.
10 Robert S. Wistrich, *A Lethal Obsession: The Longest Hatred*, New York 2010.
11 Stephen Steinberg, *The Ethnic Myth, Ethnicity and Class in America*, Boston 1989.
12 Eric Williams, *Capitalism and Slavery*, New York 1996.

13 Stephen Greenblatt, *Marvelous Possessions: The Wonder of the New World*, Chicago 1991, 74.
14 John M. Roberts, *The Triumph of the West*, Boston 1985; Eric L. Jones, *The European Miracle*, Cambridge 1981; Immanuel Wallerstein, *The Modern World System*, New York 1974.
15 Margaret Aston, *The Fifteenth Century: The Prospect of Europe*, New York 1968.
16 David Hume, "Of National Characters", in T. H. Green and T. Grose, eds., *Essays: Moral, Political and Literary*, vol. 1, London 1875, 252.
17 D'Souza, *The End of Racism*.
18 Georg Wilhelm Friedrich Hegel, *The Philosophy of History*, New York 1956, 95–99.
19 Arthur de Gobineau, *The Inequality of Human Races*, trans., A. Collins, New York 1967.
20 D'Souza, *The End of Racism*.
21 Renato Rosaldo, *Culture and Truth: The Remaking of Social Analysis*, Boston 1993.
22 Jean P. Sartre, "Preface", in Franz Fanon, ed., *The Wretched of the Earth*, New York 1963.

5 Foucault and Beyond

The Death of the God Killer

The work of Michel Foucault (1926–1984) redefines the questions, "What is modernity?" and "What is enlightenment?", and creates new interrelationships between them. Foucault took a huge task upon himself: to be the archeologist of Western culture, to examine its sexuality, its confessions, its forms of punishment, its speech, its patronizing attitude to other cultures; to analyze the relationships of power and knowledge in every ideology and organization; to be the psychologist of the psychiatrists, the historian of historiography; and to look at research disciplines known as adhesive mixtures that have become the outmoded and subtle means of retaining power.[1] He scrutinized their discourse from his professorial chair, which he called without false modesty "the chair of the history of systems of thought". He wished to be a new, up-to-date Nietzsche. If the "death of God" proclaimed the birth of a new man within aesthetics—that is, modernism—the Paris philosopher boasted of coining a new concept a hundred times more daring: the "death of man", which is the birth of post-modernism. Foucault's starting point is to be found in Nietzsche:

> Final conclusion: All the values by means of which we have tried so far to render the world estimable for ourselves and which then proved inapplicable and therefore devaluated the world—all these values are, psychologically considered, the results of certain perspectives of utility, designed to maintain and increase human constructs of domination—and they have been falsely projected into the essence of things. What we find here is still the hyperbolic naivete of man: positing himself as the meaning and measure of the value of things.[2]

Traditional Western philosophy and then the modern ideologies supposed that there is an Archimedian point from which the philosopher or the ideologist can examine reality, make a partial report on it, and propose a comprehensive solution.[3] According to Foucault, they were wrong: philosophies and ideologies are not privileged. Foucault learned from Nietzsche that philosophy and its moral and political derivatives are representatives of the will-to-power. The conclusion to be drawn is that philosophy as we know it has come to an end because of its inability to answer the great question, "What is truth?" There is no truth, said the Nietzschean Foucault: there are only fictions. There is no text: there are only interpretations. There is no reality, good or evil: there are only power structures. The social reality in which we live is always a world that we construct, an arbitrary construction of our desires, our longings, and a testimony to our will to power. The truth is that humans are beings without truth and without a fixed identity. Humans are their own project and represent the dialectical interrelationship between power and truth. Power creates truth, and truth in turn creates power.[4]

Foucault rejected the liberal and Marxist basic assumptions about the nature of the modern world because both ideologies involved a simplistic rationalization of social relationships. He revealed their contradictory nature through the Nietzschean genealogical method and exposed their deviance in the heart of modernity. If Marxism and liberalism predicated historical continuity, Foucault stressed discontinuity and historical rupture; if they claimed that liberty is a concept that can only be realized in a position of control, Foucault stressed the covert will to power in ideologies, social structures, and political institutions.[5]

Henceforth, he said, philosophy must ask, "What is the relationship between power and the creation of truth?"[6] Philosophy has to stop looking for a valid truth, and history has to stop searching for an objective explanation. The most significant thinker of the second half of the twentieth century internalized this new Nietzschean approach to philosophy and history and disseminated it. Traditional philosophy and scientific history had to give way. They had to become genealogy.

In his article "Nietzsche, Genealogy, History", Foucault represented Nietzsche's three varieties of history—monumental, antiquarian, and critical—as different forms of genealogy.[7] With regard to monumental history, Foucault thought that the glorification of a relatively heroic past usually ends in parody, and the attempt is futile. Genealogy does not reveal the truth behind the mask, for there is no such truth to be found, either revealed or hidden. The world is a world of masks, and the aim of genealogy is to study the masks: their beauty, their ugliness, their influence, and their purpose.

Antiquarian history, which is concerned with details, with everyday events and banalities, is liable to see every fact as outdated and every new idea as abnormal. And therefore, instead of looking for continuity and similarity and searching for a connection between the present and the ephemeral, genealogy reveals rupture, discontinuity, differences. Without the authority of a governing order, genealogy is able to make new beginnings.

Critical history passes judgment on the past and condemns it. Foucault rejects critical history when it assumes that one can attain historical truth. In critical history, the source of information is constantly tested. Thus, criticism rises against itself. The absolute Promethean will to knowledge and consciousness ends with the destruction of the informant. The fate of humanity in

Western history is the fate of Oedipus: in solving the Sphinx's riddle, Oedipus destroys himself and lays waste to the city.

On the ruins of "history", Foucault founded an "archaeology". History as a science has gone bankrupt because it has been shown that there is no continuity between different strata of history. Archeology is a series of discontinuous strata: "historical facts have no history".[8] Gaston Bachelard's theory of "epistemological rupture" influenced the thinking of Foucault, Claude Lévi-Strauss, and Louis Althusser, and their conclusion was that scientific thought does not develop in a straight line but leaps from one historical locality to another, from consciousness to consciousness, from revolution to revolution.[9] This conclusion was also reached by Thomas Kuhn: scientific development is not a process of continuous theoretical knowledge but a series of revolutionary developments inconsistent with one another. In each archeological stratum or historical period, there is an "*arche*", a particular quality that explains the phenomenon. The Greek "*arche*", Foucault's "*episteme*", and Kuhn's "paradigm" also apply to the findings of modern science, denoting the key, the comprehensive explanation, or the general laws governing nature.

According to Foucault, civilization is sustained by a series of accumulations of knowledge, power structures, and disseminators of knowledge. In every period, there is a certain *episteme*, and our task is to reveal the group of structures governing human activities in a particular time and place. The system, the structure, the *arche*, or the *episteme* precedes the concept of humankind and determine its actions in history. The task of science is to reveal the general laws of natural phenomena and human nature. Because one is no longer concerned with linear history—that is to say, one conceptual order developing out of another—one is left with "epistemological ruptures", successive changes revealed as breaks in historical continuity.

Two "epistemological ruptures" have taken place in modern Western history. The first was the break between the sixteenth century and the seventeenth and eighteenth centuries, which was the break between the Renaissance and the classical era. Renaissance science was passive, recorded things, and cataloged the phenomena of nature. Classical science was active, sought to build structures of knowledge and sort out phenomena in a rational way. From the recording of nature in the time of the Renaissance, there was a leap to the rational interpretation of it in the classical era. The second "epistemological rupture" took place between the seventeenth and eighteenth centuries and the nineteenth century and was a break between the scientific character of the classical era and that of the nineteenth century, which is still with us. In place of the three previous scientific categories—grammar, natural history, and the analysis of wealth—there were now three new categories: philology, biology, and political economy. From the *episteme* of representation, which was a static categorization, one went to a dynamic *episteme* of organization.

The *episteme* of the nineteenth century engendered the human as the object of science. "Before the end of the eighteenth century, man did not exist. He was a completely new creation which the demiurge of knowledge made with his own hands less than two hundred years ago".[10] Foucault did not regard man as an eternal entity but as an artificial creation, an arbitrary invention, the result of technological discourse, the fictitious "science of humanity", an illusion born at a certain moment in modern civilization. In the eighteenth century, humanity was not especially an object of science, and only in the following century did an independent and critical consciousness come into being with regard to humankind. The thinkers of the nineteenth century, however, considered the science of humanity to be a duplication of science, a superstructure, a kind of science fiction that had become outmoded.

Foucault believed that man was not a subject for thought or investigation but merely an instrument: "Western culture constructs under the name of man a kind of affirmation [...] which belongs to the positive sphere of knowledge but cannot be a matter for science".[11] The real existence of man is dominated by work, life, and language. Man is a creation of the system, an invention like any other, the result of a discourse he did not create. "The greater the incandescence of language becomes among us, the more man is doomed to perish".[12] Man as a rational and autonomous entity aspiring to liberty, choosing a good life and seeking truth is a fiction. The post-Kantian idea that man builds his own world came to an end with Nietzsche. Man, who created his God in his feverish brain, could also murder him. Foucault continued the radical line of thought of Nietzsche. Rational man who is self-created, who knows himself and what he has made, looks in the mirror and sees a hollow vessel whose contents have been emptied out by inhuman realms of discourse.

Post-modernist thinkers like Foucault, Lyotard, Barthes, Lacan, De Man, and Derrida proclaim with iconoclastic delight the dismantling of the subject. In place of it, language produces humankind like any other product, sets it up as a linguistic structure, a syntactical system, a text. Deconstruction of the text is also the dismantling of the subject. This post-modernist procedure is bound up with the death of the Promethean passion of modernity in which man constructs his reality with his own language.[13] Foucault wished to be Nietzsche's successor:

> Nietzsche indicated the turning point from a long way off, it is not so much the absence or the death of God that is affirmed as the end of man [...]; it becomes apparent, then, that the death of God and the last man are engaged in a contest with more than one round: is it not the last man who announces that he has killed God, thus situating his language, his thought, his laughter in the space of that already dead God, yet positing himself also as he who has killed God and whose existence includes the freedom and the decision of that murder?[14]

Foucault felt that the time had come to abandon humanity as a subject of study for modern science. Nietzsche's criticism of modern metaphysics and of the idea that the subject was free and rational at the same time as it was disembodied and dehumanized, shaped Foucault's view that the subject was created by power. Foucault said that if he wanted to boast, *The Genealogy of Morals* would be the title of his paper. He added that it was Nietzsche who decided to focus on power as a matter for philosophical discourse at a time when Marx chose production. Power, he said, is not an institution or a structure but "the name that can be given to an aesthetic situation in a certain society". Power is the creator of the human subject. There was a change here from the traditional approach of Western philosophy that claimed the primacy of the subject over power. Foucault's philosophy of power no longer depended on the traditional paradigm of understanding power through familiar concepts such as nature, law, and sovereignty, which was replaced by an immanent perception of power relationships, wills-to-power.

The prevailing idea in modernity is that the organization of society is dominated by the exercise of power. Power is not handed down from above or directed by a supreme will but is autonomously produced by all institutions. The strength of Foucault's thought lies in its rejection of the idea that a central omnipotent power governs society, a class, or the state. There is a rejection of belief in conspiracies as a theory of history, in a general oppression resulting from the rule and manipulations of one element in the social network, as in a cobweb. Power is everywhere, and its exercise is found in all social and political practices. Power means normalization. Foucault followed in the footsteps of the Nietzschean revolution, the essence of which was the change from the traditional criteria of good and evil, truth and falsehood to criteria of the will-to-power.

The making of modern man, the rational subject, is the result of technologies of power. In his book *Surveiller et punir* (Discipline and Punish), Foucault described the subject as "the product of a special technology of power which I have called discipline".[15] Normalization and repression are two sides of the same coin, and their purpose is to remove transgressors from the body of society. Pupils or workers who are too slow are separated from their friends and thus become marginal, abnormal, and destined to be unemployed or hospitalized in closed institutions. Society as a whole institutionalizes the mechanisms of power and consequently creates a constant separation of the normal and the abnormal, the healthy and the pathological, the permitted and the forbidden, the central and the marginal.[16] Society confines the nonconforming to prisons, sends the sick to hospitals, makes children go to school and workers to factories. General mobilization is essentially a Jüngerian concept and turns society into an industrial army.[17] The objectification of the different subjects gives society more power to control its members; a society based on technology and administration turns human beings into objects. That is the essence of bureaucracy. These complementary processes, normalization and bureaucratization, created enlightened despotism in the distant past and communist regimes in the recent past when reason was identified with power and the subject with an object.[18]

The monarch's exclusive control in the old society was exceeded by the discipline, supervision, and punishment in modern society. The policed modern society, said Foucault, operates through an infinite number of networks constituting an extremely complex system of relationships that make us wonder how it is that something that nobody completely understands can be so sophisticated in its forms of dissemination, its mechanisms, its capacity for harmonization, its systems of mutual supervision. In his three genealogical works—*The History of Madness*, *The Birth of the Clinic*, and *Discipline and Punish*—modern society was depicted as a 1984-type nightmare (1984 was the year Foucault died).[19] If Marcuse spoke in updated Marxist-Freudian terms of a depressing one-dimensional consumer society, Foucault revealed a sphere of discourse in which the discipline (in the academic sense but also in the sense of maintaining order) conditioned and determined its content and limits. In the three disciplinary systems of the eighteenth and nineteenth centuries—hospitals for the mentally ill, general hospitals, and prisons—genealogy revealed self-repression and collective introversion. The subjects, or what is left of them after their dissection by Foucault, are also assembled in locations of power: armies, factories, and schools. The system of control is shown to be a sociological institutionalization of Foucault's early *episteme*—social structures of the dominant discourse.

The system annihilates the subject. A controlling force takes charge of the social reality, and a new order is finally accepted that brings about the death of man. The genealogical exposure of the controlling force is intended to bring the old humanity and the old history to an end and create a new beginning. The victory of modernity was achieved through the enthronement of reason and the establishment of an absolute despotism. It was a despotism without a despot. This was also the underlying theme of De Tocqueville's analysis of democratic despotism, of Marcuse's one-dimensional society and Jacques Ellul's and Ernst Jünger's vision of a technological total mobilization. The new rational despotism institutionalized in an inhuman system deprives subjects of their will to negate, their self-creation, and, in short, their personality. Genealogy is a kind of opposition to this rational order of things on behalf of the other, whether the prisoner, the lunatic, the criminal, the worker, the alien, or the sick—all that are trampled underfoot by the march of reason in history that ends in universal despotism.[20] Foucault's policed society is an aspect of Kojève's "end of history".

The End of Modernity: Kojève and Baudrillard

Alexandre Kojève (1902–1968), a Russian immigrant and interpreter of Hegel in France in the mid-twentieth century, created the idea of the "end of history" and promoted it.[21] In the manuscript of the seminar "Progress in Hegel's Teaching" (1947), Kojève claimed that a significant change had taken place in man, whom he called *homo historicus*, the only living creature with a historical consciousness and an awareness of making changes in history.[22] Man, he said, creates history when he works for his subsistence and fights for his survival. The end of these actions is the end of history, and man ceases to be a historical phenomenon. History ceases to exist when man stops thinking, working, and fighting. At that point, man disappears as a historical being and becomes a creature that enjoys games, love, and art.[23]

Man as we have known him disappears at the end of history. "The end of the age of humanity, or the end of history, is the final extinction of man as pure spirit, as a free and historical individual [. . .]".[24] Here, Kojève was referring to the disappearance of wars and revolutions, the disappearance of philosophy, the disappearance of the subject. Everything else, everything that makes people happy—art, love, games—will continue forever.[25]

Kojève saw the battle of Jena in 1806 as the "end of history". Universalism, in the form of Napoleon, was victorious in that battle over the old historical alliance between feudalism and the monarchy. The ideas of the Enlightenment were spread by the cannons of the French army. The ideas of liberty and equality were now accepted. Even if democracy and prosperity did not exist in practice, they were seen as the goals of society. The acceptance of these goals to the exclusion of others put an end to the historical subject obliged to think, fight, and work. One had reached the "*post-histoire*". After the end of history, there was no return to nature or a state of animality because man remained a being with a memory. Post-modern man has moved from actions with a historical meaning to art, which in Kantian terms is a "disinterested interest".[26] Posthistorical man left a state of struggle and survival for one of enjoyment, or, in other words, he moved from modernity to post-modernity.[27]

It is not surprising if post-modernist thinkers like Lyotard and Baudrillard were fashionable in Ronald Reagan's conservative United States. These cultural critics justified moral relativism, dismissed public ethics, and social action and promoted a neoconservative philosophy. What McLuhan had and his postmodernist imitators did not have was a sense of discovery, putting forward theories of social change. Jean Baudrillard, for example, made McLuhan into a determinist. Now the media were said to represent a counterreality. In an attempt to create a countercosmology, Baudrillard went from McLuhan's technological idealism to technological nihilism.

Baudrillard, a post-modernist thinker and controversial cultural critic—an "intellectual terrorist" as he called himself—also claimed there had been a radical break with modernity.[28] Like McLuhan, he felt there was a rupture between modernity and post-modernity, just as previously there had been a rupture between premodernity and modernity.[29] Premodern society was organized on the basis of symbolic replacements, and modern society was organized on the basis of production. The end of modernity was the end of political economy and the end of the age in which production was the organizing principle of society. That was the age of capitalism and the bourgeoisie in which the workers were exploited by capital and responded with revolutionary force.[30]

We were now in a new period: one of "simulation", whose main feature was production guided by the media and based on the industrialization of knowledge. Economics, politics, social life, and culture were dominated by codes and images that controlled the consumption of goods and the conditions of daily life. The worker was no longer a force of production, but became a symbol and was judged not in relation to someone else or by his intelligence, but in relation to the system. Art, which had previously been a sphere of change or possible opposition, was adopted by politics and economics. The old boundaries between the individual and society were effaced.[31]

Baudrillard internalized and continued the poststructuralist line of criticism, which held that the "system" dominated the subject. The post-modern world was a "hyper-reality" filled with entertainment, information, and media that provided people with experiences. People escaped from the "desert of reality" to the ecstasy of hyper-reality and the new sphere of computers, Internet, and hi-tech. They became marionettes or theatrical images. Thus, subjects lost contact with reality and became fragmentary. This was the situation at the end of modernity, which was a proclamation of the capacity of man to mold and control reality. The simulation and the cult of experience created a situation requiring new forms of social theories and politics suited to the technological innovations. Modernist theory, on the other hand, was suited to a subject-object dialectic in which the subject controlled the object.[32]

In the post-modern world, the very concept of meaning, depending on fixed structures, clear limits, and accepted ideas, disappeared.[33] What one had was a carnival of reflected images, mirrors-within-mirrors, from the television screen to the screen of consciousness. Man was trapped in a world of simulation. The masses were subjected to the message of a media without a message and without a meaning. In the era of simultaneity, the classes disappeared, politics were dead, and, together with that, all dreams of release from alienation, dreams of liberty and revolution. These masses who sought spectacles, not reality, were the silent majority and signified "the end of social sentiment". Social theory lost interest in reality, in changes, in difference and entered a "black hole".[34]

The true, original reality disappeared and was replaced by a mythical reality that was beyond good and evil—a cleansed aesthetic spectacle. It was a world without meaning or content, for meaning requires a hidden aspect, but in the post-modernist reality, all was transparent, accessible, ephemeral, and incidental. "Post-modernism documents the present, the destruction of meaning and desire—the image, the mosaic-like aspect of things".[35] Modernity was the era of Marx and Freud, the era in which politics, culture, and economics embraced the concepts of desire and the subconscious. Now, when technology has replaced capital, we live in a reality of technological nihilism. Baudrillard was mesmerized with the emptiness of the post-modern world: "If the meaning of being a nihilist is reaching a point of no return, then I am a nihilist. If being a nihilist means [the disappearance of] a form of production, then I am a nihilist".[36] In Baudrillard's nihilism, there is no joy, no energy, no hope for a better future. "Nothing is left to us on which to base anything. All that remains to us is rhetorical violence". The Promethean passion of modernity gave way to nihilistic pessimism.

The Subversive Intellectual

The history of the modern Western intellectual extends from Rousseau to Foucault. Rousseau thought a "new man" could be created and popular sovereignty achieved by means of reason in the form of the "general will", although he was also aware of the self-defeating potentialities of this scheme of modernity. Foucault sought to demonstrate by means of genealogy that reason and morality were obsolete. His aim was to deconstruct the concept of man as a rational subject and subvert the idea of the continuity and unity of the human race.

Rousseau thought that because man was not rational, he had to be educated toward an acceptance of universal reason. This revolutionary idea was the basis of the modern Kantian ethic, which implies the injunction that man becomes a moral subject when he is subservient to a universal code of duty. The Kantian formula, "Dare to know! Have the courage to use your brain!" contains elements of both will and reason: the ambition of Rousseau and Kant was to unite the two. In Rousseau, one does not have a philosophy of progress but a philosophy of order. In a secularized culture, he wished to restore the unity of man and nature by means of reason, but in the period after Kant and Rousseau, this goal proved to be unattainable. Modern rational man now knows that culture and nature are not identical. Modernity is an awareness that culture is in confrontation with nature. Reason, the starting point of modern culture, which had once been the idea of understanding nature, became a Promethean will-to-power to mold it.

The Promethean rational project derives from the fact that reason, whose aim was to understand and interpret the universe in clear general terms, became a principle of power that longed to control it. Ideals of thought and contemplation became principles of organization and production. The Promethean passion changed from the use of reason and science as a conceptualization and abstraction in order to understand the world to a challenge to reorganize, rebuild, and control. The project of modernity, side by side with triumphant reason, consciously aimed at the reconstruction of man and nature. Reason ceased to be a principle of order and self-knowledge and was now associated with a will to dominate.

The revolutionary post-Kantian consciousness that engendered the idea that the world can be constructed and therefore also deconstructed by our knowledge was fully manifest in Nietzsche and Foucault, but its roots can be found in Rousseau. His first two essays but also his late work, *The Confessions*, is a genealogy in all respects. *The Confessions* is a kind of personal genealogy. Rousseau did not call his work a memoir or an autobiography but a confession, which is a means of retrospective self-discovery, a conscious inspection of one's past life. If one lived it in that way, one could also have lived it in another way. This reflective consciousness of the molding of a subject—through education, one's political community, self-knowledge—is essentially modern and anticipates Foucault by two hundred years. *The Confessions* are a testimony to a narrator who knows himself and creates himself. Rousseau is a fascinating intellectual not only in his preoccupation with social and universal matters in order to understand the "world" but also, and especially, because of his self-observation and reflection in order to understand his "me". By this, Rousseau is revealed as a representative of modernity but also as a thinker who passed beyond it.

When Jacob Talmon was asked to define an intellectual, the historian replied that an intellectual is someone who does not sleep at night and not for the reasons you think.[37] What is interesting about this definition is what is missing: it disregards the common concept of an intellectual as a moral person who defends absolute values or as a defender of truth and justice. It is a completely neutral definition. There are intellectuals who do not sleep because they are troubled by problematic thoughts of injury to human freedom; there are intellectuals whose sleep is disturbed because they have nightmarish visions of human engineering and structures of power. Sleeplessness may arise from fear of despotism but also from fear of liberty. This is the meaning of Rousseau's observations on the ambiguity of modernity. There is a modernity that seeks to further the Enlightenment, and there is a modernity that fights against the values of the Enlightenment.

It was Georges Clemenceau who, during the Dreyfus Affair on the 23rd of January 1898, gave the writers of a petition in the newspaper *L'Aurore* the name "intellectuals". A week later, Maurice Barrès, an anti-Dreyfusard writer, responded with his own scornful heading concerning the petition: "Protest of the Intellectuals". Although the term is quite a recent one, about a hundred years old, intellectuals have always sallied forth from their Platonic caves, from the Socratic markets, from the medieval monasteries, from the Paris salons, from the academic ivory towers, and from the media and sought in their feverish minds to propose a path, to return to the proper way, to demand order, to arouse criticism, enthusiasm, pity, or anger.

Post-modernist thinkers like Foucault, Deleuze, and Lyotard have tried to change the approach to the task of the intellectual. According to them, the intellectual is no longer committed to the task of counselor to the masses and critic of ideologies but has to provide tools for analysis. The intellectual has ceased to be the arbiter of truth and justice who gives voice to the oppressed. Deleuze said, "For us, the intellectual theoretician has ceased to be a subject, the representative of conscience".[38] Lyotard was even more extreme, and proclaimed "the death of the intellectuals" who presumed to speak on behalf of humanity in the name of abstract ideas and moral truths.[39] One may assume that this refers to the universal truths of the Enlightenment, for there is no other kind. Artists, writers, and philosophers are no longer accountable for the fate of humanity.

Jean-Paul Sartre, in a conversation with Herbert Marcuse, claimed that "the classical intellectual has to fight".[40] He was referring to intellectuals of a bourgeois type such as Voltaire, Zola, and Charles Péguy. Their successors today, he said, should be intellectuals who draw the attention of the public to revolutionary principles. Sartre maintained that knowledge is power, and the intellectuals therefore have to bestow their knowledge on the proletariat. From Sartre's point of view, Foucault may be considered a postrevolutionary intellectual who is uninterested in influencing the collective will, and as Foucault said:

> The task of the intellectual is not to tell others what to do. What right has he to do so? His task is not to influence people again and again or to decide what is self-evident, but to arrest people's mental habits, [examine] the way in which they work and think, reconsider regulations and institutions [. . .], participate in creating a political will.[41]

Foucault created the concept of the "specific intellectual" who focuses on particular struggles and engages in the discourse on power and constructions of power, privilege, and the will-to-power. The intellectual reveals problems and is an indefatigable subverter of established beliefs, whether utopian, ideological, or scientific. In Foucault's interpretation, the intellectual does not identify with reason or Rousseau's "general will". Her task is to discover the relationship between power and truth, which she does by means of genealogy, the search for the roots of ideas and institutions, the location of the historicity of things.

In the drawn-out discussion on the task of the intellectual, Foucault shifted the emphasis from "fixing the world" to an analysis of the technologies of control governing social institutions and shaping modern politics. The task of the intellectual is not to advocate an ideological ethos but to disassemble mechanisms of power and, step by step, to build up "strategic knowledge". The creation of a series of special local strategies is a form of subversion and opposition to the power found in many networks. Instead of providing public relations for political ideologies, intellectuals have to distrust and subvert them. They must abandon the discourse on instrumental reason and natural rights, a discourse that came from the Enlightenment and reached its zenith with the Hegelian identification of the truth with the absolute. Their indefatigable subversion of the illusions of humanism, utopian dreams, and ideological visions is expressed in a deconstruction of forms of hegemony.

The intellectual is skeptical, suspicious, subversive:

> I think that placing me as an anarchist, a leftist, a Marxist, a nihilist, an anti-Marxist, a technocrat in the service of Gaullism, a new liberal [. . .], none of these descriptions is important in itself, but if, on the other hand, one takes them together, they have a certain significance. I must admit that what they are trying to say pleases me.[42]

Foucault became interested in the question of how individuals became subjects and probed "the genealogy of the modern subject as a hostorico-cultural reality". Archives and manuscripts revealed the way the mentally ill, homosexuals, prisoners, and Eastern-European dissidents became marginal in society. From the late 1970s onward, Foucault abandoned his research on the history of insanity and psychiatric institutions for a more focused analysis of Soviet dissidents, who were shown by him to have had a place in the social order. The "dangerous individual", a class that was a creation of nineteenth-century criminology, was a structural part of the modern Soviet punitive system. *The Gulag Archipelago*, for instance, was legally created for purposes of "public hygiene". The stages of regimentation in Eastern Europe were in accordance with a process of "normalization" that distinguished medically between the healthy and the sick. Dissidence was considered a form of rebellion against a classification based on common knowledge.[43]

The analysis of political techniques and the deconstruction of the uses of power were basic to Foucault's research enterprise. Foucault explained that his aim is not to write the social history of a prisoner but the political history of the creation of 'truth'. Where political activity was concerned, Foucault belonged to the *Groupe d'Information sur les Prisons* (Group for Information on Prisons, GIP), the aim of which was to bring about a situation in which prisoners could formulate and deal with their requirements without the help of intellectuals. The intervention of intellectuals in particular struggles like the activities of the Society for the Defense of Prisoners' Rights and the Group Acting on Behalf of Prisoners changed the discourse on prisoners in France. The activity was accompanied by a number of articles in newspapers against the punitive system of the prison administration. In his reaction to the movement for prisoners' rights, in the summer of 1981, Foucault called for a reexamination of the laws and the prisons. His book *Discipline and Punish* (1975) was such a reexamination of the general approach to punishment in modern society and the relationships between the power of the authorities, the right to punish, and the execution of punishment.[44] In an article on the roots of the death penalty written in response to the Mitterrand government's move to rescind it, Foucault called for "punishment to be a matter for continual reflection, research, experimentation and transformation".[45]

The philosopher who indicated an alternative route for Western culture, who disdained it from the bottom of his heart and hated the historical person it produced, who always searched out the morbid in order to redefine the normal, who sought, by means of the insane, the criminal, the pervert, the primitive, to negate the abnormal normality of European thought, art, and language, at the end of the 1970s found a new anchor.

In the years 1978–1979, Foucault published a series of articles on the rise of Khoumeini and the Iranian revolution. Six of them were published in the Italian newspaper *Corriere della Sera* and three in the French journal *Nouvelle Obsevateur*. The connecting thread of the articles was enthusiasm for the spiritual dimension that Khoumeini and the Islamic regime had brought to politics and the fascination with the experience of the crowds in the streets. The fundamentalism coming from Iran excited Foucault and brought him to the conclusion that spirituality of this kind was needed like air by a Europe on the point of passing out.[46]

Foucault compared the Iranian revolution to the French Revolution. The long-term processes of social and economic changes began long before the turnabout of 1789, a special revolutionary event that gave people a deep experience resembling a theatrical spectacle taking place before their eyes day after day. Similarly, now, the revolutionary event in Iran was an inner experience, a kind of liturgy. Religion played a central role in the people's deposition of its sovereign. In the demonstrations, Foucault saw a parallel between a religious ritual and this expression of public retribution. As in Greek tragedy, in which collective ritual is bound up with the reenactment of the laws of justice, in the streets of Teheran one saw the political action of the dethronement of a sovereign through a collective religious ritual.

But the chief thing about the Iranian uprising was the main point of every total revolution: the attempt to create a new human. In the Iranian effervescence, Foucault discerned more than an attempt to exchange one political regime for another: it was the possibility of creating a new subjective relationship to the other. Here, the religious character of the Iranian movement of liberation was important because it created a subjective relationship to the government. In the Iranians' wish to unite, Foucault saw the vision of a new regime of truth and a new form of government.

A reader of these articles is astounded at how this thinker, who in his books tried to persuade one to be critical toward mechanisms of power, lost his critical sense and was overawed by the spectacle. An intelligent observer became one who was stunned. If the rational subject no longer exists, why should a political theology such as that of Iran not be a possible solution for modern Europe, sick, dried up, and bereft of spirituality?

Notes

1 Gary Gutting, ed., *The Cambridge Companion to Foucault*, Cambridge 2005; Leonard Lawlor and John Nale, eds., *The Cambridge Foucault Lexicon*, Cambridge 2014.
2 Friedrich Nietzsche, *The Will to Power*, trans., Walter Kaufmann and Reginald J. Hollingdale, paragraph 12, 1968.
3 S. B. Drury, *Alexandre Kojeve—The Roots of Post-Modern Politics*, London 1994.
4 Michel Foucault, *The History of Sexuality*, trans., R. Hurley, vol. 1, London 1979, 109, 133.
5 Colin Koopman, *Genealogy as Critique: Foucault and the Problems of Modernity*, Indianapolis, IN 2013.
6 Jeffrey Nealon, *Foucault Beyond Foucault: Power and Its Intensifications Since 1984*, Stanford 2007.
7 Michel Foucault, *Discipline and Punish: The Birth of the Prison*, trans., A. Sheridan, London 1977.
8 Michel Foucault, *Les mots et les choses: une archeologie des sciences*, Paris 1966, 360.
9 Gaston Bachelard, *La formation de l'esprit scientifique*, Paris 1938.
10 Foucault, *Les mots et les choses*, 319.
11 Ibid., 378.
12 Ibid., 397.
13 On Foucault's approach that examines the text in a concrete discourse, as opposed to Derrida's approach that examines the text in itself, see Jacques Derrida, *L'Ecriture et la différence*, Paris 1967.

14 Foucault, *The Order of Things*, London 2002, 420.
15 Foucault, *Discipline and Punish*, 194.
16 Foucault, *The History of Sexuality*.
17 Jean-Paul de Gaudemar, *L'Orde et la production: naissance et forms de la discipline d'usine*, Paris 1982.
18 Alain Touraine, *Critique of Modernity*, trans., D. Macey, Oxford 1995, 167.
19 Foucault, *Madness and Civilization: A History of Insanity in the Age of Reason*, New York 1988.
20 Mitchell Dean and Kaspar Villadsen, *State Phobia and Civil Society: The Political Legacy of Michel Foucault*, Stanford 2016.
21 Jeff Love, *The Black Circle: A Life of Alexandre Kojeve*, New York 2018.
22 Alexander Kojeve, *Introduction a la lecture de Hegel*, ed., R. Queneau, Paris 1947.
23 Shadia B. Dury, *Alexander Kojève: The Roots of Post-modern Politics*, Basingstoke 1994.
24 Ibid.
25 Denis Goldford, "Kojève's Reading of Hegel", *International Philosophic Quarterly*, vol. 22 (1982): 257–294.
26 Kojève, *Introduction a la lecture de Hegel*.
27 Alexander Kojève, *The Concept, Time, and Discourse*, trans., Robert B. Williamson, South Bend, IN 2018.
28 Douglas Kellner, *Jean Baudrillard: From Marxism to Post-modernism and Beyond*, Cambridge 1989.
29 Richard J. Lane, *Jean Baudrillard* (Routledge Critical Thinkers), London 2008.
30 Jean Baudrillard, *Pour une critique de l'economie du signe*, Paris 1972.
31 Idem, *Symbolic Exchange and Death*, trans., Iain Hamilton Grant, Thousand Oaks, CA 1993.
32 Douglas Kellner, "Introduction: Jean Baudrillard in the Fin-de-Millennium", in D. Kellner, ed., *Baudrillard: A Critical Reader*, Cambridge 1994, 1–24.
33 Baz Kershaw, *The Radical in Performance: Between Brecht and Baudrillard*, London 2013.
34 Baudrillard, *In the Shadow of the Silent Majorities*, New York 1983.
35 Idem, *Symbolic Exchange and Death*, 4.
36 Baudrillard, "On Nihilism", *On the Beach*, 6 (Spring 1984), 39.
37 Jacob Talmon, *Mission and Testimony: Political Essays*, ed., David Ohana, Eastbourne 2015.
38 Michel Foucault, *Discipline and Punish: The Birth of the Prison*, trans., A. Sheridan, London 1977, 7–206.
39 Jean F. Lyotard, *Tombeau de L'Intellectuel*, Paris 1984.
40 *Liberation*, 7th June 1974.
41 Foucault, "The Concern for Truth", in *Foucault: Politics, Philosophy, Culture—Interviews and Other Writings 1977–1984*, New York 1984, 211.
42 P. Rainbow, ed., *The Foucault Reader*, New York 1984.
43 Foucault, "The Concern for Truth", XX.
44 Ibid., 123–110.
45 *Liberation*, 7th June 1974.
46 Foucault, "The Concern for Truth", 221.

Epilogue

The End of Modernity?

The mutual relationship between modernity and enlightenment is explored in Foucault's essay, "What Is Enlightenment?", referring to Emmanuel Kant's article of the same name.[1] The French thinker calls our attention to the negative aspect of the German thinker's definition of enlightenment. Enlightenment is an escape or exit from a state of immaturity, associated with subjection to the other: military discipline, political power, religious authority. In the terms of the essay, because man is responsible for his immaturity, the solution can only be a change he makes in himself. Enlightenment is the use of reason, the moment when one makes use of one's reason without deferring to any authority. Kant used the German word *räzonieren*, meaning the use of reason as an end in itself, and its significance was the congruence in the Enlightenment between the universal use and the public use of reason. As soon as critical reason is internalized universally and publicly, one has attained enlightenment, and in Foucault's words, "criticism is the travel-diary of reason which has reached maturity with enlightenment, and also the opposite: the Enlightenment is the age of criticism".

Is modernity a continuation of the Enlightenment? According to Foucault, enlightenment is not a historical period but a way of relating to the world around one, to free choice, to what the Greeks called "*ethos*": the way of thinking, feeling, reacting, and behaving. The *ethos* of modernity is the consciousness of a discontinuity in time, a break in tradition, or, as Baudelaire defined it in 1863, "the temporary, the fleeting, the incidental". From the idea that modernity is an eternal presence in the momentary, a hundred years later it became imprisonment in the moment. Man, said Foucault commenting on Baudelaire, is not someone who wants to discover himself but someone who wants to invent himself: "modernity is the mission of self-creation". We must see ourselves as beings who historically were created by the Enlightenment. Thus, a few historical inquiries of a genealogical nature, as specific as possible, are required. Their purpose is not to locate the core of reason, which is found in the Enlightenment, but to establish "the present limits of the essential".

What is the connection between enlightenment and modernism? The Enlightenment was a certain moment in the history of Europe that included "social changes, political institutions, forms of knowledge, projects of rationalization of knowledge and customs, and technological changes", and humanism is a variety of subjects connected with religion, science, and politics that from the nineteenth century have been associated with value judgments in European history.

In an interview in May 1966, Foucault called for humanism to be abandoned. The most strenuous heritage that the nineteenth century left us is humanism, which was a way or behavior that used terms such as "morality", "value", and "reconciliation"—problems that in principle have no solution. Our task is to release ourselves from humanism, and in this sense our work is political work. On rare occasions, humanism and enlightenment overlap. However, one must refuse the extortionate demand that "one must either be in favor of enlightenment or against it". Foucault's conclusion was that one must reject "meta-narratives", "world-embracing, radical" projects. Criticism should be genealogical: in other words, "it will no longer be an investigation of formal structures of universal value but a historical investigation of the events that made us set ourselves up and know ourselves as subjects of what we do, think, and say".

Foucault's post-modern admonition represents the end of a long intellectual tradition in which reason was the jewel in the crown of universality. Plato was the first intellectual to want the power to carry out in practice the rational utopia he had created. The philosopher-king wished to combine political action with rational thought, politics with criticism, the Caesar with the priest. Now, political thinking shifted from Leviathan—the state, which had preoccupied thinkers from Plato to Hobbes and Rousseau—to other power points. Foucault abandoned the challenge of Rousseau and the Enlightenment of combining particular and universal thought by means of the "general will" and began to analyze the complex way in which various details shape human subjects. With the help of Nietzsche, the tradition of Rousseau, Hegel, and Marx, who sought by great radical systems to establish politicomoral communities that achieve social harmony, was abandoned. The trouble was that this desire for unity and harmony expressed in the search for the common good could only be satisfied by rejection of the "other". Foucault wanted to avoid that. In place of metanarratives, he proposed various kinds of otherness and of areas of discourse.

In this demand he was joined by Lyotard, who called for an end to great narratives. What was rejected was not the content of these ideologies but the arrogance they demonstrated.[2] Because the elements in history have no unity, there is no continuity between them, and the assertion of Western culture of the unity of the human race has to be rejected. In place of the elements that were supposed to make up history, there is a series of signs and languages without any historical or social connection. The fragmentation of human societies completely destroys the idea of any unity. This idea naturally undermines classic social thought, for people are brought up to be social beings who seek out one another. Enlightened modernity asked people to go from a state of nature to a modern condition, not the opposite. The modernist model that had dominated Western thought from the time of the Enlightenment had now reached its end. The call to promote the universality of the human family, to return to the great humanist values, or to revive enlightened conceptions has failed.

Post-modernist thought compresses human experience into the conditions of the market where people have no historical continuity, collective memory, or social solidarity. But what is humankind without meaningful rational activity? Without it, one is left with an obsessive search for identity and self-definition, which includes others only in their difference. Post-modern society is a society of "others", in which the "other" is the "other" of the "other". With the rejection of universal relationships, the special value of the humanity common to all people or "others" is also likely to disappear. This dynamic of otherness may also develop into a mutual threat, into a rupture of social relations, into a break in the continuity of history, into a social Darwinism, and into a view of mankind as conceived by Carl Schmitt: friend or foe, them or us. Society becomes a battlefield of cultures alien to one another in which there are relationships of power between men and women, black and white, religious and secular. Social conflicts and cultural wars create a human kaleidoscope. Humans are like spaceships united by cultures distinguished by their differences, cold wills-to-power in inhuman constellations.

The idea of modernity is expressed in critical self-perception and a striving for the triumph of reason, which is now in a situation of decline. There is less belief in the idea of universality, which began with monotheism, and Greek thought, which claimed that the world was made by God or was said to be run according to the principles of objective reason. This belief paved the way for the victories of universal morality, of the scientific spirit, of human rights in general, and of democracy, which came from the call for "one man, one vote". Thus, the soil was prepared for the creation of modern thought, which sought to act according to free and rational decisions. But the victory of reason also caused a transition from a rationalism of ends to a rationalism of means, and this soon became a rationalization of technology. This created a moral vacuum that was quickly filled by phenomena like charisma or violence, whose justification was their mere existence.

The Promethean century has witnessed the decline of modernity, precisely because of its success. Prometheus, having fulfilled himself, is liable in his despair to seek to call back inhuman mythical forces. Underlying the Promethean passion was modernity—man's scheme of self-creation—and enlightenment, the existence of a constant tension between the actual and the desirable, between existence and conception, between reality and the ideal. The correlation between self-creation and working toward a universal objective was basic to the constant effort to discover new horizons. Beneath the weariness, the exhaustion, and the skepticism of post-modernist criticism is a refusal to take Promethean horizons into account. At the same time, reason remains a powerful critical weapon of humankind against the idols that have come out of modernity: totalitarianism, fundamentalism, the golem of technology, genetic engineering, and a boundless will-to-power. Otherwise, the new Prometheus is liable to return the fire to the gods.

Notes

1 Foucault, "What Is Enlightenment?" in P. Rabinow, ed., *The Foucault Reader*, New York 1984, 32–50.
2 Lyotard, *The Post-Modern Condition*, trans., G. Bennington and B. Massumi, Minneapolis, 1984.

Bibliography

Aeschylus, *Aeschylus: Persians. Seven Against Thebes. Suppliants. Prometheus Bound*, trans. Alan H. Sommerstein, Loeb Classical Library, no. 145, Cambridge, MA 2009.
Agursky, Mikhail, *The Third Rome—National Bolshevism in the USSR*, London 1987.
Angaut, Jean-Christophe, "Revolution and the Slav Question: 1848 and Mikhail Bakunin", in Douglas Moggach and Gareth Stedman Jones, eds., *The 1848 Revolutions and European Political Thought*, Cambridge 2018.
Arendt, Hannah, *The Origins of Totalitarianism*, New York 1968, 454.
Arieli, Yehoshua, *Individualism and Nationalism in American Ideology*, Cambridge, MA 1964.
Aristotle, *The Politics*, New York 1981.
Aron, Raymond, *Main Currents in Sociological Thought*, vol. I, London 1965.
Aston, Margaret, *The Fifteenth Century: The Prospect of Europe*, New York 1968.
Atlan, Henri, "Preface", in Moshe Idel, ed., Cyrille Aslanoff, trans., *Le Golem*, Paris 1992.
Aust, Stefan, *Baader-Meinhof: The Inside Story of the R.A.F.*, trans., Anthea Bell, Oxford 2009.
Bachelard, Gaston, *La formation de l'esprit scientifique*, Paris 1938.
Bannour, Wanda, *Les nihilistes russes*, Paris 1975.
Baud-Bovy, Samuel, ed., *Jean-Jacques Rousseau*, Neuchâtel 1962.
Baudrillard, Jean, *Pour une critique de l'economie du signe*, Paris 1972.
Baudrillard, Jean, *In the Shadow of the Silent Majorities*, New York 1983.
Baudrillard, Jean, "On Nihilism", *On the Beach*, 6 (Spring 1984).
Baudrillard, Jean, *Symbolic Exchange and Death*, trans., Iain Hamilton Grant, Thousand Oaks 1993.
Bauer, Otto, *Die Nationalitatenfrage und die Sozialdemokratie*, Vienna 1907.
Benjamin, Walter, "The Work of Art in the Age of Its Technological Reproductibility", in Edmund Jephcott, Howard Eiland and Others, trans., Michael W. Jennings and Howard Eiland, eds., *Collected Writings*, Cambridge, MA 2002.
Benoit, Jean-Louis, *Tocqueville moraliste*, Paris 2004.
Bentham, Jeremy, *An Introduction to the Principles of Morals and Legislation*, eds., J. H. Burns & H. L. A. Hart, London 1982.
Berlin, Isaiah, *Against the Current: Essay in the History of Ideas*, ed., Henry Hardy, London 1979.
Berlin, Isaiah, "Herzen and Bakunin on individual liberty", in *Russian Thinkers*, London 1994.
Berlin, Isaiah, *Karl Marx: His Life and Environment*, Oxford 1996.
Berlin, Isaiah, *Liberty: Incorporating Four Essays on Liberty*, Oxford 2002.

Berna, Henri, *Du socialisme utopique au socialisme ringard*, Paris 2015.
Bernal, Martin, *Black Athena: The Afroasiatic Roots of Classical Civilization*, New Brunswick, NJ 1987.
Bernstein, Richard J., ed., *Habermas on Modernity*, Cambridge, MA 1985.
Bernstein, Samuel, *Auguste Blanqui and the Art of Insurrection*, London 1971.
Bertman, Christopher, *Rousseau and the "Social Contract"*, London 2004.
Bianquis, Geneviève, *Faust a travers quatre siecles*, Paris 1955.
Bibliotheque Nationale, Blanqui MSS.
Birnbaum, Pierre, *Sociologie de Tocqueville*, Paris 1955.
Blanqui, Louis Auguste, *Oeuvres de Louis Auguste Blanqui*, Editions la Bibliothèque Digitale 2012.
Blanqui, Louis Auguste, *Défense du citoyen Blanqui devant la cour d'assises*, Paris 2018a.
Blanqui, Louis Auguste, *The Blanqui Reader*, eds., Peter Hallward and Philippe Le Goff, trans., Mitchell Abidor, Memphis, TN 2018b.
Bloch, Ernst, *The Principle of Hope*, trans., N. Placie, S. Placie, and P. Knight, Cambridge, MA 1986, 1945.
Bloom, Allan, "Jean-Jacques Rousseau", in Leo Strauss and J. Cropsey, eds., *History of Political Philosophy*, Chicago 1987.
Bloom, Allan, *Closing of the American Mind: How Higher Education Has Failed Democracy and Impoverished the Souls of Today's Students*, New York 2012.
Blumenberg, Hans, *Work on Myth*, trans. R. M. Wallace, Cambridge, MA 1985.
Blumenau, Bernhard, *The United Nations and Terrorism: Germany, Multilateralism, and Antiterrorism Efforts in the 1970s*, Basingstoke 2014.
Bobbio, Norberto, *The Philosophy of Decadentism*, trans., David Moore, Oxford 1948.
Bourget, Paul, "Theory of Decadence", in *Décadence*, Essais de psychologie contemporaine, Paris 1883.
Brogan, Hugh, *Alexis de Tocqueville: A Life*, New Haven, CT 2007.
Brooke, Christopher, "Rousseau's Second Discourse, Between Epicureanism and Stoicism", in Stanley Hoffmann and Christie MacDonald, eds., *Rousseau and Freedom*, Cambridge 2010.
Byron, George Gordon, *The Works of Lord Byron*, London 1905.
Calinescu, Matei, *Five Faces of Modernity—Modernism, Avant-Garde, Decadence, Kitsch, Post-Modernism*, Durham, NC 1987.
Camus, Albert, *The Rebel: An Essay on Man in Revolt*, trans., Anthony Bower, New York 1992.
Capdevila, Nestor, *Tocqueville ou Marx: democratie, capitalisme, revolution*, Paris 2012.
Carr, Edward Hallett, *A History of Soviet Russia*, 7 vols., New York 1950.
Carr, Edward Hallett, *Michael Bakunin*, New York 1975.
Carrese, Paul O., *Democracy in Moderation: Montesquieu, Tocqueville, and Sustainable Liberalism*, Cambridge 2016.
Carver, Terrell, ed., *The Cambridge Companion to Marx*, Cambridge 1991.
Carver, Terrell and Farr, James, eds., *The Cambridge Companion to the Communist Manifesto*, Cambridge 2015.
Cassirer, Ernst, *The Philosophy of the Enlightenment*, Princeton, NJ 1951.
Chaudhuri, Nirad C., *The Continent of Circe*, Oxford 1966.
Chaunu, Pierre, *Historie et Decadence*, Paris 1981.
Chomsky, Noam, *On Anarchism*, New York 2013.
Clark, Ronald W., *Lenin*, New York 1988.

Cohen, Jacques, *La Preparation de la Constitution de 1848*, Paris 1925.
Cohen, Joshua, *Rousseau: A Free Community of Equals*, Oxford 2010.
Cohen-Solal, Annie, *Sartre, 1905–1980*, Paris 1985.
Cohn, Norman, *The Pursuit of the Millennium*, New York 1961.
Cole, George Douglas Howard, *History of the Socialist Thought*, 5 vols., London 1954–1960.
Condorcet, Marquis des, *Esquisse d'un tableau historique des progres de l'esprit humain*, Paris 1795.
Confino, Michael, *Violence dans la Violence*, Paris 1973.
Copelston, Fredrick C., *Philosophy in Russia—From Herzen to Lenin and Berdyaev*, Notre Dame, IN 1986.
Cranston, Maurice, *The Noble Savage: Jean-Jacques Rousseau, 1754–1762*, Chicago 1991.
Croce, Benedetto, *History of Europe in the Nineteenth Century*, trans., Henry Frust, New York 1933.
Daniels, Robert Vincent, *Trotsky, Stalin and Socialism*, Boulder, CO 1991.
Dart, Gregory, *Rousseau, Robespierre and English Romanticism*, Cambridge 1999.
Dean, Mitchell and Villadsen, Kaspar, *State Phobia and Civil Society: The Political Legacy of Michel Foucault*, Stanford, CA 2016.
De Gaudemar, Jean-Paul, *L'Orde et la production: naissance et forms de la discipline d'usine*, Paris 1982.
De Gobineau, Arthur, *The Inequality of Human Races*, trans., A. Collins, New York 1967.
De la Fournier X, *Alexis de Tocqueville, un monarchist independent*, Paris 1981.
De Montesquieu, Charles, *Considerations sur les causes de la grandeur des Romains et de leur decadence*, Paris 1734.
Dent, Nicholas, "Rousseau on amour-propre", *Aristotelian Society Supplementary*, 72:1 (1998): 57–74.
Dent, Nicholas, *Rousseau*, London 2005.
Derrida, Jacques, *L'Ecriture et la différence*, Paris 1967.
De Tocqueville, Alexis, "The Social and Political State of France Before and After 1989", *London and Westminster Review* (1836).
De Tocqueville, Alexis, *The Old Regime and The Revolution*, trans., John Bonner, New York 1856.
De Tocqueville, Alexis, *Oeuvres Completes*, Paris 1864–1875.
De Tocqueville, Alexis, *Souvenirs*, ed., Luc Monnier, Paris 1942.
De Tocqueville, Alexis, *The European Revolution and Correspondence with Gobineau*, ed. and trans., J. Lukács, Gloucester, MA 1968.
De Tocqueville, Alexis, *Correspondence Tocqueville-Kregorlay*, Tome XIII, vols. 1, 2, Paris 1977.
De Tocqueville, Alexis, *Democracy in America*, trans., James T. Schleifer, Indianapolis, IN 2010.
De Tocqueville, Alexis, *The Ancien Régime and the French Revolution*, Cambridge 2011.
Dolgoff, Sam, ed., *Bakunin on Anarchy*, London 2013.
Dommanget, Maurice, *Babeuf et les Problemes du Babouvisme*, Paris 1963.
Draper, Hal, "The Dictatorship of the Proletariat", in *From Marx to Lenin*, New York 1987.
Drescher, Seymour, *Tocqueville and England*, Cambridge, MA 1964.

Drury, S. B., *Alexandre Kojève—The Roots of Post-Modern Politics*, London 1994.
D'Souza, Dinesh, *The End of Racism*, New York 1995.
Duchemin, Jacqueline, *Promethe: Historie du mythe, de ses origines orientales a ses incarnations modernes*, Paris 1974.
Durkheim, Emil, "Montesquieu and Rousseau", in *Forerunners of Sociology*, Ann Arbor, MI 1960.
Dury, Shadia B., *Alexander Kojeve: The Roots of Post-Modern Politics*, Basingstoke 1994.
Edwards, Bob, Foley, Michael W., and Diani, Mario, eds., *Beyond Tocqueville: Civil Society and the Social Capital Debate in Comparative Perspective*, Hanover 2001.
Elster, Jon, *Alexis de Tocqueville: The First Social Scientist*, Cambridge 2009.
Engels, Friedrich, *Selected Works*, 3 vols., New York 1950.
Fairbank, John K. and Albert, Feuerwerker, eds., *The Cambridge History of China*, vol. 13, *Republican China 1912–1949*, Part 2, Cambridge 1998.
Fairley, Barker, *Faust: Six Essays*, Oxford 1953.
Falk, Candace and Pateman, Barry, eds., *Emma Goldman: A Documentary History of the American Years*, vol. 3, Stanford, CA 2012.
Felshtinsky, Yuri, *Lenin, Trotsky, Germany and the Treaty of Brest-Litovsk: The Collapse of the World Revolution, November 1917–November 1918*, Milford, CT 2012.
Ferro, Marc, *October 1917: A Social History of the Russian Revolution*, vol. III, London 1980.
Fichte, Johann Gottlieb, "Die Anweisung zum seligen Leben oder auch die Religionslehre", in *Sammtliche Werke*, vol. V 1806.
Fitzpatrick, Sheila, ed., *Cultural Revolution in Russia*, Bloomington, IN 1978.
Fitzpatrick, Sheila, ed., *The Russian Revolution*, New York 1982.
Foucault, Michel, *Les mots et les choses: une archeologie des sciences*, 1966.
Foucault, Michel, *Surveiller et punir*, Paris 1975.
Foucault, Michel, *Discipline and Punish: The Birth of the Prison*, trans., A. Sheridan, London 1977.
Foucault, Michel, *The History of Sexuality*, trans. R. Hurley, vol. 1, London 1979.
Foucault, Michel, "The Concern for Truth", in *Foucault: Politics, Philosophy, Culture—Interviews and Other Writings 1977–1984*, New York 1984a.
Foucault, Michel, "What Is Enlightenment?" in P. Rabinow, ed., *The Foucault Reader*, New York 1984b, 32–50.
Foucault, Michel, *Madness and Civilization: A History of Insanity in the Age of Reason*, New York 1988.
Foucault, Michel, *The Order of Things*, London 2002.
Foucault, Michel, *History of Madness*, trans., J. Khalfa, ed., J. Murphy, New York 2006.
Franks, Benjamin, Jun, Nathan and Williams, Leonard, eds., *Anarchism: A Conceptual Approach*, London 2018.
Freund, Julien, *La Decadence: Historie sociologique et philosophique d'une categorie de l'expression humaine*, Paris 1984.
Furet, François, "La Decouverte de L'Amerique", *Magazine litteraire*, 236 (Decembre 1986).
Furet, François and Ozouf, Jacques, *Reading and Writing: Literacy in France from Calvin to Jules Ferry*, Cambridge 1982.
Furet, François and Ozouf, Mona, eds., *Dictionnaire Critique de la revolution francaise*, Paris 1981.
Gannett, Robert T., *Tocqueville Unveiled: The Historian and His Sources for the Old Regime and the Revolution*, Chicago 2003.

Garaudy, Roger, "Le Neo-blanquisme de contrebande et les positions anti-leninistes d'Andre Marty", *Cahiers du Communisme* (January 1953).

Garsten, Bryan, ed., *Rousseau, the Age of Enlightenment and Their Legacies*, Princeton, NJ 2014.

Gauthier, David, *Rousseau: The Sentiment of Existence*, Cambridge 2006.

Gautier, Theophile, *Portraits et souvenirs litteraires*, Paris 1881.

Gide, Charles, *Selections from the Works of Fourier*, London 1901.

Gillespie, Michael Allen, *Nihilism Before Nietzsche*, Chicago 1995.

Golden, Leon, *In Praise of Prometheus: Humanism and Rationalism in Aeschylean Thought*, Chapel Hill, NC 1966.

Goldford, Denis, "Kojève's Reading of Hegel", *International Philosophic Quarterly*, 22 (1982): 257–294.

Goldman, Lucien, *Marxisme et sciences humaines*, Paris 1970.

Gossett, Thomas F., *Race: The History of an Idea in America*, Dallas 1963.

Gould, Stephen Jay, *The Mismeasure of Man*, New York 1981.

Gramsci, Antonio, *Selections from Political Writings*, London 1910–1920.

Greenblatt, Stephen, *Marvelous Possessions: The Wonder of the New World*, Chicago 1991.

Grey, Alexander, *The Socialist Tradition*, London 1946.

Gutting, Gary, ed., *The Cambridge Companion to Foucault*, Cambridge 2005.

Handlin, Oscar, *Race and Nationality in American Life*, New York 1957.

Harrington, C. J., *The Author of Prometheus Bound*, Austin, TX 1970.

Harvey, David, *Marx, Capital, and the Madness of Economic Reason*, Oxford 2017.

Havens, G. R., *Voltaire's Marginalia on the Pages of Rousseau*, Columbus 1933.

Hegel, Georg Wilhelm Friedrich, *The Philosophy of History*, New York 1956.

Hegel, Georg Wilhelm Friedrich, *Philosophie des Rechts—Die Vorlesung von 1919–20 in einer Nachschrift*, ed., D. Henrich, Frankfurt 1983.

Hegel, Georg Wilhelm Friedrich, "Hegel to Niethammer: Bamberg, October 28, 1808", in Clark Butler and Christiane Seiler, *Hegel: The Letters*, trans., Bloomington, IN 1984.

Herf, Jeffrey, *Reactionary Modernism: Technology, Culture and Politics in Weimar and the Third Reich*, Cambridge 1984.

Herman, Arthur, *1917: Lenin, Wilson, and the Birth of the New World Disorder*, New York 2018.

Herr, Richard, *Tocqueville and the Old Regime*, Princeton, NJ 1962.

Hesiod, *Hesiod: Theogony, Works and Days, Testimonia*, trans., Glenn W. Most, Loeb Classical Library, no. 57, Cambridge, MA 2006.

Hobbes, Thomas, *Hobbes: Leviathan (Revised student edition)*, ed., Richard Tuck, Cambridge 1996.

Horkheimer, Max and Adorno, Theodor, *The Dialectic of Enlightenment*, New York 1974.

Huizinga, Johan, *The Autumn of the Middle Ages*, Chicago 1997.

Hume, David, "Of National Characters", in T. H. Green and T. Grose, eds., *Essays: Moral, Political and Literary*, vol. 1, London 1875.

Hutton, Patrick H., *The Cult of the Revolutionary Tradition: The Blanquists in French Politics, 1864–1896*, Berkeley, CA 1981.

Huyssen, Andreas, "The Vamp and the Machine—Technology and Sexuality in Fritz Lang's Metropolis", *New German Critique*, 24–25 (1981–1982): 221–237.

Idel, Moshe, *Golem: Jewish Magical and Mystical Traditions on the Artificial Anthropoid* (SUNY Series in Judaica), New York 1990.

Illing, Sean, *Prophets of Nihilism: Nietzsche, Dostoevsky, and Camus*, Washington, DC 2017.

Issac, Jeffrey C., *Arendt, Camus, and Modern Rebellion*, New Haven, CT 1992.
Iviansky, Ze'ev, "Individual Terror: Concept and Typology", *Journal of Contemporary History*, 12:1 (January 1977): 43–63.
Jacobi, Friedrich Heinrich, *Werke III*, Leipzig 1816.
Jacoby, Russell, *Dialectic of Defeat: Contours of Western Marxism*, Cambridge 2002.
Jardin, André, *Alexis de Tocqueville*, 1986.
Jay, Martin, *The Dialectical Imagination: A History of the Frankfurt School and the Institute for Social Research 1921–1950*, London 1973.
Joll, James, *The Anarchists*, Cambridge, MA 1980.
Jonas, Hans, *Le principe responsabilite:une ethuque pour la civilization technologique*, Paris 1990.
Jones, Eric L., *The European Miracle*, Cambridge 1981.
Juillard, Jacques, *La faute à Rousseau*, Paris 1985.
Kagan, Donald, *Pericles of Athens and the Birth of Democracy*, New York 1991.
Kandiyali, Jan, *Reassessing Marx's Social and Political Philosophy: Freedom, Recognition, and Human Flourishing*, London 2018.
Kant, Immanuel, *Beantwortung der Frage: Was ist Aufklärung?*, Berlin 1784.
Kantzler, Saul, *The International Terror: Ideology, Organization, Practice*, Tel-Aviv, 1980.
Karl, Marx, "The Abolition of Universal Suffrage in 1850", *Karl Marx and Frederick Engels—Collected Works*, 10 (1978): 137.
Kateb, George, "The Political Thought of H. Marcuse", *Commentary* (1970): 18–63.
Kautsky, Karl, *The Dictatorship of the Proletariat*, Ann Arbor, MI 1919.
Kautsky, Karl, *Communism vs. Social Democracy*, New York 1946.
Kellner, Douglas, *Jean Baudrillard: From Marxism to Post-Modernism and Beyond*, Cambridge 1989.
Kellner, Douglas, "Introduction: Jean Baudrillard in the Fin-de-Millennium", in D. Kellner, ed., *Baudrillard: A Critical Reader*, Cambridge 1994.
Kelly, Aileen, *Mikhail Bakunin—A Study in the Psychology and Politics of Utopianism*, New Haven, CT 1987.
Kerényi, Károly, *Prometheus: Archetypal Image of Human Experience*, trans., R. Manheim, New York 1963.
Kershaw, Baz, *The Radical in Performance: Between Brecht and Baudrillard*, London 2013.
Kohn, Hans, *Nationalism in the Soviet Union*, New York 1934.
Kojève, Alexander, *Introduction a la lecture de Hegel*, ed., R. Queneau, Paris 1947.
Kojève, Alexander, *The Concept, Time, and Discourse*, trans., Robert B. Williamson, South Bend, IN 2018.
Kolakowski, Leszek, *Main Currents of Marxism*, trans., P. S. Falla, Oxford 1978.
Koopman, Colin, *Genealogy as Critique: Foucault and the Problems of Modernity*, Indianapolis, IN 2013.
Koppen, Karl Friedrich, *Friedrich der Gross und seine Widersacher*, Leipzig 1840.
Kropotkin, Petr, *Law and Authority*, London 1900.
Labriola, Antonio, *Essays on the Materialist Conception of History*, Chicago 1904.
Lamberti, Jean-Claude, *La notion d'individualisme chez Tocqueville*, Paris 1970.
Lampert, Evgenii, *Studies in Rebellion*, London 1957.
Lane, Richard J., *Jean Baudrillard* (Routledge Critical Thinkers), London 2008.
Lash, Scott, *Sociology of Post-Modernism*, London 1990.
Lawlor, Leonard and Nale, John, eds., *The Cambridge Foucault Lexicon*, Cambridge 2014.

Lecercle, Jean-Louis, *Jean-Jacques Rousseau: Modernité d'un Classique*, Paris 1973.
Lecourt, Dominique, *Promethee, Faust, Frankenstein—Fondements imaginaries de l'ethique*, Le Plessis-Robinson 1996.
Leier, Mark, *Bakunin: The Creative Passion: A Biography*, New York 2006.
Lenin, Vladimir, *Collected Works*, Moscow 1964–1970.
Leopold, David, *The Young Karl Marx: German Philosophy, Modern Politics, and Human Flourishing*, Cambridge 2009.
Lerner, Karl, *Der Kampt der Osterreichischen Nationen um den Staat*, Leipzig 1924.
Le Roy, Maximilien and Locatelli Kournwsky, Loïc, *Ni Dieu ni maître. Auguste Blanqui, l'enfermé*, Tournai 2014.
Lesson, Peter T., *Anarchy Unbound: Why Self-Governance Works Better Than You Think*, Cambridge 2014.
Lévi-Strauss, Claude, "Race and History", in Leo Kuper, ed., *Race, Science and Society*, Paris 1975.
Lewis, Bernard, *Race and Slavery in the Middle East*, Oxford 1990.
Leymaire, Camille, "Barbes et Blanqui a Belle-Ile", *La Nouvelle revue*, CXII (1898).
Liberation, 7 June 1974.
Lively, Jack, *The Social and Political Thought of Alexis de Tocqueville*, Oxford 1965.
Locke, John, *Second Treatise of Government* (Hackett Classics), Indianapolis, IN 1980.
Longworth, Philip, *The Making of Eastern Europe*, New York 1959.
Lorberbaum, Yair, *In God's Image: Myth, Theology, and Law in Classical Judaism*, Cambridge 2015.
Love, Jeff, *The Black Circle: A Life of Alexandre Kojeve*, New York 2018.
Lovejoy, Arthur Oncken and Boas, George, *Primitivism and Related Ideas in Antiquity*, New York 1965.
Low, Alfred D., *Lenin on the Question of Nationality*, New York 1958.
Lukács, Georg, *Lenin: A Study on the Unity of His Thought*, trans., Nicholas Jacobs, London 1970.
Lukács, György, *History and Class Consciousness*, London 1971.
Luxemburg, Rosa, *The Russian Revolution*, Ann Arbor, MI 1961.
Lyotard, Jean-Francois, *La condition post-moderne: rapport sur le savoir*, Paris 1979.
Lyotard, Jean-François, *The Post-Modern Condition*, trans., G. Bennington and B. Massumi, Minneapolis, MN 1984a.
Lyotard, Jean-François, *Tombeau de L'Intellectuel*, Paris 1984b.
MacIntyre, Alasdair, *Marcuse*, New York 1970.
Maguire, Matthew W., *The Conversion of Imagination: From Pascal Through Rousseau to Tocqueville*, Cambridge 2006.
Manuel, Frank E., *The New World of Henri Saint-Simon*, Cambridge, MA 1956.
Manuel, Frank E. and Manuel, Fritzie P., *Utopian Thought in the Western World*, Cambridge, MA 1979.
Marcuse, Herbert, *Soviet Marxism*, London 1958.
Marcuse, Herbert, *Negations: Essays in Critical Theory*, trans., J. Shapiro, Boston 1968.
Marcuse, Herbert, "The End of Utopia", in *Five Lectures: Psychoanalysis, Politics, and Utopia*, Boston 1970.
Marcuse, Herbert, *An Essay on Liberation*, Boston 1971.
Marcuse, Herbert, *Reason and Revolution: Hegel and the Rise of Social Theory*, London 1986.
Marcuse, Herbert, *Hegel's Ontology and the Theory of Historicity*, Cambridge, MA 1989.

Marcuse, Herbert, "Philosophy and Political Theory", *Times*, 44 (Spring 1993).
Marcuse, Herbert, *One-Dimensional Man: Studies in the Ideology of Advanced Industrial Society*, London 2002.
Marty, A., *Quelques aspects de l'activite de Blanqui*, Paris 1951.
Marx, Karl and Engels, Friedrich, *Marx and Engels Collected Works*, London 2010.
Mason, E. C., *Goethe's Faust. Its Genesis and Purpose*, Berkeley 1967.
Mathiez, Albert, "Notes inedites de Blanqui sur Robespierre", *Annales historiques de la Revolution Francaise* (1928).
McLellan, David, *Karl Marx: A Biography*, Basingstoke 2006.
McLuhan, Marshall, "Myth and Mass Media", *Daedalus*, 2 (Spring 1959).
Melograni, Piero, *Lenin and the Myth of World Revolution: Ideology and Reasons of State, 1917–1920*, Amherst, NY 1989.
Mendelssohn, Moses, *Ueber die Frage: was heißt aufklären?* Berlin 1784.
Meschke, W., ed., "Prometheus", in *Gedichte Goethes, veran-schaulicht nach Form und Strukturwandel*, Berlin 1957.
Meyer, P. H., "The Individual and Society in Rousseau's *Émile*", *Modern Language Quarterly* 19 (1958): 99–114.
Mill, John Stuart, *Considerations on Representative Government*, London 1861.
Mitchell, Joshua, *The Fragility of Freedom: Tocqueville on Religion, Democracy and the American Future*, Chicago 1995.
Molinier, Sylvain, *Blanqui*, Paris 1948.
Moncourt, Andre, *Daring to Struggle, Failing to Win: The Red Army Factions 1977 Campaign of Desperation*, Oakland, CA 2008.
Mumford, Lewis, *The Story of Utopias, Ideal Commonwealth and Social Myths*, Philadelphia 1972.
Namier, Lewis B., *1848: The Revolution of the Intellectuals*, New York 1946.
Nealon, Jeffrey, *Foucault Beyond Foucault: Power and Its Intensifications Since 1984*, Stanford 2007.
Neher, André, *Faust et le Maharal de Prague: Le mythe et le réel (Questions)* (French Edition), Paris 2015.
Neidelman, Jacob, *Rousseau's Ethics of Truth*, London 2017.
Nelson, Robert J., "The Quarrel of Ancients and the Moderns", in Denis Hollier, ed., *A New History of French Literature*, Cambridge, MA 1989.
Neuhouser, Frederick, *Rousseau's Critique of Inequality*, Cambridge 2014.
Ngcobo, S. B., "The Bantu Peoples", in G. H. Calpin, ed., *The South African Way of Life*, New York 1954.
Nietzsche, Friedrich, "Beyond Good and Evil", in Walter Kaufmann, ed. and trans., *The Portable Nietzsche*, New York 1968a.
Nietzsche, Friedrich, *The Will to Power*, Walter Kaufmann and Reginald J. Hollingdale, trans., New York 1968b.
Nietzsche, Friedrich, "Twilight of the Idols", in Walter Kaufmann, ed. and trans., *The Portable Nietzsche*, New York 1968c.
Nietzsche, Friedrich, *The Gay Science*, Josefine Nauckhoff, trans., Cambridge 2001, paragraph 347.
Nietzsche, Friedrich, "The Antichrist", in Walter Kaufmann, trans. and ed., *The Portable Nietzsche*, New York 1976. Available at https://www.amazon.com/Portable-Nietzsche-Library/dp/0140150625#reader_0140150625
Nietzsche, Friedrich, *Digitale Kritische Gesamtausgabe Werke und Briefe*. Available at http://doc.nietzschesource.org/de/ekgwb (accessed 30 November 2018).

Nisard, Desire, *Etudes de moeurs et de critique sur les poetes latins de la decadence*, 2 vols., Paris 1888.
Ohana, David, *Homo Mythicus*, Eastbourne 2009.
Ohana, David, *The Dawn of Political Nihilism*, Eastbourne 2012.
Ohana, David, *The Nihilist Order: The Intellectual Roots of Totalitarianism*, Eastbourne 2016.
Orr, John, "German Social Theory and the Hidden Face of Technology", *European Journal of Sociology*, XV:2 (1974): 312–336.
Page, Stanley W., *The Geopolitics of Leninism*, New York 1982.
Palmer, Philip M. and More, Robert P., eds., *The Sources of the Faust Tradition, From Simon Magus to Lessing*, London 1936.
Parsons, Talcott, *The System of Modern Societies*, Englewood Cliffs, NJ 1971.
Pierson, George Wilson, *Tocqueville and Beaumont in America*, New York 1938.
Pitkin, Hanna Fenichel, *The Attack of the Blob—Hannah Arendt's Concept of the Social*, Chicago 1981.
Plato, *The Dialogues of Plato*, Republic, Book X, trans., B. Jowett, Oxford 2005.
Plato, *Laches. Protagoras. Meno. Euthydemus*, Loeb Classical Library 165, Cambridge, MA 1977.
Plekhanov, Georgi V., *Fundamental Problems of Marxism*, London 1969.
Pokrovsky, Mikhail, *Russia in World History*, ed., R. Szporluk, Ann Arbor, MI 1970.
Pons, Silvio, *The Cambridge History of Communism*, Cambridge 2017.
Proudhon, Pierre Joseph, *Qu'est-ce que la propriete?* Paris 1840.
Proudhon, Pierre Joseph, *La Revolution sociale demontree par le coup d'etat du Deux Decembre*, Paris 1852.
Raggio, Olga, "The Myth of Prometheus—Its Survival and Commonplace", *Journal of Warburg and Courtauld Institutes*, 21 (1958): 44–62.
Rainbow, P., ed., *The Foucault Reader*, New York 1984.
Rauschning, Hermann, *The Revolution of Nihilism*, New York 1939.
Read, Christopher, *Lenin: A Revolutionary Life*, London 2005.
Reeves, Richard, ed., *American Journey: Traveling with Tocqueville in Search of Democracy in America*, New York 1983.
Reginster, Bernard, *The Affirmation of Life: Nietzsche on Overcoming Nihilism*, Cambridge, MA 2006.
Richardson, Joanna, *Baudelaire*, London 1994.
Ricœur, Paul, "Qu'est-ce qu'un texte? Expliquer et Comprendre", in *Hermeneutik und Dialektik*, vol. II, Tubingen 1970.
Ridd, T. J., *Goethe* (Past Masters), Oxford 1984.
Rigby, T. H., *Lenin's Government: Sovnarkom 1917–1922*, Cambridge 2008.
Ritter, Alan, *Anarchism: A Theoretical Analysis*, Cambridge 2010.
Roberts, John M., *The Triumph of the West*, Boston 1985.
Roberts, William Clare, *Marx's Inferno: The Political Theory of Capital*, Princeton, NJ 2018.
Rosaldo, Renato, *Culture and Truth: The Remaking of Social Analysis*, Boston 1993.
Rosen, Stanley, *G. W. F. Hegel: An Introduction to the Science of Wisdom*, South Bend, IN 2000.
Rosenaw, Eliyahu, "Rousseau's Émile, An Anti-Utopia", *British Journal of Educational Studies*, XXVIII:3 (1980): 212–224.
Rougerie, Jacques, *Proces de Communards*, Paris 1964.
Rousseau, Jean-Jacques, "Introduction", in Allan Bloom, trans. and ed., *Émile, or On Education*, Book V, New York 1979.

Rousseau, Jean-Jacques, *On the Social Contract* (Hackett Classics), trans. Donald A. Cress, Indianapolis, IN 1988.

Rousseau, Jean-Jacques, "The Social Contract", in Victor Gourevitch, ed. and trans., *The Social Contract and Other Later Political Writings*, Cambridge 1997.

Rynolds, Vernon, Falger, Vincent S. E., and Vine, Ian, *The Sociological Ethnocentrism*, Athens, GA 1987.

Salmon, Jean-Jacques, *Le destin technologique*, Paris 1922.

Sartre, Jean-Paul, "Preface", in Franz Fanon, ed., *The Wretched of the Earth*, New York 1963.

Schaeffer, Denise, "The Utility of Ink: Rousseau and *Robinson Crusoe*", *The Review of Politics* (2001): 121–148.

Schelling, Friedrich Wilhelm Joseph, *Einleitung in die Philosophie der Mythologie oder Darstellung der rein-rationalen Philosophie in Schellings Werke*, ed., Schroder M., 6 vols., Munich 1927–1928.

Schiller, Friedrich, "The Theosophy of Julius," in *The Works of Friedrich Schiller*, IV, *Poems and Essays*, New York 1906.

Schlegel, August Wilhelm, *Prometheus*, 1979; appeared first in Friedrich Schiller, *Musen-Almanach*, Tubingen 1798.

Schleifer, James T., *The Making of Tocqueville's Democracy*, Chapel Hill, NC 1980.

Scholem, Gershom, "The Golem of Prague & the Golem of Rehovoth", *Commentary* (January 1, 1966).

Scholem, Gershom, *Origins of the Kabbalah*, trans., Allan Arkush, Princeton, NJ 1987.

Scholem, Gershom, *The Messianic Idea in Judaism and Other Essays*, New York 1995.

Schoolman, Morton, *The Imaginary Witness: The Critical Spirit of Herbert Marcuse*, London 1980.

Schumpeter, Joseph A., *Capitalism, Socialism, and Democracy*, New York 2008.

Scott, James C., *Two Cheers for Anarchism: Six Pieces on Autonomy, Dignity, and Meaningful Work and Play*, Princeton, NJ 2012.

Sebestyen, Victor, *Lenin: The Man, the Dictator, and the Master of Terror*, New York 2017.

Sharpe, Lesley, ed., *The Cambridge Companion to Goethe*, Cambridge 2006.

Shaw, Bernard, *Fabian Essays in Socialism*, CreateSpace 2017.

Shelley, Mary, *Frankenstein: Or the Modern Prometheus*, San Diego 2015.

Sherwin, Byron L., *The Golem Legend*, New York 1952.

Simmons, John A., *On the Edge of Anarchy: Locke, Consent, and the Limits of Society*, Princeton, NJ 2014.

Smith, J., Moncourt, André and Churchill, Ward, eds., "The Red Army Faction", in *A Documentary History*, vol. 2: *Dancing with Imperialism*, Oakland, CA 2013.

Sontheimer, Kurt, *Das Elend Muserer Intellectuellen*, Berlin 1976.

Sorel, Georges, "Jean-Jacques Rousseau", *Le mouvement Socialiste*, XXI (Juin 1907): 507–532.

Sorel, George, *The Illusions of Progress*, trans., J. Stanley and C. Stanley, Berkeley, CA 1969.

Spengler, Oswald, *The Decline of the West*, 2 vols., trans., C. F. Atkinson, New York 1947.

Sperber, Jonathan, *Karl Marx: A Nineteenth-Century Life*, New York 2014.

Spitzer, Alan Barrie, *The Revolutionary Theories of L. A. Blanqui*, New York 1957.

Stalin, Joseph, "The Foundations of Leninism", Reptd, in B. Franklin, ed., *The Essential Stalin*, London 1924.

Stalin, Joseph, "Lenin as the Organizer and Leader of the Russian Communist Party", in Lenin, ed., *Selected Works*, vol. 1, Moscow 1950.
Starobinski, Jean, *Jean-Jacques Rousseau—Transparency and Obstruction*, Chicago 1971.
Starobinski, Jean, *Jean-Jacques Rousseau, La Transparence et l'obstacle*, Paris 1982.
Steinberg, Stephen, *The Ethnic Myth, Ethnicity and Class in America*, Boston 1989.
Sterinberng, Jonathan, *Bismarck: A Life*, Oxford 2013.
Sternhell, Zeev, *La Droite revolutionnaire, 1885–1914*, Paris 1978.
Sternhell, Zeev, *Anti-Enlightenment Tradition*, trans., David Maisel, New Haven, CT 2009.
Stokes, Curtis, *The Evolution of Trotsky's Theory of Revolution*, Washington, DC 1982.
Stoppard, Tom, *The Coast of Utopia*, New York 2002.
Suny, Ronald Grigor and Martin, Terry, eds., *A State of Nations: Empire and Nation-Making in the Age of Lenin and Stalin*, Oxford 2001.
Talmon, Jacob, *The Origins of Totalitarian Democracy*, London 1952.
Talmon, Jacob, *Mission and Testimony: Political Essays*, ed., David Ohana, Eastbourne 2015.
Tardy, Jean-Noël, *L'Age des Ombres. Complots, conspirations et sociétés secrètes au XIXe siècle*, Paris 2015.
Theen, Rolf H. W., *Lenin: Genesis and Development of a Revolutionary*, Princeton, NJ 2014.
Thomson David, *The Babeuf Plot*, London 1947.
Todorov, Tzvetan, *On Human Diversity: Nationalism, Racism, and Exoticism in French Thought*, Cambridge, MA 1993.
Touraine, Alain, *Critique of Modernity*, trans., D. Macey, Oxford 1995.
Tridon, Gustave, *Les Hebertistes*, Paris 1864.
Trotsky, Leon, "The Russian in Lenin", *Current History*, 19 (1923–1924).
Trotsky, Leon, *Literature and Revolution*, ed., William Keach, Ann Arbor, MI 1960.
Trotsky, Leon, *The Permanent Revolution and the Results and Prospects*, New York 1962.
Trotsky, Leon, *Out Political Tasks*, London 1980.
Trousson, Raymond, *Le theme de Promethee dans la literature europeenne*, 2 vols., Geneva 1964.
Tsemah, Adah, *Alexis de Tocqueville on England*, Notre Dame, IN 1951.
Tudesq, André-Jean, *La Democratie en France depuis 1815*, Paris 1971.
Varon, Jeremy, *Bringing the War Home: The Weather Underground, the Red Army Faction, and Revolutionary Violence in the Sixties and Seventies*, Oakland, CA 2004.
Vattimo, Gianni, *The Transparent Society*, Cambridge 1992.
Venturi, Franco, *Roots of Revolution*, London 1969.
Villa, Dana Richard, *Teachers of the People: Political Education in Rousseau, Hegel, Tocqueville, and Mill*, Chicago 2017.
Vladchos, Georges, "L'influence de Rousseau sur la conception du contrat social chez Kant et Fichte", in *Études sur le "Contrat Social" de J.-J. Rousseau*, Paris 1964.
Volkogonov, Dmitri, *Lenin: A New Biography*, New York 1994.
Volpe, Galvano della, "Critique marxiste de Rousseau", in *Études sur le "Contrat Social" de J.-J. Rousseau*, Paris 1974.
von Balthasar, Hans Urs, *Prometheus: Studien zur Geschichte des deutschen Idealismus*, Heidelberg 1947.
von Rad, Gerhard, "The Origin of the Concept of the 'Day of Y'", *Journal of Semitic Studies*, 4 (1959): 97–108.

Wallerstein, Immanuel, *The Modern World System*, New York 1974.
Warth, Robert D., *Leon Trotsky*, Boston 1977.
Webb, Sidney, *Socialism in England*, Trieste 2017.
Weber, Max, *The Protestant Ethic and the Spirit of Capitalism*, trans. Stephen Kalberg, Oxford 2010.
Weitling, Wilhem, *Garantien der Harmonie und Freiheit*, Berlin 1908.
Welch, Cheryl B., ed., *The Cambridge Companion to Tocqueville*, Cambridge 2006.
Wells, Roger, *Insurrection: The British Experience 1795–1803*, Gloucester, MA 1986.
Wendling, Amy, *Karl Marx on Technology and Alienation*, Basingstoke 2009.
Werblowsky, Raphael Judah Zwi, *Lucifer and Prometheus—A Study of Milton's Satan*, London 1952.
Wessel, Leonard P., *Prometheus Bound: The Mythic Structure of Karl Marx's Scientific Thinking*, London 1984.
Wheeler-Bennett, John W., *Brest-Litovsk: The Forgotten Peace, March 1918*, New York 1971.
Wiener, Philip P. and Fisher, John, eds., *Violence and Aggression in the History of Ideas*, New Brunswick, NJ 1974.
Williams, David Lay, *Rousseau's Social Contract*, Cambridge 2014.
Williams, Eric, *Capitalism and Slavery*, New York 1996.
Wilson, Francis G., "Tocqueville's Conception of the Elite", *The Review of Politics*, IV (1949): 271–286.
Winnington-Ingram, Reginald Pepys, *Studies in Aeschylus*, Cambridge 1983.
Wistrich, Robert S., *A Lethal Obsession: The Longest Hatred*, New York 2010.
Zimmerman, M. E., *Heidegger's Confrontation with Modernity: Technology, Politics, Art*, Bloomington, IN 1990.
Zunz, Olivier and Kahan, Alan S., eds., *The Tocqueville Reader: A Life in Letters and Politics*, Oxford 2002.

Index

Abendroth, Wolfgang 189
Adams, John Quincy 61
Aeschylus 4, 25n6
Africa 198–199, 201
al-Andalusi, Said 198
Allgemeiner Deutscher Arbeiterverein 117
Althusser, Louis 206
American Revolution 37
Amis de la Verite 116
Amis de Peuple 116
anarchism 169–172
Ancien Régime et la Révolution, L' (The Ancien Régime and the Revolution) (de Tocqueville) 61–62, 64–65, 132–133
Antichrist (Nietzsche) 34
anti-Semitism 199–200
Aquinas, Thomas 42
À Rebours (Against the Grain) (Huysmans) 108
Arendt, Hannah 16, 54
Argument, Das (journal) 189
Arieli, Yehoshua 12
Aristotle 182, 198
Armenia 149
Aron, Raymond 15, 24
Augustine 14
Austria 158
Azerbaijan 149

Baader, Andreas 188, 190–191
Baader-Meinhoff 188–193
Babeuf, Gracchus 101–102, 115, 170
Babeufand 116
Bachelard, Gaston 206
Bacon, Francis 36, 114
Bakunin, Mikhail 3, 171, 174–179, 189, 196

Barbés, Armand 100–101
Barrat, Odion 95
Barrès, Maurice 213
Barricade, La (Bourget) 108
Barthes, Roland 207
Bataille, Georges 17
Baudelaire, Charles 107, 109, 218
Baudrillard, Jean 210–211
Bauer, Otto 121, 147, 149–150
Berkman, Alexander 172
Berlin, Isaiah 174
Bernstein, Eduard 117, 119, 171
Birth of the Clinic, The (Foucault) 209
Black Order 192–193
Blade Runner (film) 24
Blanc, Louis 84, 97
Blanqui, Jérôme 116
Blanqui, Louis Auguste 2, 97–102, 116, 170
Blanquism 97–103, 116, 119, 176
Bloch, Ernst 196
Bloom, Allan 11, 42
Blumenberg, Hans 18
Bolsheviks 3, 14, 98, 117, 119–121, 142, 146–147
Borochov, Ber 147
Bourget, Paul 107–109
Bruno, Giordano 21
Buonarotti, Filippo 170
Burke, Edmund 71
Byron, Lord 8

Cabet, Étienne 97
Călinescu, Matei 105
Campanella, Tommaso 114
Camus, Albert 18–19, 179, 196
capital 94
capitalism 64, 100, 106, 113, 119, 121–122, 146, 148, 151–152

Carbonari 116
Carnot, M. F. Sadi 172
Carr, E. H. 174
caste system 199
Central Republican Society 101
Chartists 116–117
Chernyshevsky, Nikolai 195
China 122, 198
Civil War in France, The (Marx) 138–139
Civitas Solis (Campanella) 114
Class Struggle in France, The (Engels) 90
"Class Struggles in France, The" (Marx) 129
class warfare 86, 90–96
"Class Warfare in France" (Marx) 95
Clemenceau, Georges 98
"Club Blanqui" 98
Cold War 192
"Collapse of the Second International, The" (Lenin) 160
Columbus, Christopher 200–201
communism 17, 113, 147; *see also* Marx, Karl
"Communist Manifesto" (Marx and Engels) 82, 94
Condorcet, Marquis de 13
Confessions, The (Rousseau) 212–213
Confino, Michael 174
Considérant, Victor 97
Considérations sur le gouvernement de la Pologne (Considerations on the Government of Poland) (Rousseau) 55
Contrat social, Le (The Social Contract) (Rousseau) 31
"Contribution to the Critique of Political Economy" (Marx) 127
Cooperative Magazine 114
Coppola, Francis Ford 109
Cramer, Philibert 45
Crimea 164
Crime and Punishment (Dostoevsky) 195
"Critique of Political Economy, A" (Marx) 130, 150
Croce, Benedetto 95
Croissant, Klaus 188
Cromwell revolution 114

Dagestan 149
Damnés de la terre, Les (The Wretched of the Earth) (Fanon) 202
decadence 105–109

Decline and Fall of the Roman Empire (Gibbons) 106
Degeneration (Nordau) 107
Deleuze, Gilles 213
della Mirandola, Pico 21
De Man, Paul 207
Democracy in America (de Tocqueville) 59, 61, 75; *see also* de Tocqueville, Alexis
democratic tyranny 63–78
Derrida, Jacques 17, 207
Descartes, René 12, 36
Description of the Beginnings of Political Economics (Blanqui) 116
de Tocqueville, Alexis 2, 17, 32, 54, 59–78, 81–89, 115, 126, 128, 132–133, 176, 185, 209
Devils, The (Dostoevsky) 178
dialectical materialism 112–113
"Difference Between the Philosophy of Nature of Democritus and Epicurus, The" (Marx) 112
Diggers 114
Discipline and Punish (Foucault) 209, 215
Discourse on the Origin and Foundations of Inequality Among Men (Rousseau) 114
"Discourse on the Sciences and Arts" (Rousseau) 35, 37
Discours sur les sciences et les arts (Discourse on the Sciences and Arts) (Rousseau) 30
Doktor Faustus (Mann) 7
Dostoevsky, Fyodor 178–179, 195
Dreyfus Affair 200, 213
Durkheim, Émile 78
Dutschke, Rudy 189

education 32, 36–37, 44–56, 150–151
"Eighteenth Brumaire of Louis Bonaparte, The" (Marx) 130, 136
Elijah of Chelm 20
Elizabeth of Austria 172
Ellul, Jacques 32–33
Émile (Rousseau) 2, 14–15, 31–32, 35, 44–52
Engels, Friedrich 82, 90–91, 112, 118, 124, 131, 139, 153, 160
Enlightenment 1, 6, 10–16, 30, 32–33, 35, 37, 44, 69, 125–126, 196, 198, 201, 213, 218–219
Enráges 116, 169

Ensslin, Gudrun 188–189
Epimetheus 5
equality 53–54, 112
Eros and Civilization (Marcuse) 181
Estonia 164
ethnocentrism 199
existentialism 15

Fabian Society 117
Fanon, Frantz 202
Farrakhan, Louis 202
Fathers and Sons (Turgenev) 195
Fauré, Gabriel 84
Faust 7–8, 22
Faust and the Maharal of Prague (Neher) 22
February Revolution 88, 90–93, 124
feudalism 151–152
Feuerbach, Ludwig 170
Fichte, Johann 6
Finland 149, 151
Fleurs du Mal, Les (The Flowers of Evil) (Baudelaire) 107
Foucault, Michel 17, 19, 204–209, 213–216, 218–219
Fourier, Charles 116, 170
"France Before and After 1789" (de Tocqueville) 83
Franco, Francisco 172
Frank, Jacob 191
Frankenstein, or the Modern Prometheus (Shelley) 19–20
Frankfurt School 15, 22, 32, 123, 180–181
Frankism 191
freedom of association 66
French Revolution 16, 34, 37, 52–56, 60–61, 63–65, 82, 85, 88, 114–116, 118, 124–133, 169–170, 215–216
Freud, Sigmund 32, 38, 186, 211

Gautier, Théophile 107, 109
Georgia 149
German Enlightenment 12
German Ideology, The (Marx and Engels) 118
"German Ideology, The" (Marx) 131
Gibbons, Edward 106
Gillespie, Michael Allen 18
GIP *see Groupe d'Information sur les Prisons* (Group for Information on Prisons) (GIP)
Girondins 169
Glaucus 39–44

gnostics 191
Gobineau, Artur de 84, 201
Godwin, William 169–170
Goethe, Johann Wolfgang 7–8
Goldman, Emma 172
Golem 20–23
Gotha Program 120
Gramsci, Antonio 120, 122
Gray, John 116
Groupe d'Information sur les Prisons (Group for Information on Prisons) (GIP) 215
Guarantees of Harmony and Freedom (Weitling) 171
Guizot, François 61, 86

Habermas, Jürgen 15, 17
Hall, Charles 116
Hébertistes 116
Hegel, Georg 8–9, 15, 32, 44, 74, 112, 127–128, 181–182, 201, 219
Heidegger, Martin 17
Helvétius, Claude Adrien 13
Hercules 5
hermeneutics 3–4
Herzen, Alexander 117, 174–175, 195
Herzen, Natalia 176
Hesiod 4
Hill, Christopher 162
historicism 11
historiography 123–127
History of Madness, The (Foucault) 209
Hobbes, Thomas 11–12, 41–42, 219
Hodgkin, Thomas 116
Holocaust 201
Holy Family, The (Marx) 128
homogeneity, of population 153
"How to Profit from One's Enemies" (Plutarch) 30
Hughes, Stuart 196
humanism 45
Humbert I of Italy 172
Hume, David 3, 201
Huysmans, Joris-Karl 108

idealism 6
Idel, Moshe 22
imperialism 121, 123, 135, 148, 150, 156–157, 159
"Imperialism, the Highest Stage of Capitalism" (Lenin) 156–157
India 198–199
Industrial Revolution 82, 115

Inegalité des races humaines, L' (The Inequality of Human Races) (Gobineau) 201
inequality 36, 39–40, 43
Iran 215–216
"Irish Rebellion of 1916, The" (Lenin) 162

Jacobins 102–103, 120, 131–132, 169, 175
Jesuit Order 174–179
Jews 199–200
Joll, James 170
Jünger, Ernst 184, 196, 208
"Junius Pamphlet, The" (Lenin) 158

Kant, Immanuel 12, 15, 17, 32–33, 106, 192, 212, 218
Kapital, Das (Marx) 112
Karakosov, Dmitry 176–177
Kautsky, Karl 117, 119–120, 146–147
Kerensky, Fyodor 147
knowledge, in Rousseau 49–50
Koestler, Arthur 16–17, 186
Kojève, Alexandre 209–210
Konkret (journal) 189–190
Koppen, Karl Friedrich 6
Kossuth 102
Kropotkin, Peter 171, 174
Kuhn, Thomas 206

Labriola, Antonio 120
Lacan, Jacques 207
Lamartine, Alphonse de 97
Lang, Fritz 24
language 180–181
Langueur (Verlaine) 105
Latvia 164
Lavrov, Pyotr 117
law: in de Tocqueville 70–71; in Rousseau 114
Ledru-Rollin, Auguste 97
"Left-wing Communism, An Infantile Disorder" (Lenin) 153–154
Lenau, Nickolaus 7
Lenin, Vladimir 3, 113, 118–120, 147–148, 150–165, 171
Leninism 97–98, 122, 146–151
Levelers 114
Lévi-Strauss, Claude 4, 32, 206
Lewis, Wyndham 196
liberalism 16, 113, 205
Link, Werner 189
Lithuania 164

Locke, John 13–14, 42–43, 116
Louis Napoleon 3, 59, 85, 88, 94–95, 124, 133–138
Louis-Philippe 85–86, 91, 99
Louis XIV of France 65
Louis XVI of France 60–61, 169
Lucifer and Prometheus (Werblowsky) 8
Luddites 115
Lukács, György 123
Luxemburg, Rosa 121
Lyotard, Jean-François 19, 207, 213, 219

Maharal of Prague 20
Main Currents in Sociological Thought (Aron) 24
Mallarmé, Stéphane 108
Mann, Thomas 7
Maoism 122
Mao Zedong 122
Marcuse, Herbert 17, 75–76, 122–123, 180–186, 209, 213
Marighella, Carlos 189
Marinetti, Filippo Tommaso 196
Marx, Karl 2–3, 6, 9, 14, 32, 34, 43, 73, 75, 77–78, 82, 86, 90–96, 112–142, 148–149, 153–154, 160, 162–163, 183, 186, 211, 219
Marxism 16, 97–98, 115, 117, 119–123, 147, 205
Mayakovsky, Vladimir 196
Mazzini, Giuseppe 102, 122, 192
McKinley, William 172
McLuhan, Marshall 210–211
Meinhoff, Ulrike 188–191
Mendelssohn, Moses 12
Metropolis (film) 24
Mickiewicz 102
middle class 82–84
Mill, John Stuart 61, 71, 82
Milton, John 8
Modernism, Decadence, Kitsch, Postmodernism (Călinescu) 105
Mon Faust (My Faust) (Valéry) 7
Montesquieu 69–70
More, Thomas 114
multiculturalism 201–202
Munzer, Thomas 114
Mussolini, Benito 196
mutualism 171
myth 4

Namier, Lewis 97, 116
Napoleon 83

Napoleon III *see* Louis Napoleon
nationalism 16, 121, 146–152, 161–165
National Socialism 201
nature 13–14
Nechayev, Sergei 176–179
Neher, André 22
neotechnology 25
New Atlantis, The (Bacon) 114
New Left 123, 190
Newton, Isaac 12, 36
Nietzsche, Friedrich 9–10, 17, 24, 32–34, 37–38, 50, 52, 108–109, 194, 204–205, 207–208, 219
"Nietzsche, Genealogy, History" (Foucault) 205
nihilism 10, 17–18, 24, 108, 194–197, 211
Nihilism Before Nietzsche (Gillespie) 18
Nisard, Désiré 107, 109
Nordau, Max 107
Norway 154

Ogarev, Nikolai 195
One-dimensional Man (Marcuse) 75–76, 180–181
"On New Democracy" (Mao) 122
On the Middle Class and the People (de Tocqueville) 84, 115
"Organization, The" 176
Orwell, George 16
Owen, Robert 84, 114, 116

Pandora 5
Paradise Lost (Milton) 8
Paris Commune 118, 120, 124, 138–142
Peasants' Rebellion 114
Péguy, Charles 213
People's Vengeance 178
Pestalozzi, Johann Heinrich 14
"Philosophical Art" (Baudelaire) 107
Philosophical Discourse of Modernity, The (Habermas) 17
"Philosophy and Critical Theory" (Marcuse) 180
Philosophy of Law (Hegel) 8
Pisarev, Dimitri 195
Plato 5, 15, 31, 36–39, 52, 169, 182, 219
Plekhanov, Georgi 117, 119
Plutarch 30
Poland 149, 157
political science 11–12
Politics (Aristotle) 198

presidential elections, in de Tocqueville 67–68
primitivism 14
Principle of Hope, The (Bloch) 196
progress 14
"Progress in Hegel's Teaching" (Kojève) 209–210
Project pour l'éducation de M. de Sainte-Marie (Project for the Education of Monsieur de Sainte-Marie) (Rousseau) 44
Prometheus 3–10, 30, 112–113, 212, 220–221
Protagoras (Plato) 5
Proudhon, Pierre Joseph 88, 170–171
Psalms, Book of 20

Quinet, Edgar 55

racialism 16
racism 198–202
RAF *see* Red Army Faction (RAF)
Ranner, Karl 121
Raspail, François-Vincent 97
Rauschning, Hermann 196
Ray, Michelle 188
reason 11, 13
Red Army Faction (RAF) 188
Redhardt, Reinhard 189
Reeve, Henry 81
Réflexions sur la violence (Reflections on Violence) (Sorel) 108
religion 63–64
Renaissance 105–106, 114
Renner, Carl 150
revisionism 119
Revolution of Nihilism, The (Rauschning) 196
Ricardo, David 116
Richardson, Joanna 107
Ricoeur, Paul 3–4
Rise of Totalitarian Democracy, The (Talmon) 196
Robespierre, Maximilien 34, 53, 102–103, 169
Röhl, Rainer 189
Romanticism 6
Rous, Jacques 169
Rousseau, Jean-Jacques 2, 11–12, 14–15, 30–56, 56n2, 114, 212–213, 219
Russian Revolution (1905) 120
Russian Revolution (1917) 119–120, 132, 162–163

Saint-Simon, Henri 34, 84, 100, 114, 116, 170
"Sanity of Art, The" (Shaw) 107
Sartre, Jean-Paul 188, 191, 202, 213–214
Schelling, August Wilhelm 6
Schiller, Friedrich 8
Schmitt, Carl 220
Scholem, Gershom 24
Schopenhauer, Arthur 38, 108
Schulz, Bruno 22
science: God vs. 15; Golem and 21–22; political 11–12
Scott, Ridley 24
Scottish Enlightenment 12
secularization 11
selfishness 43–44
Serbia 158
sex 186
Shaw, Bernard 107
Shaw, George Bernard 117
Shelley, Mary 8, 19–20
Sismondi, Jean 129
Soboul, Albert 54
"Social and Political Situation in France Before and After 1789, The" (de Tocqueville) 82
Social Contract, The (Rousseau) 34–35, 51–53
Social-Democratic Party (Russia) 117–118, 160
socialism 16, 81–89, 113–118
socialization 43
Société des Familles 100
Société des Saisons 100–101
Society of Fraternal Democrats 117
Socrates 15, 25, 38
Sorel, Georges 35, 108, 171–172, 196
Southeimer, Kurt 190
Soviet Marxism (Marcuse) 181
Spinoza, Baruch 42
Stalin, Joseph 113, 120, 147–149
Starobinski, Jean 43
Stirner, Max 170
Surveiller et punir (Discipline and Punish) (Foucault) 208
Switzerland 151
Syndicalism 116–117

Tailor's Dummies (Schulz) 22
Talmon, Jacob L. 51, 76, 196, 213
Taylor, Frederick Winslow 121
technological determinism 182–184
"Theory of Decadence, A" (Bourget) 107

Thompson, William 116
totalitarianism 16–19, 191–192, 196
"Toward a Critique of Hegel's Philosophy of Judgment" (Marx) 127–128
tribalism 199
Trotsky, Leon 18, 120–121, 163–164, 172
Turgenev, Ivan 195
Turgot, Anne Robert Jacques 14
twentieth century 1–2
Twilight of the Idols (Nietzsche) 33
tyranny, democratic 63–78

Ukraine 156–157, 164
universalism 210
Utopia (More) 114
utopias 114, 116

Valéry, Paul 7
Verlaine, Paul 105
Voltaire 13, 34, 53, 106–107, 213

Wagner, Richard 109
"War and Russian Social Democracy, The" (Lenin) 160
weather 24–25
Webb, Sidney 117
Weber, Max 11, 16, 78
Weitling, Wilhelm 171
Werblowsky, Zvi 8
"What Is Enlightenment?" (Foucault) 218
"What is property?" (Proudhon) 170–171
What Is to Be Done (Chernyshevsky) 195
Widmann, G. R. 7
Wilde, Oscar 108
Wilson, Woodrow 163
Winstanley, Gerrard 114
Work on Myth (Blumenberg) 18
World War I 93, 157–161, 163–164
World War II 192

Young Europe 116
Young Hegelians 170
Young Russia 176

Zeno 169
Zeus 4–6
Zola, Émile 213
Zulu 198–199